Labor Rights Are Civil Rights

POLITICS AND SOCIETY IN TWENTIETH-CENTURY AMERICA

Series Editors

WILLIAM CHAFE, GARY GERSTLE, LINDA GORDON, AND JULIAN ZELIZER

A list of titles in this series appears at the back of the book

Labor Rights Are Civil Rights

MEXICAN AMERICAN WORKERS IN TWENTIETH-CENTURY AMERICA

Zaragosa Vargas

PRINCETON UNIVERSITY PRESS

PRINCETON AND OXFORD

Library of Congress Cataloging-in-Publication Data

Vargas, Zaragosa
Labor rights are civil rights / Mexican American workers in twentieth-century
America / Zaragosa Vargas.
p. cm.—(Politics and society in twentieth-century America)
Includes bibliographical references and index.
ISBN 0-691-11546-X (cloth : alk. paper)
1. Mexican Americans—Employment—History—20th century. 2. Labor
movement—United States—History—20th century. 3. Mexican Americans—
Civil rights—History—20th century. I. Title. II. Series.
HD8081.M6V36 2004
331.6′272073′0904—dc22   2004042852

British Library Cataloging-in-Publication Data is available.

This book has been composed in Sabon

Printed on acid-free paper. ∞

www.pupress.princeton.edu

Printed in the United States of America

10 9 8 7 6 5 4 3 2 1

For Zaneta

Con los probes de la tierra
Quiero yo mí suerte echar
(With the poor people of this earth,
I want to share my lot.)
   —JOSÉ MARTÍ, *Guantanamera*

Contents

Acknowledgments

I HAVE BENEFITED enormously from great teachers and colleagues, whom I count as my dear friends, in the years I spent writing this book. This study began at the University of Michigan in a graduate seminar on the New York intellectuals offered by Alan M. Wald. Alan contributed to my development as a scholar with his thorough knowledge, critical guidance, and example of intellectual rigor. You have my respect, Alan, for your seriousness of purpose and commitment to social justice. I have also had the good fortune of receiving advice, guidance, support, and inspiration from David Montgomery. David read all the manuscript and led me to shape central arguments. David, your astute criticism and advice strengthened this book. I owe an immense debt to my colleague Nelson Lichtenstein. Nelson read several chapters, made insightful suggestions on their organization, and pushed me to clarify issues. Alan, David, and Nelson, your contributions to this book are beyond measure. I express to you my deepest gratitude.

I am most appreciative of those numerous librarians and archivists across the nation who helped me identify collections: the staff at the Franklin D. Roosevelt Presidential Library, the Herbert Hoover Presidential Library, the National Archives, the Texas Labor History Archives at the University of Texas at Arlington, and the New Mexico State Records Center and Archives. Special thanks to: Christine Marín, Chicano Studies Library, Arizona State University; Les Orear, Illinois Labor History Society; Margo Gutiérrez, Mexican American Collections, University of Texas at Austin; Patrick Dawson, Chicano Studies Library, University of California at Santa Barbara; Teri Robertson, Southern California Library; David Marshall, Special Collections, California State University at Northridge; Barbara Dey, Colorado Historical Society, Denver; Claudia Rivers, Special Collections, University of Texas at El Paso; and Harry Rubenstein, Museum of American History of the Smithsonian Institution.

I am grateful to those individuals who helped me with the illustrations that appeared in this book: Carolyn Cole, Los Angeles Public Library Photo Collection; Ann Greenwald, Instructional Resources, University of California, Santa Barbara; David M. Hays, Western Historical Collections, University of Colorado at Boulder; Kenneth Kennedy Johnson, Photoduplication Services, Library of Congress; David Lamb, Special Collections, Notre Dame University; Rebecca Lintz, Stephen H. Hart Library, Colorado Historical Society; Steve Neilson, Minnesota Historical

Society Library; Dolores B. Olivarez, Institute of Texan Cultures; and Robert P. Spindler, Arizona State University. I wish to acknowledge Juan Vicente Palerm and the staff of UC-MEXUS for a research grant that provided me with assistance in completing major portions of the research for this study.

Friends have shaped this project through their support and encouragement: Gabriela Arredondo, Luis L. Arroyo, Albert Camarillo, Neil F. Foley, Colleen O'Neill, Vicki L. Ruiz, and Devra Weber. I especially want to thank Howard Brick, Douglas H. Daniels, Ramón Favela, Robbie Lieberman, Anne M. Martínez, Paula Rabinowitz, José Sánchez, and Rudy D. Torres for their friendship over the years. One more time, I extend a soul handshake and hug to all my black Marine brothers whom long ago I had the honor and privilege to serve with in Vietnam. Thank you all for instilling in me your civil rights and revolutionary values and for making me an honorary soul brother during our time together.

Portions of this book appeared previously in academic journals. An earlier version of chapter 3 first appeared in the *Pacific Historical Review* (vol. 66, no. 4, used here by permission of the University of California Press). Portions of chapter 6 and the Conclusion appeared in the *New Mexico Historical Review* (October 2001). Thanks to Brigitta van Rheinberg, Kathleen Cioffi, Alison Kalett, and everyone else at Princeton University Press who aided in the publication of this book. I am particularly grateful for the attention Brigitta gave to this project and for helping me turn an unwieldy manuscript into a polished book. In this regard, Ellen Barber, my copy editor, provided sound advice and improved the manuscript immeasurably. I owe a special debt to Linda Gordon, coeditor of the series. Linda offered important suggestions for improving the manuscript and strongly supported this project.

Finally I want to thank my wife, Zaneta, my best friend, for her infinite love and encouragement and support over the years. This book and everything else would not have been possible without you. Zaneta, your loving and meaningful care and understanding have helped me to heal from the hell of war. You are my everything.

Abbreviations

AAA	Agriculture Adjustment Act
AFL	American Federation of Labor
ANMA	Asociación Nacional México-Americana
ASARCO	American Smelting and Refining Company
BWA	Beet Workers Association
CAMW	Committee to Aid Mexican Workers
CATL	Latin American Confederation of Labor
CIO	Congress of Industrial Organizations
CIO-ADC	Congress of Industrial Organizations Anti-Discrimination Committee
CIO CARD	Congress of Industrial Organizations Committee Against Racial Discrimination
CIO PAC	Congress of Industrial Organizations Political Action Committee
CPUSA	Communist Party of the United States
CTM	Confederación de Trabajadores Mexicanos
CWA	Civilian Works Administration
FEPC	Fair Employment Practices Committee
FERA	Federal Emergency Relief Act
FLMPA	Fabens Laboring Men's Protective Association
FTA	Food, Tobacco, Agricultural, and Allied Workers of America
HUAC	House Un-American Activities Committee
ILD	International Labor Defense
ILGWU	International Ladies' Garment Workers' Union
ILWU	International Longshoremen's and Warehousemen's Union
INS	U.S. Immigration and Naturalization Service
IPP	Independent Progressive Party
IWW	Industrial Workers of the World
LULAC	League of United Latin American Citizens
NAACP	National Association for the Advancement of Colored People
NBGA	National Beet Growers Association
NFLU	National Farm Labor Union
NIRA	National Industrial Recovery Act
NLRA	National Labor Relations Act
NLRB	National Labor Relations Board

NMU	National Miners Union
NRA	National Recovery Administration
NYA	National Youth Administration
OCIAA	Office of the Coordinator of Inter-American Affairs
OPM	Office of Production Management
OWI	Office of War Information
PCM	Communist Party of Mexico
PWOC	Packinghouse Workers Organizing Committee
SDC	Spanish Defense Council
SLDC	Sleepy Lagoon Defense Committee
SRA	State Relief Administration
SWOC	Steel Workers Organizing Committee
TUEL	Trade Union Educational League
TUUL	Trade Union Unity League
TWOC	Texas Agricultural Workers Organizing Committee
UAW	United Auto Workers
UCAPAWA	United Cannery, Agricultural Packing, and Allied Workers of America
UE	United Electrical
UFC	United Front Committee
UFWA	United Furniture Workers of America
UMWA	United Mine Workers of America
UPWA	United Packinghouse Workers of America
USWA	United Steel Workers of America
WILPF	Women's International League for Peace and Freedom
WMC	War Manpower Commission
WPA	Works Progress Administration

Labor Rights Are Civil Rights

> There is only one remedy left. . . . We of the laboring class
> must organize.
> —MAXIMINO JUÁREZ, Tejano worker

ON MEMORIAL DAY 1937, thousands of steel workers and their families approached the gates of the Republic Steel mill in South Chicago. Thirty-one-year-old Guadalupe (Lupe) Marshall participated in the strikers' demonstration. Marshall came with her family to Chicago from Mexico in 1917. A volunteer social worker with Hull House, Marshall was active in the expanding Chicago labor and civil rights movement. The Mexican[1] female activist had been arrested two years before for participating in a steel worker demonstration. Marshall was one of the two hundred women who took part in the march on the plant, a demonstration one journalist described as having a "holiday atmosphere." Many women had their children with them, and the young ones ate ice cream and popsicles as a bevy of speakers addressed the crowd prior to the march. As the jubilant marchers proceeded to the Republic Steel plant, the situation suddenly changed from semifestive to deadly serious.

> The police advanced toward us in a running step and were closing their ranks and crowding us, pushing us back all this time. Somebody hollered, "Mayor Kelley said it is all right to picket." Others said, "We have got our rights." I said to one of the officers in front of me . . ."There are enough of you men to march alongside these people to see that order is kept." . . . An officer . . . directly in front of me . . . had his gun out [and he] laughed real sarcastically in my face. . . . I was still talking to these officers in front of me when I heard a dull thud toward the back of my group, and as I turned around there was screaming . . . and simultaneously a volley of shots. It sounded more like thunder. I heard that and I couldn't . . . believe that they were shooting. . . . I turned around to see what was happening and the people that were standing in back of me were all lying on the ground face down. . . . I saw some splotches of blood on some of the fellows' shirts.[2]

Marshall tried to escape from the advancing police indiscriminately swinging their clubs, but the road was blocked by stunned strikers. She saw one demonstrator being bludgeoned by a policeman. Each time the striker tried to get up, the policeman would club him mercilessly. A very

Figure I.A. Chicago police mowed down strikers during the Memorial Day Massacre. Mexican American labor organizer Guadalupe Marshall pleading with the police to stop the merciless killings. The black line across the image is a police baton. (Courtesy of Illinois Labor History Society).

distraught Lupe Marshall screamed at the policeman, "Don't do that. Can't you see he is terribly injured?" Suddenly someone struck Marshall from the back and knocked her down. She tried to get up, but several police struck her in the back with clubs; then someone picked her up and took her to a patrol wagon. As Marshall was led to the police wagon, she stared in disbelief at men lying all over the field. Some of them were motionless. Others were groaning. Their heads were covered with blood, and their clothing was bloodstained. Sixteen men were packed in the patrol wagon with Lupe Marshall. All of them were seriously wounded. After driving around the city, the patrol wagon finally reached Burnside Hospital. Marshall saw other patrol wagons come up to the hospital. Among the strikers coming into the hospital was a woman with a small child who had been shot in the heel and in the leg. Though bleeding badly from the blows she had sustained at the hands of policemen, Lupe

Marshall went into the hospital dining room, gathered tablecloths and napkins and a pitcher of water, and began to put wet packs on the wounded strikers.[3]

Chicago steel worker Max Guzmán was one of the two strikers carrying American flags in the march that fateful Sunday. Police clubbed the twenty-six-year-old Mexican steel worker in the head as the first shots were fired, and he went down. Terrified protesters frantically fleeing from police passed Guzmán, lying dazed and bleeding on the ground. The fallen steel worker tried to pick himself up, but he was struck a second and third time by another policeman, who then grabbed him by his jacket and threw him into a patrol wagon. Guzmán was held at the South Chicago Police Station for nearly three days. While in lockup, Guzmán was fingerprinted and interrogated by the police. They asked him what he had done with the weapons. When the police told the steel worker he was a communist troublemaker, Guzmán responded that he did not know what the word *communist* meant. Although Guzmán had been in Chicago since 1920, he was not a U.S. citizen. Learning this, the police threatened Guzmán that they could send him back to Mexico anytime they felt like it.[4]

Hundreds of other Mexicans manned the picket lines during the disastrous 1937 Little Steel strike, like mill workers Philip Morengo and Max Luna from Indiana Harbor, Indiana, who came to South Chicago to join the protest. These men were among the strikers and supporters beaten, arrested, and murdered by police at South Chicago's Republic Steel plant during the infamous "Memorial Day Massacre." The unionization drives by the Steel Workers Organizing Committee (SWOC) of the Congress of Industrial Organizations (CIO) found a receptive audience among the Spanish-speaking steel workers, who made up 5.4 percent of the Great Lakes region's steel workforce. Mexican steel workers from the mills in South Chicago, Illinois, and in East Chicago, Indiana Harbor, and Gary, Indiana, flocked to SWOC. In fact, Mexicans were the first ethnic group to completely organize. SWOC became a vehicle through which Mexicans could contest racial discrimination in work assignments, wages and hours, and promotions.[5]

Not much is known about the heroic role of Spanish-speaking blue-collar workers in the Little Steel strike action and in the larger CIO insurgency to organize the nation's basic industries that has been evoked by labor historians. Mexicans rose up in a series of strikes in the 1930s, and although these actions were overshadowed by the major conflicts involving Anglo workers, the strikes epitomized in microcosm a host of issues central to the Spanish-speaking population of the United States. At this time, Spanish-speaking workers took up the struggle to improve their social and economic condition as a rise in ethnic and class consciousness coalesced into campaigns to organize. Racism, ethnicity, and nationalism were central principles to the Mexican working-class struggle that erupted throughout the Southwest as any deference that existed among Mexicans vanished. In fact, it was Mexicans on the huge fruit and vegetable farms of California who initiated the massive strike wave that swept across the nation in the 1930s.

Mexican women likewise gained a voice and added a noteworthy dimension to the incipient union movement. Spanish-speaking women provided crucial support during strikes through explicit action. They held the picket line sometimes for months on behalf of their male kin. When the strikes were over, the women continued to lead the struggle for unemployment relief as members of Unemployed Councils, neighborhood relief committees, and auxiliaries. Advanced in their understanding of social and economic issues, Spanish-speaking workingwomen in Chicago, Detroit, San Antonio, Los Angeles, and other communities took part in relief demonstrations, resisted eviction efforts, dealt with demeaning relief workers, and led the fight for social insurance. As workers in the fields, in canneries and packinghouses, and in garment shops and cigar factories, Mexican women developed a consciousness of common interests that fueled the movement toward unionization and then political action.[6]

Protest backed by collective action was axiomatic. This immersion in labor activism by Mexicans broadened their political horizons as class-conscious workers, for in the early years of the Depression they also broke the fetters that bound them to the paternalistic control of the Mexican consuls. Loyal to their privileged class backgrounds and interests, these Mexican officials were untrustworthy: they acted as brokers between employers and Mexican workers; frequently colluded with employers in strikebreaking; operated in opposition to American unions, which had to counter the consuls' class-laden nationalist claims; attempted to sway Mexican unionists away from the Left-led labor movements; and condoned as well as assisted in the federal roundup and deportation of Spanish-speaking labor activists.[7]

The Communist Party of the United States is controversial in American history because of its Stalinist, undemocratic past. Nelson Lichtenstein and other historians, however, acknowledge that the party was a strong force for self-organization and actualization in immigrant and racial communities. The exemplary fight waged by the Communist Party of the United States for the real economic needs of the jobless and working poor, its leadership role in the difficult task of organizing migrant farm workers, and especially, its forceful opposition to racism and its legal battles on behalf of Mexicans through the International Labor Defense, attracted a considerable cross section of Spanish-speaking workers. The Communist Party is of great importance in *Labor Rights Are Civil Rights* because it contributed significantly to Mexican organizing and action, just as Spanish-speaking workers added much to the party in terms of its multiracialism.

Radical views like anarchism, socialism, and communism were familiar to the progressive elements of the Mexican communities by the turn of the twentieth century. In fact, many early Spanish-speaking communist recruits, like the blacks who joined the party early on, were nationalists of various stripes. According to Devra Weber, the most visible Spanish-speaking radicals, who rose to leadership positions in the party, were those who had been influenced by the Mexican and Russian revolutions. Another politicizing factor was the workers' uprisings during and after World War I, such as the copper strikes in Arizona initiated by the Western Federation of Miners and the coal strikes in Colorado led by members of the Industrial Workers of the World (IWW). Admittedly, these ideologies and events did not push large numbers of Mexican American radicals into the party orbit, but these factors did strengthen their belief that change was probable within the milieu of working-class unity and could release them from their purgatory of exploitation and oppression. A discussion of the communists is thus crucial, because in the next twenty years communists and communist sympathizers frequently participated in the leadership of key Mexican American unions and left-wing organizations like the Asociación Nacional México-Americana (ANMA).

The early New Deal labor legislation became the impetus for the first phase of Mexican labor insurgency, and the creation of the CIO in 1935 ushered in another wave of rank-and-file labor organizing. Mexican Americans had become actively conscious of both the positive and negative roles of the government in their everyday lives. They became educated in the function of mass pressure in obtaining amelioration of their condition from the government. The National Recovery Administration (NRA) kindled the hopes of Mexicans, who felt the government had now begun to recognize their right to organize. In the Southwest, Mountain States, and Midwest, union organizers targeted Mexican workers in mining, agriculture, food packing, steel, and auto work. Although the early unions, and later the CIO affiliates, were hardly consistent in eliminating racial barriers to hiring, promotion, and equal treatment on the job, the union movement for Mexicans became a powerful catalyst to remove the shackles of economic and political as well as racial subordination. Years of bitter anger and deep frustration transformed many Spanish-speaking labor actions into crusades against the abuses Mexicans suffered as workers and as American citizens.[8] The labor struggles of Mexicans were inseparable from the issue of civil rights, because whether the worker upheavals succeeded or failed, the labor movement set in motion important changes. Just as racial discrimination led Mexicans to pursue the righteous path to unionism, it pushed them into the struggle for social justice.[9]

Studies of American workers and the 1930s labor movement have largely ignored the role of Mexican Americans in this era's union drive; however, several historians have explored certain aspects of this neglected working-class experience. For example, *Cannery Workers, Cannery Lives* by Vicki Ruiz documents the history of Southern California Mexican women cannery workers in the CIO affiliate United Cannery, Agricultural, Packing, and Allied Workers of America (UCAPAWA). Mario T. García devotes a section of his *Mexican Americans* to the activists who formed the Congress of Spanish-Speaking Peoples (Peoples' Congress). *Bitter Harvest* by Cletus Daniel chronicles the attempts at unionization by California farm workers. And Devra Weber in *Dark Sweat, White Gold* analyzes the relationship between economic structure, human agency, and the state in shaping the early California agricultural workforce.[10]

This book, *Labor Rights Are Civil Rights*, brings the struggle of Mexican workers to light during the years when they initiated a broad-based movement aimed at making fundamental changes in their social, economic, and political status. I argue that in the period encompassing the 1930s and the World War II years, Mexican Americans initiated a labor and civil rights movement that was the precursor of the early civil rights movement of the postwar years, which formed the foundation of the modern Chicano movement. The fundamental questions my book addresses are similar to those posed by historians such as Robin D. G. Kelley, Elizabeth Faue, Dolores Janiewski, Lizabeth Cohen, Gary Gerstle, Michael Honey, Robert Korstad, and others who have studied labor upheavals among workers, white and black, men and women. How did Mexicans choose their terrain of struggle? What were the grievances of workers in strike actions and the tactics and strategies implemented? Why was community-based unionism important in building labor movements? What was the role of Mexican women as workers and as rank-and-file labor organizers? How was racial inequality contested? What was the significance of racial, ethnic, and national identity as a social and cultural force in mobilizing class consciousness and in establishing organizing tactics among Mexican workers? And how did the Spanish working classes fashion their struggles for fair employment and civil rights during the World War II years?

I outline and address several important themes in *Labor Rights Are Civil Rights*. The plight of Mexican farm workers at the dawn of the Great Depression is a central theme of chapter 1. Despite their diverse work experiences, Mexican workers found their job opportunities greatly influenced by the pattern of rapid regional specialization in agriculture. More than in any other region in the United States, agricultural expansion in the Southwest was large-scale and labor-intensive. It was linked to the huge irrigation projects brought on line through federal land reclamation programs undertaken at the turn of the century or through private land development. The Texas lower Río Grande Valley and Winter Garden area, Arizona's Salt River Valley, and the California Imperial Valley became major specialized farming regions. All of these regions were coupled to huge labor reserves of Mexican seasonal migratory workers, whose basis was a family wage system long abandoned in other labor sectors.[11]

Chapter 1 provides three case studies to show that, irrespective of whether Mexicans worked in Texas agriculture, Colorado beets, or California factory farms, their condition was deplorable and got progressively worse with the onset of the Depression and the repatriations and deportations the economic crisis triggered. Mexican migrant farm labor was a transnational movement involving both Mexican Americans and Mexican nationals that created interstate, regional, and international arrangements of labor migration. The task of forming and sustaining strong worker organizations within the Mexican community was impeded. Economic controls coercive in nature, as in Texas and Colorado, where they were the most terrible by any measure, and low wages hampered the maintenance of unions and strike funds. Like their black counterparts in the Deep South, most Mexican migratory farm workers were too poor, too geographically dispersed, and too vulnerable to oppressive controls at the beginning of the Great Depression to rise up in common struggle.[12] A key weakness was the ever-pressing demand for cheap Mexican labor from across the border, which sustained the necessity for oppression to ensure agricultural labor requirements.

Detailing this major segment of the Mexican working classes and discussing the political context of the early Depression years to discern what economic and social conditions Mexican workers faced provides background to repatriation, which is the focus of the second half of chapter 1. As the Great Depression deepened and many employers cut back on both labor and wages, the options for Mexican workers narrowed considerably and they flooded into the cities to seek relief. The strong objections of Anglos discouraged Mexican participation in assistance programs. It is at this time that the notion of the illegal alien gained notoriety, transforming Mexican workers into potential fugitives of the law unless they procured proper documentation. Tragically, repatriation victimized Mexicans who were U.S. citizens, legal residents who entered the country before there were official measures to confirm their legal immigration, and individuals unable to show proof of their legal status because of poverty.

It was the New Deal that inspired Mexican farm workers to organize, since many believed that the legislation would protect them against growers who wanted a labor force subservient to their objectives. In an unprecedented action, Mexicans were now demanding better wages and working conditions because they were particularly encouraged by President Roosevelt's guarantee of labor organizing and collective bargaining.[13] However, Southern Dixiecrats weakened key New Deal reforms by exempting agriculture and domestic work from the National Labor Relations Act and the Social Security Act. The deathblow for the Mexican American working classes, largely consisting of farm workers, was their exclusion from the Fair Labor Standards Act reform in 1938. Agreements between farm workers and employers were never formalized, and the federal government failed to recognize the farm worker unions. Knowing farm workers did not enjoy the right of collective bargaining, growers used every means of coercion and legal suppression to put down worker insurrection, including collusion with the Immigration and Naturalization Service and the U.S. Border Patrol. Indeed, deportation was an advantage held in reserve until needed. The history of Mexican labor conflict in the 1930s thus offers an object lesson in the ways the state was employed to repress worker militancy. The federal government, as witnessed by its ruthless methods of repression in handling labor disputes and its intimidation and interception of those who were undocumented or legal U.S. residents, hindered more than helped the struggle of Mexicans for rights, dignity, and equality. Nevertheless, in the absence of significant political activism, the labor movement remained the central organizing base out of which Mexican American protest activity emerged.

The American Federation of Labor blocked the entrance of Mexican workers into American unions, many of which maintained racially separate locals, and reinforced divisions within the American working classes. Chapter 2 presents a history of several labor struggles in the era of the National Industrial Recovery Act (NIRA). It first focuses on the organizing campaigns by Mexican farm workers in Texas, Colorado, and California, all of which proved difficult for the reasons outlined in chapter 1. In Texas, the struggle by workers was the more desperate because they had to face the Texas Rangers, who had been the most brutal in their dealings with Tejanos (Texas Mexicans). Still, the new opportunities for organizing initiated by the NIRA spurred Mexican American industrial workers to organize. The continued rural-to-urban migration within the Southwest and Midwest regions ultimately afforded them a stronger organizing context within which they could mobilize. Using the NRA code violations as an organizing tactic, Mexican female cigar workers and dressmakers went on strike. It was Mexican women workers who first challenged the long-standing problem of labor surpluses produced by the flow of women commuters from Mexico into border cities like El Paso, a situation that neutered unionism as well as the strategic advantage that would be available to both Tejanos and Mexican nationals if they formed an alliance against their nemesis.

Radicals played a prominent role in forcing this labor action. A better understanding of Mexican American labor radicalism is needed, particularly the complicated ties to communist-related unionism. Spanish-speaking workers brought radical traditions into the Communist Party that included old and new forms of collaborative action, some of which were unorganized and spontaneous strategies; Mexican working people maintained a sense of racial identity and solidarity; and the role of women in this radicalism was prominent. The party shaped and was shaped by Mexican working-class radicalism, of which cultural and national identity was a key element. Communist activity among Mexican workers is introduced and discussed in chapter 2 with an examination of the protracted Gallup, New Mexico, coal strike of 1933. This strike took place in the important Third Period (1929–33) of the party's revolutionary unionism, when communists took over the leadership of many labor struggles and embarked on a worker offensive against employers.[14]

The Mexican coal miners of Gallup launched their strike under the auspices of the radical National Miners Union (NMU). At this time, employers in the Southwest were as rabid in their hatred of Reds as they were rabid in their hatred of Mexicans. In the prevailing climate of repression, coal operators Red-baited the workers, the state governor declared martial law, and a reign of terror was launched against those identified as supporters of the NMU. The miners were blacklisted, denied relief, and subjected to deportation. The Immigration and Naturalization Service targeted labor leaders belonging to La Liga Obrera de Habla Español, who together with NMU members, were hounded out of the country on charges of communism. A pattern developed that would characterize many of the strike actions by Mexican workers during the period under study. Time and again, the allies of employers—the Immigration and Naturalization Service and the U.S. Border Patrol—broke up labor strikes and carried out searches and arrests of Mexican workers.

How the institutional frameworks of the New Deal and the CIO, and the character of particular Left-led unions determined the mobilization of Mexican workers in their opposition to abuse, as well as their successes or failures, represents another important theme of *Labor Rights Are Civil Rights*. CIO organizing by Mexican Americans is the focus of chapter 3, which begins with the onion strike outside Laredo, Texas, in 1936 led by La Asociación de Jornaleros. The significance of the onion strike is that it marks the beginning of transborder organizing by Left-led unions in the United States and their counterparts in Mexico. Prodded by the Communist Party of Mexico, the Communist Party of the United States took up the task of organizing Spanish-speaking workers, helping them obtain relief, fighting against discrimination, protesting police violence, and defending them against deportation.

During the Great Depression, Mexican American women were prominent as leaders of radical labor and civil rights movements. The way the party envisaged the class struggle opened up areas for Mexican American working-class women. The party's early ventures into labor organizing ignored the majority of Spanish-speaking women because, like the majority of black women, they were concentrated in domestic work and agriculture. Working through a variety of communist-led mass organizations, from the International Labor Defense to the Congress of Spanish-Speaking Peoples, the Communist Party eventually produced a noteworthy group of Mexican American women leaders, who included María Solis Sager and Emma Tenayuca (Texas), Luz Salazar (New Mexico and the Mountain States), and Guadalupe Marshall (Chicago).

Emma Tenayuca played a key role in organizing San Antonio's Tejano workers by leading demonstrations and strikes for relief work and organizing relief workers to contest job discrimination. More important, Tenayuca reaffirmed the message that their struggle was part of the struggle of all Mexican workers for civil rights. In chapter 3, I assess Emma Tenayuca's role in community and labor organizing as well as her activities in the Communist Party as its ablest Mexican American spokesperson. The focus of this chapter is the challenge of Mexican American agrarian unionism centered on Emma Tenayuca, as well as a united effort by a major union, the United Cannery, Agricultural, Packing, and Allied Workers of America, in Southern California. Chapter 3 ends with a discussion of the initial CIO union drive by Mexican American workers in Los Angeles.

Chapter 4 examines the campaign by the International Union of Mine, Mill, and Smelter Workers (Mine-Mill) to organize Mexican nonferrous metals workers in the Southwest, focusing on the union drive in El Paso, Texas, during the years 1939–43. The nonferrous metals industry suffered from oversupply and depressed prices, which resulted in cutbacks in production and employment. Owing to disputes, the copper industry operators could not reach agreement on an NRA code. Unemployment and widespread deprivation eclipsed long-existing wage differentials between this mining region and other regions. Given the prevailing open-shop atmosphere, unionism in the nonferrous metals industry was nonexistent. For most of the 1930s, Mine-Mill was at low ebb and the membership declined. However, despite infighting and disputes with the AFL, the NIRA collective bargaining provisions and the copper code led to the restoration of interim local unions at some southwestern mines and metal processing refineries.

Mexicans and Mexican Americans made up over half of the 15,000 miners and smelter workers employed by Phelps Dodge, Nevada Consolidated, Anaconda, and American Smelting and Refining Company

(ASARCO) in the Southwest. All the Spanish-speaking miners worked as low-wage common laborers, lacked seniority provisions, were subject to company domination, and outside the workplace were victims of pervasive discrimination. Given the oppressive conditions, there was little optimism that a successful labor movement could arise in the southwestern copper industry. Mine-Mill possessed a history of rank-and-file militancy, and the Southwest region's Mexican miners and smelter workers embraced it. Drawing on the ancient conflict between aggrieved Mexican workers and the mining companies, Mine-Mill tapped a core of activism among these minority workers, who were just as indignant about the social discrimination they endured, which reflected the larger racial climate of the Southwest region. Mine-Mill represents an institution in which Mexicans could actually advance their labor and civil rights in a New Deal context. Mine-Mill's interracial unionism proved successful in cross-border alliances and was equally crucial to the union's success in building its locals.

According to historians of American communism, the American Communist Party, in unity with the Comintern's Seventh World Congress, called for a Popular Front against fascism, de-emphasized its Marxist ideology, and eventually supported Roosevelt's New Deal coalition. Indeed, in a few short years, the party had made a great transformation. Slogans about "social fascists" and building a "Soviet America" were replaced by efforts to carve a niche for the party in the mainstream of the American reform tradition. Communists joined mainstream civil rights organizations in greater numbers. Spanish-speaking left-wing organizers served as the primary force behind the Mexican American coalition effort in the Congress of Spanish-Speaking Peoples, a Popular Front organization that emerged at about the same time as the fall of Madrid to the fascist armies in March 1939. The leftists also used their influence in the CIO and in the Workers' Alliance of America to bring Mexican Americans into similar progressive organizations behind President Roosevelt.

World War II profoundly affected Mexican Americans. Disproportionate numbers fought overseas as a result of unfair draft selection; others entered wartime employment and, despite resistance, for the first time held skilled jobs. They also became a focus of wartime hostility. An early Mexican American civil rights movement emerged during World War II as the wartime experience and the growing power of the black vote elevated the importance of civil rights in national politics. At the same time, the Communist Party's sudden shift to an extreme antiwar position, the Dies Committee's investigation into "un-American" activities, and the rising anticommunism among CIO leaders all weakened the party's base of support on the eve of World War II.

The struggles by Mexican Americans for full citizenship during the World War II emergency is another theme I take up in *Labor Rights Are Civil Rights*. In fact, the potential for racial equality reached fruition during World War II. Chapter 4 shifts to the labor scene in Los Angeles, which now had the nation's largest Mexican population, made up overwhelmingly of blue-collar workers, who in 1941 were swept up in the ferment of one of the largest CIO-led strike waves. With the start of the war, many Mexican Americans migrated to war mobilization centers to seek work in the defense plants. CIO unions educated workers about federal standards and policies and labor grievances. Taking on greater roles in rank-and-file and community activism through CIO-supported civil rights associations, Mexican American workers brought new meaning to the relationship of labor and civil rights.[15] As a product of the Popular Front and the CIO labor organizing drives, the Congress of Spanish-Speaking Peoples worked to incorporate Mexican Americans and Mexicans into American life and citizenship through political mobilization. In Los Angeles, a coalition of progressive CIO unions and left-wing activists assisted the Peoples' Congress in combating racial and ethnic strife. An important activity of the Peoples' Congress was confronting the profascist organization of the Sinarquistas.

World War II represented a turning point for Mexican American workers, whose demand for equality in the workplace and in the nation as a whole made them the chief actors in the struggle for civil rights. This heightened consciousness was brought about by the opportunities for political and economic advancement afforded by New Deal labor legislation, the government's patriotic wartime propaganda, the President's Committee on Fair Employment Practices hearings on discrimination, and the bloody interracial violence that swept America's cities in 1943. The entry of Mexican Americans into the CIO unions and their fight against shop floor discrimination served as an important catalyst in the unfolding struggle for social and political advancement by this fast-growing, urban working-class population. As always, Mexican American women played as important a role as the men in mobilizing and leading support for the cause of civil rights.

Chapter 5 focuses on the overall experiences of the Mexican American community during World War II. Like blacks, Mexican Americans combined the fight against fascism abroad with the struggle for civil rights to achieve racial and social equality at home. Mexican Americans came to realize that they needed the help of the federal government to gain rights as American citizens and called on it to intervene. The federal government's policies regarding Mexican Americans were shaped more and more by foreign policy decisions. The new context of international pressures, urbanization, and full employment made federal authorities deeply sensitive to the outbreak of racial disturbances such as the Los Angeles Zoot Suit Riots. President Roosevelt therefore used the FBI and various arms of military intelligence to infiltrate Sinarquista fund-raising cells operating in the United States. However, race relations were not a centerpiece of Roosevelt's domestic policies. Nor did race relations strike a responsive cord among white Americans: they resisted what little assistance was given to racial minorities. Despite all the official dogma about equality, there was no coordinated and concerted government effort to deal with racial discrimination. In the end, government enforcement measures were unresponsive to the realities of race relations in the Southwest. The Mexican Americans were kept in their place as excluded and exploited second-class citizens—they were the last hired for defense work, were discriminated against in federal job training programs, were assigned mostly unskilled jobs, and had to cope with the larger issue of racism. Segregation barriers in most cities of the Southwest were strong. Anglos maintained the racial status quo and therefore resisted fair housing, and federal housing apartheid policies led to related social problems, such as the segregation of schools. Along with black workers, Mexican Americans fought against the widespread discrimination in defense work, sought to increase and expand job opportunities and end discrimination in the unions, and moreover continued to participate in the pursuit of full equality. In so doing, Mexican Americans helped change the character of race relations in the United States.

Mexico declared war against the Axis powers on May 28, 1942, and quickly began fulfilling its wartime commitment to America by providing tens of thousands of agricultural contract workers, tankerloads of oil, and massive amounts of other crucial war matériel as well. Over the next three and a half years of war, the economic and military links forged between Mexico and the United States would define relations across the Río Grande for decades to come. Mexican immigrant labor, bilateral trade, energy sharing, and security cooperation are all modern-day issues that were first confronted by Mexico and the United States as wartime allies sixty years ago. As will be seen in my discussion of the Mexican contract labor program, labor representatives questioned the contract labor program's impact on domestic farm workers, while Mexican Americans were concerned that the braceros would take away jobs and contribute to more racial discrimination.

Chapter 6 recounts the efforts of Mexican Americans to organize for equality in the postwar years because they were not enjoying the fruits of peacetime economic expansion. Most continued to be employed mainly in agriculture at low pay and under miserable conditions. In the industrial workplace, Mexican Americans experienced job loss as a result of low seniority and layoffs. Unemployment was demoralizing, and there was deep-seated discontent among those Mexican American blue-collar workers who had work because they were relegated to the worst unskilled and semiskilled positions with the lowest pay. Owing to a renewed race hatred, Mexican Americans still suffered violations of their rights. Police violence against Mexican Americans, who were widely identified as lawless, continued to fuel great bitterness in the Mexican American communities, where the residents were overcharged for run-down housing and suffered other inequities, such as the high numbers of youth pushed out of school. School dropout rates increased because teachers in the overcrowded urban schools believed Mexicans were inferior and thus less capable of learning. The nation's second-largest minority was socially segregated from Anglos, another sign of the deepening racial polarization of America.

In the postwar years, the Mexican American struggle for full citizenship increased. Unions once again were invaluable in the successful grassroots mobilizations, for they served as vehicles for empowering Mexican Americans to fight for their civil rights. Mexican American trade unionists were at the forefront of the movement in advocating economic and social equality. In seeking to reverse the declining fortunes of their unions, Mexican Americans participated in demonstrations and strikes for full employment and higher wages during the conversion to a peacetime economy. The struggle for equality concentrated on expanding Mexican American employment and ensuring decent jobs, and it began as a fight to make the FEPC permanent. Mexican American trade-union activists pushed for antidiscrimination laws at the state level, demanded shop floor seniority and wage parity from local unions growing racially conservative, sought to repeal the Taft-Hartley Act, and led community-based struggles for equality. Protests in the communities addressed the controversial issue of wanton police abuse; protestors also called for better housing, schools, and other adequate services.

Amid frequent charges of communism and in an atmosphere of racist antialien hysteria, Mexican Americans demonstrated their determination to cross the color line to advance the cause of labor and civil rights. To be sure, the heightened sense of identity and the welling up of consciousness among the Mexican American people were dashed by the rise of the Cold War. McCarthyism, including the purge by the CIO of left-wing unions, many with a sizable racial minority membership, impeded the Mexican American civil rights movement. The union campaigns on behalf of Mexican Americans would be defeated by Taft-Hartley and the Red Scare crackdown on outspoken dissenters in a broad assault against civil liberties. Mexican Americans were harassed and intimidated, and their credibility was compromised when they were denounced as subversives. These men and women thus paid a high price for their resolve to realize their goal of racial equality. Meanwhile, traditional Mexican American civic leaders who shunned direct action were similarly put on the defensive by reactionaries and hard-line civil rights opponents.

Another disturbing factor, and a more immediate menace than the Red Scare, were the legions of work-starved *mojados* who posed a direct threat to the living standards, health, and education of Mexican Americans. Together with the Mexican contract labor program that began in 1942 and would continue over the next twenty-two years, the influx of *mojados* rapidly increased the number of Mexican nationals in the United States. Unemployment and underemployment as a result spread among the Mexican American working-class population. The attendant deportation frenzy created by the McCarran-Walter Act through "Operation Wetback" to deal with an unraveling contract labor program further racialized Mexican Americans, already the victims of a hostile environment.

Yet Mexican Americans were no longer willing to accept their inferior status, as is indicated by the rise of a grassroots movement for full equality. The first change in the political scene came from the emergence of vocal groups working for greater Mexican American participation in the political process. The newly formed all–Mexican American organizations educated community members on current issues, registered them to vote, and pressured the major political parties for fair representation. I conclude that the period extending from the New Deal years to the postwar era was a turning point for Mexican American demands for civil rights. Specifically, the activism that flowed out of the CIO union movement laid the groundwork for the rise of a postwar Mexican American civil rights movement. *Labor Rights Are Civil Rights* will help reveal this hidden legacy of Mexican American workers and their numerous contributions to the American labor and civil rights movement.

We Are the Salt of the Earth: Conditions among Mexican Workers in the Early Great Depression Years

> Bowed by the weight of centuries he leans
> Upon his hoe and gazes on the ground,
> The emptiness of ages in his face,
> And on his back, the burden of the world.
> —EDWIN MARKHAM, *The Man with a Hoe*

> If there were two less Mexicans in our country the same
> number of Americans would have jobs.
> —IRATE ANGLO RESIDENT, April 22, 1930

ABOUT 1,422,533 Mexicans lived in the United States in 1930, a figure representing a 75 percent growth in the Spanish-speaking population since the last census counts in 1920. Three-fourths of the population was concentrated in the southwestern states of Texas, Colorado, New Mexico, Arizona, and California. Relatively young and made up of large families with many American-born children, the Mexicans' specific economic and social importance rested with their use by employers solely interested in exploiting their labor and subjected to an extreme form of economic exploitation. By the turn of the twentieth century most Mexicans in the Southwest had been systematically incorporated into an emergent working class, and many found themselves increasingly serving in the agricultural sector and subjected to an extreme form of economic exploitation. Because of its proximity to the United States, Mexico supplied an enormous number of migrants to the United States. The majority of these migrants were transnational, migrating to the Southwest, usually to find employment, while maintaining community membership in the home country. Southwestern agricultural interests, which by now were quite used to getting their way with the federal government, opposed any immigration legislation they perceived as likely to curtail the supply of Mexican workers and financially ruin them. There were few obstacles to the introduction of imported Mexican laborers because growers used the power of the state to shape the economic order of the Southwest and create a dependent labor force. Mexican labor became a structural feature of the

Southwest economy, growing in tandem with the economy's expansion. Employers integrated the Southwest's tradition of racism into the edifice of labor relations to guarantee efficiency and powerlessness. Racism inexorably determined how the Mexican would be employed, and racism's political, cultural, and legal underpinnings made it difficult, but not wholly impossible, to mount collective resistance against this situation of near total subjugation. There was no question that Mexicans were one of the most disadvantaged groups in the United States.[1]

Planting and harvesting many fruit and vegetable crops was extremely labor-intensive. This physically arduous work was very often performed by seasonal and migrant farm labor. Several migrant streams supplied this labor in the Southwest. The Texas stream represented the largest entity of migrant workers and was made up of Tejanos who were based in south Texas. Several hundred thousand Tejano migratory workers contributed to the agricultural economy of Texas throughout the year on a seasonal basis. These workers followed the crops throughout the state; some followed the crops northward, traveling to the midwestern states. The Mountain States stream originated in Mexico; the migrants crossed through or resided in the border town of El Paso, Texas, then migrated to the beet fields of Colorado, where they became an important component of the agricultural workforce in that state. The West Coast stream consisted primarily of workers who were Mexican nationals and those who were residents of communities in Southern California or along the California border. The number of seasonal and migratory farm laborers was difficult to determine. Out-migration and the different strategies by which Mexican farm workers would attempt breaks with the old order depended on the structural arrangements of production relations in the distinctive economic regions of the Southwest.

With the start of the Great Depression, the deteriorating economic conditions increased racial tensions in areas with large Spanish-speaking populations. The widespread unemployment deepened Anglo racial animosity toward Mexicans; Anglos idled by the economic crisis condemned Mexicans as the root cause of unemployment and other attendant ills. In the widespread anti-Mexican agitation, Anglos blamed the Mexicans not only for taking jobs, but also for increasing the American taxpayers' burden and for competing with more deserving local Anglo residents for scarce social resources. Mexican immigrants were made the universal scapegoats of inept government actions to improve conditions for the growing number of poor people during a time of economic depression. Resembling the "Negro Removal" campaigns of the mid-South, though minus the ugly violence, a drive to thin the ranks of the Mexican laborers was mounted in both rural and urban settings. Mexican immigrants faced the dire prospects of apprehension and deportation aimed at impeding immigration from Mexico. Local and state authorities and soon the federal government all took part in organizing and coordinating the drive to send the workers back to Mexico.[2] Mexican Americans were directly affected by the anti-alien climate and were subject to blanket suspicion as these practices intensified. Along with legal residents they were interdicted by the U.S. Immigration Bureau, denied access to social services, or else faced barriers intentionally created to discourage their participation in relief assistance.

The "Big Swing": The Peregrinations and Tribulations of Tejano Cotton Harvesters

By 1929, the Southwest was producing 40 percent of America's supply of fruits and vegetables. In Texas, food production ranked first among all industries in this state, and over half of the farmland in Texas was planted in cotton. Tejanos were the chief source of labor for the Lone Star State's fruit and vegetable harvests and its giant and overlapping cotton harvest seasons. Tejanos lived principally in the lower Río Grande Valley in south Texas, in central Texas including the city of San Antonio, in the Winter Garden area of southwest Texas, and in the El Paso district in west Texas. However, most of the workers came out of south Texas, the largest reservoir of cheap labor in all of the United States. All these areas of Tejano concentration functioned as labor reservoirs for large-scale agriculture and truck farming and for similar hand labor outside the state. Moreover, with more than half of the 2,100-mile border the United States shared with Mexico running along the Río Grande in Texas, a steady stream of job-hungry immigrants from Mexico crossed the border or were brought across into the Lone Star State and complemented and reinforced the Tejano labor force. The extremely high number of Tejanos in south Texas, together with the importation of great numbers of immigrant workers from Mexico subservient to the wants of employers, preserved labor relations and broke the bargaining power of the region's Spanish-speaking workers.[3]

America was thoroughly racially segregated, and nowhere in the Southwest was prejudice more pervasive than in Texas, where Tejanos lived as subordinate members of society. Holding the Tejano workers back was a powerful combination of Anglo growers and ranchers and local officials forbidding any organization of Tejanos. Mimicking Southern Jim Crow racism, this system, whereby Tejanos bore the brunt of Anglo contempt, produced a form of labor control that fluctuated with the seasons of agricultural production. As with the Deep South's black workers, economic opportunity was extremely narrowed for Tejanos because Anglos controlled all resources. Growers and their cronies had command of the courts, the sheriffs' offices, and the justices of the peace, and utilized the Texas

Rangers, who monopolized armed force in south Texas to sustain control over Tejano and Mexican national alike. The possibility of collective action by Tejanos was all but eliminated by these coercive measures employed by the Anglo ruling class. In addition to de facto segregation, which cancelled upward mobility, civil rights, and political power, American-born Tejanos competed directly with Mexican immigrants for jobs and, because of their large numbers, faced substantial anti-Mexican prejudice.

Cotton cultivation had assumed a central economic importance in Texas by the early twentieth century. The Tejanos who streamed into the cotton areas of the Gulf Coast, central, and north central regions of Texas at first were an insignificant factor, because of the Anglo and black share-cropper and tenant families still on the area farms who provided the labor for chopping and picking but remained idle the rest of the year. However, beginning in 1915 the sharecropper and tenant system was overturned through the introduction of agricultural modernization techniques such as tractor-driven and other machinery for planting and cultivating crops. Great numbers of Tejano migrant workers at this time moved into these Texas cotton-growing regions, though bypassing areas where pockets of black and Anglo sharecroppers still remained. In a narrow belt of land stretching from Greenville and Dallas in the north to San Antonio in the south, large-scale cotton plantations likewise developed based on the use of machinery. More and more sharecroppers and tenants were being displaced from the land by the expansion of mechanized large-scale cotton farming, which dramatically speeded up crop sowing and cultivation and thereby reduced the need for year-round resident labor. However, mechanization did not affect the man-hour requirements of cotton harvesting, which became wholly dependent on massive numbers of itinerant workers brought in by labor contractors from the lower Río Grande Valley. The black and Anglo sharecroppers and tenants were unable to compete with the low-wage Tejano laborer. Dispossessed, the former became day laborers in Houston, Dallas, and Fort Worth and supplemented their low wages with whatever relief they could obtain. Government-sponsored crop reduction programs introduced in the 1930s would ultimately collapse the Texas tenant-sharecropping system.[4]

As labor costs declined through mechanization and as cotton prices rose rapidly during the World War I years, there was a permanent shift to wage work as cotton farmers took full advantage of Mexican labor. Farmers at one time had paid sharecropper and tenant families $800 for the year but now paid migrant families only $250 a year for the cotton harvest. The greatest cotton migrations in the Southwest occurred in Texas, due mainly to the staggered cotton planting, cultivating, and harvesting periods, which ranged from the south Texas border region to the High Plains area in the Texas Panhandle. Also, cotton as a major cash crop provided employment at the lowest wage rate to the largest number of workers—three-fourths of them Tejano—over a longer period of time than all other agricultural enterprises. The demand for pickers took place during the harvest seasons all over the Texas cotton regions, lasting six to ten weeks in each cotton area. As the following account shows, the cotton harvest began first in south Texas, then moved on to east and central Texas, and culminated in the northwestern part of the state.[5]

The staggered cotton-harvesting season in Texas began around mid-July in Cameron, Willacy, and Hidalgo Counties in the lower Río Grande Valley. Workers entered this area from the nearby small towns or migrated down from San Antonio, a major supply center of Tejano labor. Other Tejanos, upon completing the area onion harvest in the northern part of the state, migrated down through central Texas to the south Texas cotton district. The gatherings of workers grew huge as the labor crews took to the main highway to the lower Río Grande Valley. Many moved into the large-scale cotton-producing area of Nueces and San Patricio Counties, joining local Tejanos on the cotton farms, some with several thousand acres of planted cotton requiring more than 5,000 pickers to do the back-breaking, tedious hand labor while fighting the fierce, blazing sun.[6]

Once they picked the cotton in Nueces and San Patricio Counties, some of the peripatetic families traveled northeast to the cotton farms in Wharton and Fort Bend counties and to those in the coastal county of Brazoria, located south of Houston. Meanwhile, other workers followed migration routes running through and beyond these two areas. The anxious crews of Tejano workers moving out of Wharton and Fort Bend Counties traveled northward toward the state's largest cotton district, around the cities of Dallas and Fort Worth, where this particular migratory route terminated. From the Nueces and San Patricio cotton district another of the Tejano migratory routes led northwest through the cotton district located between Corpus Christi, Austin, and San Antonio. Exhausted, some Tejanos headed to the huge barrio in San Antonio's West Side to wait for the harvest season to commence in another cotton-growing area. From San Antonio, these workers migrated into central Texas, another stream of migrants flowed directly north to the cotton farms between Abeline and Wichita Falls, and yet another stream of workers flowed northwest into the new High Plains cotton area surrounding the city of Lubbock (dubbed the "cotton capital") that included Lynn, Dawson, Terry, and Hockley Counties. On the eve of the Great Depression, between 35,000 and 50,000 Tejanos migrated into the High Plains area to harvest cotton totaling 1,130,713 bales. The area tenant farmers, who at one time operated more than half the cotton farms, were rendered obsolete; they were displaced by the combination of rapid mechanization and great numbers of Tejano workers. Hardworking and skillful, tens of thousands of Tejanos harvested the cotton so fast on the huge farms that the cotton gin could not keep up with them. The El Paso district in west Texas was another high cotton production area. The seventy-mile-long irrigated cotton area stretched along the upper Río Grande Valley and surrounded the city of El Paso. Most of the pickers were local Tejanos and Mexicans from Ciudad Juárez trucked in from El Paso. Because unemployment was rife in the border area, the uncertainty of work forced these laborers into the low-wage field work.[7]

The army of Tejano cotton pickers completed the succession of cotton harvests in late November and early December and disbanded. Some Tejano families moved on to New Mexico and Arizona, while others traveled to California and Washington, to the Mississippi Delta, and to northwest Ohio. Most of the migrants returned to their home base in the Winter Garden area or to the lower Río Grande Valley to work the various winter vegetable harvests. These were followed by the onion harvests, which began in May in Webb County, then in Nueces and San Patricio Counties in the lower Río Grande Valley, and in June in north Texas around Dallas and some of the surrounding counties. The short onion harvests paid less than fifty cents a day, but guided by the principle of "work or starve," the Tejanos took this work. Upon finishing the onion harvest in north Texas, the Tejanos migrated back down through central Texas into the lower Río Grande Valley. Here they joined other work crews for the beginning of the cotton-harvests, once again repeating the whole migration cycle within Texas. The exact number of Tejano migrants who harvested cotton was unknown owing to the fluctuation in a worker's migration patterns determined by harvest conditions and other opportunities for farm work. Workers who drifted into a cotton area remained for the entire cotton-harvesting period; others came in for short intervals, while still others stayed briefly, heard of better cotton, and worked long enough to make money to wander on.[8]

The cycle of the Texas cotton harvests, that is, the day-to-day pace and patterns of work, the irregularity of work at low wages, perpetual debt, and the playing out of the insidious dynamics of race and class, greatly influenced Tejano life. Families and extended family members made up the work crews that varied in size from twelve to as many as twenty workers. For enduring unbearable working conditions under a hot sun, Tejano cotton pickers earned between $225 and $600 per season. However, by the early 1930s the most efficient Tejano families were earning the equivalent of a dollar a day per season. Much of this money went to pay off cash or credit advances, food, gas, and other expenses. Tejano families were cheated out of their pay by greedy cotton farmers and unscrupulous labor contractors and as a result were broke when the harvest season ended. Some became stranded in distant parts of Texas because they could not pay for their return trip home. Once home, further credit advances for food or housing drowned Tejanos in debt. Credit, which enticed many Tejanos into debt, also made them more obedient to orders. Because the growers wanted a labor force totally subordinated to their objectives, the workers were further debilitated by socially enforced sanctions that included debt peonage. Emerging throughout the South during the post-Reconstruction years, debt peonage was used to restrict the movement of workers. A long-established Texas custom held that a Tejano worker had to pay off his debt to a grower before moving on to another employer or else languish in jail. In Willacy County in the lower Río Grande Valley, the customary punishment was to make Tejanos work off their debts by picking cotton. Peonage was enforced through the use of guards, the isolation of the workers on out-of-the-way farms, "No Trespass" and other posted warning signs, cooperation of sheriffs and police officials, and outright terror. During constant "labor shortages," other Tejanos were randomly charged with vagrancy, a law sanctioned to exact involuntary labor from Tejanos. Labor contractors drove Tejanos in their work through a combination of wheedling, threats, and mistreatment. Workers who were not U.S. citizens were instilled with the fear of being deported. Growers exploited this fear. They turned Mexicans over (usually before payday) to local law or immigration officials who purposely manipulated the law to the workers' disadvantage. Those workers who dared complain about working conditions were also deported.[9]

These were the arrangements by which Tejanos were tied to cotton picking. Admittedly, there were instances of individual acts of resistance, but the deployment of the Texas Rangers ensured that any attempted uprising would be crushed with an iron hand. This is why few Tejanos came out collectively on strike to demand an increase in wages or better working conditions.

As was the lot of most migrant workers, living conditions for cotton pickers were deplorable. At their home base in south Texas, housing for Tejanos typically consisted of a dilapidated two-room "box house" with an outdoor privy. Very few pickers owned their homes, as most lived in their houses rent-free or else rented. As the migrant families followed the crops, they occupied sheds, barns, and shacks without toilet facilities or running water for cooking, bathing, and washing clothes. Others set up makeshift camps wherever they chose a site. Most of the families lived in roadside squatters' camps or near the edge of the cotton fields and furnished their own tent or shelter and household goods. Water was free when growers provided it, or else the pickers drew their water from nearby abandoned wells and rivers. The pickers scavenged for fuel. The abysmal living situation was made worse by overcrowding because growers generally advertised for more workers than needed, or because work-

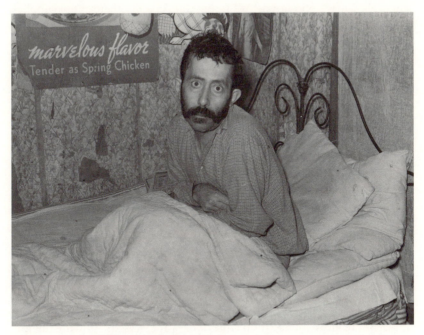

Figure 1.A. Tejano worker with advanced case of tuberculosis, Crystal City, Texas, 1939. The high rates of sickness and death owing to poor nutrition, contaminated drinking water, and unsanitary living conditions added to the misery of Mexican American agricultural workers. (FSA 8b21044—Courtesy of Library of Congress).

ers out of habit arrived in advance of the start of the picking season. Because of the congestion, combined with rains, cold weather, hard work, and a poor diet, the settlements were ravaged by diseases such as small-pox, typhoid, and scarlet fever that threatened the health of migrants and that of the local population as well. The local Anglo populace disliked the congregation of Tejano workers on the margins of towns. This is why the workers were kept confined to the migrant camps so they would not drift into town to frequent grocery stores, picture shows, and taverns. All of this served as proof of the Tejano migrant worker's lowly status. One reason for the extensive use of Tejano labor rather than Anglo labor in some sections of Texas was that Anglo landowners hated seeing "white people living that way."[10]

Poverty was exacerbated by illiteracy, a damning indictment of Anglo racism. Illiteracy was caused by poor school attendance, because eco-nomic necessity forced cash-starved parents to put their children to work in the fields. Also, many parents did not have birth certificates for their children. They could not afford to buy books and other school supplies, and most migrant children were poorly clothed and lacked shoes. Parents chose to keep them out of school rather than endure insults from hostile teachers and heckling and teasing by classmates. Ill health attributed to malnutrition and harsh physical work was also a contributing factor in low school attendance. The state's compulsory school attendance law was not enforced, or else was ignored, so that in some counties the school term for migrant children lasted just three to four months. Although many Mexicans in the Southwest region could not read or write, illiteracy was greatest among Tejanos. More than a third had never attended school, in contrast with 10 percent of the state's blacks; 40 percent dropped out before the third grade; and just 5 percent of Tejanos had gone beyond the fourth grade, in comparison to 14 percent of blacks and 90 percent of Anglos. Illiteracy was greatest in the lower Río Grande Valley.[11]

Poverty, ill health, and ignorance were therefore the terrible consequences for Tejanos of being nearly owned by Anglo farmers completely indifferent to their plight. Rendered defenseless by Jim Crow, and with no organizations to espouse their cause owing to the demise of the rich associational life of mutual aid and fraternal organizations that had nurtured and increased ethnic solidarity since the turn of the century, working-class Tejanos found all avenues of escape closed. As with migrant workers generally, Tejanos would have to wait until the late 1960s for the federal government to focus attention and resources on their unfavorable working and living conditions and on the education of their children. Similar situations of despair existed in the Tejano working-class sections of San Antonio, Laredo, and El Paso when migrants poured into these cities during the winter off-season. As the Great Depression unfolded, more and more Tejanos fleeing rural poverty sought refuge in these urban centers, but they would have great difficulty finding work and obtaining relief from their distress.

To supplement their awfully low earnings from itinerant farm work, many Mexicans desperately sought work in urban centers at the end of the harvest season or during bad harvests. However, the rural migrants who arrived in the cities were soon rendered destitute by unemployment and suffered dreadfully because of the squalid and crowded living conditions in Mexican working-class districts. Unable to afford rent for a house or a room, the arrivals doubled up with kin and friends. This in-migration to the cities resulted in more overcrowding and heightened job competition, all of which made Mexicans susceptible to pauperization.

San Antonio, Laredo, and El Paso were all major urban hubs for Tejano labor. Known as the "Queen City of the Southwest," El Paso was the most important port of entry for Mexican immigrants. After San Antonio and Los Angeles, El Paso had the nation's third largest Mexican population, and it was bound to the slums of the city's east and south sides. In these exclusively Mexican working-class districts, the overcrowding, made awful by poor sanitation, combined with the fact that residents were too poor to buy food because of chronic unemployment, produced high death rates from tuberculosis and other fatal diseases. An important demographic characteristic impinging on the welfare of El Paso's Mexican Americans was that the city's Spanish-speaking population was mostly foreign born. In 1920, over three-fourths (77 percent) of the Mexicans residing in El Paso were foreign born; ten years later, 64 percent of this border city's Mexican population remained foreign born. In addition to de facto segregation, which cancelled upward mobility, civil rights, and political power, American-born Tejanos faced substantial prejudice because Anglo El Pasoans misidentified Mexican Americans as Mexicans and perceived all Mexicans unsympathetically as foreigners. The deeply entrenched anti-Mexican hostility served to repress labor, forced Mexican Americans to distance themselves from their immigrant counterparts in all matters of association, and by doing so stymied the development of working-class alliances.[12]

The railroads, retail and wholesale houses, construction firms, urban services, the American Smelting and Refining Company, and cotton production formed the basis of El Paso's economy. Unorganized reserves of Mexican labor from both El Paso itself and Ciudad Juárez, directly across the border, supported this economy. Constituting over half of El Paso's population, Mexicans were restricted to so-called degraded "Mexican jobs," which paid less than the jobs Anglos held and less than similar work performed by Mexicans outside the El Paso border district. El Paso's Anglo businessmen and their allies the public officials sustained this racially segmented, dual-wage labor market. Mexican women, including those from Ciudad Juárez who commuted daily to El Paso, provided another ample source of cheap labor, for which they received less remuneration than the men.[13] Female workers were economically indispensable to the local labor markets; competition among the women, as among the men, was differentiated along lines of nationality and citizenship, further dividing them and reinforcing their economic inequality.

With retail and clerical jobs for the most part closed to them, the Mexican women essentially took work Anglo women were unwilling to accept. Many of the Tejanas worked in the local commercial laundries performing wash work that was undercompensated; characterized by hot, damp, and poorly ventilated working conditions without sanitary facilities; and punctuated by periodic layoffs and speedups. From the late nineteenth century until World War II, domestic work, marked by long hours and low pay, was the single largest source of employment for Mexican women. Taking advantage of El Paso's abundant labor supply of Mexican women, Anglo housewives hired them as maids to clean their homes, cook, do laundry, run errands and shop, and care for their children. The fact that Mexican women worked exclusively as maids racialized domestic work and pushed already low wages for this labor further down.[14]

El Paso's labor situation remained relatively unchanged during the 1930s. Because on one level collective action is a product of local circumstances, union organizers would face the same formidable problem in the city that plagued their predecessors—winning over and attaining unity with a large population of Mexican nationals who hampered labor organization. Tejanos and Mexican nationals would have to find common ground and forge ties with one another for unionization to succeed. A similar surplus labor problem of Spanish-speaking workers distinguished San Antonio.

A huge floating population of semi-urban Tejano workers accounted for San Antonio's tight labor market, as well as for its highly dense Mexican quarters on the West Side. This slum area teemed with Mexicans; it was the most heavily congested area with the worst living conditions in the entire Southwest, a virtual death trap. As in El Paso's densely packed Mexican working-class slums, the high death rates among Tejanos from San Antonio's Westside resulted from the ravages of tuberculosis and other poverty-related diseases. In 1930, Mexicans made up nearly half (47.8 percent) of San Antonio's total population, which, like El Paso's, consisted largely of immigrants. Seventy percent of the city's Mexican population had immigrated to the United States between 1911 and 1930, while 20 percent had arrived between 1900 and 1910. Fifty percent of San Antonio's Mexicans worked as common laborers in manufacturing, trade, and transportation, and, more significantly, over two-thirds of the city's Mexicans did not have full-time work. The few employment opportunities available in San Antonio cast women in the role of family breadwinner. Almost three-fourths of the city's Mexican females worked as domestics or as factory operatives on a seasonal basis in the cigar and garment shops (40 percent and 44 percent, respectively) and in the pecan-shelling industry, San Antonio's largest employer of Mexican labor. Organizing their workplaces along racial and gender lines and completely ignoring health and safety conditions, the cigar companies, garment shops, and pecan-shelling sheds relentlessly exploited the abundant, all-Mexican workforce.[15]

Tejanos lived in similar social and economic circumstances in the border city of Laredo, where they made up 80 percent of the population, many of them immigrants from Mexico. The lack of work produced a high jobless rate almost year-round, and when Laredo's Tejanos did work in the existing nonagricultural jobs, it was for the lowest wages in the country. Pay for women was even lower. Although Laredo served chiefly as a reservoir for Tejano migratory labor and notwithstanding other barriers to organization and action, an incipient group of Tejano activists made this city a major focal point of labor and political activism.[16]

Located on or in close proximity to the border and possessing large immigrant populations, El Paso, San Antonio, and Laredo all offered Tejanos poverty, slums, and unemployment or underemployment. Tejanos began to protest that workers from Mexico lowered their living standards, contributed to other social ills, and held back labor organization. As the 1930s unfolded, union organizers from both sides of the border cooperated in the difficult task of organizing this labor force and awakening a sense of mutual commitment. Given the nature of the labor market, the activists realized that ties of class and culture were far more important than national differences because such animosities undermined the potential for solidarity. Organizing had to include Mexican nationals if Tejano workers were to gain a strategic advantage against their fate. Nonetheless, labor organizers worked hard, exhorting the Tejanos in the fields, and they responded solidly to the message of unionism.[17]

"In the Land of Bondage": Colorado's Mexican Sugar Beet Workers

In contrast to the highly competitive small cotton and truck farms in Texas, the nation's sugar beet–growing industry was highly capitalized, large-scale, and dependent on government controls. It was characterized as well by the racial composition of its seasonal workforce, consisting of large Mexican family units who, like serfs, bound themselves to the beet growers through contracts for the longest period of work of all crop production. Two-thirds of the workers settled in the sugar beet–growing areas or migrated to the beet farms from nearby cities and towns. Beet work drew migrants from the economically hard-pressed villages of northern New Mexico; the working-class barrios of Denver; Lincoln and Omaha, Nebraska; Minneapolis and St. Paul, Minnesota; and El Paso, San Antonio, and Fort Worth, Texas. Whereas the sugar companies had previously recruited the workers using their own agents or through employment agencies contracted for this purpose, on the eve of the Great Depression growers and growers' associations had taken over the recruitment of the beet workers.[18]

Invariably, Colorado Spanish-speaking beet workers felt the weight of racial discrimination, the evils of child labor, widespread illiteracy, harrowing living conditions, chronic ill health, and eternal poverty. Colorado's Mexicans were trapped in a migratory cycle linked to beet production, bound to an onerous form of stoop labor by seasonal contracts and dependent on relief for six months out of the year to avoid starvation. The full dimensions of the Mexican beet worker's tragic story unfolded in Colorado.

The Great Western Sugar Company dominated sugar production in Colorado; by 1930, Great Western was producing 80 percent of Colorado beet sugar, representing nearly half of the nation's beet sugar market. The area of the South Platte River Valley in northeastern Colorado was the nation's largest producer of sugar beets with the heaviest beet-producing areas located in northern Colorado's Weld, Larimer, Logan, Adams, and Boulder Counties. Each harvest was dependent on a labor force of 20,000 workers, three-fourths of them Mexicans and Mexican Americans, who thinned and harvested 110,000 acres of sugar beets valued at over $12 million. Governed by the paternalism of the sugar companies, the Spanish-speaking beet workers were tolerated as a necessary nuisance, for they did stoop labor Anglos would not do. No matter how much Anglos needed work, they "would not crawl," that is they would not contract to perform the long hours of high-paced, backbreaking, low-wage work.[19]

Great Western Sugar carried on a well-financed recruitment program that targeted the Spanish-speaking labor pool in the region encompassing southern Colorado and the northern New Mexico areas made up of Mexican American families who, losing their land base through eviction, had made the transition to wage work. To avoid competition for labor from other sugar companies, Great Western requested that its workers migrate a month in advance of the start of the blocking and thinning season. Due to the expense of bringing in labor from the border area, the company sought to make its workforce year-round residents. Until work began, Great Western tried to find jobs for its beet workers, usually by making arrangements with coal companies operating mines nearby. The northeastern Colorado sugar beet region was a coal-mining area, and because the lignite mines produced coal for home heating purposes, the operation of the mines meshed with the downtime in beet work. Furthermore, as one of Colorado's largest coal consumers, the sugar processing factories influenced the mine companies' hiring policies. Unenlightened in the matter of labor relations, the coal companies hired an excess of Mexicans in order to create a labor surplus and keep wages low as well as to heighten racial tensions, thwart open rebellion, and inhibit unionization. With mine jobs racially and ethnically determined, Mexican coal diggers did the heaviest and most dangerous work. Some of the beet workers sent to the mines fell sick or were crippled through accidents, and indebtedness to the coal companies through script payments assured that the men would not leave the coal district.[20]

Families constituted from 75 to 90 percent of the sugar beet labor force that worked in a beet-growing area extending from northern Colorado northwest through parts of Nebraska, Wyoming, and Montana. Extra workers were recruited to hasten the harvesting of sugar beets and to maintain the poverty wages. Seasonal contracts ensured the same workers would be recruited just one time and be obliged contractually to the sugar corporations to work both periods of blocking and thinning and then harvesting. In other words, the labor contracts maintained rigid labor discipline.[21]

Most of the labor contracts were printed by the Mountain States Beet Growers Marketing Association, which represented 40 percent of the region's growers. Written in English and Spanish, the contracts' specific terms and conditions, which even determined labor relations for workers hired through oral agreements, were fixed in advance by sugar company officials and the growers. The company made the final decision on the price of beets and labor costs and was the sole mediator in disputes (through a company field representative) between the grower and the laborer. Embracing the labor of all family members able to work, the contract obligated the beet worker to both spring and fall work seasons but did not guarantee payment upon completion of the job. Because growers first paid off their debts to bankers, loan companies, and other creditors and thus sometimes fell short of money, the contracts extended store credit until the company was able to pay its workers. Since workers often arrived at the beet farms broke or with little cash before the start of the work season and were without funds until they completed all the work, the sugar company advanced the workers credit, store credit being more common than cash advances. Accumulated credit advances inevitably consumed the workers' pay. In essence, the contract labor system perpetuated a form of debt peonage that served to maintain labor discipline.[22]

The labor contract did not set a time for ending the harvest season. Under the contract's so-called "hold-back clauses," the loss of a dollar per acre if work stopped bound beet workers through the winter until the entire beet crop was harvested. The contract permitted the grower to hire extra labor if the beet workers failed to maintain a high work pace, regardless of illness or inclement weather, the cost of which was deducted from the workers' pay. Workers dealt with this exploitive aspect of the labor contract by getting extended family members or friends to help them speed up completion of the beet work and as compensation shared their pay with them.[23]

Beet workers put in the most hours per day of all farm workers, literally toiling from sunup to sundown. The families began work as soon as there was sufficient light and worked into the evening until it was too dark to see. The U.S. Children's Bureau found that half of all workers put in more than twelve hours per day during thinning and toiled more than eleven hours per day during harvesting. Sugar beet workers were employed for only fifty days during a six-month period, the labor-intensive work being limited to blocking and thinning and then harvesting. The sugar companies alotted the workers about a month of "free" time for traveling to and from the sugar beet area. This one-month block of unpaid time became a grievance during the early 1930s, as wages for beet work declined and as hard-pressed workers found it increasingly difficult to pay for food, gasoline, and other costs.[24]

The intense exertion of hand labor was the key element in sugar beet work. The task of blocking and thinning was one of the most backbreaking and dirtiest kinds of field labor. It required working in a stooped position, though some workers did this work kneeling or by moving through the rows on their hands and knees, a practice giving rise to the term "crawl." Beet work was governed by the calculus of time: get the fields thinned quickly to permit a long growing season and pick the beets before the ground freezes. Since the sugar beets were left in the ground for as long as possible to obtain maximum sugar content, beet harvesting was usually performed when freezing weather and snow were frequent.[25]

The imperative of having as many workers in the field as possible required the labor of women and children, who were required to maintain the pace of the lead worker. Women's work in the beet fields took precedence over all their other work responsibilities. The degree and amount of labor women performed and whether or not they had assistance depended on the size of the extended family. As was the custom, women toiled in the fields during their pregnancies, often going without prenatal care, and prepared meals taken to the fields; they washed the family's clothes by hand and performed other chores on the weekends. Once their babies were born, the women took the babies with them to the fields. Children minded the newborns. To help support the family, children entered the fields at an early age. Child labor contributed about a third of the income from beet work. A 1935 survey disclosed that 9 percent of six- to eleven-year-old Mexican children and 50 percent of those twelve and thirteen years old worked alongside their parents blocking, thinning, and harvesting beets. A contemporary observer estimated that in blocking and thinning an acre of beets, a young child "crawled" on his or her hands and knees through 26,136 feet of rows, or a distance equal to a little over five miles. Beet work took a psychological and physical toll on young Mexican children, aging them prematurely. Children ten or twelve years old were aged well beyond their years because they did the hard work of adults.[26]

Most of Colorado's Mexican beet workers were illiterate, some never having attended school in their lives. In Weld County, half the fourteen- and fifteen-year-old children of Mexican beet families on relief had less than a fifth-grade education, and half of the sixteen-year-old beet workers had less than a third-grade education. No systematic provisions existed for verifying the age of children or for inspecting beet fields for child labor violations. Because their labor was needed in the beet fields, many children were kept from regular school attendance. The children missed a third of each school year, and four-fifths who attended school regularly fell behind, so that by 1925, almost two-thirds of the children had fallen three years behind in school. In 1928, 5,000 Mexican children worked in the beet fields in violation of Colorado's school laws, with one-fourth missing more than two months of the school year. Children of migrant families were absent from school more frequently; their school attendance dropped by half in September, October, and November, during the harvest season, and again during the part of June when the beet plants were thinned. When in school, Mexican students were put in "opportunity" and Americanization classes: they were deemed "retarded" because many lacked sufficient English skills. The students were also perceived as social pariahs—because of their migratory lifestyle, the Mexicans came to school poorly clothed, often shoeless, dirty, and disease infested. Local school officials ignored compulsory school laws or issued unauthorized school exemptions to keep Mexican children out of school and in the beet fields. County school board officials, many of them local sugar growers who wielded considerable influence and expressed little concern about the use of child labor, opined that Mexican migrant children were in Colorado to work. Besides, they believed beet work had a "definitive educative value." The main factor keeping Mexican children out of school was blatant racism. As one school official pointed out, the "respectable white people . . . did not want their children to sit alongside dirty, filthy, diseased, infected Mexicans." It was suggested that the Mexicans bring their own teachers to teach the children, but only at times when it did not interfere with beet work. There was widespread sentiment in favor of setting apart the young Mexicans by placing them in separate schools. Thus, as Sarah Deutsch makes abundantly clear in her seminal study of the Mountain States region's Mexicans, the long-established educational system in Colorado's sugar beet districts helped to sustain Mexicans as marginal labor from generation to generation.[27]

In the middle of June 1934, New Deal field investigator Lorena Hickok saw the same young Mexican children toiling silently and for long hours in northern Colorado's beet fields who had previously been reported on by other investigators. Hickok noted that over half the children under age fifteen worked more than nine hours a day. One Mexican American mother told Hickok her children had started work when they were six. A ten-year-old Mexican American girl, thinning beets alongside her older brothers and sisters and parents, told the investigator she began working "in the beets" when she was eight. "What time do you start in the morning?" asked Hickok. "Oh, maybe 6 o'clock, maybe earlier," replied the child matter-of-factly. "And what time do you get through at night?" queried Hickok. The Mexican American girl answered: "Six o'clock only sometimes it's seven, and sometimes it's dark. I get pretty tired sometimes when it's getting dark."[28]

The sugar companies built up a resident labor supply of families in the Colorado beet districts to eliminate the expense of recruiting and moving single male workers to and from the beet districts, which amounted to several hundred thousand dollars. The growers preferred to hire families; they had a stabilizing effect on the labor force and made it possible to avoid the services of devious labor contractors. Each Mexican family in essence constituted a small contracting company. Living conditions for the families were inhumane. As one contemporary pointed out, there were no standards for the housing of sugar beet workers "equal to the standards fixed for the housing and care of cattle." The families lived in overcrowded, run-down shacks with poor sanitation and contaminated drinking water, a veritable breeding ground for typhoid, pneumonia, influenza, and tuberculosis. The dangerous, disease-ridden environment, in combination with malnutrition caused by a poor diet and the lack of proper clothing, contributed to a high infant mortality rate. These awful living conditions were well known to outside observers like the U.S. Children's Bureau, but the economically and politically powerful Colorado sugar companies had convinced state and local officials that the Mexican workers did not deserve better, and therefore nothing was done to alleviate their acute suffering.[29]

Since the Mexican families who remained year-round in the beet-growing districts could not get work, the males went to work in the state's coal mines, headed to Pueblo's steel mill, or migrated to Wyoming to find work as sheepherders. The lack of work pushed many families into nearby towns, where they lived on credit or on what money they managed to save, but they soon exhausted their meager resources and as a last resort applied for relief. For Mexicans, this forced necessity was degrading and belittled their dignity as workers. That Mexicans should have access to relief assistance was bitterly opposed, because according to public opinion this was a privilege reserved for deserving whites. The seeds of a process that restricted a host of social services for Mexicans had been planted, and these policies of exclusion spread to include denial of social services to Mexican Americans and those who were legal residents of the United States. Nevertheless, as work evaporated during the New Deal years, the ranks of Mexican beet workers who stayed in the city year-round and relied on relief surged.[30]

The influx of sugar beet workers increased the number of Mexicans living in Denver's three barrios from about 2,000 to over 8,000 in the 1920s, and the number grew higher in the 1930s. Three-fourths of the

Figure 1.B. Bands of Mexican American migrant families lived in makeshift accommodations consisting of overcrowded sheds, barns, shacks, and tents without toilets or facilities for washing, bathing, or cooking. (Thomas Mahony Collection, Courtesy of University of Notre Dame Archives).

families left from the city each spring to work in the beet fields. Contempt for Mexicans was growing steadily among Anglos, who despised the "greasers" and denounced Mexicans and Mexican Americans alike as foreigners. Riled by the implied threat of a resident population of indigent and sickly Mexicans living in squalor, infuriated by the public relief expenditures for their care during the winter, and resentful of the sugar companies for perpetuating their presence, local Anglo residents intentionally made it hard for Mexicans to establish any kind of a foothold. Ku Klux Klan cross burnings and "White Trade Only" and "No Mexican Trade Wanted" signs posted in restaurants, barbershops, and movie theaters were frightening reminders of the Anglos' hostility toward the unwanted Mexicans.[31]

Over the years, beet growers and sugar processors had lobbied loudly not to restrict immigration from Mexico, arguing that the sugar beet industry could not survive without Mexican labor. By denying the Mexican an "agricultural ladder" and all other opportunities for economic advancement, sugar company spokesmen had assured Congress that, a peon in Mexico, the Mexican would remain a beet worker in the United States. This policy to confine Mexicans to a caste-like existence, to handle them as farmers saw fit, applied to the state's American-born Mexicans as well. Colorado Spanish-speaking sugar beet workers were trapped in a never-ending cycle of low-wage seasonal labor, credit, debt, and relief. Thus, disenfranchised Spanish-speaking beet workers by the end of the Great Depression would become reduced to unemployed wards of the state subsidized for half the year by relief. Lorena Hickok, upon the completion of her visit to northern Colorado, rightfully concluded that the plight of the Mexican beet workers resembled that of the poor Southern black and white sharecroppers and tenants in the Cotton Belt. The only marked difference Hickok noticed was that the exploitation of Cotton Belt workers was not as well organized as the exploitation of Mexican workers by the sugar companies.[32] In the wake of the coalfield wars, Colorado was already fraught with instances of rural conflict, and very soon its beet fields, strongholds of rural community, would serve as the site for an uprising. In California, where the West Coast stream of Mexican migrant labor thrived, growers likewise devised strategies to control and exploit Mexicans in the state's vast agricultural fields.

SUMMER IN THE COUNTRY: CALIFORNIA'S MEXICAN FARM WORKERS

Labor-intensive, specialized fruit and vegetable crop production in California grew in the twenties, so that by 1929 more than a third of all large-scale farms in the western states were located in California. This concentration of specialized farms produced an intricate pattern of intrastate migration routes and a high ratio of farm workers who were exclusively nonwhite. Whereas in 1929 approximately 25 percent of all people employed in agriculture in the United States were wage laborers, the ratio was nearly 60 percent in California, which had the highest proportion of all states. California's rich variety of successive harvests included the winter-month vegetable harvests in Imperial County and the harvesting and packing of citrus fruits in the state's southern counties. In the spring, summer, and fall, migrant farm workers harvested fruits and vegetables in the Coastal Valley, the San Joaquin Valley, and the Sacramento Valley and then returned once again to the citrus crops in the southern part of the state. Sharp peaks and lows in labor demand, weather conditions, and wage rates based on piece work determined the migratory routes followed by tens of thousands of workers and their families in the West Coast migrant stream.[33]

Scholars note that from the beginning, California truck farms were large-scale undertakings with huge labor needs. As a result, California growers imported armies of cheap, single, male Chinese, Japanese, East Indian, and Filipino laborers headed by a labor contractor. Unlike the more expensive and unreliable Anglo worker, the so-called fruit tramp, these groups were hard-working and tractable and, because of their nationality and race, became subject to full exploitation by those who used their labor and kept each group in its place through segregation. The pattern for employment for the Mexican in California dovetailed with that of these previous racial groups, with the exception of packinghouse work because of the predominance of white male itinerant workers.[34]

With the proximity of the border ensuring a steady infusion of job-starved workers from Mexico, Mexicans became the foundation of the industrialized labor relations in California crop production. Mexican work gangs drawn from area towns and cities had been used for many years in Southern California agriculture. However, during the 1920s the use of Mexican labor on California's large-scale farms increased and became the basis of the state's seasonal migratory labor force. It was the accessibility of additional workers in nearby Mexico and along the border that facilitated the economic exploitation of Mexicans in a way that was not true of Chinese, Japanese, Filipino, or other labor imported from across the Pacific Ocean. Like Texas cotton farmers and Colorado sugar companies, California growers lobbied strongly to maintain free access to Mexico's workers, arguing that the state's agriculture would collapse without this labor, which, of course, was always in short supply.[35]

The growing importance of Mexican workers to California agriculture was indicated by the fact that while in 1915 Mexicans made up only 7 percent of all workers in migratory labor camps inspected by the California Immigration and Housing Commission, in 1929 they represented over 31 percent of this state's migratory workers. A 1928 study of the nonwhite labor used in California's intensive crops noted that Mexicans constituted more than half of the workers in the production of grapes and deciduous fruits, three-fourths of the workers in citrus fruits, and over 60 percent of the laborers in truck farm production. Because large-scale farming dominated California, nine of ten farms of more than 640 acres used Mexican labor deemed vital and essential to the farms' profitability. Grower associations organized regionally into private labor bureaus, recruited workers, and fixed wages, thus guaranteeing low labor costs. Each year the regional labor bureaus estimated the number of workers needed in the area, recruited and distributed these workers to growers, and set wage rates. In this way, competition for workers at peak periods of demand was eliminated and wage rates were standardized at the lowest level.[36]

California had its own version of the Texas "big swing" and of the migratory routes Mexican American workers had established in Colorado organized along the lines of family work units. In California, however, demand for farm workers varied with the specific harvest seasons of each successive crop. To ensure high profits, more labor was recruited than needed at peak harvest seasons. Although growers complained persistently of labor shortages, the opposite was true; during the 1920s California was plagued by an oversupply of farm labor hired at the lowest wage. Constant movement characterized the life of these migrant families as they followed the crops in efforts to obtain as many successive workdays as possible. Crop and weather conditions and other factors worked against them in procuring steady field work. The work crews made up of families moved together in car and truck caravans through California's fruit and vegetable districts, spending one-third of the year seeking work and living in over five different places. Notwithstanding California's child labor and compulsory school attendance laws, children slaved alongside their parents in the orchards and fields to maximize the money earned through piecework.[37]

While the farm workers were on the road, their homes were temporary roadside camps or those they constructed on vacant lots on the edges of small towns, all of which lacked sanitary facilities and clean water. Everywhere the Mexican migratory worker went in California, they were decried as being dirty, diseased, ignorant, and helpless, a persistent danger to the health and welfare of the local Anglo communities. Due to racism and their grimy physical condition from working, "those dirty Mexicans" became a commonly accepted appellation used to characterize the dark-skinned and sullied field migrants. With nativist animosity rising during the Great Depression and further heightening ethnic tensions, the word "foreigner" was added to the list of soubriquets that defined and defiled the Mexican.[38]

When idle during the off season, Mexican farm workers headed to Los Angeles to find jobs as day laborers, thereby further glutting the city's labor market and its already thickly settled Mexican working-class quarters. Given the nature of certain kinds of farm work and the requirements of gang labor, a vast proportion of the Mexicans who swelled the areas were single men. The 134,300 Mexicans in Los Angeles in 1928 represented 10 percent of the city's total population and its largest single racial group. However, moving to Los Angeles did not result in improved conditions, for segregation was rampant in the city. Experiencing widespread discrimination in public services, recreational facilities, and education, the migrants were essentially confined to the city's "Mexican" sections with the highest rents and the poorest homes. Infant mortality rates were three times that for Anglos, and one-third of the tuberculosis cases under charity care in Los Angeles County came from the Mexican community. Racism restricted Mexicans to the dirtiest and lowest-paying jobs as common or unskilled laborers, a discriminatory pattern of employment in place for more than half a century and which the AFL endorsed with unanimity. Mexicans were denied better work even as the local economy became diversified with the arrival of auto, aircraft, and rubber and steel companies that created a job boom. The lot of Mexican wage earners in antiunion Los Angeles consisted of eking out their existence as day laborers or being confined to the meanest jobs as unskilled workers while enduring oppressive working conditions and low pay, accentuated by frequent harassment and occasional beatings at the hands of the police for those who stepped out of line.[39]

Notwithstanding the growth and diversification of its manufacturing base, Los Angeles County remained a major agricultural producing and processing center. Garden farms surrounding Los Angeles expanded with the city's growth to meet the demand of its residents for fruits and vegetables. Likewise, food processing steadily expanded because of new technological developments. Reflecting similar patterns in El Paso, Laredo, and San Antonio, Los Angeles employers actively recruited Mexican women and children to maintain a cheap, docile surplus labor pool. The women were disproportionately assigned to unskilled work in the packinghouses and canneries, followed by the clothing and needle trades, other light industries, and the commercial laundries, or they worked as domestics. Women made up three-fourths of the workers in the state's canneries and packinghouses, where wages were set by the shipping and marketing organizations. In 1928, Mexicans made up almost a fourth of the Los Angeles cannery workforce (23.5 percent). However, because canning was a seasonal industry, work lasted only ten to eleven weeks per year. During the peak summer processing season, California's canneries employed from 60,000 to 70,000 workers, while in the winter months the workforce shrank to 10,000 to 13,000 food processors. Mexican women cannery workers in Los Angeles were more fortunate; they enjoyed a long work season because the city was a canning hub for Southern California agriculture. However, they were concentrated in "women's occupations"—washing, grading, cutting, canning, drying, and packing—all very fast-paced piecework production that paid $16.55 per week. On the other hand, men held nonintensive positions as warehousemen and cooks and earned wages averaging $26.64 per week. As historian Vicki Ruiz has noted, Mexican women food-processing operatives were a diverse workforce and included young, single daughters, newly married women, middle-aged wives, and widows. The younger Mexican American women replaced older immigrant women when the latter could no longer keep up with the fast work pace. Kin networks extended from the family to the community and into the workplace, forming an integral part of work life and contributing to a collective identity shaped by the cannery work culture. As with other Mexican women employed in industrial work, organizing by cannery workers would be family and community based. Unlike farm workers, the women cannery workers would benefit from minimum wage protection through New Deal labor legislation.[40]

Aside from canning, extensive seasonal employment in garment factories provided work for wage-earning Mexican women in Los Angeles. In the 1930s the women's clothing industry employed 6,024 women and children. Mexican women holding unskilled and semiskilled jobs made up 75 percent of the labor force. Seasonal work, labor turnover, speedup, and homework characterized the very competitive clothing industry. An open-shop environment, a worker surplus, and very soon the sharp rise in unemployment created a situation the heartless garment employers quickly exploited to their advantage. There was no question that the drudgery of Mexican women enriched the garment industry of Los Angeles, as it does in the present era. As one 1930s labor organizer concluded, "thousands in [the] industry slaved under the most degrading and humiliating conditions, with no control of hours and wages; no place to go for the redress of grievances." During the Great Depression, when male breadwinners lost their jobs or could not find work, family poverty pushed additional women into the area workforce, opening the way for more worker abuse.[41]

Outside of these seasonal industries, the majority of Mexicans in Los Angeles enjoyed few job opportunities. Together with the great mass of farm workers who wintered in the city, Mexicans represented a huge surplus labor population in Los Angeles that, as the decade of the twenties closed, teetered on the edge of deprivation. These circumstances compelled the city's most economically hard-pressed Mexicans to depend on relief. They made up over 25 percent of Los Angeles public relief cases, over half the budget of the private Bureau of Catholic Charities went to aid indigent Mexicans, and in adjacent Orange County, Mexicans represented nearly half the relief cases of the Orange County Aid Commission.

As labor scholar Ernesto Galarza observed at this time, depressed wages, overcrowding, slums, social and racial discrimination, and large relief caseloads characterized life for Mexicans in both rural and urban areas. The fear of becoming entangled with immigration officials; the isolation from American cultural, political, and social institutions; the reluctance of many communities to take responsibility for the Mexican people's housing, health, education, and relief problems; and the seasonal nature of their work were the circumstances that kept the Mexican always moving about. Under such conditions, it was impossible for Mexicans to build a stable life. Moreover, denied the opportunity to learn English, Mexicans could not understand laws and regulations or labor contracts, and they were banned from organizing to defend themselves as workers. Ostracized, Mexicans consequently remained apart from the larger American society. During the depression of the 1930s, Mexican agricultural workers, along with women who performed domestic work, were excluded from New Deal labor legislation, and in many instances the federal programs, administered at the local level by hostile officials, reinforced the racial divisions found in the Southwest.[42]

The Great Depression Hits the Mexicans of Texas and the Western States

The surplus of farm labor in the Southwest was a consequence of the deliberate and systematic overrecruitment of labor complemented by the strong pattern of transnational migration whereby immigrants from Mexico worked seasonally in the United States and spent the rest of the year in Mexico. The final result of this process of labor force formation, underscored by the factors of race and nationality, was the Mexicanization of the Southwest, which greatly expanded seasonal and labor-intensive agriculture and gave rise to internal labor migration to the cities during the lulls at the ends of the harvests as workers sought jobs, then relief, to compensate for their idleness. However, the Great Depression upset the traditional streams of Mexican labor migration as the employment situation in the United States changed from one of constant labor shortages to one of acute labor surpluses. In the Southwest, Mexican farm workers, miners, smelter workers, and railroad maintenance and repair men underwent reductions in workdays and wages or lost their jobs as employers discharged them.

As noted, cotton was of immense commercial importance in Texas, but beginning in the late 1920s, Texas cotton growers faced the problem of a growing surplus of American cotton, falling prices, and low demand because cheap cotton from Egypt, Brazil, and India was flooding the world market. U.S. cotton exports had fallen from eleven million bales in 1927 to seven million bales in 1930, a decline of over 15 percent. In the following two years, the U.S. domestic cotton surplus increased more than 60 percent, from six million bales (in 1931) to nearly nine million bales (in 1932), while cotton prices fell to a record low of 5.7 cents per pound. As prices continued to tumble and the need for labor shrank, cotton pickers experienced a simultaneous decline in wages and a precipitous rise in unemployment.[43]

The drop in domestic cotton prices led Texas state legislators to pass the 1931 Cotton Acreage Control Law, resulting in a 50 percent reduction in cotton acreage. A prototype of the AAA's plow-under policy, the state law stipulated that Texas farmers could plant no more than a third of their land in cotton, nor could they plant cotton on the same acreage for two consecutive years after 1933. Moreover, counties with a high proportion of land in cotton, such as those in south Texas, had to reduce their production by half in 1932 and 1933. For example, cotton acreage was reduced from 254,000 acres to 90,000 acres in Nueces County and from 155,000 acres to 55,000 acres in San Patricio County. Though a lawsuit invalidated the Cotton Acreage Control Law, the legislation had a great impact on the Tejanos who harvested the state's cotton crop. The contraction of the labor market pushed additional American-born Tejanos to head for urban centers to search for work as day laborers, while Mexican nationals crossed the border and returned to their homes in Nuevo Laredo, Piedras Negras, and Ciudad Juárez. For these workers, returning home to Mexico was a viable alternative to spreading unemployment, deprivation, potential hunger, and living under constant fear of apprehension and removal.[44]

Tejano migrant workers faced unemployment in Texas, and the safety valve that beet work in the North provided was threatened by the fact that northern sugar companies had reduced their labor needs by as much as a third to a half. Actually, there was a labor surplus in the northern beet fields because growers tapped the reserves of Mexican workers in the area cities. In some beet districts, the workforce increased by 35 percent, so that by 1933 it was a third larger than in the 1920s but earning 7 percent less because the labor surplus spurred the sugar companies to implement draconian measures. The companies reduced acreage allotments, paid one rate for all beet work, eliminated credit, and no longer arbitrated labor disputes. There was now no one to mediate between the hard-pressed farmers being squeezed by the sugar companies and the powerless beet workers, resulting in more mistreatment for the latter. Having established their dominance over both farmer and beet worker, the sugar interests astutely lobbied the federal government to raise tariffs on foreign sugar to safeguard their monopoly on the national sugar market. The sharp lobbying paid off because in 1930 President Herbert Hoover raised the duty on foreign sugar, thus guaranteeing an annual sugar quota for domestic sugar producers. The spreading deprivation pushed more and more frantic Mexicans to seek relief assistance, but because of the nativist backlash, their requests for aid in most instances were held back or denied altogether. Much like the measures implemented by Mississippi Delta planters to reduce the black population during the 1960s, a plan was adopted to hound the Mexican out of the country. This was done by pushing the Mexican to starvation by cutting back relief or denying them assistance. The labor of the Mexican would not go unexploited, however. Certain growers maintained a reserve of Mexican labor without assuming care for them for the whole year through an arrangement with public relief officials. The plan was to allot Mexican families a small token of relief during the off-season in fruit and vegetable production and then cut them off when the harvest season started. The growers' behavior toward their Mexican workers was shameless as ever.[45]

In the Midwest, discontinuing relief assistance to sugar beet workers became an imperative, and it was accomplished by overburdened county relief agencies imposing new residency requirements. Applicants now had to prove one-year county or state residence. This prerequisite immediately eliminated thousands of Tejano migrant workers, since they lived in the beet-growing area only part of the year. Their plight became desperate. Families had no assurance they would be paid for the spring beet-thinning season; the financially strapped grower could not pay the families until the fall and so were encouraging their workers to get on relief. By 1932, most beet work was paid for in cash from loans northern growers secured from the Reconstruction Finance Corporation. Through an arrangement with the sugar companies, county and city welfare departments provided beet worker families with grocery orders through the summer and fall, but only if the workers harvested a specified number of beet rows. The public relief agencies reimbursed themselves for the food allotments by securing a lien on a family's wages. However, the paltry grocery orders proved hardly adequate for families on the verge of starvation, forcing reluctant relief agencies to supplement these with additional assistance in kind. Unable to support themselves on beet work, additional families were driven by sheer hunger to request relief. In sum, this represents the outlines of a specific policy implemented throughout the Great Depression, and that was timing the allocation of relief and work relief to Mexicans with the start of the fruit, vegetable, and cotton harvests as a way to discipline this workforce and to keep them in the fields.[46]

As a result of newly imposed residency requirements, Spanish-speaking New Mexican migrants in the same way were denied relief. About 7,000 to 10,000 Mexicans from northern New Mexico at one time performed seasonal wage work out of state, but now only 1,800 to 2,500 workers held jobs, with sheepherding accounting for more than half of this work. Even the skilled sheepherders (along with cowpunchers) lost their jobs because ranchers now gave preference to in-state workers. The lack of work forced the migrants to return home, where they relied on family, friends, and mutual aid societies for help. However, the deepening economic crisis increased destitution and forced more Spanish-speaking New Mexicans on the verge of starvation onto already swollen relief rolls. Representing almost half of New Mexico's population, Mexicans made up 80 percent of the state's relief load.[47]

Beet laborers in Colorado found themselves in even more dire circumstances. An early freeze ruined almost all the western sugar beet crop in 1929, making it the "worst year in beet history," and in its wake left beet workers jobless. The ensuing drought between 1930 and 1935 slashed the western region's sugar beet harvest by about 50 percent, from 242,000 acres to 140,000 acres, and forced nearly half of Colorado's 15,000 beet workers out of work. The new contracts signed by the Mexicans lucky enough to find work stipulated that they would be paid less than half what they previously earned per acre of beets. Moreover, farmers no longer allowed beet worker families to winter on the farms. Deprived of shelter during the off-season, half the beet workers in northern Colorado streamed into Denver and nearby towns. The forlorn, hungry, and sick families added to the joblessness and overcrowding in the Spanish-speaking working-class districts and further strained the city and county public and private relief rolls. In Huerfano and Las Animas Counties in southern Colorado, the 3,489 Mexican American families on permanent relief accounted for more than a fifth (21.7 percent) of the state's relief recipients. Meanwhile, other despairing Mexicans left the beet fields and returned home to southern Colorado, northern New Mexico, and Texas, doubling up with relatives and friends, barely holding out against imminent starvation.[48]

A similarly stark situation of joblessness unfolded for Mexican migrant farm workers in Southern California as growers reacted to the drop in market prices for fruits and vegetables by cutting back on plantings. In 1929 in the Imperial Valley, one year after the strike by cantaloupe workers over wages and working conditions was smashed through mass arrests and deportations, the cantaloupe harvest fell from 14,378 to 6,055 boxcars, and the valley's lettuce harvest dropped from 12,608 to 6,356 boxcars. Cotton production in the San Joaquin Valley was also impacted by the crisis. As wages fell, angry pickers responded by refusing to harvest the crop at the price set by the San Joaquin Valley Agricultural Labor Bureau. In September 1931, the opening of the fruit-canning season curtailed some of the unemployment in the state. However, except for Los Angeles cannery workers, a large surplus of fruit pickers and cannery workers remained unemployed throughout California. By January 1933, California's farm labor surplus stood at an estimated 2.36 workers for each farm job. The inflated labor market triggered an exodus of about 15,000 work-starved Mexicans from California to other states in search of work. The hard times apparently did not stop the sugar companies from flooding the labor market with more workers, because in Los Angeles five labor agents representing sugar companies in the Mountain States and Midwest were busy recruiting Mexicans and shipping these workers by rail to the beet fields of Colorado, Wyoming, Nebraska, Minnesota, and Michigan. Other job-hungry Mexicans left Los Angeles on their own to pick cotton in Arizona. However, finding only poverty wages in these areas, all the workers returned to Mexico. The circular migration process that began in the early twentieth century had broken down as a result of the economic crisis.[49]

As a final resort to fend off looming hunger, California's Mexican families who counted on seasonal farm work for their livelihood were forced to seek relief assistance. In Orange County, a major citrus production area, the lack of work forced underfed Mexican families to ask for some kind of public support. Having exhausted all their resources, many of the desperate families had been feeding themselves by sifting through garbage for food scraps. Threats of relief cutoff combined with the offer by local officials of free transportation to the border persuaded about 2,000 indigent Mexicans to leave Orange County. Out of work, denied relief, and facing starvation, thousands voluntarily left California. Most were single males. The Mexicans remaining in the state and barely eking out an existence now faced competition for work, first from local workers and then from the influx of out-of-state workers. The growing labor surplus led to more wage cuts and more demands for relief.[50]

Jobless and homeless transients streamed into California and contributed to the growing unemployment problem in the state. In September 1931, the railroads entering California and the inspection stations operated by the U.S. Agriculture Department reported that about 1,000 transients entered the state each day. Moreover, their numbers were increasing by 15 percent per month, so that between 100,000 and 200,000 jobless itinerants were expected to arrive by the start of winter. All of them were of working age, 80 percent between the ages of sixteen and twenty-four years, with most going to the southern part of the state. California state officials chose not to publicize the amount of money or the amount of work relief earmarked for the unemployed, fearing that doing so would lure more transients to the state. Unbeknownst to the transients, they were ineligible for county relief, public work, or charity because they were not California residents.[51] Without work, the very subsistence of Mexicans depended on getting relief, especially for those families with large numbers of children and elderly dependents. Viewed with growing disfavor and frightened that they would be identified and deported because they lacked residency, many Mexicans avoided applying for public or private assistance.

WORK, LEAVE, OR STARVE: LIMITING RELIEF TO MEXICANS

The Mexican migratory worker had met the short-term requirements of seasonal agricultural work. Like birds of passage, the Mexicans had gone to work when needed and left when no longer needed. Thus on the eve of the Great Depression it was widely believed that Mexicans would not stay in the United States but return to Mexico if afforded the opportunity. This happened during the 1920–21 depression, when local officials paid for transporting unemployed Mexican workers and their destitute families back to Mexico as an inexpensive alternative to giving them relief. In the early 1930s, spreading joblessness and utter desperation were forcing additional Mexicans on the public dole, and in some locales they constituted the bulk of relief applicants. The prospect of providing relief to indigent Mexicans threw Anglos into a panic. For Anglos, this merely confirmed their convictions all along that relief removed the incentive for Mexicans to look for work. The relief rolls grew as budget allocations fell sharply, anti-Mexican hostility mounted in both rural and urban areas, and the virulence culminated in a program of Mexican removal. A great cataclysm befell the Mexican community.[52]

Caving in to pressure from disgruntled Anglos being thrown out of work, some employers stopped hiring Mexicans while others fired them, including those who were American citizens or permanent residents, and replaced them with Anglos, who swallowed their pride and took the demeaning "Mexican" jobs. As nativism increased, public officials and organized labor eagerly lent their support to stop Mexicans from getting work in urban employment sectors. In 1930, the El Paso City Council passed an ordinance barring immigrants from work on city-funded construction projects, and early the next year the newly organized Unemployed American Voters League pushed local employers to dismiss their immigrant employees. The new restrictions denied work to American-born Tejanos who, hard pressed for work, probably welcomed the measures nonetheless as a means to curb labor rivalry from Mexican nationals. The AFL Central Labor Union formally endorsed both the city's provision and the Unemployed American Voters League's call for excluding all immigrant workers from public and private employment. At the state level, laws were enacted mandating that only married men and those with dependents who were American citizens be allowed to work highway construction and other public works projects. While this legislation applied to all aliens, it was specifically designed to remove longtime Tejano employees from state-funded road construction jobs.[53]

In New Mexico, the influx of out-of-state migrants prompted state relief agencies to deny transients public assistance, and this was followed by passage of a law limiting the hiring of nonresidents on public works projects to 15 percent. This legislation, however, penalized thousands of Mexican Americans who worked and lived outside the state as seasonal laborers but now could not find work. Denied relief in those states where they had previously worked for many years, these migratory workers returned to New Mexico only to be told by relief officials that due to their absence they were ineligible for aid. Because of discrimination, Spanish-speaking New Mexicans, who made up 80 percent of the state's relief recipients, would soon have difficulty obtaining federal work relief, and what work relief they did get was undesirable and low paying.[54]

Because of the fiscal crisis and the growing xenophobia, further denying Mexicans the benefits of white society now included denying them relief. Notwithstanding the ancestry of many of Colorado's Spanish-speaking residents, Colorado Anglos viewed Mexicans with contempt and believed they were favored for work relief but were undeserving because they were not "Americans." Moreover, an opinion widely embraced by Colorado Anglo residents and relief officials alike, such as the secretary of the National Reemployment Service of Las Animas County, was that once Mexicans got on the dole, they would become dependent on public assistance and refuse to work. The fact that Mexicans got federal relief at all only hardened these biases.[55]

In Los Angeles, Mexicans made up more than a fourth of all city residents on public assistance (excluding private charity) because they accounted for 25 percent of the poverty in Los Angeles County, which was collapsing under the weight of the fiscal crisis. During 1929–30, the County Welfare Department spent $2,469,519 for relief and in the next fiscal year spent $4,209,725, a huge one-year increase of 70.5 percent. For the 1931–32 year, however, the Los Angeles County relief budget was reduced to $3,346,050. This decreased by half the number of Mexican families (2,247 of 18,730 families averaging four persons per family) the County Welfare Department was caring for. No doubt, the 50 percent reduction in the number of Mexican public relief cases was caused by irate residents pressuring officials to give preference to American citizens. The cause for this alarm was that the number of persons on relief in Los Angeles had doubled. Now 4 percent of Los Angeles residents were receiving county assistance, whereas normally only 1–2 percent of the city's population depended on public relief. Also, the average length of a county relief case was now eight months and was projected to increase to twelve months. Because of the city's emerging fiscal crisis, many Los Angeles residents sought aid from private charities. In 1931, seventeen private charities were assisting 12,883 families, a remarkable 91 percent increase over 1930. Despite shrinking budgets, Mexicans represented a third of the 51,123 private charity cases. All of these were Catholic charity cases because the proposed unemployment relief program for Los Angeles called for residents of the Catholic and Jewish faiths to get aid from their respective relief organizations. The number of people in the city in need of assistance kept growing; however, the Community Chest of Los Angeles could raise only 85 percent of its $3.2 million budget and now included unemployment relief. Facing this budget reduction, the city's Catholic charities cut the food allowances for Mexican families by 25 percent yet reduced food allocations for Anglo families by only 10 percent. The recent $220 million bond issue for the construction of the Colorado River aqueduct was expected to provide employment for 10,000 men in Los Angeles for six to seven years. However, as with all other public works projects, Mexican U.S. citizens were systematically denied this work. City work relief went only to worthy white American citizens of the Los Angeles metropolitan area.[56]

The state of California had not adopted a plan for meeting the relief problem, and Mexicans were overrepresented on the relief rolls. In August 1931, the California legislature passed the Alien Labor Act, which served to eliminate the remaining Mexicans assigned to the various state highways and building construction projects. In an action reflecting the AFL's position that Mexicans were fatal to the federation, organized labor in Los Angeles pounced on the Mexican as a target for removal. The threatening catchphrase went out over the city: "Employ no Mexican while a white man is unemployed. Get the Mexican back into Mexico regardless by what means." No thought was given to the legal status of the Mexican. It was a question of color, not a question of citizenship or legal right.[57]

"SEND THEM BACK TO WHERE THEY CAME FROM": THE REPATRIATION CAMPAIGN UNFOLDS

As work became scarce, the jobless Mexican seeking relief suddenly became a very visible and conspicuous social problem. The presence of so many Mexicans on the dole raised a cacophony of public complaints, while relief officials charged just as loudly that the destitute families were needless tax burdens. With greater frequency, Mexican Americans were denied assistance because public relief officials confounded their citizenship status with that of Mexican nationals. Southwest employers had become strongly addicted to Mexican labor, and they argued otherwise. Recognizing the advantages Mexicans offered by their seeming willingness to work for low wages under bad conditions, employers had integrated Mexicans into the region's economy under their terms. As with Southern blacks, systematic retaliation and the weight of racism rendered Mexicans incapable of mass resistance through work stoppages or through strikes and protests. Because employers had devised ways to handle them, the powerless Mexicans were easily exploited. In calling for an open border, growers argued that the economy of the Southwest greatly depended upon Mexicans to do the difficult, unpleasant work refused by Anglo workers as a matter of course. Potential government action to close the border presented grower interests with a dilemma, and they took decisive action. They testified before a congressional committee that Mexican labor was not competing with American labor; on the contrary, because the aliens performed the menial labor vital to the agriculture of the Southwest, they had actually created job opportunities for American workers outside agriculture. Given the fact that the U.S. government played a role in encouraging Mexican immigration, Southwestern employers received support in their arguments from the U.S. Departments of Agriculture and Interior. Officials from both these federal government agencies did not want any legislation to disrupt the region's labor supply. Testimony by the Interior Department's Director of Reclamation Economics revealed that nearly $38 million in federal monies had been invested in irrigation projects benefiting farmers relying exclusively on Mexican labor. The government official cautioned that any halt to Mexican immigration would make it financially impossible for the farmers to pay for this irrigation service in the form of a special tax and very likely would require them to seek federal relief. If employers could not do without the cheap labor of the Mexicans, local officials could not afford to keep them on the dole. A practice soon emerged that became widely used in the Southwest, the brainchild of growers who wanted assurances that their fruit and vegetable crops would be harvested on time. Relief officials in agricultural growing areas gave tacit cooperation and undertook a specific plan of assistance. By removing Mexican families from welfare rolls in the spring and fall, state, county, and local governments could save on relief expenditures and guarantee that the workers would return to the fields during the planting and harvesting season. Any relief recipient who refused to work or who raised protests would be removed permanently from the dole. However, the Mexicans who complied, got off relief, and accepted work found it difficult to obtain assistance afterwards.[58]

Notwithstanding these attempts to keep the border open and hold on to a Mexican labor reserve with little if any expenditure for its care, the federal government interceded to subdue public unease over Mexican immigration. Foreshadowing practices undertaken in the postwar years, public officials from the president to the labor secretary through several policy initiatives manipulated the immigration issue by drawing on ideas of citizenship, community, and national identity. This rhetoric served to maintain plentiful numbers of Mexican workers while supporting the impression that the United States kept hold of its borders.[59]

Congress passed the Immigration Act of 1929, making unlawful entry into the United States punishable as a misdemeanor. The U.S. State Department moved to cut back Mexican immigration by tightening administrative procedures. It instructed American consuls in Mexico to enforce the existing regulations concerning contract labor and the literacy tests and, citing the precedent of a nineteenth-century statute, urged them to prevent Mexicans from entering the United States who would "likely . . . become a public charge." The State Department's administrative restrictions on Mexican immigration would remain in force throughout the 1930s. The U.S. Immigration Bureau expanded the U.S. Border Patrol and began a general program to curb immigration. Furthermore, the 1929 Immigration Act allowed the federal government and other public agencies favoring more aggressive and punitive measures to carry out a "federal deportation campaign" to remove foreign aliens. It is at this time that the notion of the illegal alien gained universal distinction, transforming Mexican workers into potential fugitives of the law unless they procured proper documentation. At first, the campaign targeted individuals who were in the country illegally, but it was soon directed specifically at Mexican immigrants. To deflect attention from his inability to deal with the unfolding economic crisis, President Herbert Hoover publicly denounced the Mexican as one of the causes of the Depression, and in so doing made the Mexican the object of an official federal removal program. Tragically, repatriation victimized Mexicans who were U.S. citizens, legal residents who entered the country before there were official measures in place to confirm their legal immigration, or residents unable to show proof of their legal status because of poverty. The last lacked birth certificates or other vital documents to prove their American citizenship or continuous residence. The escalating anti-Mexican campaign that at once criminalized the Mexican worker was widely approved by national organizations, including, of course, the anti-immigrant and racist American Federation of Labor.[60]

The AFL placed pressure on the U.S. Labor Department's Immigration Bureau to act with expediency. Along with the passage of national legislation in 1929 to curb immigration from Mexico and the U.S. State Department directives, the Immigration Bureau imposed a regulation upon workers seeking employment in the United States that required them to post a bond. Mexican women seeking work as domestics were also required to post a bond. The exceptions were immigrants who were skilled workers or professionals and married couples of which either spouse was an American citizen. However, bonds were required of married couples if one of the spouses was a legally admitted alien who resided in the United States. Unskilled immigrant workers or their prospective employers had to post a $1,000 bond. This bond request unquestionably posed considerable financial hardship for many Mexican immigrants. The sum equaled the amount of money an impoverished Mexican farm worker and his family could earn over a two- to three-year period. (To put it in perspective, the $1,000 bond was the equivalent of an auto worker's annual wages during the prosperous times of the 1920s.) Moreover, each family member had to pay the $5 filing fee for a visa petition. This meant each family member submitted a visa application with a $5 filing fee and needed to post a $1,000 bond if they planned to work in the United States.[61]

The national labor federation also pressured the U.S. Immigration Bureau to seek out and apprehend Mexicans, ordering them to produce citizenship papers or evidence of legal U.S. entry. The Immigration Bureau swiftly and efficiently carried out its assignment to empty the Mexicans from the United States. According to one witness of the government assault on the Mexicans, "For a time officers of the department would arrest Mexicans by the truckload; they would drive up in front of a store or poolroom and fill the truck, take them [in] for questioning and . . . thousands of them have been deported." Because of the industrial nature of the Depression, the Midwest was hard hit by the economic crisis. In Chicago's Stockyards district, in Detroit's working-class neighborhoods, and in other midwestern blue-collar areas, federal immigration agents staged mass raids to search for and arrest Mexicans in violation of the immigration laws. Complementing this federal deportation drive were locally initiated repatriation programs hastily organized by county and city officials working in tandem with public and private relief agencies. City police staged their own sweeps of working-class neighborhoods and, without warrants or advance warning, sometimes forced their way into the homes of Mexicans to arrest individuals. The dragnets created a climate of bewilderment and fear that encouraged quick departure and at the same time succeeded in making immigrants a favored political scapegoat. This intimidation, along with misinformation about legal procedures, generated considerable controversy though little overt opposition. The defenseless Mexican communities could do nothing but return to Mexico. Those who stayed were Mexican Americans or legal residents, but they lived in intense fear. In a prefiguring of episodes of terror in the contemporary era, Mexicans remained in hiding, venturing out only to get food. They did not complain to police or go to the hospital if they or family members were sick or dying. They hid from view, relying on their networks of kin and friends for help rather than relief agencies. Failure to hide almost assured deportation.[62]

Newly appointed secretary of labor William N. Doak implemented the policy of removing aliens illegally in the country. The well-publicized nationwide raids by Immigration Bureau agents had an ulterior political purpose; they reflected Doak's determination to carry out President Hoover's plan to create a distraction as a way to counter organized labor's unfriendly attitude toward his administration and perpetuate the growing perception that Mexicans took scarce jobs and much-needed welfare away from worthy Americans. Labor Secretary Doak accordingly fabricated a figure of 400,000 immigrants in the country illegally. Eliminating these immigrants through deportation meant jobs for white Americans, an endeavor Doak reasoned would certainly please organized labor. To curry favor with employer interests, the U.S. Labor Department began monitoring strikes in which workers who were foreign nationals were involved. Strike leaders and picketers were singled out, arrested, and subjected to deportation by conspicuous Immigration Bureau agents. This ruthless method of repression led to numerous instances of strikebreaking by American as well as Mexican officials and the subsequent interception, arrest, and deportation of Mexican and Mexican American union activists. Those suspected of having communist ties were especially singled out for immediate arrest and expulsion. At the same time, the U.S. Border Patrol colluded with ranchers and growers by allowing the latter to fetch Mexican workers during strike situations and labor shortages.[63]

Doak steadfastly defended his agents against the rising charges of misconduct and abuse, including arbitrary beatings, stating that saving jobs for white American workers was far more important than the numerous civil rights violations taking place as federal agents ruthlessly hunted down Mexicans, many of whom were American citizens, legal residents, or individuals without the means to legalize their citizenship status. Most local and state officials adamantly shared Doak's sentiments, for they were looking for ways to remove the Mexican worker and his family from the dole. One of these officials adding to the nativist fervor was Charles P. Visel, newly appointed coordinator of the Local Citizens' Unemployment Relief Committee of Los Angeles. Visel strongly urged the U.S. Labor Department to send more immigration officers to Los Angeles and Southern California because local police and sheriff's office personnel could not apprehend individuals fast enough, owing to the large Mexican populations. Most of the Mexicans targeted for removal were the scores of jobless agricultural and other seasonally employed immigrant workers wintering in the city, but the dragnet caught many legal residents, and these were arrested as well.[64] Because Texas contained the nation's largest Mexican population and posed a potentially serious relief problem, more Mexicans were repatriated from this state than from any other region.

In Texas, the problem of Tejano destitution was quite serious and was compounded by the large number of Mexican nationals in the state, the result of the past actions of employers who wanted to maintain high levels of surplus labor. Thousands of Tejano tenant farmers were forced off the land in south and central Texas. Texas legislators, among them powerful growers from the ravaged cotton districts, made no effort to find jobs for the displaced cotton pickers. They preferred having them rounded up and run across the border. One focal point of the repatriation drive in central Texas was Karnes County, located southeast of San Antonio and home to 11,500 Tejanos wholly dependent on cotton cultivation. The problem in Karnes County was that in addition to the cotton reduction program, land was being taken out of cotton production when the new cotton district emerged in the Texas Panhandle. The Spanish-speaking population of Karnes County reflected the Tejano population generally. It was made up of first- and second-generation Tejanos, and those who were non-U.S. citizens were longtime Texas residents; they were mostly of working age; very few had an education beyond the fourth grade (over a third had never attended school); large families prevailed (one-third had four to five dependents); and the Tejanos harvested cotton in the county and across the state.[65] In late fall of 1931, Tejano cotton pickers and their families, representing over a third of Karnes County's Tejano population, gathered at Karnes City and left for Mexico. Ten thousand additional Tejanos left for Mexico in November and December. The pace of repatriation quickened because thousands more were expelled as government "roundups" were undertaken in San Antonio, Houston, El Paso, and other Texas cities where many Tejanos desperate for work had flocked and now posed a potential social problem as they sought help from publicly funded services. Of the 345,839 Mexicans repatriated to Mexico, more than 70 percent left from Texas. The large drop in cotton production in Texas, the fact that the state provided little relief to its indigent residents, and the long-standing bad feelings toward Mexicans no doubt hastened their removal.[66]

Relief was not a viable option in Texas. Made up of conservative Democrats who voted on the basis of the economic interests of their constituents, the Texas legislature failed to appropriate general revenue funds for relief purposes, and it also voted down a mandatory constitutional amendment that would have allowed the issuance of bonds to raise revenues for local relief agencies. Tejanos fell victim to the repressive climate being created by the U.S. Immigration Bureau, in addition to the lean times ushered in by the AAA that eliminated hundreds of thousands of acres from cotton production. Not only were Tejanos driven from the land by the cotton reduction program, but the workers were cheated out of receiving AAA crop reduction subsidy checks by malicious growers because many worked for the locally administered New Deal agencies that dispensed these subsidy checks. If Tejanos complained or sought legal recourse, they were threatened with either repatriation or eviction. Idleness in the end, made Tejanos susceptible to arrest.[67]

The unfolding repatriation drives coincided with the highly publicized expulsions in Los Angeles, Chicago, Detroit, and other urban areas with large pockets of Mexicans. Impatient with the federal government, some local communities took matters into their own hands and got rid of the Mexicans. Beginning in 1930 and continuing through 1935, Colorado relief agencies, aided by funds provided by Mexican consulates, repatriated about 20,000 Mexicans. Many American-born adults and children without proper identification were removed in the sweeps. However, the Great Western Sugar Company, protected by the newly passed sugar tariff, made sure enough Mexicans remained in the state to harvest its beets. The sugar company implemented a system of forced labor that served as a way of redistributing available labor in order to meet its needs. Hunger and fear soon became everyday companions of the Mexican American beet workers. In an unusual arrangement, these families received just enough county relief to carry them through the winter without starving

Figure 1.C. The Hoover administration seized on the bad state of the economy to scapegoat Mexicans. Mexicans being repatriated from Morenci, Arizona. (MP CM 79—Christine Marín Photograph Collection, Chicano Research Collection, Courtesy of Arizona State University Libraries).

or freezing to death, and then they were cut off relief when the beet season started and left to survive on their low earnings. In Colorado, New Mexico, and Arizona thousands of Mexican miners and railroad workers lost their jobs. From the mining district around Globe and Miami, Arizona, several hundred Mexican copper miners and their families returned to Mexico. Others left for the Salt River Valley to pick cotton, adding to the surplus of workers resulting from the influx of out-of-state transients desperate for work.[68] As in Texas, the drop in cotton prices pushed Arizona growers to slash their workforce. Without work, thousands of Mexicans in Phoenix and in the surrounding Salt River Valley dependent on cotton cultivation were picked up by federal agents and returned to Mexico. Those who remained were U.S. citizens or resident aliens, but they confronted two problems. The first was competition from hundreds of unemployed copper miners and the 1,000 transients the Arizona State Committee on Unemployment Relief assigned to work in the cotton fields. The other problem was the idleness and indigence of Mexicans that followed when the cotton harvest ended in early winter, which exposed them to apprehension and arrest by U.S. Border Patrol agents scouring the streets and countryside for aliens.[69]

In April 1930, the jobless rate among Mexicans in Los Angeles stood at 14 percent, and it climbed to 20 percent by year's end: one in five workers in the city was now unemployed. Between 3,000 and 5,000 Mexicans initially requested transportation to Mexico, but as these Mexicans departed, others from different parts of Southern California made their way to Los Angeles. In early January 1931, a press release in various city newspapers in Southern California warned that federal and local authorities would target Mexicans in a deportation campaign to begin on January 6. By printing this notice, local newspapers deliberately heightened the level of panic sweeping through the Mexican colonies of Los Angeles and Southern California as a way to hasten the departure of Mexicans. Repatriation momentarily halted when California growers intervened. Because growers relied exclusively on Mexicans to harvest their fruits and vegetables, they viewed the repatriation campaign as a costly inexpediency that could potentially disrupt the harvesting and processing of fruits and vegetables, all worth millions of dollars. In addition, numerous private construction companies in Los Angeles were dependent on Mexican labor. The army of out-of-state transients could not be depended on as a substitute for the hard-working and competent Mexican laborers because these white men were unreliable and demanded higher wages. Employers in the city therefore pressured the Los Angeles Chamber of Commerce to pull back its support for repatriation and called on public and private officials to restore calm in the frantic Mexican community. Owing to the strong ties between local urban industrialists and landowners in the San Joaquin and Imperial Valleys, the Los Angeles business community insisted on a modicum of protection for Mexican workers. Business leaders had already made it widely known that they wanted a well-regulated relief program to assist Mexicans without disturbing this labor's availability during the fruit and vegetable harvests. Such egregious business practices would make Mexican workers more highly motivated, so they would perform better. Nonetheless, the campaigns of indiscriminate raids and intimidation by U.S. Bureau of Immigration officers succeeded in terrorizing the Mexican population of Southern California, causing about 40,000 to leave the state. A third of the Mexican population of Los Angeles returned to Mexico. Most of the repatriates were single males recently arrived from the surrounding farming regions or from Mexico who had not found work. U.S. citizens, legal residents, and those with documentation made up the majority of the grief-stricken Mexicans remaining in the city of Los Angeles.[70]

Because of the industrial nature of the national economic crisis that produced mass layoffs in steel, meatpacking, railroad, and auto work, the Midwest's urban blue-collar Mexican communities bore the brunt of the

repatriation drives. In Milwaukee, Chicago, Gary, and Detroit, local officials removed Mexican families from the dole, intentionally made it difficult for them to obtain relief, or denied public assistance to Mexicans
altogether. Business interests set the tone early on. Some industrial employers who had actively recruited Mexicans during the World War I
labor shortages now claimed no responsibility for their plight. For instance, Horace S. Norton, the head of U.S. Steel's Gary Works, president
of Gary's Chamber of Commerce, and an outspoken supporter of Mexican repatriation, flatly denied that U.S. Steel had recruited Mexicans to
Gary. His pointed remarks very likely expressed the indifference of other
area industrial employers: "I personally know that no Lake County industrial concern made any effort to get [Mexicans] to come here. The majority just drifted in."[71] A few northern companies came to the defense of
their Mexican employees, according to historian Dionicio Valdés, not out
of compassion but rather as a matter of existing paternalistic practices.
Auto magnate Henry Ford laid off Mexican autoworkers and rehired
them when full car production resumed at his plants. However, Ford's
generosity benefited him, since it meant these autoworkers had to endure
extreme speedup and ruthless workplace repression at reduced pay. Because of its longtime heavy reliance on Mexican labor, the Santa Fe Railroad Company protected its local Mexican enclaves by claiming they were
U.S. citizens. Although most individuals and organizations did not actively speak out or publish against the oppressive measures directed at
the Mexicans, a handful of church officials, social workers, and radical
organizations came forward and criticized the call for Mexican expulsion.
Presbyterian Church leader Robert N. McLean, who had worked among
Mexicans throughout the 1920s, was especially critical of the U.S. Border
Patrol. McLean charged this federal agency had previously allowed Mexicans to cross freely into the United States whenever employers claimed
labor shortages, but now its agents were staging mass dragnets to apprehend these workers, often with employer collusion. Chicago Federation
of Settlements president Lea D. Taylor also complained to Labor Secretary
Doak about the deportation raids staged by the U.S. Immigration Bureau.
Federal agents arrested large numbers of foreign-born Chicago residents,
and only a few were in violation of the immigration laws. Taylor stated
that some Chicago citizens perceived the arrests as a deliberate drive upon
the unemployed foreign worker legally in the country. For its part, the
Communist Party argued that repatriation was imperialistic and racist.
Accurately condemning the repatriations as "gigantic wholesale illegal
kidnappings," the party's International Labor Defense in numerous instances aided Mexicans, especially before, during, and long after strike
actions, when the workers were singled out for arrest and removal.[72]

CAUSES AND CONSEQUENCES OF MEXICAN REPATRIATION
AND DEPORTATION

Mexican repatriation during the Great Depression was not a uniform undertaking but rather multifaceted. One facet entailed Mexicans leaving voluntarily by crossing the border into Mexico, such as those workers living in the Imperial Valley, southern Arizona, El Paso, and the lower Río Grande Valley in Texas. Many were seized nonetheless as they crossed into Mexico. Other immigrants requested and received assistance from willing Mexican consular officials, who had been given a directive and money for allocations from the Mexican government for this purpose. In many communities, prorepatriation committees were established and mobilized by Mexicans to coordinate the removals. Another aspect of repatriation, as we have seen, involved the U.S. Labor Department, which had jurisdiction over the U.S. Immigration Bureau. Labor Department agents in staged raids or acting individually were directed to seek out and repatriate Mexicans who could not prove legal residency. Finally, repatriation involved local county and city officials. Facing dwindling funds for relief assistance, these latter officials got rid of Mexicans who became a "public charge." However, as in the 1970s, government agents deferred to the manpower needs of ranchers and growers; in exchange for favors or bribes, the agents released detained Mexicans to them and kept other ranches and farms off-limits to searches and seizures.[73] The following examines the various causes that led to the repatriation of Mexican workers during the early years of the Great Depression, a time when many Mexicans who were legal residents or American citizens became innocent victims caught in a legal imbroglio.

Mexicans were detained and taken into custody by officials of the U.S. Immigration Bureau and the U.S. Border Patrol and returned to Mexico if they were in violation of either the 1917 or 1924 Immigration Act. That is, Mexican foreign nationals could be deported if, at the time of their arrest, they had entered the United States by land other than at a designated port of entry, or if they possessed an expired immigration visa. The aliens could be released on a $500 bond or on their own recognizance if they agreed to appear for a hearing ordered by the U.S. Immigration Bureau to give cause why they should not be deported.[74]

In light of the nationwide repatriation drive, many Mexicans, in evident fear of expulsion, rushed to establish proof of continuous residency. To do this, Mexicans had to prove they had been in the United States since 1920 or since the date of immigration or, in the case of those who returned to Mexico and then reentered the United States, the last date on which their passport was renewed. Letters of recommendation showing proof of residency or proof of employment were required as supplementary evidence.[75] The workers had to show the month and year they established their residence in the country, or else the month and year in which they began and terminated their employment and returned to Mexico. Mexicans employed by the railroad, mining, automobile, and steel companies had little trouble furnishing this information, since most of these corporations maintained employment departments. However, most Mexicans worked for fruit and vegetable growers, who did not keep accurate employee records because they hired the workers through a labor contractor. Longtime workers, that is, those who entered the United States more than ten years previous to 1920, had a far greater problem establishing proof of residence or employment. In such cases, poor or nonexistent record keeping or the death of a former employer or landlord became contributing factors for detainment. Along with the fact that U.S. immigration laws were not stringently enforced in the past, some employers refused to provide their Mexican employees with service letters, and this ultimately resulted in problems for the worker. Eighty percent of Mexican workers lived in company housing and because of the itinerant nature of their employment could not prove continuous residency in one location. The discretion exercised by U.S. Immigration Bureau inspectors and their arbitrary actions were also factors. Some of these federal officials would not accept oral statements or written affidavits from breadwinners or family members in proving continuous residence or for verifying employment. Nor would they accept letters from landlords dated one month to over six months from the time the worker quit his job or vacated his residence, and letters not written on letterhead stationery were likewise rejected as valid evidence. Furthermore, many Mexicans were very reluctant to come forward to prove their legal residency because they had entered the country surreptitiously or feared or mistrusted the sinister immigration officials. Many of the agents were former Texas Rangers and local sheriffs and deputies and thus longtime practitioners of legalized violence when dealing with Mexicans.[76]

Legal residents who had registered with the U.S. Immigration Office upon entering the United States later discovered that their records had been misplaced or lost. They now faced the bureaucratic dilemma of proving that registration with the U.S. Immigration Bureau took place, as in the case of sugar beet worker Luis Guerra from Louisville, Colorado. Luis had registered with the U.S. Immigration Office on March 27, 1917, shortly after entering the United States, and because of the wartime conditions, Luis had also registered with the Louisville draft board. Nonetheless, fifteen years later, on May 20, 1932, amidst labor unrest in the area beet fields caused by a strike, U.S. Immigration Bureau agents detained the Guerra family in northern Colorado. The Guerras had returned to the northern sugar beet fields from the coal mines in southern Colorado because coal operators, in their relentless chase after profits, cut wages and implemented work-share schemes so that miners were earning about $125 per year. Since the Guerras could not come up with proper identification, the family was repatriated. Writing from Mexico, Luis pleaded with Catholic officials in Colorado for help in returning to the United States: "I can prove that I know how to respect the laws of the United States as well as [that I am an] honest working man." With the hard times he and his family experienced in the southern Colorado coal mines fresh on his mind, the repatriate offered a caution to other Mexicans seeking work as coal diggers in Colorado's coal mines: "If there is any way to do it, all the Spanish-speaking people should be warned to keep away from the Colorado coalfields. The conditions are worse than ever . . . [and] there is no assurance that they will receive their pay . . . at all."[77]

Other legal residents were repatriated for failing to renew their passports, like Arizona copper miner Alberto Mora. After fourteen years of work in the copper mines around Bisbee and Prescott, Alberto and his American-born wife returned to Mexico in 1930 when all the area mines closed. Alberto had proof of legal admission into the country and continuous residency since 1916, but the copper miner had failed to renew his passport following a short stay in Mexico. When records verified their repeated claims of American citizenship, immigration officials allowed Alberto's wife and children to return to Arizona, at which time Mrs. Mora began the long process of bringing her husband back to the United States. To do this, she had to pay the fine for her husband's passport violation and prove that he would not become "a public charge nor solicit nor live off charity."[78]

As noted, the U.S. Immigration Bureau apprehended Mexicans who crossed into Mexico to wait out the economic crisis. For example, American authorities nabbed copper miner Ricardo Gonzales on August 24, 1933, as he attempted to cross into Mexico at the small town of Acala, just south of El Paso. The unemployed miner had worked for the Chino Copper Company in Arizona for five and one-half years, until September 1927, when the recession that year caused him to lose his job. For the next six years Ricardo worked sporadically, and by February 1933, the ex–copper miner could not find any more work and gave up searching. As he crossed into Mexico, U.S. immigration authorities, present in great numbers because of the outbreak of a cotton strike in the El Paso district, picked him up and detained him, pending proof of residency. Railroad worker José García and his American-born wife were longtime residents of Santa Fe, New Mexico. From June 1926 to June 1928, José worked for the Southern Pacific Railroad near Midlake, Utah. In September 1928, José obtained work with the Utah Copper Company Mines at Bingham

Canyon, Utah. He held this job for three years but because of the Depression was discharged on January 11, 1931. Returning to New Mexico, José could not get relief assistance for himself and his family because he had been working outside the state since 1926. In April 1932, U.S. immigration officials took the ex–railroad worker into custody at El Paso as he was attempting to cross into Mexico.[79]

Mexicans were invariably on the move, hoping to procure steady work, staying in some locations only one or two days, several weeks, or a few months. This constant peregrination made it difficult for workers to show proof of continuous employment and residency. Proving residency was a problem because many workers lived communally to save on living expenses, a practice especially common among the single men. Problems also arose when workers could not find records of their employment, sometimes because they falsified names on job applications. Mexican American repatriates could not establish proof of U.S. citizenship or residence because they could not recall the towns and cities where they were born or where they had been baptized. The needed information very often was unavailable because names were filed incorrectly or misspelled or because of improper record keeping. Catholic parishes did not record baptisms or there was poor record keeping, since priests were frequently transferred from one parish to another. Furthermore, Mexicans could not afford to copy and notarize these vital records.

In their eager rush "to get rid of Mexicans," some local administrators intentionally processed American-born citizens and legal residents for repatriation. The experiences of the seven-member Godina family of Longmont, Colorado, clearly illustrate the innumerable wrongful mistakes resulting from hasty repatriation schemes implemented by county and city officials. The Godinas were among the 20,000 Mexican indigents repatriated from Colorado to Mexico by state relief agencies in 1932. Mrs. Godina was an American citizen and so were her five children. Although born in Mexico, Mr. Godina was a legal resident; he had lived in Longmont since he was a child. The Godina family was living in Ciudad Juárez, Mexico, scarcely surviving, when the National Catholic Welfare Conference in El Paso was contacted on their behalf. Shortly thereafter, the Godinas were assisted in returning to their home in Colorado.[80]

As did certain employers and private relief agencies, a few state and local officials helped repatriated Mexicans search for vital records in their attempt to return to the United States. They mailed blank birth certificates to the repatriates in Mexico, along with instructions for them to contact individuals in the United States who were present at their birth to fill out the certificates. In Arizona, the Division of Vital Statistics of the State Board of Health assisted Mexicans needing copies of their birth certificates, and in similar fashion, the state of New Mexico assisted with verification of birth records by furnishing "Affidavits for a Correction of Birth and Death Record." Some individuals also came to the aid of Mexican repatriates. One of these was Cleofas Calleros of El Paso. Calleros directed the Southwest office of the National Catholic Welfare Conference and in addition served on the El Paso County Board of Welfare and Employment, which operated the city's Welfare Bureau and administered FERA relief funds.[81] Assigned to direct relief for El Paso, Calleros was able to persuade U.S. immigration authorities to accept a wider variety of proof of employment and residency from Mexican nationals. Calleros efficiently reduced the paperwork in processing immigration cases, and he helped Mexicans with their visas, legal residency applications, and petitions to become U.S. citizens. In this regard, Calleros stopped the practice by notary publics of swindling Mexicans by charging them exorbitant rates to establish their legal residency, and he secured back pay for Mexicans repatriated to Mexico. The numerous services rendered by the tireless Cleofas Calleros proved helpful to more than 30,000 Mexicans in an area extending from Brownsville, Texas, to San Diego, California, and as far north as Detroit, Michigan. All these examples of compassion were exceptional because few came forward to assist the harried Mexicans.[82]

The repatriation of destitute Mexicans was not the cost-saving measure local and state officials had hoped to achieve; in fact, the opposite was true. For example, the National Catholic Welfare Conference reported that in El Paso over six hundred new cases would be added to the local relief rolls as a result of Mexican families' losing their breadwinners to repatriation. Another study disclosed that it would cost $90,000 to deport 1,200 Mexican aliens; however, these deportees would leave behind 1,478 dependents eligible for public relief totaling $147,000 because they were U.S. citizens or legal residents. Also, 80 percent of the deportees would be eligible to obtain nonquota preference for reentry, since their wives, children, and other relatives were citizens or legal residents of the United States.[83]

The growing backlog of federal deportation cases awaiting final action ultimately resulted in a reassessment of repatriation procedures. This policy change likely came about in 1933, when President Roosevelt combined the Burea of Immigration and the Bureau of Naturalization into the Immigration and Naturalization Service. To give relief organizations an opportunity to study and submit their deportation case reports, the U.S. Justice Department delayed deportation proceedings until July 1, 1934. These federal officials were reviewing nearly 600 cases to avoid deportation where family separation would cause severe hardship. The cases of 1,100 aliens jailed for immigration law violations were reduced to 400, and these individuals were released to the custody of their families at a savings to the government of $150,000. In addition, new labor secretary Frances Perkins requested that all social services agencies be consulted to allow them to review cases to determine hardship and assist those cases worthy of consideration. There were further changes in federal policy. The $500 bond for violation of American immigration laws and the $1,000 bond to procure work were each reduced to $150. Essentially, the Immigration and Naturalization Service (INS) was carrying out the policy initiative of the Roosevelt administration regarding appropriate treatment by federal inspectors of persons seeking admission to the United States. In sum, the Roosevelt administration would not tolerate any misconduct by INS inspectors in the form of unreasonable, unjust, cruel, harsh, or discourteous treatment toward the immigrants.[84]

Unfortunately, this agenda was not as benevolent in those sections of the country with large Mexican populations; the INS continued to violate the civil rights of Mexicans. Those who engaged in labor organizing and strike actions especially faced constant scrutiny in addition to bullying and harassment by INS and Justice Department officials. For the remainder of the Great Depression, the Spanish-speaking community lived in fear of these officials. What's more, the climate of scathing anti-Mexican sentiment created intense polarization, producing a sweeping suspicion toward foreigners, irrespective of their legal status, and a quite hostile form of scapegoating, which linked housing congestion, strained relief services, and social ills to the large presence of Mexicans.

What public officials and American citizens alike failed to realize or understand, but which employers were fully aware of, was that by the 1920s Mexicans had become the mainstay of the economy of the Southwest, dominating low-wage agricultural, mining, railroad, construction, and service sector work. Living and working conditions for the Mexican laboring classes were uniformly dreadful, whether in agricultural fields, the mines, or the city sweatshops. Years of confinement to low-wage labor, however, took its toll. There was outright disregard for the despised Spanish-speaking workers confined to the squalid, disease-ridden slums, and illiteracy was widespread, especially hindering children's advancement in American society. It seemed that Americans, if they noticed the Spanish-speaking population at all, were only interested in the Mexican as a laborer but barred him from any kind of action to protect his interests as a worker. Rejected from participation in the cultural, social, and political life of the United States, Mexicans were judged unassimilable and thus had failed to take their place in American life. Mexicans were considered not to belong to a community and therefore were thought devoid of civic duty. The belief that Mexicans could not and should not hold public office accounted for the fact that few served as elected officials, including on local and county relief agency boards. This had dire consequences for Mexican Americans during World War II. They were kept off the all-white local draft boards, and casualties among Mexican American overseas were extraordinarily high. Because of this general hostility toward them, very few Mexicans became naturalized U.S. citizens. They had learned the hard lesson that the advantages afforded to U.S. citizens were denied to Mexican Americans, who, despite the halt in immigration from Mexico, remained eternal victims of discrimination and were rendered outsiders by the prevailing nativist mind-set.

The hardships of the Great Depression raised alarm about the great numbers of Mexican immigrants entering the United States each year, even though thousands of aliens unable to find work returned to Mexico. Mexicans were noticed when they became a relief burden, yet very few were deemed eligible for assistance, including children and the aged, who generally made up most of the relief cases. Many local relief boards attempted a host of schemes to disqualify Mexicans for assistance; it was believed that starving the indigents would force them to return to Mexico. The consensus was that Mexicans had no place in America's social life. From 1930 to 1935, 345,839 Mexicans were repatriated or deported back to Mexico, with the years 1931 and 1932 representing the peak of the expulsions, when more than a third (138,519) of them were sent back. As Ernesto Galarza correctly observed, repatriation was nothing more than the wholesale disposal of human labor below the border. That the intensive repatriation dragnet gathered up Mexican Americans is indicated by the fact that more than 80 percent of the repatriates from California were American citizens or legal residents. Thousands of these individuals, stranded in Mexico, would eventually attempt to return to the United States. Many did so in the 1940s as contract laborers through the newly implemented Bracero program, while others volunteered for military service when the United States declared war on Japan.[85]

With the coming of the Roosevelt administration, the number of Mexican deportations declined by 50 percent. Deportation was reevaluated though it did not stop, as Spanish-speaking labor activists soon learned, because it had become a widely used practice in the Southwest to muzzle dissent. Nor did racism stop against Mexican Americans: those who obtained work with New Deal programs faced wage and other kinds of wholesale discrimination. Overall, the dismal plight of Mexican Americans and an increase in measures against them provided the context for an appeal to spirited collective action to mount common claims against injustice. Many embittered albeit resolute Spanish-speaking workers took up the call to organize and took center stage in the struggle that commenced in the Southwest.[86]

Gaining Strength through the Union: Mexican Labor Upheavals in the Era of the NRA

> Workers who refuse to strike for justice . . . are signing their death warrant.
> —COLORADO STRIKE LEADER JOSÉ VILLA

> United, we all defend ourselves.
> Disunited, discrimination will pursue us more and more.
> —LA LIGA OBRERA DE HABLA ESPAÑOL

IN THE EARLY YEARS of the Great Depression, the hostile attitudes toward Mexicans only became worse. Mexicans became the scapegoats for the nation's growing joblessness. The degradation of the Mexican people resulted from the rapid increase in unemployment, the denial of relief assistance, and acute discrimination. The working conditions for Mexicans were unvaryingly terrible, whether in the agricultural fields, the sweatshops, the factories, or the mines and smelters. Mexican workers were on their own and at the mercy of their employers, who implemented or increased dangerous and exploitive labor practices to ensure the maximum amount of cheap labor.

Although it supported trade unionism in Mexico, the AFL for the most part shunned the Mexican. At the onset of the Great Depression, the AFL lent its support to drive the Mexican worker across the border. Along with backing anti-immigration legislation in state legislatures and in Congress, the AFL stood firm on prohibiting immigration during times of unemployment. The AFL's position all along was that Mexican immigrants lowered living standards for American workers and weakened unions. Organized labor charged that during labor disputes Mexicans were deployed as strikebreakers, as they were at the turn of the century in the mine wars in Arizona and Colorado, in the 1919 steel strikes in Chicago and Gary, and in the 1921–22 railway strikes in Kansas City. While unduly portraying Mexican labor as weakening AFL organizing drives, the federation neglected to state that its international unions, through their constitutions, bylaws, and established practices, routinely excluded Mexicans from membership. Dominated by all-white craft unions, the intransigent federation made few attempts to unionize the

Mexican laborer, and when it did, unionization meant segregated locals. It had also failed to get Mexico's Confederación Regional Obrera Mexicana (CROM) to cut off the flow of Mexican labor into the United States. In an extension of its policy of blocking attempts at advancement by unskilled black, immigrant, and women workers, the AFL had reached an arrangement whereby low-wage common labor would be the domain of the Mexican worker. Through a plan of containment adhered to by the all-white state labor councils, the AFL acted to prevent the spread of Mexican labor into industrial employment and the skilled crafts and trades. Only when the CIO began competing aggressively with the national federation for members would it reluctantly reach out to the Mexican working classes.[1]

No strong and effective Mexican American civil rights organization existed to advance a coherent program on behalf of the Spanish-speaking of the Southwest. LULAC was a weak and ineffective institution and moreover was disengaged from Mexican workers. LULAC was aware of the profound growth of the Spanish-speaking population produced by two decades of uninterrupted immigration from Mexico and especially of the harmful consequences it had on American-born Mexicans. In January 1930, LULAC lent its voice to the growing anti-immigrant sentiment when this organization sent representatives to Washington, D.C., to testify before the congressional committee holding hearings on Mexican immigration. If immigration from Mexico was left unchecked, the LULAC spokesman argued, it would sharpen discrimination against American-born Mexicans and block their economic advancement. But which group of Mexican Americans did LULAC have in mind? From different economic and educational backgrounds, LULAC's elite middle-class Mexican American leadership was inclined to ignore the plight of the poor Mexican workers. Having embraced the mantle of respectability, LULAC advocated its own version of the black middle-class doctrine of "racial uplift" and assimilation. Along with its values and aspirations, its accommodationist outlook reflected the self-interest of its conservative professional and business-class leadership at the expense of workers who joined this organization. Blinded by class, LULAC distanced itself from the Mexican wage earner at a time of utmost need for unity. Basing Mexican American identity on class allegiances, LULAC essentially launched itself on a course separate from the concerns and needs of the Spanish-speaking working classes.[2]

Without labor and civil rights leadership and reeling from the twin scourge of mounting discrimination and the economic crisis, the Mexican worker would need other allies. Mexican workers sought aid from within their own ranks and reached across racial lines to progressive Anglos. The latter, individuals committed to supporting the laboring classes and

Figure 2.A. The Communist Party boldly confronted the anguish of the Mexican people. Workers marching on May Day for better working conditions, Phoenix, Arizona, 1930. The banner reads: "Join the Communist Party." (CP SPC 156: 559—Odd Halseth Photographs, Arizona Collection, Courtesy of Arizona State University Libraries).

interracialism to the fullest, were developing a following dedicated to the principles of direct action.

In the early 1930s, communists played a major part in provoking the unrest among the Mexican workers in the Southwest. Instructed to respond to the rising level of discontent, the Communist Party initiated strikes and mass demonstrations and set up cells in factories and mines in preparation for a future revolutionary upsurge. Organizers from the Trade Union Unity League (TUUL) met with the aggrieved Mexican workers and explained to them the implications of the ongoing economic crisis. Though it rarely formed lasting unions, the TUUL nevertheless pursued its goal of organizing Mexican workers, leading them in strike actions, and exposing them to the principles of class struggle. Moreover, through its Unemployed Councils and the International Labor Defense, the Communist Party helped Spanish-speaking workers obtain relief, mounted additional legal activities, provided legal aid to fight against discrimination and protest police violence, and defended the workers against deportation.[3]

The Communist Party courted Spanish-speaking workers to join its ranks and those of its left-wing organizations. In this regard, the party was prodded by the nascent Communist Party of Mexico (PCM), which began to stress to its American counterpart the worsening conditions among Mexican workers in the United States. Given the PCM's fledgling status, most Mexicans probably came into the party orbit in the United States. Others became fellow travelers who traversed a radical path. They identified themselves as anarcho-syndicalists, were former IWW members, or were staunch unionists who embraced a socialist orientation.[4]

In their work with Mexicans as an oppressed national minority, the communists had no equivalent of the ambitious Southern strategy of self-determination outlined for blacks. The party would have to reevaluate its understanding of race issues beyond a black-and-white context and consider the complexities of race, ethnicity, and nationality in order to accommodate the interests and needs of Mexicans, who formed the main labor force in the Southwest and were behind the labor upheavals unfolding in the region. The communist organizers soon discovered that, as with Southern blacks, dry Marxist doctrine and lofty revolutionary aims counted less than their antiracist stance and willingness to lend their organizing talents to the Mexicans' cause. Notwithstanding, the communists earnestly took on the task of organizing the Spanish-speaking workers and empowered them by cultivating their radical tendencies.[5]

As the dominant racial/ethnic group in the Southwest, Mexicans provided the main support for strike actions and led some of the hardest and longest-fought labor struggles in the region. Through the NRA, Mexicans believed they had an opportunity to advance their interests and gain protection through organization.

The announcement under the National Industrial Recovery Act of minimum hours and a sixteen-dollar-a-week minimum wage came just as farm worker wages reached their lowest level in forty years; $1.05 per day, or 11.1 cents per hour. The New Deal labor legislation had no provisions for agricultural workers, largely as a consequence of Roosevelt's appeasement of Southern Democrats and the influential farm bloc. Nevertheless, the rising expectations of government support through Section 7a prompted the mostly poor and politically impotent agricultural workers to contest wage grievances and bad working and living conditions through a massive wave of labor strikes. Sixty-one agricultural strikes erupted in seventeen states and involved 56,800 farm workers, with most of them striking in California. Practically all these work stoppages broke out in farming regions where migrant labor predominated and in proximity to urban-based labor movements from which the striking farmers got additional support. Most (85 percent) of the labor disputes were over wages, followed by work hours and then work conditions. Work stoppages for union recognition were a comparatively new aspect of the labor protests.[6] The majority of these striking agricultural workers were Mexicans.

Organizing farm workers has remained a tremendous undertaking ever since the Industrial Workers of the World first carried out this task early in the twentieth century. The seasonal nature of farm work and migration prevented effective organizing, and low wages hampered farm workers in maintaining their incipient unions and boosting their meager strike funds. When farm worker unions secured a strike settlement, agreements with employers were never formalized, and they lasted just a short time; moreover, federal officials failed to acknowledge farm labor unions in the labor arbitration disputes. Growers fiercely opposed unions because they were promoted by radicals or outside agitators who fomented revolution and communist principles. This fact and the nonwhite makeup of the farm labor force led to violent attacks on farm worker unions as being un-American and foreign and thus a threat to tradition and order. Once assured that farm workers did not enjoy collective bargaining rights under the New Deal labor legislation, growers used all legal and forceful means to thoroughly crush threats to their harvests and to deport the instigators.[7]

California's huge and dramatic agricultural strikes, which brought national attention to the low wages and bad working conditions in the fields, have been well documented by scholars. However, the histories of California farm labor strife have tended to obscure similar militant strike actions by Mexicans elsewhere in the Southwest. The following examines the walkouts by Tejano cotton pickers in the El Paso cotton district, by Colorado beet workers, and by Spanish-speaking female domestic, tobacco, and garment workers in El Paso, San Antonio, and Los Angeles in the era of the NRA. The El Paso cotton strike demonstrates the immense difficulty Tejanos faced in building agrarian unionism along the Texas-Mexico border, while the beet strike illustrates the impediments to radical collective action. The domestic, tobacco, and dressmakers' strikes, on the other hand, show that the era's militant unionism and the New Deal labor legislation awakened Spanish-speaking women to the working-class activism taking root in the urban centers of the Southwest. The women proved capable of wide-ranging action as they coordinated their activities through a unionism that flowed from their everyday networks. Public opinion was solidly against their efforts to gain union recognition, and employers organized and deployed their resources to smash the strikes. A radical brand of unionism was clearly obvious in the huge agricultural strikes Spanish-speaking workers waged in California. Radicalism was also manifest in the protracted strike carried on by Mexican coal miners in Gallup, New Mexico, which is also a subject of this chapter.[8] Hundreds of workers signed up with the Communist Party and other progressive organizations. This perceived direct rebellion against the authority of the state of New Mexico gave the coal operators of Gallup and government leaders an excuse to blame Mexicans for labor unrest and to supply lawful grounds for their expulsion. As a result of the change in INS policy to target labor activists, Mexican unionists were arrested on the grounds that they were communists who essentially called for the use of force to overthrow the government. In the government's effort to undermine support for labor strikes, Mexicans were arrested, detained, and deported. Despite the violence and repression that rained on them, the solidarity of the Mexican workers never wavered.

Revolt in the Cotton Fields: Tejano Pickers Strike the El Paso Cotton District

In 1931, organizing by Tejano cotton pickers unfolded in the El Paso cotton district—the "Cotton Paradise," as the El Paso Chamber of Commerce promoted it. The workforce was made up of workers who traveled to the farms from El Paso and its environs. Wage cuts to forty cents per one hundred pounds of picked cotton, combined with the drop in cotton's market price and widespread worker discontent, triggered spontaneous work stoppages across the cotton district. Lacking leadership and coordination, the walkout by the workers was badly managed and proved no match for the forces marshaled by the cotton growers to put down the strike.[9]

Threatened with the loss of the cotton crop, area growers, assisted by the newly expanded U.S. Employment Service (USES), at first responded to the walkout by hastily recruiting scabs. The cotton growers then organized into associations and began plotting the suppression of the strike. In their support of the cotton farmers, El Paso authorities immobilized the Tejano cotton pickers and forced them into the fields by denying them work on a county-funded construction project and, as further pressure, announced a vagrancy roundup. City police officers spread the warning "Work or jail" in the streets, and their dragnet singled out Tejano cotton pickers on relief and those making applications for aid. Tejanos arrested and taken into custody could choose to pick cotton or serve a sentence on the city chain gang. City truant officers aided the cotton growers by letting Tejano children miss school to make them available for picking. U.S. Immigration Bureau officers helped execute the vagrancy law, an indication that the city statute was being imposed solely to net Tejanos for strikebreaking duty. The presence of federal immigration agents and the ongoing repatriation drive were proof that deportation had become a fact of life along the border. The federal agents earnestly pursued their task of apprehending Tejanos; the agents went into the fields, hunted down the Tejano cotton pickers, and arrested them at will. Growers responded to the sudden labor shortage by recruiting more strikebreakers and thus easily suppressed the strike. In the face of formidable odds, including those posed by the growers' new partnership with El Paso law enforcement officers and the U.S. Immigration Bureau, the strike failed because it lacked leadership, was poorly planned, and was hastily implemented. Two years later, the pickers walked out again, this time better prepared and organized by the Fabens Laboring Men's Protective Association (FLMPA).[10]

At this time, progressive working-class ethnic associations, farmer and worker groups, and Left-led organizations continued to carry on a struggle for unionism. An independent labor body, the FLMPA was a vestige of the Land League of America movement of the pre–World War I years, which promised for its adherents land distribution and a revamped land rental policy. About 1,000 Tejano laborers from various mutual aid societies and Socialist Party labor federations belonged to the Land League and imbued it with interracialism. However, the Land League movement waned in the post–World War I years. It succumbed to irregular dues payments by its poor members and the repressive power of cotton interests, but it was particularly undone by the intense antisocialist sentiment and racism at war's end that saw radicals arrested and aliens deported.[11] In 1933, the FLMPA drew on the social ferment building among Tejano workers in the El Paso cotton district against the cotton growers' oppression. As the FMLPA launched its organizing drive among the cotton pickers, the newly constituted Immigration and Naturalization Service, armed with information supplied by the growers and under their instruction, tactically deployed its agents to intimidate workers by staging raids.

In the fall of 1933, before El Paso area growers had set the wage rate for picking cotton, the FLMPA called a strike and announced a series of demands: one dollar per hundred pounds of cotton for pickers working full-time, seventy-five cents per hundred pounds of cotton for part-time pickers, and an improvement in working conditions in the fields. Regarding the last, the FLMPA in a letter to U.S. Labor Secretary Frances Perkins explained that the Tejano cotton pickers slaved thirteen to fourteen hours a day, many going without pay because they were deep in debt to a company store, and endured terrible living conditions that bordered on bondage. The FLMPA expanded its strike with assistance from the United Citizens' Civic League, a progressive group of El Paso Tejanos who met with cotton pickers in Ysleta, Socorro, Fabens, and other surrounding towns in an effort to gain solidarity. As the strike spread to more farms, numerous cotton pickers joined in willingly, while others very likely were forced to join the strike or warned not to return to work. These actions provoked the growers, who reacted by identifying and then firing all workers sus-pected of belonging to the FLMPA. Other cotton farmers, growing anx-ious that their crop might rot in the fields if left unpicked, followed suit and rid their fields of pro-union pickers. Those workers who had accumu-lated substantial debt at the company store because of the rising prices were forced to remain on the farms and harvest the cotton. Opposition to the strike intensified. Growers would not accede to the strikers' de-mands and were going to teach Tejanos a lesson. Cotton farmers went after the pickers with whips and armed their field bosses with shotguns. This steady torrent of violence pressed some of the workers back into the cotton fields. El Paso County Sheriff Chris P. Fox and his deputies stood ready to crack down on the striking workers, whom Fox labeled as radi-cals.[12] The cotton growers had launched their coordinated counterattack.

Refusing to answer the FLMPA's complaints of violent repression, El Paso County's assistant attorney at the behest of growers issued a stern warning to the labor association: its members would be prosecuted if they continued to harass and intimidate the workers into walking out. The growers next sought the help of the relief departments. Public as well as private relief agencies announced that assistance would be denied to all cotton workers out on strike and that those already on relief would be taken off the dole. In a reflection of the dominance of state governments in the South, the political influence of the cotton growers extended to the state capitol in Austin. Violating state policy, wherein work relief was provided to rural residents, Texas government officials notified welfare agencies in outlying districts that all able-bodied persons would be ineligi-ble for work relief. Additionally, the head of the American Red Cross, at the behest of farmers, announced that the distribution of clothing to indigents would be postponed until the picking season ended. In their collaborative efforts to crush the strike, cotton growers essentially de-prived strikers of food, work relief, and clothing. The collusion between area growers and local, county, and state officials once again involved the federal government. USES official J. R. Martin declared that unless there was a noticeable labor surplus in El Paso County, his agency would pro-hibit travel to adjacent Hudspeth County, adding that any exodus of workers would be stopped "with shotguns if necessary." In a final move against the FLMPA, the INS deployed its agents for deportation duty.[13]

In late September, the vice-chairman of the El Paso Relief and Employ-ment Board issued a report announcing that 60 percent of the Tejano cotton pickers were subject to deportation. Accustomed to mixing Mexi-can nationals and Tejanos to drive down wages, speed up the work, and create dissension, the cotton growers split the ranks of the strikers ac-cording to citizenship status. Along with endorsing the local NRA board's decision to employ only U.S. citizens and legal aliens on government relief projects, cotton growers agreed to cooperate with the INS in the apprehension and deportation of Mexicans found working in their fields without proper identification. The INS immediately launched a series of sweeps of the cotton fields around El Paso to roundup these individuals. Once more, the long-standing complicity between growers and federal immigration officers along the border came to light. On the surface, such agreements appeared incompatible with the needs of the growers, who, like the strikers, understood the important role played by undocumented workers in reversing labor shortages. However, by publicly announcing their intention to work with U.S. immigration officers, growers kept nonstriking cotton pickers in line with the threat that any trouble from them would result in their immediate expulsion. Replacement workers could always be found across the border in Ciudad Juárez.[14]

The repression exerted on the FLMPA put a stop to the workers' revolt in the El Paso area cotton fields. Worn down, the FLMPA finally agreed to a compromise and called off its strike. The walkout that had extended, on and off, over a two-year period gained the Tejano cotton pickers a ten-cent pay increase. Specifically, the workers would pick cotton at the rate of fifty cents per hundred pounds, so long as growers raised their pay with foreseeable increases in the market price of cotton. However, the workers were made no promises either of future wage increases or of improvement in working conditions, including doing away with the company store.[15]

Though short-lived, the FLMPA filled the vacuum created by the lack of a union presence among El Paso's Tejano cotton pickers, who confronted growers fully intent on using all their resources to suppress the strike, including the divide-and-conquer strategies of local, county, state, and federal authorities. The failed cotton strike did not dash the rising hopes of El Paso's Tejano workers. The NRA labor legislation had heightened expectations, and as a result, Tejano workers mobilized themselves to improve their own and their families' conditions, just as the Colorado beet workers did. The same concerns over conditions and wages also motivated the Colorado beet workers to participate in direct labor action.

RADICAL LABOR UNREST IN THE COLORADO BEET FIELDS

Organizing efforts by northern Colorado beet workers can be traced to the 1927 coal strike led by the ever-ready IWW as the bankrupt and battered United Mine Workers of America abandoned the area coalfields to concentrate on organizing campaigns in the East. Support came from multiple sources: the agitation for direct action by the IWW included the propaganda and education campaigns carried on by Spanish-speaking anarcho-syndicalists, socialist radicals, and participants in the earlier coal wars, with cooperation from progressive elements within the Colorado State Federation of Labor.[16]

During the coal strike, IWW organizers had turned to the Mexican beet workers for support, but none came. However, as winter set in and money ran out for food, fuel, and other living expenses, the hard-pressed beet workers, gathered in towns and beet colonies, had a change of heart and asked the IWW to send organizers. By late January 1928, the IWW claimed fourteen beet worker locals with 1,700 members (excluding women and children) in Weld, Larimer, and Boulder Counties. Meanwhile, in Denver, beet workers affiliated with the IWW formed La Liga Obrera de Habla Español (the Spanish-Speaking Workers' League). Branches were soon established in Colorado and in New Mexico. Organizing along lines of ethnicity and class, La Liga quickly emerged as the most important Spanish-speaking worker organization in the Mountain States region. It agitated for relief, raised funds, and was active in strikes. In the meantime, progressive voices within the Colorado State Federation of Labor persuaded the national federation to provide for a paid organizer. The AFL sent veteran Tejano organizer Clementino N. Idar, who set up union locals in the beet colonies of Colorado, Wyoming, and Nebraska, gaining more than 10,000 members. Not all the beet workers embraced the strategy of fostering unity through joint struggles, as some wanted to form all-Spanish-speaking independent organizations. This reflected the national and ethnic divisions that then existed among Colorado's Spanish-speaking workers but which would vanish with the commencement of the repatriation of Mexican nationals in the state.[17]

In August 1929, following a convention held at Fort Lupton, the beet locals set up by the tireless organizer Idar were brought together as the Beet Workers Association (BWA). The BWA applied for an AFL charter. The charter would be granted only if the BWA maintained itself as a stable and self-sufficient organization. However, the incipient farm labor association fell apart. Idar fell ill, and this brought a halt to organization by the AFL in the beet fields. Furthermore, funds evaporated, and an early freeze ruined the sugar beet crop, combining with the unfolding economic crisis to cause a worker surplus in the fields. Furthermore, disputes between northern beet growers and Great Western Sugar led to a 50 percent reduction in beet acreage, and this in turn led to a wage cut that further affected labor demand. Communists sensed opportunity as unemployment worsened in Colorado. Organizers were sent into the cities and towns to spread dissent among the beet workers, as well as to furnish modest sums of money and provisions to help them fend off hunger as the Depression worsened.[18]

In March 1932, there were 55,000 workers out of work in Colorado, triple the number unemployed in 1930. This figure did not include the state's 25,000 Spanish-speaking beet laborers; they had been carried on the relief rolls for so long the state of Colorado listed them as destitute rather than unemployed. By summer, the number of Colorado unemployed workers increased to 65,000, and the number of Mexican Americans on relief rolls likewise showed a rise. Beginning in late 1930, Spanish-speaking communists from Denver began organizing beet workers into locals of the Agricultural Workers Union (AWU). Colorado beet workers had threatened strike actions nearly every year, and in 1932 they rose up and launched a general strike. In addition to a wage increase, the beet workers demanded an end to withholding pay, fair hiring policies, the right to union negotiations, work relief, adequate housing, drinking water, and garden plots. The sugar companies and the growers refused to bargain, and they had the support of county and local officials in stalling negotiations by canceling worker meetings and arbitrarily jailing union leaders. Despite these troubles, the ranks of organized beet workers grew, and conferences were held to conduct educational discussions, pass resolutions, and build worker coalitions.[19]

Left-wing Spanish-speaking beet workers formed the United Front Committee (UFC), a coalition affiliated with the TUUL's Cannery and Agricultural Workers Industrial Union that followed the principles of third-party ideology. Most of the beet workers brought together in the UFC were ex-Wobblies, belonged to La Liga Obrera de Habla Español, or came from mutual aid and fraternal organizations, and some were members of the recently formed Spanish American Citizens Association (SACA), which the year before had helped organize 15,000 Mexican Americans living in Denver. The UFC called a general strike for May 16, following a wage reduction in the northern sugar beet district. Borrowing a tactic the IWW had employed during the 1927 coal dispute, union members caravanned through the beet field districts in trucks and cars to spread word of a general strike. Once again, women found common cause with the men in class struggle and played key roles as participants, lending strength and enthusiasm to the strike and mobilizing strikers by utilizing traditional support networks for protest. Strong, widespread strike solidarity resonated in the Spanish-speaking colonies and the beet worker camps, with the most backing coming from the coal camps adjacent to the beet districts. Tensions mounted as the strike unfolded. Relief was denied to workers who refused to cross the picket lines. This resistance prompted Weld County sheriff's deputies to patrol the farms near the coal mine area to force workers into the fields. A series of arrests set off a wave of open-air protest meetings, one of which was hosted by Greeley's Mexican colony, a center of union militancy. That violence had been advocated at this meeting by radical partisans provoked local farmers to arm themselves against the Red menace and call on law officials to make more arrests of the belligerents. This show of force broke the strike's momentum, as peace officers brandishing guns and clubs hunted down, captured, and arrested leading members of the strike. Charged with vagrancy and intimidation, the workers were jailed and served twenty- to thirty-day terms. Deportations of the UFC's more militant Spanish-speaking members served as a weapon to break striker morale. The sustained armed terrorism and harassment eventually won out: two weeks later the beet fields were quiet. The beet workers abandoned the strike and returned to work at the former wage rate, defeated, though not entirely demoralized.[20]

From the outset, the 1932 Colorado beet strike was plagued with Red-baiting and arrests, as well as dissension within the UFC's ranks over strategy and tactics. The strike was ill timed, launched at the beginning of the thinning season. A labor surplus in the beet fields, the result of mass unemployment among the Mexicans and their elimination from the relief rolls, was another reason for the strike's failure. Wage and other demands were excessive, and the strikers refused to accept less than a total victory, reflecting the influence of the UFC's more militant leaders. The strikers had attempted through a general strike to extend and coordinate the walkout over the entire beet district, encompassing the Arkansas Valley in southern Colorado and the beet counties in the northern part of the state. Food provisions to feed the strikers and their families were scarce because the UFC did not receive the supplies promised through the Workers' International Relief Fund in New York City. Legal assistance from the ILD proved inadequate for the large number of strikers arrested and detained. Finally, the Mexican beet worker colonies had been exposed to a storm of terror and violence by roving bands of sheriff's deputies and U.S. Immigration Bureau agents that probably included threats of eviction from the beet camps. This repression forced the strikers to back down, undermined morale, and reduced pressure on the growers to seek an immediate negotiated settlement.[21]

In any event, the statewide beet strike produced several long-range results. The appeal for solidarity by UFC organizers instilled confidence in the beet workers; many who had been radicalized through exposure to mass action continued to organize. The survival of about eight AWU beet union locals, along with La Liga Obrera de Habla Español, further sustained solidarity into the 1940s. Many of the workers joined SACA and made it the largest pro-labor Mexican American organization in Colorado. Colorado's Spanish-speaking working classes were united as American citizens. Their aspirations were raised by the New Deal reforms, which many believed would redress their long-standing grievances. Mexican American workers took exception to the fact that they were denied New Deal–administered work relief, but they well understood their predicament, in which growers used relief as a weapon to undermine the workers' bargaining power. Specifically, labor activists had revealed to them that when workers were denied relief, job competition increased and wage rates fell. Labor organizers would utilize the tactic of securing relief assistance to their advantage five years hence.[22]

In May 1933, relief monies became available in Colorado through the Federal Emergency Relief Administration (FERA). The Colorado FERA received 85 percent of its funds from the federal government, with the remainder coming from local communities. Because of fiscal problems, Colorado's FERA program was administered from Washington, D.C.[23] The work program provided through the Civilian Works Administration (CWA) for those on relief employed 33,000 during the 1933–34 winter. Under a steady stream of accusations, all Mexican American CWA job applicants were required to verify their citizenship status to be eligible for this work relief. Moreover, Mexican Americans were removed from work relief programs at the beginning of the beet-planting season and then again at the start of the beet harvests on the simple assumption that, owing to their surnames, they were beet laborers. The anti-immigrant hysteria, the deep-seated racial sentiments of many Anglos, and increasing public pressure to keep Mexicans off relief, an issue that aroused considerable anger among Anglos, accounted for these actions. A process had unfolded that restricted social services for Mexican Americans.[24] Two-thirds of Colorado's Mexican American families headed by a nonnaturalized U.S. citizen were denied assistance. As the Depression wore on, it became harder and harder for Colorado's Mexican Americans to get assistance, given the tightened restrictions, the dwindling funds, and the angry nativist environment.[25]

Federal government policies sorely affected Colorado's sugar beet workers. Depressed sugar prices caused by the glut in the world's sugar market, in addition to the natural ravages brought about by droughts, wracked Colorado's sugar industry. At first, the sugar companies doubted the remedy of AAA acreage restrictions to offset the falling sugar prices, fearing this federal program would further reduce their profits. The prevailing climate of uncertainty, however, finally convinced the sugar interests that the government subsidy program was the solution to their lost profits. Colorado sugar companies soon became the largest beneficiaries of AAA subsidies, receiving 40 percent of the $15,526,943 in federal monies paid to the state's farmers. This cash windfall did not trickle down to the poverty-stricken beet workers, who likely were cheated out of their AAA subsidy checks by the sugar companies.[26] A 1934 government survey of the beet districts in Boulder and Weld Counties revealed that area conditions had been bad for the last three years. Because the AAA's planting reduction program prevented beet workers from receiving a sufficient allotment of sugar beet acreage, the families were forced to rely on relief for survival even when they were employed. Although officially barred from state and local relief, the beet workers qualified for the FERA's transient relief program and other federal relief, despite the one-year residency requirement. However, bowing to the powerful sugar companies, state and local relief officials continued to arbitrarily cut beet workers off relief before the start of the beet-growing season. This policy and the ongoing recruitment of out-of-state workers created the intended labor surplus in the beet fields that further depressed worker wages. In Weld County, the nation's largest sugar-producing region, the Great Western Sugar Company was directly involved in the distribution of federal relief. All of the 1,000 beet families that were entitled to relief first had to be approved by field representatives of Great Western.[27]

Toiling for poverty wages under conditions described by contemporary observers as approaching industrial slavery sustained the Spanish-speaking beet workers' penury. For example, the annual cash income of beet workers in Weld County, including relief, averaged a miserable $78 per year per person, or one-fourth the minimum amount needed by a family of four. In addition to buying food, beet workers needed to pay for clothing, supplies, fuel, doctor bills, etc. To obtain their fair share of relief and to improve conditions on FERA work relief projects, communist organizers, with help from La Liga Obrera and the Colorado State Labor Federation, organized beet workers into Unemployed Councils. However, this was a short-lived affair: in 1934, government assistance in Colorado disappeared altogether after Harry Hopkins eliminated FERA-administered relief to farm workers. Hopkins made this decision based on the evidence that federal relief was actually serving as a subsidy to the wealthy sugar companies. In 1935, the state of Colorado withdrew direct relief for transients and restored the one-year residency requirement for relief eligibility. Denied their right to bargain collectively and relying greatly on federal relief for survival owing to their low wages, Colorado Mexican farm laborers were now recognized as welfare beneficiaries, not as wage earners.[28]

Federal intervention through the Jones-Costigan Act of 1934 reactivated unionism among beet workers. The Jones-Costigan Act called for the equitable division of federal sugar returns among beet processors, growers, and farm workers. In order for beet producers to continue receiving federal benefit payments for production adjustments, under the Jones-Costigan Act, the sugar companies had to set minimum wage standards for beet work as well as stop the use of child labor. Meanwhile, left-wing organizers revived and took control of the Beet Workers Association and rallied Colorado beet workers to agitate at the government hearings. In addition, the Independent League, the Spanish American Protective League, and other newly established nonsectarian organizations aided in another organizing drive by the state's beet workers. This action rejuvenated activism among

Mexican American sugar beet workers and maintained national focus as well on their desperate plight.[29]

Mexican women who entered service sector employment or took unskilled and semiskilled work in urban low-cost goods manufacturing were incorporated into a labor force segmented along lines of race, ethnicity, and gender. The ravages of the Great Depression, the New Deal reform legislation, and the era's militant unionism thrust these Spanish-speaking workingwomen into significant collective organizing for the first time and in doing so helped forge the history of Mexican labor organizing in the 1930s.

In Unity There Is Strength: Strikes by Tejana Domestic, Cigar, and Garment Workers

The issues of poverty, migration, and cheap labor among Mexicans in the Southwest had a feminized aspect due to the expansion of women's work in the service and industrial sectors, which reflected the restructuring of the Southwest economy. It was devalued and marginalized work that was informal, undercompensated, unprotected, and stigmatized as "Mexican work." The growing number of Mexican workers now in southwestern urban areas resulted in major organizing drives and, as collective strength increased, turned the cities into centers of labor ferment. Far from being fearful and submissive, the women were prominent in the labor struggles that took place. They engaged in strikes not only to win higher wages and better working conditions, but also because they conceptualized their resistance struggle as contesting racial, ethnic, and gender conflict. The unionization efforts in El Paso, San Antonio, and Los Angeles examined and discussed in the following section dramatically illustrate that while these women workers endured racial and gender oppression, they were strong union supporters, were receptive to union organizing, and were effective organizers. Their strikes signaled the fact that Mexican insurgency had begun in the cities.

The newly passed NRA spurred El Paso's Tejana wage earners to launch organizing drives. Their favorable reaction to the new organizing opportunities inspired labor organizer Charles Porras to remark that they desired "to obtain, through . . . appeals for fair play what the NRA has given other groups." Working long hours for less than half of what their male counterparts earned made it impossible for working-class Tejanas to support themselves or their families. Most of the women laborers were paid less than five dollars for six days of work, some working nine or more hours a day. Moreover, the anti-immigrant climate placed the underpaid Tejanas at great risk of exploitation; they could not demand their rights or negotiate for better wages and working conditions for fear of retaliation, such as blacklisting, if they complained. The deepening crisis of the Great Depression, the promise of the NRA, and pressing family needs nonetheless brought the battle over stagnant wages to the fore.[30]

Because Anglo women would be offended by performing servile labor, almost all of El Paso's paid domestic workers were Mexican women, either from the city or from Cuidad Juárez, who toiled in Anglo homes as day workers or in live-in arrangements. Many had started cleaning houses at a young age. The women suffered class and racial oppression at the hands of protective American housewives, who nonetheless exploited them and paid them little. Gifts of food and discarded clothes marked these caring Anglo housewives, who expected and demanded loyalty, devotion, and deference from their Mexican domestic help. The Spanish-speaking domestic workers occupied an unfair work setting that was difficult to organize, and unions eschewed them. The Asociación de Trabajadoras Domésticas (Association of Domestic Workers, or ADW) undertook the difficult task of organizing domestic workers to help them gain their rights. This grassroots organizing addressed the specific needs of Mexican workingwomen who struggled to support their families on low-wage temporary or part-time domestic work.

The ADW specifically challenged the long-standing problem of competition for work from the plentiful and relatively cheap surplus of Mexican women commuters who crossed the border to do housework in El Paso. The strong demand for cheap labor in El Paso, where wages were higher than in Mexico, acted as a magnet to attract Mexicans, who had little trouble getting work as maids. Through an informal network, in place since the turn of the century, which Anglo housewives tapped for labor, thousands of Mexican immigrant women were hired as maids to clean houses, cook, and look after children. The fact that they were unsure of their rights and unable to speak or understand English made these Mexican nationals easy to exploit. Past attempts had failed to stop Mexican women from Cuidad Juárez from coming into El Paso to work as scab labor. During the 1919 laundry workers' strike, AFL organizer Clementino Idar met with the El Paso U.S. immigration inspector and persuaded this federal government official to confiscate the commuters' passports. However, the commercial laundry owners contacted the Mexican consul for assistance. Maintaining close relations with local employers and acting for the welfare of his fellow citizens of Mexico, the Mexican official ordered the U.S. immigration inspector to return all the passports, allowing the women once again to cross the border freely in both directions. To deal with the steady flow of this labor across the international bridges, the ADW established an employment bureau. Requiring women domestics to register with an employment bureau could regulate domestic work and

ensure that Tejanas received preference in hiring. Although the NRA legislation did not cover domestic work, El Paso's domestic workers continued
to organize, and the women received assistance from the Brigada Mexicana de Propaganda de la NRA (the Pro-NRA Mexican Brigade) and the
El Paso Central Labor Union. For years the latter had dealt unsuccessfully
with the problem of surplus labor caused by an open border.[31]

Domestic workers were likely emboldened by the unfolding strike in
the El Paso cotton district because many of the striking pickers were relatives or friends; membership in the ADW climbed to more than 700
within a month and was expected to double through further organizing
drives. The domestic workers began a mass letter-writing campaign to
demand that employers pay them one dollar more per week than they
currently earned. After several weeks without domestic help, 169 desperate Anglo housewives, not quite inured to the physical demands of home-
making, reluctantly agreed to increase their employees' pay. The ADW
continued its strike. In the meantime, labor organizer Charles Porras met
with U.S. Border Patrol officials. Following the lead previously taken by
AFL organizer Idar, Porras convinced the officials to cut the hours of operation at the international bridges to interrupt the flow of about 1,800
women from Ciudad Juárez, the source of unfair labor competition. Assisting Porras was El Paso's Central Labor Union. It contacted officials in
Washington, D.C., and requested that they reduce the time the international bridges linking Ciudad Juárez and El Paso stayed open.[32]

Angered by the pay revisions the ADW was demanding and by the
prospect of losing access to cheap domestic help, El Paso housewives
began their own protest. A number of them called a meeting with U.S.
Immigration Bureau officials and insisted that labor organizer Porras, a
U.S. citizen, be deported. The El Paso Chamber of Commerce intervened
on behalf of the unhappy housewives, since its members likewise wanted
uninterrupted access to cheap labor from Mexico. Knowing the NRA had
no provision for domestic labor, the Chamber of Commerce urged the
U.S. Border Patrol to extend the hours of operation of the international
bridges, which it did. This action immediately disrupted the work stoppage by the ADW.[33]

The issues of low wages and bad working conditions for domestic work
remained unresolved. A 1934 survey by the El Paso League of Women
Voters revealed the continuing pattern of extreme wage disparity. In one
case, a Spanish-speaking domestic worker who was supporting a family
of five was paid approximately fifteen cents a day, and in another case, a
maid had been paid ten cents a day over a two-year period. A Texas State
Department of Vocational Education study of the working conditions of
El Paso domestic workers confirmed these findings of excessive wage exploitation and substantiated as well the contempt of Anglo women for

Mexican women. Haughty El Paso housewives saw no reason to pay Tejana domestic workers decent wages when they could hire Mexican maids from Ciudad Juárez full-time for a dollar a week and part-time maids for half this amount. Besides, El Paso Anglos blamed poor Mexicans for their plight and maintained that the maids were lazy; the Tejanas were "welfare Queens," preferring the dole to domestic work. The housewives' complaints that they were "losing their maids to the relief rolls" were corroborated by a U.S. Employment Services report. It revealed that 65 percent of the 500 domestic workers registered with this agency were on relief. However, investigators failed to note that the grocery orders were keeping these poorly paid workers and their families from starving.[34] In accordance with the widely held racist stereotypes regarding freeloading Tejanas, El Paso County officials tightened relief measures to disqualify Tejana applicants and make them available for domestic service. Two months after the USES issued its report, and with the full cooperation of employers and local and federal officials, the El Paso Relief Board ordered that any woman who refused to accept work or who had accepted work be cut from relief. The absence of NRA minimum wage provisions for domestic work forced Tejanas into a quandary of work or starve—or work *and* starve, because by taking the poorly paid domestic work the Tejanas accepted slow starvation, and if they were dropped from the relief rolls, they would go without food. El Paso's Tejanas were publicly condemned for refusing domestic work, while Mexican women from across the border were equally scorned for accepting low-paid domestic work in the Queen City, since the employment of these "cheap" Mexican maids swelled the number of Tejana relief cases in El Paso.[35]

The Great Depression cast a long shadow on Mexican Americans. Victimized by racism, exploited by employers, and subject to deportation because they were treated as perpetual foreigners, they were denied the rights enjoyed by other U.S. citizens. As with race and ethnicity, differences based on national identity were part of the social conventions of the Southwest. These distinctions were amplified as employers and local officials subjected Mexican Americans to blanket suspicion regarding their citizenship or used them as a wedge, as in the case of the El Paso cotton strike, to divide Tejanos from Mexican immigrants. Throughout the Southwest and Midwest these conceptions of national identity and citizenship polarized the Spanish-speaking community, whose composition, because of the national repatriation campaign, was shifting from Mexican to American-born. Yet the claim of working-class Americanism was canceled out in the case of Mexican Americans by the prevailing Anglo belief that Mexicans of every status were one and the same. Nationality, along with race and low wages, thus marginalized Mexican Americans as second-class citizens. The U.S.-Mexico border was becoming a contested terrain shaped by changing individual and collective definitions of Mexican culture, ethnic identity, citizenship, and national loyalty. Demographic changes brought about by the new immigration law and the recent repatriation drives that greatly reduced the number of Mexicans in the United States, combined with the long-standing xenophobia directed at Mexicans, helped create one basis for a new group consciousness among Mexican Americans. The activities of the ADW in El Paso highlighted the conflicting dynamics of national and ethnic identity and citizenship as highly contentious issues surfacing among the Spanish-speaking population that would shape the priorities of collective action in the 1930s. Notwithstanding the low expectations of some Mexican Americans regarding the NRA, the national legislation roused most to carry on their struggle against marginalization. The NRA sparked organizing efforts by Tejana cigar and garment workers in San Antonio, who dared to make a better life for themselves and their families by challenging their exploitation at the workplace through courageous and tough militant actions that confounded their employers. Once again, abusive and greedy Anglo bosses deployed indiscriminate violence to derail the union movement.[36]

The labor force of the Finck Cigar Company of San Antonio, like that of other cigar makers, had been feminized. The relatively skilled but poorly paid Tejana tobacco workers had been subjected to speedup in the work because of the economic crisis. The workers who walked out in August 1933 were led by Mrs. W. H. Ernst. In the thirty-day strike the Tejana strikers drew an outpouring of support from the huge West Side barrio, from a smattering of pro-union forces, and from a few enlightened Anglos. As the strike unfolded and workers were discharged, the mayor of San Antonio intervened on behalf of Finck and imposed a settlement on the workers. The mayor told the women strikers that Finck would improve low and inadequate wages and poor working conditions and rehire them if their strike leader did not return to work. The union agreed to this concession, but it was soon betrayed: only a few of the strikers were taken back, while Finck dismissed the most active protesters to undermine organizing efforts. Ernst called another walkout, and she and two other cigar workers were immediately arrested and put in jail.[37]

Ignoring the NRA codes for cigar work, Finck promptly revised the quota of cigars his female workers were required to bunch and roll. The workers responded by filing a grievance against their underhanded employer. They charged the cigar maker with raising the production quota to make it virtually impossible for them to reach and ordering them to pack badly rolled cigars (the "roll-overs") without paying them for this work. The women also accused Finck of fining workers a penny for every minute they arrived late to work, and they charged that the washroom facilities at his cigar plant, consisting of three faucets for 375 workers, were wholly inadequate. Finck went off the NRA standard and immediately cut wages.[38]

Almost one year later, the Finck Cigar workers struck again. The majority had chosen not to work under the awful conditions. Anticipating a fierce assault from hostile sheriff's deputies accustomed to roughing up "Meskins," the Tejana strikers placed one hundred of their most militant and fearless union members on the picket line. Predictably, the women were set upon by baton-wielding sheriff's deputies, who broke up their picket line, arrested about two-thirds of the female strikers, and jailed them. The brutal suppression by law officers failed to sow panic among the extremely militant women cigar workers or to break their resolve: each time a striker was released from jail, she returned to the picket line, only to be taken prisoner again. One of the young women arrested and jailed for holding the line was sixteen-year-old Emma Tenayuca, who in four years would orchestrate the huge strike by the city's Tejana pecan shellers. The arrest of strike sympathizers like Tenayuca indicated that the women cigar workers were relying on strong neighborhood networks to keep the strike supplied with fresh recruits. Untold numbers of Tejanas were also vulnerable to deportation, and to break their morale and resistance, the authorities threatened the Tejana strikers and family members with expulsion. Deputies invaded the workers' homes and, using insulting language, sternly warned the Tejanas that if they refused to return to work, they and their families would be sent back to Mexico. The Mexican consul's office did nothing on behalf of the striking women cigar workers. Nor did LULAC; its members were likely shamefaced about the unruly actions of the striking Tejanas, but they also stayed out of the fray for fear of the wrath of the Anglo power structure. Because of the suppression by the sheriff's department, the strike collapsed, but violence and harassment failed to make the women cigar rollers return to work. This caused little consternation for Finck. The women were dispensable, given the growing number of unemployed Mexicans in San Antonio who desperately sought work, owing to their need for money to buy food and to pay their rent. The walkout improved working conditions for the replacement workers. Dreading the fury local peace officers could unleash (having witnessed what happened to the workers they replaced), the new hires feared for their safety and their jobs and remained silent on the union issue. Inspired by the cigar workers' strike and the NRA legislation, Tejana garment workers struck in 1934.[39]

The Texas garment industry grew during the 1930s largely as a result of the use of cheap, though skilled, Mexican female labor engaged in homework. Between 15,000 and 20,000 Mexican women needleworkers sewed clothing in their homes for ten to fifteen hours per day under an unfair piece-rate system. San Antonio's children's clothing industry employed only Mexican women needleworkers, and their situation was precarious. In the spring of 1934, the ILGWU chartered the Infants' and Children's Wear Workers' Local 180 and the Ladies' Garment Workers' Union

Figure 2.B. Unions achieved significant benefits for Mexican American workers. Teresa B. Espinoza (right) and other members of the International Ladies' Garment Workers' Union demonstrating in San Antonio, Texas. (No. 103-2— Courtesy of Elma V. Espinoza, Institute of Texan Cultures at UTSA).

Local 123. The drive to organize San Antonio's garment workers began at the A. B. Frank plant, but management quickly shut down production when the ILGWU organized its workers. The Halff Company fought the union drive by converting from dress to shirt manufacturing to avoid union jurisdiction, while at the Dorothy Frocks Company negotiations halted with the sudden death of the owner, who had been favorable to the union effort. Dorothy Frocks' new owner absolutely refused to negotiate with Local 123, which called a strike in May and picketed Dorothy Frocks for six months. The striking Tejana garment workers, angry over the devastating effects of unemployment, low wages, and long hours, stalked, laid in wait for, and attacked women who remained at work. Some of the scabs had their faces slashed with broken glass and were publicly stripped of their clothes. The women strikers were also assaulted by employers and their hired goons armed with blackjacks and clubs, but each time the garment workers bravely defended themselves against the attacks. The strikers lost the strategic initiative when the Dorothy Frocks Company relocated to Dallas, where the strike was resumed by the Dallas ILGWU local. Dorothy Frocks signed a contract in November 1936, but by this time Local 123 had ceased functioning in San Antonio.[40]

For the first time Tejanas felt a collective sense of importance as workingwomen, the value of unionism, and an awareness that they were in the vanguard of the larger insurgent labor movement in America. Rank-and-file leaders were empowered by their calls for improved wages and working conditions, for which they were willing to confront a torrent of abuse from Anglos, risk physical violence, and go to jail. The cigar and garment workers' strikes set an example that let other Tejano workers know what could be done. These early walkouts served as rehearsals for the subsequent CIO drive in 1938, at which time Tejanas would add the call for social justice and full citizenship for Mexican Americans to their fight for economic equality, and this would have the effect of further involving the Tejano community directly in their struggle.

LEARNING THE LESSONS OF RANK-AND-FILE TRADE UNIONISM: THE LOS ANGELES GARMENT WORKERS' STRIKE

The NRA triggered a pervasive sense of hope among the Mexican working classes, and it bore some results for workers in Los Angeles. Nationwide, the labor movement opposed employer efforts to roll back the gains won since the passage of the NRA. In Los Angeles, workers and their respective unions took a stand against these attacks and increased organizational work to bring in new members. One of the groups of workers in the city resisting the employer offensive was women dressmakers. In the fall of 1933, about 2,000 dressmakers from eighty garment shops walked out under the banner of the International Ladies' Garment Workers' Union. Through their labor, the dressmakers had made the Los Angeles ladies' garment industry a $3 million enterprise and one of the city's fastest-growing businesses. Three thousand dressmakers held unskilled and semiskilled jobs in hundreds of small dress shops in the downtown garment district, a workforce that more than doubled to nearly 7,500 workers at the height of the season, when additional workers hired on. Mexican women constituted three-fourths of the dressmaker workforce; the rest were Italian, Russian, Jewish, and Anglo women. Although it did not win the kinds of gains achieved by the male cloak and suit makers, the Los Angeles dressmakers' strike is credited with initiating industrial unionism among blue-collar Mexicans in this notoriously antiunion city.[41]

Garment work was typically seasonal and marked by fluctuation, circumstances that were intensified by the economic crisis of the Great Depression. The sweatshop conditions inside the poorly ventilated garment shops of Los Angeles were reportedly among the nation's worst, and so were wages. Employers ignored both the California minimum wage law of sixteen dollars for a forty-eight-hour week for dressmakers and the NRA dress code minimum wage of fifteen dollars. As a result, 40 percent of the dressmakers made less than five dollars a week. Moreover, hourly employment records were falsified, workers did not get paid for dead work, and through a kickback system the dressmakers turned over part of their wages to the employer. Making matters worse were speedup, unequal work distribution owing to favoritism, and homework, which further degraded family life. During the busy season, factory owners hired workers, then laid them off, and overhiring further lowered wages and contributed to worker instability, which prevented union organizing. However, when garment workers did attempt to organize, they were quickly fired and blacklisted. The desire to remedy these bad working conditions amplified organizing activities by the ILGWU, and so did the passage of the California Industrial Recovery Act, which brought the state's garment industry in line with the NRA codes. Like other workers, the dressmakers mobilized around the issue of NRA code violations.[42]

In late summer 1933, a group of union-minded Los Angeles dressmakers approached veteran labor organizer Rose Pesotta for help in launching a union drive in the city's garment shops. Pesotta took their case to ILGWU president David Dubinsky, who granted the garment workers a union charter on September 16 and an advance for organizational expenses. Returning to Los Angeles that fall, Pesotta explained to the dressmakers that they faced several obstacles detrimental to organizing: a large pool of surplus labor made up of out-of-state workers, who had been lured to Los Angeles by promises of work; the extant disunity in the dress shops caused by employers exploiting the ethnic diversity of the workers to foster division and suspicion; and the fact that the mostly male ILGWU national officers and those in Los Angeles lacked faith in the untested Mexican women's ability to take on the organizing task. True, the dressmakers lacked education in rank-and-file trade unionism, but they soon gained it under the expert tutelage of Rose Pesotta and her Spanish-speaking lieutenants.[43]

Affiliated with the newly chartered ILGWU Local 96, the dressmakers undertook a full-scale organizing drive to bring the union to the Los Angeles garment industry. This was no easy task. The garment shop owners brought in plainclothes officers from the Red Squad to make certain that workers reported to work. Spanish-speaking ILGWU union organizers went into the neighborhoods to talk to the workers about the union, defying employers who had threatened they would report workers who joined the union to U.S. immigration officials. In light of the intense fear the deportation drive had sown in the city's Mexican working-class communities only a year ago, and despite outreach by the ILD, many Spanish-speaking dressmakers were reluctant to become active in unionization. The ILGWU organizers instilled confidence in the dressmakers by assuring them that the union's lawyers would fight against this strikebreaking tactic. The ILGWU stepped up its educational and social program campaign—essential to organizing in the Mexican community—through Spanish-language radio broadcasts, the distribution of bulletins and leaflets, and social gatherings open to "members of all unions, regardless of their classification." Through their kinship and other social networks, women in turn spread word broadly about workers' views, the ILGWU, and the pending strike.[44] Heretofore, with the exception of the TUUL, no other labor organization had done this kind of extensive mass work among the city's Spanish-speaking working classes, who were inspired as never before to build their labor movement. However, it was the Mexican dressmakers who were involved with the planning of the strike from the start, provided much of the support, and led the way in union organizing.

On September 27, two days after the cloak makers met, 1,500 spirited dressmakers held their meeting in Walker's Theatre to discuss grievances and vote for a general strike if employers failed to meet their demands. The dressmakers were seeking the elimination of homework, a remedy for the dispute over time cards, a minimum wage in line with the NRA dress code, union recognition, a thirty-five-hour work week, and election of shop chairmen, and the female workers demanded that future shop disputes be addressed jointly by union and employer representatives. The dress manufacturers ignored all these demands, as well as a request for a meeting. Casting aside Dubinsky's earlier warnings that the garment industry had entered its slowdown period and that the ILGWU national office could ill afford to support a sustained strike, and buoyed up by support for a general strike from the Los Angeles Central Labor Council, the dressmakers walked out on October 12.[45]

The Mexican women were being indoctrinated into the principles of American trade unionism. The ILGWU activated its various strike committees, and the dressmakers reported to the strike headquarters as instructed. Here the workers were registered and organized by shop, each shop elected a chairperson, and the women were given identification cards for meals, groceries, and weekly cash benefits. By day's end, all the city's garment workers had registered with the ILGWU. Over 1,100 workers walked out. Tactics such as parades, food drives, and union propaganda were integral to the ILGWU's community-building efforts. The numbers of strikers picketing the dress factories and their calls on other coworkers to join the strike were direct challenges to the employer injunction against picketing. Because of outbreaks of violence, the Los Angeles Police Department deployed its Red Squad unit into the garment district. Officers arrested strikers en masse while providing protection for those passive workers remaining in the shops. Five days later, on October 17, the cloak makers signed a separate agreement that won them union recognition and a closed shop. Unfortunately, this agreement did not address the grievances of the women dressmakers. Communists within the ILGWU and from the Left-led TUUL's Needle Trades Workers Industrial Union (NTWIU) were stirring up dissension, an indication that the walkout was marked by the infighting of rival groups. These dissidents, who mingled with the dressmakers so that no nonunion workers took the place of the strikers, were attempting to assert their authority over the strike. Formed in 1929 when communists left the former ILGWU Local 65, the NTWIU was stalwartly against Roosevelt's New Deal.[46]

The Merchants' and Manufacturers' Association (MAM) acted decisively to break the strike. MAM provided antistrike services to the garment employers who belonged to the Associated Manufacturers of Los Angeles, a MAM affiliate. For example, Bristol Limousine was hired to transport scabs to and from the garment shops. Policemen lined up and loaded the cars with strikebreakers, and the limousines also served as ambulances to transport those individuals beaten by the strikers to the hospital. Union recognition was the main step necessary to protect dressmakers from NRA code violations, company unions, and employer discrimination. The garment employers stood firm against the demands for pay raises and the closed shop, claiming most of their workers did not want unionization. The union members suspected the NRA local office was scheming with antiunion forces and buying time for employers. In a repetition of the experiences of San Antonio's Tejana cigar workers, many dressmakers were fired or locked out for their union activities. The Mexican dressmakers did not falter. Gaining momentum, the walkout was having an impact on the women, and more joined the ILGWU.[47]

As it unfolded, the garment strike developed a daily routine and gained support from a broad range of labor and political groups. For example, shop meetings were held daily at strike headquarters, where speakers such as socialist leader Norman Thomas addressed the women strikers and rallied them. A delegation from the American Youth Congress walked the picket line with strikers on South Broadway. Several NTWIU members, in violation of a city ordinance, passed out handbills, blocked the sidewalk, and jeered, booed, and shouted disparaging epitaphs at the scabs. Strike delegations marched to the offices of the NRA and the State Labor Commission to press their demands and went to City Hall to complain of police-instigated interference and violence. About 2,000 dressmakers were honoring the strike but under trying circumstances; many strikers had their home utilities shut off for nonpayment, while others were on county relief. The latter risked losing relief because the county was still eliminating Mexicans from the rolls. To alleviate some of this hardship, the ILGWU issued strike benefit cards, which allowed the women to borrow money to pay their rent. In addition, many pro-union community members stepped forward with much-needed food donations.[48]

The striking garment workers proved tough under pressure and supported each other in the struggle. Ignoring a temporary injunction, more than 1,000 picketers held the line. The women continued to press their demands on the picket line, urging their coworkers to walk out, though they knew that plainclothes officers from the Red Squad were present to prevent picketing and attempt to halt the sporadic clashes between strikers and scabs caused by the strong current of pro-union sentiment. Women strikers who fought it out on the line were arrested for unlawful picketing, disturbing the peace, using foul language, and battery. The city's newspapers were for the open shop. A spate of biased and sensationalist news stories focused on instances of strikers throwing tacks and tomatoes at cars transporting scabs to the garment shops and on the strikers' assaulting of scabs. Because of the heightened strikebreaking activity, the city attorney and the local NRA executive endorsed the reassignment of one hundred police officers to the garment district. The MAM and the Los Angeles Chamber of Commerce, both against the closed shop, likewise approved this action.[49] This only strengthened the solidarity of the dressmakers. Their resolve and the overall conduct of the strike dispelled any lingering doubts on the part of the ILGWU's male leadership that the women were not up to the task of union organizing.

On October 30, the garment manufacturers and the ILGWU agreed to have a federal arbitration board settle the strike, which ended one week later on November 6. The arbitration board ruled that all dressmakers who walked out could return to work without penalty; wages and working hours were to follow the new NRA dress code, which provided for collective bargaining and no homework or child labor; and the board granted the women employees the right of union representation and arbitration of any future disputes. Although the dressmakers failed to gain union recognition, the ILGWU chose not to challenge this decision. The arbitration board's ruling was submitted to the rank and file for a vote, and it became effective on December 28. Just as ILGWU president Dubinsky forewarned, Los Angeles dress shop owners took advantage of the industry slowdown, returned to the low wage scale, and denied work to employees who participated in the strike. Complaints of continued firings, intimidation, and discrimination were turned over to the NRA arbitration board, but it did nothing to remedy these violations. Meanwhile, the NTWIU attacked the ILGWU leadership for "selling out" the dressmakers to "the treacherous class collaboration politics of the AFL and the 'Socialist misleaders.' " The communists scolded the garment workers: "Instead of using your splendid struggle to beat the bosses . . . your officials handed you over to the mercy of an arbitration board. . . . Arbitration never gave anything to the workers. Struggle on the picket lines did." The dressmakers finally savored the victory of their union movement when an agreement was reached between ILGWU representatives and employers. The union won recognition, wages in accordance with the NRA dress codes, and health and disability benefits. ILGWU membership grew to 2,460 by 1935, almost half with Local 96 affiliation. The garment strike gained a sense of dignity, respect, and strength for the dressmakers and laid the foundation for the dressmakers' union in Los Angeles.[50]

The Mexican dressmakers initiated the union drive in the garment industry and helped lead it, but they remained marginalized in their local owing to the control wielded by the entrenched male leadership of the ILGWU national office, which was steeped in craft unionism and did not take women's needs seriously. Mexican women made up 75 percent of the union's membership, but only six of the nineteen officials elected to the first executive board of Local 96 were Mexican women. The local's male leadership did not build on the earlier union efforts. Moreover, ILGWU president David Dubinsky reneged on his promise to issue a separate charter for the 600 Mexican union members because the national office was more concerned with solidifying its position in the garment industry. As the base of the American labor movement shifted from the community to the workplace, women were cast in a secondary role within labor. The exceptions were those women in Left-led unions. Nevertheless, as scholars correctly claim, the 1933 Los Angeles dressmakers' strike was the first major experience of the city's Mexican female workers in American trade unionism, and it clearly demonstrated that they were capable trade union activists.[51] More important, the women advanced in their understanding of social and economic issues through training and expert advice in collective bargaining.

FOR THE UNION: LOS ANGELES FURNITURE WORKERS ORGANIZE

Furniture manufacturing was one major Los Angeles industry that underwent the shift to industrial unionism. Promoters of the open shop, the city's furniture manufacturers exploited the largely nonunionized, low-wage, and racially stratified labor force consisting of Mexicans and blacks, who worked the most dangerous jobs despite experience and seniority. For example, Frank Lopez, a worker who would later play a leading role in the United Furniture Workers of America, sorted springs at the Nachman Spring Corporation and earned eight dollars a week for sixty-seven hours of hazardous work. The onset of the Great Depression intensified racial tensions among the stratified workforce in furniture making, but it also created the conditions necessary for a movement away from craft unionism.[52]

Taking advantage of new opportunities for organizing offered by the NIRA, communist organizers challenged the AFL in the Los Angeles furniture industry, which had previously been limited to skilled white workers. In early June 1933, several carloads of men and others on foot, numbering about forty workers, almost all of them Mexicans, approached the Universal Furniture Manufacturing Company. Most of the labor agitators were from the Brown & Salzman Furniture Factory, a union shop. They had come to the Universal plant to tell the upholsterers that the Upholsterers Union had met and agreed that once Congress approved the NRA, they would vote to call a general strike of all the upholsterers in the city. Heartened by the radical convictions of union campaigners, the upholsterers from the Sterling and the Soronow Furniture plants and from other furniture companies walked out and began picketing the shops. They belonged to the TUUL-affiliated Furniture Workers Industrial Union and were led by Mexican TUUL unionists. Local 10 of the Furniture Workers Industrial Union pushed the AFL to engage in industrial unionism. In May 1934, when the Sterling Furniture Company announced a 15 percent pay cut, the entire workforce walked off the job. Taken aback by this new-found interracial solidarity, which helped roll back the wage cuts and strengthened pro-union sentiment, the Sterling Furniture Company's exasperated officials asked the white upholsterers who walked out: "What are you fellows fighting for those Mexicans and unskilled workers for?" This activity by upholsterers and other industrial workers in Los Angeles reflected the wave of strike actions to secure the benefits granted to workers by the NRA and labor's subsequent defensive efforts against the growing anti-NRA employer offensive. It was clear that Mexican workers would strike to achieve their ends and that an activist phase had begun.[53] In the meantime, a protracted strike in Gallup, New Mexico, by mostly Mexican coal miners unfolded under the red flag of communism.

"Are You a Bolshey?": The 1933 Gallup, New Mexico, Coal Strike

The nearly four-month labor conflict of the coal miners of Gallup, New Mexico, was part of the huge miner upsurge in the spring and summer of 1933 following Roosevelt's newly implemented NRA. The miners confronted strikebreakers, law officials, deportations, loss of company store credit, debt, hunger, and evictions. The Gallup miners built their strike apparatus with the assistance of communist organizers from the Left-led National Miners Union (NMU). Flushed with their victory in a similar campaign in Carbon County, Utah, the communists strictly obeyed the party line of building revolutionary unions. The chief aim of the Gallup coal strike, therefore, was "the revolutionization of the striking workers," not just the gaining of "material results." The NMU, moreover, viewed the Gallup strike as an opportunity for a rapid mass recruitment of coal miners into the Communist Party.[54]

The problems of New Mexico's coal industry reflected the 60 percent decline nationwide in commercial coal mine production. The widespread unemployment among New Mexico's 3,500 coal miners, over half of them in the Gallup coal district, resulted from a cut in coal prices, rising transportation costs, and competition from natural gas from Texas. In August, half of Gallup's miners were out of work. None of the coal miners worked full-time; they were on a two- to three-day workweek. Wages had declined by 45 percent. Gallup area mine operators had made four consecutive wage cuts in 1933 alone.[55] Workers faced the company "weigh man," nonpay for "dead work," favoritism, and the blacklist. Racial discrimination in work assignments such as loading coal and pick work, which paid lower wages and offered no avenue for mobility, was a major complaint of the Spanish-speaking miners. The men did not like it. Nor did they like being pressured to patronize the company store, where they bought food, clothing, and other life necessities and were charged for the dynamite, powder, and percussion caps they used in their work. Through this unfair credit system the coal companies exerted control and discipline over the poorly paid employees. Dormant wages and sporadic pay, along with intermittent coal production, inevitably trapped the miners in debt. The fact that Gallup miners only worked part-time rendered them ineligible for relief. Those miners who could not prove their citizenship were denied relief assistance. In the series of reprisals against the Spanish-speaking miners who went on strike, this exclusionary policy spread to include denial of services to American-born citizens and legal U.S. residents.[56]

There was growing restiveness among Gallup's coal diggers, who had walked out before to improve their working and living conditions. New Mexico's mining towns had union exposure extending back to 1882, when the Knights of Labor attempted to organize coal miners in New Mexico and Colorado. The Knights held particular resonance for the native-born New Mexican miners. Their kin had transformed the Knights of Labor into the Caballeros de Trabajo, whose rallying cry was "protection for the worker against the monopolists." Las Gorras Blancas emerged at this time, a highly secretive band of 1,500 masked riders who undertook guerilla activities against the large landowners, destroying hundreds of miles of fences, thousands of railroad ties, crops, and farm buildings and implements. The last coal miners' strike in 1922 was led by the UMWA, which in that year was waging a nationwide coal strike. The environment of labor unrest shaped the miners' mutual aid and fraternal societies into militant organizations. In seeking revenge against members who betrayed the strike, benefit societies expelled members who scabbed and denied benefits to the relatives of members who died while strikebreaking. Owing to the strikers' militancy, and in the prevailing climate of "100 percent Americanism" roused by the fear of immigrants, bolshevism, and labor, New Mexico's governor declared martial law. The governor also sought to invoke the Sherman Anti-Trust Act against the striking Gallup miners, who in protecting their common interests were in restraint of trade. The 1922 Gallup coal strike failed against this mighty antiunion opposition. This unsuccessful strike experience, during which the miners went without relief, had no legal aid, and were defenseless against the blacklist, produced a bitter current of sentiment against a declining UMWA and John L. Lewis's despotism. In 1933, the communist-led National Miners Union exploited this discontent and awakened the miners to radicalism.[57]

The Guggenheim-Morgan interest, the Kennicott Copper Company, the American Smelting and Refining Company, and the Santa Fe Railroad owned GAMERCO. GAMERCO held sway over the other coal companies and controlled local and state officials. The state governor, the National Guard, and the courts cooperated to put down any insurrection by the coal miners. Indeed, such influence reflected the greater power management wielded over labor in the West, where historically worker disputes were settled by brute violence. Because of a legacy of worker exposure to radical and militant unionism, mine operators and other em-

Figure 2.C. The Communist Party was almost a lone political voice in supporting the struggles of the Mexican people. In 1935 the International Labor Defense called for vindication of the Gallup coal miners. "Save the Gallup Workers" Bulletin, Gallup Defense Committee, Santa Fe, New Mexico, October 12, 1935. (MSS512—Denver Gallup Defense Fund, Courtesy of Colorado Historical Society).

ployers in the western region believed strikers posed a dangerous threat and required military intervention, thus placing the role of the state on management's side. Moreover, New Mexico's mining corporations expected a return on the taxes levied against them, which in the 1930s totaled more than $3 million. Though rich in natural resources, New Mexico was one of the poorest states in the union, with one of the nation's worst relief programs. Until the arrival of federal monies, New Mexico had not allocated state funds for the increasing number of unemployed workers, the farmers losing their homes and lands, and the many out-of-state transients arriving in the state.[58]

Because of the economic crisis, relief provisions in New Mexico were cut back considerably in April and again in May 1933, further squeezing the state's workers. The growing demand for food and clothing allotments and the general sense of injustice attributed to the state of New Mexico and employers triggered hunger marches by the Unemployed Councils in July. With banners and slogans the marchers demanded milk and shoes for children; a three-dollar cash allotment for workers and their spouses; free rent; no shutoffs of water, light, or gas; no evictions or foreclosures; that relief stations be open all day; and that striking farm workers in the Pecos River Valley of Chaves County be given relief disbursements. The Unemployed Councils brought attention to the plight of New Mexico's jobless. The need for assistance was greatest among New Mexico's Mexicans, as most were out of work and were generally discriminated against in relief and relief work assignments. Spanish-speaking organizations like the Spanish American Club of Clovis also protested this rampant discrimination and pressed the state governor to have Mexicans "treated with equal rights as all citizens."[59]

Gallup's coal miners learned that the NRA granted workers the right to organize unions and bargain collectively with employers. The UMWA's betrayal in the 1922 strike and the knowledge that John L. Lewis was signing "no-strike contracts" in the East—agreements which gave mine owners the right to fine miners two dollars a day for striking—prompted Gallup miners to look for alternative leadership. News of the strike being waged by coal miners allied with the NMU in Carbon County, Utah, generated renewed enthusiasm for activism. In light of the resurgence of the reactionary nativist rhetoric of the early 1920s, one NMU principle especially appealing to Gallup's Mexican and Slavic miners was that the organization "unites and organizes all miners, white, colored, native, and foreign born." However, race and class hatred roused the violence that was aimed at this communist union, and the coal companies used the Red union's interracialism to split the white miners from the Mexicans.[60]

As previously noted, progressive worker-based ethnic associations, farmer and worker organizations, and Left-led groups at this time continued to carry on a struggle for unionism. In this climate of insurgency, Gallup's Spanish-speaking coal miners got help from the militant La Liga Obrera de Habla Español. With local branches throughout Colorado and New Mexico, La Liga had more than 10,000 members representing one-third of the 34,816 Spanish-speaking workers in these two states. In 1928 and again in 1932, La Liga had carried down news to New Mexico's Spanish-speaking communities of the coal and beet strikes in Colorado. La Liga secured injunctions preventing the eviction of 7,000 Spanish-speaking small landholders; became politically active at the state level with the defeat of a syndicalism bill; and, in addition to its union work, collaborated with the Unemployed Councils to obtain relief for the Spanish-speaking. The work of La Liga was undertaken at the risk of deportation, a fact well known to its members, who fought for labor and social justice. In the prevailing racist and antiradical climate, the coal operators charged that Spanish-speaking workers who agitated for labor reform and unionism were communists and foreign aliens from "Old Mexico," and they threatened them with deportation. Notwithstanding, the NMU, guided by the principle that the outcome of a strike depends on clear, decisive, and rapid action, would attempt to avoid an ill-timed spontaneous strike against wage reductions while it organized its relief and legal aid apparatus in preparation for mobilizing the miners against the coal operators.[61]

The Red Menace: The National Miners Union Enters Gallup

Born out of the "Save the Union" movement, the National Miners Union was founded in Pittsburgh, Pennsylvania, in September 1928 as part of the Communist Party's dual union strategy. The NMU's goal was to wage a class struggle against capitalism through trade union work, an objective the party reaffirmed in July 1933 at its Extraordinary National Conference in New York City. The NMU invaded the jurisdiction of the UMWA, competed with it for members, and united workers across race and gender lines in its offensive to replace the UMWA. The coal mines in southern Utah and New Mexico became the focal point of NMU organizing after its defeats in the western Pennsylvania, eastern Ohio, and West Virginia coalfields in 1931 and in Harlan County, Kentucky, in 1932. The NMU entered the fray around Gallup greatly weakened by its most recent involvement in the coal strike in southern Utah and its other previous strikes.[62] The UMWA was also conducting a major recruiting drive. As a way to divide the miners, the coal operators made the mistake of momentarily stopping the UMWA from organizing the coal camps by partly encouraging the NMU. This allowed the NMU to gain control of several of the mining camps; national Communist Party functionaries came in, and the party brought in its auxiliaries, the International Labor Defense, the Workers International Relief, and the Young Communist League. Communist leaders further instigated the desperate miners to pursue the strike. They had little trouble convincing the miners that their plight was caused by blatant employer tyranny, exploitation, and racism, as opposed to the hard fact that the national coal market was in precipitous decline.[63]

The NMU assigned husband-and-wife team Robert F. Roberts and Martha Roberts to conduct the initial organization of the Gallup miners. Prior to arriving in Gallup, the Roberts team had been helping organize Spanish-speaking and Anglo farm workers in the Pecos River Valley.[64] It was here that the Roberts team made contact with local radical leaders, who helped them get in touch with the most militant elements among the coal miners in Gallup. La Liga Obrera probably spread word of the pending arrival of the two NMU organizers through its networks in the Spanish-speaking community. The Communist Party believed it was necessary to build a union with mass membership. Therefore, once in Gallup, the Roberts team assessed the situation, devised an appropriate strategy, and began to publicize their presence among the coal miners, first by assuring the coal diggers they were not UMWA organizers, and then by building NMU solidarity through informational leafleting, meetings, and house-to-house canvassing. Working fifteen to eighteen hours a day, the Roberts team did the groundwork. They searched out the most active coal miners and helped to organize NMU local unions in each of the mines. Just as in previous strikes, the NMU organizers set up grievance and strike committees in the Gallup coal district to which miners were assigned "regardless of union affiliation" for the purpose of letting the miners themselves conduct the strike. They next set up Unemployed Councils and women's auxiliaries and youth sections of the NMU. It was necessary to make women an important and acknowledged force in the NMU. Martha Roberts went to the homes of coal miners to talk directly to the women and strengthen their confidence. With preparation now virtually completed by the field organizers, and understanding the connection between the NMU and the Communist Party and its concept of class struggle, these miners and their wives became the party nucleus. Three additional NMU organizers came to Gallup. These were Pat Toohey, NMU executive board member and editor of the *Coal Digger*, and Colorado labor organizer Dick Allender and his brother Harry "Spike" Allender from Utah. Denver attorney George Kaplan, the ILD secretary, had arrived earlier to provide legal assistance. Kaplan's arrival had been followed by that of Charles Guynn, organizer of the Carbon County strike.[65]

Perceived as dangerous outsiders, the NMU representatives immediately came under suspicion in Gallup. City Mayor Watson, who was on the company payroll as the doctor at the GAMERCO mine, obtained information on the NMU from Labor Secretary Green, Assistant Labor Secretary McGrady, and UMWA boss John L. Lewis. The three labor chiefs had wired Mayor Watson as well as Governor Arthur Seligman, warning them that the NMU was communist and affiliated with William Z. Foster's TUUL. Two years earlier, Lewis had used the threat of communist influence in the coalfields to appeal to Hoover and the Congress for collective bargaining recognition for the UMWA and government-administered price production controls for coal. The UMWA president added that the NMU had no stable membership and no contracts with the country's mining industry, which was true. The best alternative for the Gallup miners, therefore, would be for them to make a contract agreement with the UMWA, thereby promoting a legitimate relationship with the coal industry. Pressure was immediately placed on the NMU; Governor Seligman passed on this information to the military officer he soon put in command of the National Guard troops in Gallup. The Gallup city council issued ordinances restricting the NMU from holding fund-raisers, and following the lead of the coal operators, Gallup officials commenced a smear campaign against the union. The partisan *Gallup Independent* poisoned the air by running a series of articles denouncing NMU leaders as "known and avowed communists."[66]

NMU organizers at first denied then openly defended the charges of communism with a barrage of propaganda. William Dietrich from the party's district office in Denver arrived in Gallup and attacked the Red Scare campaign and the use of troops. As hundreds of National Guard troops looked on, Dietrich, through an interpreter, pledged to the miners that the party would aid them in their struggle, just as it had aided the Spanish-speaking beet workers in Colorado the year before through its United Front Committee. In keeping with the policy to form a party basis—"that the first thing to be considered is the building of the Party"—the NMU launched an educational campaign to recruit additional miners to build cadres. The potential members had already been talked to by the Robertses and by members of the party nucleus but were given further explanation of the party, what it stood for, its relation to the potential strike, its role in the NMU, and so on. Within a short time the NMU, through its various union committees, brought 150 coal miners into the party (100 more miners would join after the strike), and in addition, 100 boys and girls joined the Young Communist League. Years of racial exclusion and intense labor conflict were the special factors that led the Mexican coal diggers to embrace the communism of the NMU.[67]

The NMU executive board committee called a strike for Tuesday, August 28, 1933, and activated the strike committee. Meanwhile, the UMWA announced that it would challenge the NMU for union recognition in the coal district. The next day, miners affiliated with the NMU shut down the five coal mines around Gallup. As McKinley County sheriff's deputies (probably on company payrolls) and company gunmen stood by, 1,000 strikers and sympathizers hurried into position and set up a twenty-four-hour picket line around the GAMERCO mine. The women's and children's auxiliaries were set up for the purpose of involving families in the strike. A member of the Women's Auxiliary and a leader of the strike, Mrs. Dominica Hernández became one of the most visible of these activist women. She organized the coal camp women in support of their husbands. These women stayed on the picket line for five months. After the strike, Mrs. Hernández continued to lead the workers in struggles for unemployment relief and other demands. Plans for relief at first included soliciting support from local businesses and boycotting those that refused, then expanding requests for relief outside the mining district. Notwithstanding all these preparations, and even though it had trained local coal miners to fill leadership positions, the NMU lacked a firm base and a sufficient number of organizers to carry on a protracted strike in the coal district. The Gallup walkout was supported in large part by the sheer will and determination of the Mexican coal diggers and their white ethnic allies. The Red union's emphasis on the great importance of working-class solidarity as the best and most effective means to resolve the miners' issues, including combating racial discrimination, rallied the men. The NMU representatives assured the Mexicans that the party would confront their national oppression by fighting against any deportation actions on the part of the coal companies in partnership with the U.S. Immigration Bureau and Mexican consular officials.[68]

GUNS, BAYONETS, AND CLUBS: MARTIAL LAW DESCENDS ON GALLUP

New Mexico Governor Seligman immediately denounced the strike, imposed martial law in McKinley County, and ordered state militia units to Gallup. The mine companies, the UMWA, local officials, and the Santa Fe Railroad had pressured the governor to take this retaliatory action because of existing circumstances. GAMERCO furnished electrical power to Gallup, some of it used to pump the city's water supply. This dependence on GAMERCO for water led Gallup's residents to support the mine owners and to back the request for the state militia to be brought in to protect their electricity. The coal for the Chino copper mines in Arizona came from the Gallup coal district, which also supplied the Santa Fe Railroad with its fuel. As part owners of the Gallup coal mines, the Santa Fe Railroad threatened to convert to fuel oil if the strike cut off its coal supply. Martial law thus descended on Gallup. Brigadier General Osborne E.

Wood, the commander of the military district that included the Gallup area, was placed in charge of the troops. An officer experienced in strike-breaking, the general had served in the 1919 Boston police strike, and the Lawrence textile strike, the Great Steel Strike, as well as the Allentown silk and Denver tramway strikes. General Wood enforced martial law in Gallup by prohibiting gatherings without a permit, picketing, and free speech and assembly; he replaced civil rule with military rule, including tribunals and court-martial. Following their strict orders, troops patrolled the streets and enforced an 8:00 P.M. curfew. Entrance to the mines was by military permit only. Machine gun units and the National Guard cavalry and infantry were brought in.[69]

Aware of the high risk involved in confronting this show of force activated against them, the miners pursued a peaceful resolution. Experienced in union negotiations, Gallup miners outlined their demands and grievances in a letter to Governor Seligman written by A. Alvarado of the NMU's Sub-District Board. Using the NRA to their advantage even though the NMU had repeatedly denounced it, Alvarado explained in the letter that the main reason the coal operators rejected negotiations was that the NRA did not recognize the NMU. Alvarado reminded the governor that Section 7a stated that employees have the right to join and belong to any organization and to deal through representatives of their own choosing without their employer's (or its agents') interference, intimidation, or coercion. The Mexican American union leader further articulated that the coal operators were violating this section of the NRA through their activities to force the miners into the UMWA. On behalf of his fellow strikers, Alvarado asked the governor to withdraw the military forces from the Gallup coalfields, since there was no justification for their presence, adding that the coal companies were using the state militia as a strikebreaking tool. Alvarado ended the letter by informing the governor that a strike delegation would be traveling to Santa Fe to meet with him about this and other problems related to the strike, and he expressed his hope that the governor would receive this delegation.[70]

Outside relief was crucial to the strike, and it came from a variety of sources. Miner families who grew gardens and raised small livestock now shared their food with all the miners. Despite opposition by the Gallup Chamber of Commerce and the local NRA board, both of which threatened to remove the Blue Eagle Card if they contributed, Gallup merchants donated food and money to the union's relief committee. The storekeepers empathized with the striking miners because many had immigrant roots themselves and probably had family or friends who were coal miners. Sympathetic restaurant owners also fed strikers. Further support came from the radical Farm Holiday Association of Colorado. Its members collected food and brought it to Gallup, as did Nebraska and Wyoming chapters of this progressive organization. However, the demand for relief outpaced contributions, and it would remain a problem throughout the duration of the strike. After repeatedly raising the issue of more assistance, the Communist Party's district office in Denver placed the United Front Committee in charge of relief work for the Gallup strikers.[71]

Eluding roadblocks, carloads of strikers left Gallup to expand the protest and solicit funds. These delegations held protest meetings in Albuquerque, Santa Fe, Las Vegas, Roswell, Clovis, and other New Mexico towns and appealed to the residents for assistance. Others went to Colorado's coal and farm districts, to El Paso, to the Arizona copper mining districts, and to Los Angeles. The NMU gained support, and the majority rallying behind the striking miners were Spanish-speaking workers. Pressured by its rank-and-file membership, the New Mexico Federation of Labor came out in support of the NMU strikers, as did the Albuquerque Central Labor Union. The latter was probably pushed by the Carpenters' Union, with its large Mexican American membership. In defiance of their employer, Mexican American rail workers in the Railroad Brotherhoods of Las Vegas demanded that National Guard troops be recalled from Gallup. Meanwhile, Unemployed Councils in Denver, Walsenburg, and Salt Lake City, all labor strongholds, watched over local employment agencies to prevent the recruitment of scabs. Through prodding from ILD attorney David Kaplan, the ILD mobilized workers nationwide on behalf of the strikers, enlisting progressive unions, farmers' associations, and the unemployed in this cause.[72]

Revolutionary Unionism at Work

Five hundred state militia guarded the mines, the tipples, and Highway 666, and passage to any point was through these armed troop ranks. The NMU dealt with this problem by devising various forms of picketing: mass picketing wherever possible, house-to-house picketing in the mining camps, and picketing by squads on Gallup's downtown streets. Picketing was organized on a group system. Each mine had a picket captain who was responsible to the executive board and the strike committee. Each of these mine captains had ten to twenty "lieutenants," who in turn were responsible for the rank and file. Information could be relayed to the entire strike body within an hour by word of mouth through these picket committees.[73] At first, the most effective were the house-to-house and squad pickets, but the National Guard countered this strategy by quarantining the city's working-class sectors and patrolling the roads. Soldiers also accompanied the scabs in the trucks and cars to and from the coal mines so that strikers and strike sympathizers would not harass or intimidate them. This was countered by an outbreak of car vandalism, as strikers scattered nails and spikes on streets and roads, saboteurs damaged or removed rails underground in the mines, and participants engaged in other acts of collective resistance. In addition to the strike committees, the Communist Party maintained its own organization of the strike. Each mine had a communist cell, to which a group of strikers was assigned and which took up situations with the strike committees. Through this system, rapid decisions could be transmitted despite martial law, treachery within worker ranks could be prevented, and men could be mobilized for picketing or mass demonstrations.[74]

The coal operators would not capitulate, and in a show of clear defiance the NMU for its part rejected the NLRB recommendation for arbitration. C. W. Grubbs, the NRA administrator for Southern California, New Mexico, and Arizona, did not recognize the NMU, so he refused to negotiate with the Red union. However, Grubbs met with members of the miners' executive committee on September 5 to get the strikers to return to work and await the passage of the coal code. The NMU turned down this proposal, arguing that the coal operators would retaliate against the miners taking part in the strike by firing all of them. Grubbs next called in the strikers by language groups—Spanish, Greek, Slavic, etc.—to try to convince them to return to work and take up grievances later. Grubbs told the men the same thing he had told the NMU executive committee, that he would deal only with mine "employees," the scabs, in line with NRA guidelines. Having been prepared beforehand, spokesmen for each group of miners rejected Grubbs's plan. The NRA representative left the meeting disgusted with the strikers, whom he denounced as "unreasonable."[75]

The NMU reorganized the union's relief and defense committees and recruited additional picket captains and picket squads. The National Guard commander had granted the NMU permission to meet at the Mentmore schoolhouse and, as with all worker gatherings, assigned National Guard spies. NMU organizer Dick Allender was the featured speaker, with the popular union secretary Juan L. Ochoa translating into Spanish what the Anglo communist had to say. Because fears had been raised concerning evictions, Allender first addressed this question. He informed the strikers that all persons ordered to move out of company housing had been granted ten more days to remain in their homes. The strikers learned that about one hundred men, most underage, were working at the GAM-ERCO mine but were not meeting production, mining only three coal cars per day, as opposed to the normal daily output of sixty cars. Allender assured the gathering that the strike remained strong, aid was being received from throughout the country, and public sentiment was turning in their favor, and he told the strikers they should hold fast until their demands were met. The party member reported that the NMU strike committee had met with the governor for six hours and had made some progress. In closing, Allender cautioned the strikers to maintain peace on the picket lines; he warned that any outbreak of violence would be proof that the state militia was needed and moreover would turn public sentiment against the strikers.[76]

The NMU began a concerted effort to sign up the miners of the Mutual mine, stressing to these men that settlement of the strike at this mine would force the Mentmore and the Allison mines to capitulate. Such an arrangement would entrench the NMU in two or possibly three or four mines, bring pressure on GAMERCO, and thereby alleviate long-range relief needs. Unless the NMU settled at least three of the mines, the coal operators would force the miners into the UMWA. The mine companies were individually owned, had separate coal markets, and competed with one another as well as with companies outside the coal district. There was no mine association in Gallup; the mines were under the general leadership and counsel of Horace Moses of GAMERCO. This is why the NMU was determined to divide the coal companies, to exploit the differences between them so as to destroy their defense. However, one weakness of this plan was that the settled mines might begin to fill the coal orders of the seized mines, thus preventing the NMU from striking the mines again. The arrests of the strike leaders changed this strategy.[77]

Horace Moses reported to the governor that the mines in the Gallup district were operating at only 30 percent capacity but nonetheless were filling the coal orders of the Santa Fe Railroad and the Chino copper mines. Moses acknowledged that 550 miners remained on strike. There were bitter feelings between the employed miners and those on strike. The former were Anglos and belonged to the rival UMWA, while the latter were Mexican Americans, Mexicans, and white ethnic "foreigners," all of them members of the NMU. The strike resurrected and amplified the long-time racial and ethnic animosity that underlay conditions in the mines as well as in Gallup's mining communities. Moses believed there would have been serious disturbances and certainly bloodshed had the governor not ordered the state militia into Gallup. He was convinced that the strikers would have marched on the mining camps and that a pitched race battle would have erupted between the striking NMU miners (foreign) and the men currently working (Anglo).[78]

To force the strikers to return to work, in early October, General Wood arrested the entire NMU leadership for inciting insurrection against the state of New Mexico. Those arrested were ILD attorneys George Kaplan and Clarence Lynch, NMU organizers R. F. Roberts and Spike Allender, William González and A. C. Alvarado of the NMU Sub-District Board, and Mentmore mine strike leader J. C. Walker. The men were escorted to the Ceremonial Stockyards, which served as the military stockade.[79] The release of the jailed leaders now became a condition of the strike settlement. The NMU told its members it was prepared to close down the schools should more strike leaders be arrested and that they should anticipate serving picket duty at the Ceremonial Stockyards. The NMU suspected that local officials had contacted the Mexican consul general of El Paso and NRA representative Grubbs to begin a round up of the Spanish-speaking miners supporting the strike. Just as the NMU suspected, local officials called in the Mexican consul general from El Paso to convince his countrymen to return to work. The Mexican miners knew the consul general had come to isolate and remove the leadership of Gallup's Mexican community. The consul general raised the issue of communist activity and threatened these individuals and all those who refused to return to work with deportation. The coal operators gave their compiled lists of communist enemies to the consul general. Strike leaders Alejandro Correo and Eziquio Navarro were apprehended and taken to the Ceremonial Stockyards to await deportation to Mexico. This turn of events failed to persuade the Mexicans to quit the strike, for the NMU rallied behind them, telling the men not to be fooled into thinking they would be sent back to Mexico. This insolence infuriated Major Moore, who believed ignorant Mexicans could not conduct the strike on their own. The major bluntly told the strikers, "Someone is giving you directions. You are under the authority of . . . Communists."[80]

Encouraged by this display of worker solidarity, the NMU district board wired Governor Seligman and gave him twenty-four hours to release the strike leaders, warning that it would spread its strike to the mines around Raton, Dawson, and Madrid. With their leaders jailed, the miners decisively took over more control of the strike. Their demands now wisely included as a condition of settlement the immediate release of the strike leaders.[81]

The coal operators of the Allison, Mentmore, and Mutual mines told their striking employees that replacement workers would be hired when the mines reopened. Trying to intimidate the striking Mexican miners, the manager of the Mentmore mine warned them that if they did not return to work, they would be deported. Again the Mexicans remained undaunted and stayed out of the mines. Meanwhile, negotiations between the NMU and the Mutual mine resumed, and a settlement was expected soon. The Southwestern mine agreed in full to the strikers' demands, and these men went back to work. This allowed the rest of the strikers to stabilize their organization to prepare for future struggle. The walkout was having some effect on coal production in the region: a report came in from Arizona that GAMERCO had increased the price of its coal by forty-two dollars per ton, and the union learned that coal operators were beginning to worry about the possibility of a coal shortage. Meanwhile, disobeying martial law, a picket line of about 400 strikers and sympathizers, made up mostly of women and children, formed at the Ceremonial Stockyards to protest the arrests.[82]

CLASS AGAINST CLASS: THE GALLUP COAL STRIKE ESCALATES

In mid-October, Lieutenant Governor A. W. Hockenhull became state governor upon the death of Arthur Seligman. The new governor requested that Gallup coal operators meet with him to arbitrate the strike, which was now in its seventh week. Some of the coal operators turned down the governor's request for a meeting. Convinced of the necessity and possibility of a positive outcome, five representatives from the NMU were en route to Santa Fe to confer with the governor.[83] In Gallup, a confrontation between strikers and the state militia was about to unfold. Strikers milled around the gas station on the corner of GAMERCO and Maloney Avenues to hear a speech by Herbert Benjamin of the National Unemployed Council of New York, the organizer and leader of the First and Second National Hunger Marches on Washington, D.C., in 1931 and 1932. Informed of the unlawful gathering, Colonel C. G. Sage of the 111th Calvary arrived and ordered the strikers to disperse. The colonel reminded the crowd that a state regulation required permission from the military before meetings could be held, thus the gathering was in defiance of military authority. Sage had Herbert Benjamin arrested and escorted to the Ceremonial Stockyards, where he joined the other strike leaders, who now included Juan L. Ochoa, Alejandro Correo, and Eziquio Navarro. Within a block of the Stockyards, foot soldiers and a tear gas squad appeared in anticipation of civil unrest.[84]

Reinstatement of the miners fired for going on strike was delaying settlement of the labor dispute, according to the miners' delegation meeting with Governor Hockenhull in Santa Fe. NMU attorney Charles Guynn told Hockenhull the miners wanted to negotiate a settlement but the coal operators had steadfastly refused to meet with them. Guynn reiterated the original demands of the miners and outlined several others the governor could act on immediately to end the strike: withdraw the National Guard, whose presence, the union attorney claimed, had never been necessary; restore civil rights, including the right to hold meetings and fundraising events to aid the strikers; and release the arrested strike leaders. Guynn charged the National Guard with partiality to the mine owners. Miners had been denied their civil rights, some miners and their families had been physically intimidated, and strikebreakers were trucked to the mines under the protection of armed troops.[85]

The mine operators who subsequently met with Governor Hockenhull demanded that National Guard troops remain in Gallup to keep the mines open, pointing out that if the state militia were withdrawn, federal troops would have to be brought in to maintain the peace. In reference to the NMU, the governor told the coal operators that violence and bloodshed had marked similar strike actions across the country, except at Gallup because of the state militia's presence.[86]

New Mexico was in the throes of an economic crisis, and Governor Hockenhull was attempting to settle a major labor dispute in the state's coalfields. The labor turmoil presented him with a series of dilemmas. The governor's main concern was the desperate financial conditions caused not only by the strike but also by keeping the state militia in Gallup. New Mexico was a Republican state opposed to the New Deal programs. This is why the mine operators believed the federal government, through its NRA activities, was responsible for the Gallup strike. On the other hand, the mine owners reasoned that because of such federal intervention, it seemed logical that an appeal be made for federal troops to replace the National Guard. The governor responded that federal troops would not be brought in until the state militia was withdrawn. One mine official suggested to the governor that additional deputies be sworn in and used in place of the state militia, but Hockenhull immediately dismissed this, citing the enduring troubles between deputies and strikers. The governor added that he would try to reach an agreement acceptable to all parties and bring an end to the strike.[87]

Attempting to remain neutral, the governor told the coal operators he wanted to get the strike settled fairly for all parties involved, but he also wanted to stop the expenditure for the National Guard, which was costing the state about $500 a day. The mine operators informed the governor that the area railroads preferred fuel oil because it was cheaper, and as a result there was a strong possibility that the Chino copper mines would either close or convert to gas as fuel. In the context of the economic hard times, this would result in a further financial loss to the whole Gallup coal market and to New Mexico as well. If the Gallup mines shut down, New Mexico would lose a sizable tax revenue and all the mine workers, not just the strikers, would be forced onto relief. This would be an even greater expense to the state than maintaining the National Guard in Gallup, where gunfire erupted.[88]

Three men were wounded by shotgun fire in two outbreaks of violence after the NMU launched a house-to-house picketing campaign against the Mutual mine because the coal operator refused strikers' appeals for a settlement. The wounded strikers were Lucio Ruiz and Victorio Correo, the latter the brother of NMU strike leader Alejandro Correo, under arrest and awaiting deportation. The men were hit by two shotgun blasts while standing at a downtown intersection, one blast striking Ruiz's right side and chest and the second blast hitting Correo in the leg. National Guard officers were unable to determine who fired the shots but said they had two suspects. The two miners and the residents living nearby were all questioned, but none knew who fired the shots.[89]

Violence flared once more as the strike wore on into November. In defiance of martial law, a contingent of 200 protesters demanded the release of Herbert Benjamin from the McKinley County jail. At a signal, they quickly formed a column four abreast and began their march to the meeting in front of the Gallup courthouse. The crowd marched up the courthouse steps, but the doors to the jail were locked. Someone called for the troops, and when they arrived the strikers began to fight with the soldiers. Guardsmen arrested six strikers and hurried them away to the military stockade. The crowd greeted the order to disperse with boos. Holding their ground, the troops threw tear gas bombs, which made the crowd flee. High winds rendered the smoke bombs ineffective, however, and a handful of defiant strikers picked up the bombs and hurled them back at the soldiers. The protesters continued to defy orders to disperse but at last withdrew to the opposite side of the street. The 111th Cavalry arrived, but the strikers held their positions, forcing the mounted soldiers to ride into them. Women armed themselves with clubs, and several men hurled rocks. More troops arrived. Rocks hit several of the guardsmen, including Captain W. P. Martin. A club-wielding striker hit another officer. Upon dispersing the strikers, mounted patrols were posted throughout downtown Gallup. Tensions were rising in the ranks both of the strikers and of the state militia as the coal strike teetered on the verge of civil disorder.[90] To back down now not only would undermine the morale in the coal camps but would also reduce pressure on the coal operators to seek a negotiated settlement.

A Pyrrhic Victory: The Gallup Coal Strike Ends

On November 27, the NMU voted to end the strike. In a letter addressed to Governor Hockenhull, the NMU announced that "all striking miners now in settlement of the strike condition will return to work under the agreement between the miners and the operators, as soon as work is available under said agreement." Governor Hockenhull suspended martial law in Gallup, not because he believed all danger of further labor disturbance had passed, but because martial law was simply bleeding the state treasury. Over $115,000 in state monies had been spent to keep the National Guard in Gallup. All NMU "outside" leaders remained in the custody of the military in McKinley County, San Bernalillo County, and the State

Penitentiary in Santa Fe until they signed statements promising to leave New Mexico immediately and stay away for a year. These men at first refused to sign, until it was agreed that two NMU organizers be allowed to remain in Gallup to settle the union's internal affairs. A week later, the governor honored this request, but only after the NMU assured him that its two leaders would not incite further trouble. The NMU withdrew from Gallup, and local miners confidently assumed full control.[91]

The euphoria of the miners' victory quickly evaporated. Dead work remained a problem, and no agreement had been reached on the issue of dirty coal, as it was left out of the contract. Despite a modest wage increase, pay for miners remained based on assigned work area. This mostly affected the Mexican coal diggers, since they occupied the worst mining jobs. Use of company scrip remained in place, in violation of the NRA codes. Though it was illegal to do so, the coal operators blacklisted employees who had gone out on strike and evicted them from company-owned housing as well. The McKinley County Welfare Association was providing relief to the families of miners who had been on strike; however, the breadwinners could not obtain work with the CWA as the governor originally promised. On the other hand, federal work relief was given to the men who scabbed during the strike. Employer reprisals were evident: three-fourths of the miners involved in the strike were without work. Conditions in and around the Gallup mining area had changed very little.[92]

The Communist Party hailed the Gallup strike as a victory emblematic of the new worker consciousness. The strike had demonstrated that the NMU could rebuild itself and challenge the UMWA. However, it was an empty victory because, as elsewhere, the communist activists, as William Z. Foster charged, failed to put emphasis on the "daily problems and demands of the aggrieved coal miners" and instead fell back on "general slogans and similar agitation." The result of this Left-led mine strike in Gallup was the same as elsewhere: unemployed and blacklisted miners formed the cadres the party intended to leave in its wake. In December, a national party conference on mining decided to abandon the NMU and instead work within the UMWA. The NMU's fortunes as a communist front organization were shaped by events unfolding in Europe. The end of the Third Period arrived after Hitler became German chancellor in 1933. Now in a united front against fascism, the party abandoned and broke up its dual labor organizations and ordered workers to unite under the AFL. In March 1935, the communists convened the Committee for the Unification of Trade Unions.[93]

The NMU was maintained until about February 1935, at which time the coal miners voted to join the UMWA as a body. UMWA representative Nicholas Fontacchio accepted this action, and the locals were issued charters of the UMWA. There was reluctance at first from Gallup miners formerly in the NMU to join the UMWA, a union they had criticized and fought against just months before. Many were eventually persuaded to join. The diehard miners who chose to remain in the NMU were reelected to office in the union locals of the Southwestern and Allison mines. This kept the leadership in the hands of the rank-and-file pit committee, limiting the power of the UMWA officials. The long-standing racial tensions heightened hostility toward Mexicans, most of whom had joined the NMU and gone out on strike. The Spanish-speaking feared for their future and as a defensive measure joined the Unemployed Councils and the ILD.[94]

The concern of the communists who came to Gallup was obtaining the greatest amount of publicity without regard to the harm this would cause to the miners who joined them, and thus they used whatever means were necessary to advance their interests. Foster had emphasized the importance of "partial demands" and working in united front arrangements with other trade unionists, including those in AFL unions. Instead, the NMU resorted to revolutionary speech making rather than focusing on explicit examination of industrial issues. The demonstration by the Left-led UFC at the Capitol Building in Santa Fe on January 15, 1934, displayed the party's commitment to promoting its leftist revolutionary agenda. Communists used the issue of relief to stage demonstrations that in turn were used to recruit new members into the party. This demonstration followed a similar rally in Denver in late December 1933, when 2,000 unemployed men, mostly Mexicans, led by United Front Committee agitators invaded the Colorado legislature to protest the cutbacks in FERA relief funds announced by Harry Hopkins. On January 15, about 2,000 jobless workers crammed the galleries of the New Mexico legislature, with Mexicans again making up the majority of the unemployed demonstrators. House members tried repeatedly to transact business but were disrupted by the demonstrators. Led by William Dietrich, various UFC speakers took the floor and chastised the legislators well into the evening. When it was his turn to speak, Dietrich mounted the rostrum and boldly announced, "I am a Communist; these are my comrades with me. You fellows have acted the fools here long enough while these people are hungry and relief money has run out." This apostle of revolution warned: "Let me tell you fellows something. You haven't more days here. We will be making the laws here before long if you don't sit up and take notice."[95]

For the year 1933, FERA direct relief in New Mexico had totaled $594,947, and as noted, much of this relief went to the state's poor Spanish-speaking residents. In Gallup, more men were thrown out of work by the decline in coal production. Those miners on FERA relief projects struggled to support their families. The McKinley County FERA announced a wage reduction on its relief projects. FERA project workers organized against the planned wage reduction, demanded that local residents be given preference in hiring, and called for an end to discriminatory practices in determining family need. They were led by Juan L. Ochoa, a leader of the Gallup strike who had spent most of his time in the military stockade for his activities in trying to improve the working conditions of his fellow miners. Ochoa was now a UMWA member, and he also belonged to the State Committee of the New Mexico Unemployed Council. To avert a statewide strike by FERA employees, the wage dispute went into arbitration and the previous rate was restored. This action served to fuel further opposition to radical organizations in New Mexico. New Mexico chapters of the Elks, the Veterans of Foreign Wars, and the American Legion received endorsement by their respective national offices to begin an anticommunist campaign. Local Anglo citizens quickly joined the protests. Although Anglos expressed little interest in the fate of Mexicans, they especially resented the extension of New Deal relief to foreign aliens, a race-coded complaint directed at Mexicans. About 500 of these patriotic citizens signed a petition to end the aid.[96]

Anglos frowned at the sudden growth of the numbers of the Spanish-speaking who appeared on the relief rolls. Most of these new applicants were Mexicans who had previously migrated to work out of state. Moreover, the Mexican miners were still perceived as a threat in Gallup. A series of coal miner walkouts and increased activity by the local Unemployed Council continued to focus the town's attention on the NMU. Anglos were outraged by the NMU's rhetoric of class conflict and socialist revolution. To them, the NMU was a tawdry band of outsiders and troublemakers, cursed communists and foreigners from Mexico who should be punished, brutally if necessary.[97]

THE BIG PAYBACK: THE CRUSADE AGAINST FOREIGNERS AND SUBVERSIVES

Additional Spanish-speaking miners joined the Communist Party. They were angry because the strike settlement did not produce the results they had fought for; because there was flagrant discrimination in the distribution of New Deal relief; because the coal mine operators absolutely refused to rehire former strikers, many of whom were blacklisted in retaliation for their communist union activity; and also because there was no work. By now, Mexican American and Mexican coal miners like Juan L. Ochoa and Jesús Pallares were closely identified in the minds of Anglos with the Communist Party and with its tendency to court violence through confrontation. Such a face-off took place on April 4, 1935, after 300 Mexican miners and their families were evicted from the Chihuahuita miners' camp. In GAMERCO's five-year leases, the homeowners were guaranteed title to all improvements on the land. However, after the 1933 strike, many homeowners who participated in the walkout were perfunctorily blacklisted, while others lost their jobs because of the ongoing depression. State senator Clarence Vogel, who dabbled in prostitution, had acquired title to Chihuahuita, and he filed suit to evict the residents. Vogel had set out to sell the land to the homeowners at ten to fifteen times its value. In spite of former company agreements, the new sale contracts specified that all improvements to the land became part of the realty. Any settler who refused to sign or, after signing, fell behind in payments would be evicted at once without compensation for their home or other improvements. By this transaction, 300 Mexicans and their families were threatened with the loss of their homes. The miners from Chihuahuita believed they owned the houses they had built and paid for and were unaware that the leases they had signed contained a clause sanctioning the coal company to evict residents without notice. An antieviction bill was killed in the New Mexico state legislature largely through Vogel's efforts.[98]

The workers fought off the evictions until March 1935, when the first warrant was served on Victor Campos. His furniture was dumped into the street. Hundreds of angry workers assembled to replace Campos's furniture in his house. Eziquio Navarro, released from custody but still awaiting deportation, Victor Campos, and Mrs. Lugardita Lavato took action; all three were arrested on charges of breaking and entering and jailed. Protesters marched to the jailhouse to demand the release of Navarro, Lavato, and Campos and were met by tear gas. Deputies and sheriffs panicked and opened fire on the protesters. The gunfire killed coal miner Ignacio Velarde and wounded five other protesters, one of them seriously. Sheriff Carmichael was killed in his deputies' crossfire. In a veritable frenzy of Western justice, forty-eight people were charged with murdering the sheriff. "John Doe" warrants were issued, and dozens of men were deputized and stormed Chihuahuita to apprehend the accused killers. In a retaliatory action, over one hundred Mexicans and Mexican Americans were subsequently deported by U.S. immigration agents.[99]

In the April 4 roundup by the deputies, all of the militant and active members of the union were arrested, including Joe Bartol, president of UMWA Local 6821, and Juan L. Ochoa and William Gonzales of the same local. With one exception, the entire pit committee of the Allison camp was arrested, and the same action took place in GAMERCO. Nicholas Fontacchio of the UMWA seized on the opportunity given him by the arrests to eliminate the suspected militants and other troublemakers and regain control of the UMWA locals. At this time when the locals should have met to immediately mobilize in defense of Bartol, Ochoa, Gonzales, and the rest of the workers, Fontacchio strategically made the statement that none of the workers arrested was a member of the UMWA.[100]

The wholesale raids and arrests that followed were perpetrated by Anglos who had come into Gallup from the "country" with the desire to avenge the death of Sheriff Carmichael. Forty ex-servicemen from the town of Farmington in San Juan County, directly north of Gallup, were among the men deputized and who participated in the reign of terror against the miners, whom they beat, chased, and treated like animals. Other indications of the organized effort of communist suppression, as well as connections to right-wing organizations in Gallup, included deputized men who belonged to the United Patriots of America and the Young Democrats. Their conviction that they had joined a righteous crusade against foreigners and subversive scum was realized when during the invasion of Chihuahuita deputies found incriminatory communist literature.[101]

In Gallup, Sheriff Dee Roberts handed out rifles indiscriminately to hundreds of mine gunmen, adolescent boys, and riffraff with the directive "Go get the union members." The armed deputies raided and wrecked homes, arrested miners without warrants, and got children out of school for questioning. The interrogations took place behind closed doors guarded by armed men; miners were threatened, brutalized, and beaten with fists and rifle butts. Some of the coal diggers had their union cards seized or were robbed of their savings, and the thugs also pocketed the pitifully small savings of the unemployed organizations. A total of 600 miners were rounded up and detained for questioning, and 200 were jailed before the end of the day. This included sixteen women and small children, who were jammed into two small jail cells. Company bosses came into the jailhouse, fingered the most militant and active leaders, and framed them to deprive the workers' organizations of the last of their leaders. By the time of the preliminary hearing, forty-eight men were charged with first-degree murder. The prosecutors based the trumped-up charges on a statute passed in 1854, fifty-six years before New Mexico entered statehood. Meanwhile, federal immigration agents arrived and began rounding up workers, holding them incommunicado for deportation. This action helped to further break up workers' organizations and, more important, deprived the defense lawyers of valuable defense witnesses.[102]

In 1934, the International Labor Defense reported that the San Francisco General Strike marked the beginning of the drive against the foreign-born worker in the United States, particularly against those active in the labor movement and in working-class political organizations. Government officials knew that the cases of these persons could not stand up to judicial scrutiny and thus they could easily be deported. In the case of Mexicans, the new government policy initiatives interlocked with prevailing racist attitudes toward this minority group. For example, after participating in an unemployment demonstration in Phoenix, Arizona, on September 6, 1934, Marie Gonzales was arrested and held for deportation on charges of membership in the Communist Party. The twenty-two-year-old activist, who had been in the United States since she was a year old, was deported on January 26, 1935. Thirty-seven-year-old Tejano Abundio Arias was arrested April 22, 1935, and charged with membership in the Communist Party. Arias's case was initially dropped because of public protest; however, the Tejano was suddenly deported from Texas on June 4, 1935, charged with being in the country illegally. Arias had legally entered the United States in 1902. Forty-one-year-old coal miner Julio Herrera was arrested in September 1934 while organizing for La Liga Obrera in Española, New Mexico. Herrera had been arrested five months earlier in southern Colorado. Having legally entered the United States in 1908, Herrera was held for deportation on charges of being in the country illegally. The coal miner was deported in April 1935, leaving his wife and stepson behind to fend for themselves.[103]

Summary deportation thus became an alternative to standard judicial punishment in Gallup. It offered the city a way of quickly eliminating so-called undesirables, particularly the rebellious Mexicans who opposed the policies of the coal companies and of the government. The expulsions did not spare women and children. Thirteen adults and seventeen children left Gallup bound for El Paso for final deportation to Mexico. Five of the men were being deported on charges of membership in the Communist Party. Another group of deportees consisting of eight to ten families was scheduled for departure, while two additional families left voluntarily, the FERA paying for their passage.[104] The INS targeted Spanish-speaking labor leaders affiliated with the state's radical element, focusing their attention especially on La Liga Obrera de Habla Español.

Meanwhile, the American Civil Liberties Union demanded that seven of the women defendants, all of whom had children, be released from the murder charge. New Mexico State Attorney General Frank L. Patton refused. He sought vengeance against all individuals who praised Russia. On May 30, 1935, the state attorney general in a public address scolded the people of New Mexico for their "lethargy and unconcern" in opposing communism and exhorted them to "stamp out" the doctrine. Two weeks later, on June 14, the state attorney general again called upon New Mexicans to "take up the cudgels and smash the vipers," adding, "we [are] prepared to do everything to oppose communism."[105]

Gallup's Spanish-speaking community lived in constant fear of the INS as the number of deportations increased. Many labor activists apparently could also be removed if they were without work, because INS agents worked out a policy by which, having identified persons as being "politically undesirable," they systematically searched for a basis on which to expel them. Therefore, Mexicans were formally deported for taking relief when the real reason was that they were working in support of the rights of labor. That the threat of deportation loomed large in Gallup was revealed in letters native New Mexicans wrote to state officials seeking protection. A letter a Mexican American coal miner's wife wrote to Governor Clyde C. Tingley in 1936 succinctly illustrated what happened to Mexican Americans who advanced the interests of the workers. The letter writer pleaded with the governor:

> In the name of our Mexican colony I am asking you for protection. . . . Our persecutors are the immigration officers who deport us and treat us like criminals. All . . . this has happened since the strike of 1933. We made an error to affiliate in the party of bad ideas, but I think in the United States there is free speech. All this makes us think that there is a plan against the Mexicans. I want you to help us all you can for we were born in the United States and have children born here too.[106]

In industry after industry during the early years of the Great Depression there were strikes and the threat of strikes. Mexican workers were encouraged by the labor struggles and by increasing acceptance of the NRA. They felt the time had come to take direct action. Many of the walkouts involved Mexican women workers—farm workers, laundry workers, domestics, cigar workers, and dressmakers, who were in a worse bargaining position than the men. The Mexican strikers could no longer endure discrimination in the workplace, having their work undervalued and their dignity assaulted because of their race. They were aware of the grave injustices continuing against them as the most exploited and oppressed sector living in the Southwest. The government consciously targeted and demonized Mexicans, while Anglo society branded Mexican women as lazy and licentious. Whatever Mexicans faced as a people, it was much worse for Mexican women. Therefore they joined and formed unions, went on strike, and took part in protests to demand the same rights as other workingwomen. It was an occasion for Mexicans to oppose their degradation as workers, to protest against low wages and the inhumane conditions in which they did their work, and to challenge their and their families' destitute living conditions. The strikes united Mexicans in simultaneous action, demanding an end to low wages and excessive work while showing the urgent need for equality, the need to oppose the personal devaluing that went along with racial inequality. The early strikes waged by Mexican workers and their various demands presented these aggrieved workers with their first opportunity to participate in a well-articulated response to injustice.

Mexican workers sought to establish new unions, to assert Section 7a, the right to choose among competing unions, including those with non-AFL affiliation. Communists found fertile soil in Gallup, New Mexico. Mexicans went not to communism but to communists, because they promised to bring self-determination. The short-lived odyssey of the Gallup coal miners through the Communist Party instilled in them the imperative of class struggle. Although the National Miners Union gave voice to the miners' demands, the coal diggers found out too late that working-class struggle meant a struggle on communist terms. Pilloried as Reds, the coal miners suffered a bitter defeat in this strike and faced subsequent retaliation, intimidation, deportation, and other injustices for standing up for their rights, as workers and as Mexicans.

Mexican Americans responded to the hard times and heightened racial hostility with increased militancy. Communists actively fought for Mexican American rights as in the case of the agricultural strikes and the walk-out by coal miners in New Mexico, and they were a driving force in the Peoples' Congress. In the late 1930s, Mexican Americans demonstrated other examples of radicalism.

CHAPTER THREE

"Do You See the Light?": Mexican American Workers and CIO Organizing

> Let the workers organize. Let the toilers assemble. Let their crystallized voice proclaim their injustices and demand their privileges. Let all thoughtful citizens sustain them, for the future of labor is the future of America.
>
> —JOHN L. LEWIS

> Was I in a state of panic or fear? No. I was pretty defiant. [I fought] against poverty . . . high infant death rates, disease and hunger and misery. I would do the same thing again.
>
> —EMMA TENAYUCA

THE 1930s witnessed a tremendous upsurge in labor organizing as a movement swept the United States to establish industrial unions that would organize all workers: the Congress of Industrial Organizations. The CIO would have a long-lasting effect on the political, economic, and social life of Mexican Americans, who made up the Southwest's main labor force in the harvesting, processing, and canning of fruits and vegetables, as well as in mine, smelter, railroad, garment, and other factory work. Spanish-speaking workers were oppressed and exploited, very few were in skilled positions, they routinely earned much less than Anglos, and their work was dangerous and physically exhausting. The aggressive CIO campaign gained fervent supporters among these masses of aggrieved Mexican workers, for they understood that it could help them overcome their disadvantaged status. The CIO opened up its ranks to them because they were crucial to the unionization of the Southwest. Helping the CIO in the creation of a mass movement and pulling such campaigns together were talented Spanish-speaking organizers, many of them leftists eager to forge a labor movement capable of remaking society. Their commitment and skill and vision of social justice aroused Mexican workers to organize into unions.

The support Mexican Americans gave to industrial unionism was a radical step at the time and was probably most eagerly felt in the organizing of agricultural workers. However, the fact that wages in agriculture were low militated against the unions. Low wages and small incomes made it harder for Mexican agricultural workers to pay union dues and to hold out through a strike. In addition, attempts at unionization once again were squelched by racism and the repressive power wielded by powerful growers' associations and their lackeys.

Strident antiunionism was especially pronounced in Texas, where the mere act of organizing and demanding labor rights was perceived as a form of revolt. Notwithstanding, social ferment began to build among Tejanos as a result of the prolonged suffering of the Great Depression, low wages, racial injustice, and the promotion of unionism by labor insurgents as part of the incipient CIO movement. The recent strikes in El Paso and San Antonio demonstrated the growing resistance by Tejanos to their oppression and showed that Tejanos possessed the courage and capacity to sweep away the twin yokes of class and racial oppression.

This chapter argues these points, first focusing on the walkout by Tejano onion pickers on farms outside Laredo over a wage dispute. The growers refused to bargain. Specifically, the growers believed that conceding to the strikers' demands would lead to the breakup of the old *patrón* (feudal) system, under which Tejano families, toiled for poverty wages. The growers especially resented that Tejanos agitated under the protection of the American flag for a wage scale 300 percent higher than that accorded to Mexicans across the border in Mexico. In Laredo, city officials refused to meet with the all-Tejano Unemployed Council and banned Tejanos from holding pro-labor parades and rallies, thereby stopping the mobilization of mass support.[1] This chapter also notes that the Laredo onion strike signaled the building of solidarity across the United States-Mexico border. Tejanos and other Spanish-speaking workers in the Southwest now had as allies the pro-labor Cárdenistas, who brought agrarian reform to Mexico and by decade's end would nationalize Mexico's oil industry. The activities of the Confederación de Trabajadores Mexicanos (CTM) centered on building links with Spanish-speaking workers in the Southwest based on a common set of demands and struggles. By providing support and advice in promoting cross-border solidarity, the CTM had a profound impact on the CIO union movement in the Southwest border region.

The CIO's efforts to organize Tejano workers in Texas were constrained by racism and stiff grower opposition, in combination with a right-wing climate that resisted the further expansion of radicalism. In 1938, Anglo right-wing politicians formed the Texas Regulators, whose specific goals were restoring states' rights and propping up the supremacy of the white race, both of which allegedly were being "destroyed by the Communist-controlled New Deal."[2] Despite this repressive environment, Tejanos continued to organize, and they scored a major victory in the San Antonio pecan shellers' strike. The strike's impact was felt throughout San Antonio and the rest of Texas, and it influenced other unionization campaigns in the Southwest. For Tejanos, social equality was as much at issue as labor rights; they now focused their efforts on the organization of the community. Moving in the direction of labor rights and civil rights, Tejanos engaged in direct action protest to dramatize their cause.

Individuals who were Communist Party members or supporters played a vital role in initiating and leading the struggle to unionize San Antonio's Tejano workers. This chapter focuses on Emma Tenayuca, a Tejana who came out of the Left, demonstrated exceptional leadership and organizing skills, and was a principal organizer of the pecan shellers' strike. Her views, which reflected the most progressive thinking in the Mexican American labor movement, especially on issues of race and class, give some insight into left-wing politics in labor at this time.

Tenayuca organized the Tejanos of San Antonio's West Side in fights for relief and for union rights. Her gains were achieved by agitating around immediate issues of concern to Tejanos: unemployment relief, the right to organize unions, higher and equal wages, and racial justice. The series of unprecedented protests and marches to demand unemployment relief brought thousands of Tejanos out. These protests were impressive given the level of repression in Texas at the time. Anyone organizing against racism or for union rights was targeted for violence by the police and the much-hated Texas Rangers, Anglo lawmen who could not tell the difference between good Mexicans and bad.[3] Tenayuca quickly earned a reputation among Anglos as a menace. She was challenging a carefully constructed system of racism designed to exploit Tejano workers more effectively. Tenayuca was feared and hated because she threatened to destroy this structure and called for Tejano unity and equality. San Antonio's self-serving Mexican American middle class was particularly reserved when it came to challenging segregation in the city. No one in San Antonio had made an attempt to organize poor Tejanos for their rights.

Emma Tenayuca proclaimed the cause of unionism and explained to the Tejano people of San Antonio's West Side why they should endorse this movement. Tenayuca's organization of pecan shellers was a struggle for improved wages and working conditions, and it also became a battle against Jim Crow. In this regard, I note that Emma Tenayuca had a far-reaching objective: to rethink and articulate the issue of nationhood by writing, with her husband, Homer Brooks, "The Mexican Question in the Southwest." Although Tenayuca and Brooks never declared that Mexican Americans and Mexicans in the United States constituted a nation along ethnic and racial lines, they did call for their self-determination based on a common working-class identity.

The CIO brought in thousands of Mexican American workers as new members. Support for the CIO was most effective in the organizing of

Mexican American cannery and food processing workers. One of the most important CIO unions in the Southwest was the United Cannery, Agricultural, Packing, and Allied Workers of America (UCAPAWA). As this chapter makes clear, the work of this union was valuable particularly among impoverished urban Mexican American women workers in Southern California, who labored in the canneries and food processing plants under terrible conditions. The women workers became transformed through the process of building the union, and many of them showed talented leadership and organizing skill.

That workers in large cities were more highly organized than those who lived elsewhere applied to Mexican industrial workers of the urban centers of the Southwest. This chapter concludes with an examination of the CIO organizing drive in Los Angeles, which integrated the city's Mexicans into the new interracial union movement and advanced their employment in industries organized by CIO affiliates. Race dominated the history of the Southwest and was a major factor in labor relations. Mexican American unionists encountered impediments bound up with racial and other social problems, with the structure of industry, and with opposition from employers who used race as a weapon against unions. As we shall see, national CIO union leaders realized the importance of the Spanish-speaking worker in organizations, but local affiliates did not readily accept the unions' racial policies.

The Labor Offensive in South Texas and Cross-Border Organizing

In April 1935, labor strife broke out in south Texas when about 3,000 Tejano onion pickers walked out of the fields over low wages. The strikers were from Laredo. Since the early twentieth century, Laredo had been a traditional center for agitation by pro-labor groups, a number of which had their headquarters there, and for several Tejano civil rights groups and newspapers that periodically issued manifestos to publicize the Tejano's struggle for justice and self-determination. As will be noted, Laredo became a launching pad for an eventual labor offensive in south Texas, demonstrating that Tejanos and Mexicans were already in contact with one another. The onion pickers were led by Juan Peña and José Jacobs from La Asociación de Jornaleros, founded in Laredo in 1933 and made up of workers belonging to all-Mexican AFL affiliates. Peña and Jacobs were both capable individuals who conformed to the same ideological orthodoxy. A WPA employee, Peña served as the local chapter secretary of the League Against War and Fascism. Like Peña, José Jacobs was also an agitator. The self-employed Jewish photographer had ties to the Unemployed Councils and the Workers' Alliance of America and distributed ILD literature in support of the Scottsboro Boys, as well as copies of the *Daily Worker*. The two labor organizers and the workers they led faced growers who staunchly opposed unionization.[4]

Tejanos in the Laredo area annually harvested 2,400 to 3,000 railway cars of Bermuda onions, bumper crops valued at more than $2 million. The profits received by the onion growers resulted in several thousand Tejanos going out on strike for higher wages. With Juan Peña and José Jacobs in charge, strikers were stationed along U.S. Highway 83 leading to the onion fields just outside Laredo in the direction of the lower Río Grande Valley. For four days there was a flurry of activity on the picket lines, and strikers blocked the highway, allowing passage only to automobiles and trucks filled with strikers. The growers soon let it be known that they regarded any interference in the onion harvests as an act of mutiny. They contacted the Webb County district attorney's office, which instructed deputy sheriffs to escort under arms—including a machine gun—several trucks of scabs across the strikers' cordon. The growers were determined to chase off the strikers, who they feared would either dynamite or burn down the bridge and spread the labor troubles to the onion fields in adjacent Willacy County. Because of the volatile situation, the district judge contacted the state governor to intervene, and as an extra measure, the judge ordered that Texas Rangers be stationed in the area. Six Rangers armed with pistols and rifles soon arrived and opened U.S. Highway 83. The ruthless and brutal Rangers were eager for a confrontation and, as expected, were unforgiving in their handling of the rebellious strikers. Convinced the Rangers would break the strike, the onion growers refused to meet with the strike committee.[5]

Cooler heads prevailed, and a conciliator from the U.S. Labor Department was called in by the Laredo Chamber of Commerce to evaluate the situation and persuade Peña and Jacobs to get the workers to return to the onion fields. The conciliator advised the signing of individual contracts with two large onion growers offering to pay union-scale wages. Peña and Jacobs refused. They wanted a contract to cover the entire onion-growing district. The strikers' belligerency enraged the growers, who responded by lowering wages to the previous rates, sums they already considered "too much." For their part, the Texas Rangers thought the proper way to end the walkout was to drive the workers back into the fields. The next morning Rangers arrested fifty-nine strikers, but the men were released because the growers preferred that they be put to work rather than allowed to freeload about the jail. The Rangers departed, having antagonized not only the workers but the growers as well, who complained that the Rangers had arrested the wrong workers and let the entire radical element escape. The strikers eventually voted their walkout "off," and soon several thousand men, women, and children were back at work bunching Bermuda onions.[6]

The Laredo strike was part of an offensive launched by Tejano and Anglo labor and community activists to bring the CIO campaign to the Texas agricultural fields. The onion strike marks a departure from previous labor actions because of the workers' new outlook on their situation as a result of activists merging a Popular Front perspective with the New Deal populist culture. Moreover, they believed the immediate need was for joint action with the labor movement in Mexico to bring their plans to fruition. This marked a significant new phase in the labor movement's basic character. Mexican American workers were making international labor solidarity a priority, since assistance in the form of guidance and organizers now came from Mexico's newly formed Confederación de Trabajadores Mexicanos. In solidarity with the CIO in its organizing drives in Texas and the rest of the Southwest and Midwest, the CTM would make use of the willingness of Mexican Americans to assist in its promotion of a "*CTM del norte*" (a CTM of the North).[7]

Encouraged by the growing role of Mexicans in strike actions and the militancy they showed, the CTM began building networks among Spanish-speaking workers in the Southwest and Midwest to facilitate a formal alliance. Mexico's Communist Party (PCM) shared this interest in forging alliances with Spanish-speaking workers in the United States. In January 1936, CTM leader Vicente Lombardo Toledano, representatives of the PCM, the Mexican Railway Union, and the Mexican Labor Congress, and other labor leaders attended the CTM sponsored Convention of Mexican Workers in the United States held in Dallas, Texas. It is here that the groundwork was set for linking the CTM with progressive elements within the American labor movement. The CTM spokespersons met with labor and progressive organizations in San Antonio, Laredo, St. Louis, New Orleans, San Diego, and elsewhere. In late spring, another labor delegation from Mexico toured the United States to strengthen the legitimacy of the CTM and that of newly elected Mexican president Lazáro Cárdenas.[8] As part of the CTM's campaign to organize agricultural workers in Mexico, officials from the powerful Oil Workers Union of Mexico and from other Mexican labor unions visited Los Angeles in July 1936. They urged Mexican farm workers to join local agricultural unions and promised financial support to the citrus strikers in Orange County. Moreover, Vicente Lombardo Toledano established El Colegio de Obreros in Mexico City to train cadres of union organizers for the labor movement in Mexico and in the United States. Plans were launched to bring Mexican Americans to El Colegio de Obreros on scholarships funded by the CTM. The Tejanos who left for training at El Colegio were María Solís Sager and Emma Tenayuca, who on their return to Texas rejoined the labor movement.[9]

Local Mexican American leaders, the rank and file, and pro-labor community groups supported the cross-border labor networking and enthusiastically pushed it along. A trend began of including CTM unionists in organizing drives in agricultural and industrial labor sectors with large numbers of Mexican Americans. In Laredo, La Asociación de Jornaleros welcomed the CTM's offer of assistance in the organizing campaign in south Texas. In El Paso, Mine-Mill allied itself with the CTM in a successful organizing drive among Spanish-speaking smelter workers. The fact that advisors from the CTM were intimately involved in the planning and execution of strikes soon became a subject of controversy.

Through the work of Juan Peña, La Asociación de Jornaleros was now AFL Agricultural Workers Union No. 20212 (AWU). Many AWU members belonged to the Unemployed Councils and the Workers' Alliance of America, and some held joint membership in Mexican unions. Moreover, the AWU made contacts with militant elements as far away as Corpus Christi. To stem the tide of growing militancy among Laredo's Tejano workers, city officials quickly denounced the AWU as being dominated by communists and foreign aliens and ordered the sheriff's department, the Texas Rangers, and the U.S. Immigration Bureau to constantly shadow AWU members. Nevertheless, in early March 1936, the AWU convened a meeting to discuss plans and mobilize support for an upcoming labor offensive in south Texas. Two weeks before, a similar meeting had been held in San Antonio by Tejano laborers who organized as the Confederación de Obreros Mexico-Americanos y Mexicanos (Confederation of Mexican American and Mexican Workers). All this activity was related to the groundwork of the CTM in establishing cross-border links with the American labor movement.[10]

The AWU debated its strategic options at a meeting held at Laredo's Salón de Obreros (Workers Hall) attended by 250 workers and presided over by Mexican Consul Juan B. Richer. AWU members made several speeches, and the talks revealed not only the depth of labor solidarity but also the fact that Tejano leaders and workers were beginning to coalesce around the key issues of racial discrimination and other mistreatment, including the indiscriminate persecution of Mexicans by the INS.[11] The federal agents in attendance submitted their reports to local officials and growers, who were closely monitoring the AWU's activities. The agents reinforced their prevailing suspicions and anger by noting that the AWU's communist inclinations had included desecration of the American flag.[12]

Determined to destroy the Red AWU, Laredo officials the following week empanelled a grand jury to investigate the charges of subversion. The district attorney set the tone of the hearings by warning, "Nobody will be allowed to preach communism in Webb County," adding that those who did would be prosecuted, beaten, and run out of the county.

No indictments were made, but the eight labor leaders called in to testify were harangued, bullied, treated with open contempt, and told they would be subject to a second grand jury hearing, if necessary. The local newspapers contributed to the smear campaign through a flurry of editorials calling for the deportation of all "Bolsheviks, Communists, and Radicals," in a direct reference to the inflamed speeches made at the meeting. Unfazed by the threats, the workers gathered again, though a much smaller crowd attended. Assistance to the Tejanos from the CTM was growing. A report by immigration officials intimated that six representatives from Mexico's Labor Department were going to arrive in Laredo within several days to assist the AWU in its organizing campaign.[13]

The AWU's mission was to mobilize and unite the nearly 30,000 Tejano farm workers in south and southwest Texas, an objective requiring a joint effort by many unions and the CTM. Toward this end, the AWU invited labor elements in Texas and in Mexico to a conference in Corpus Christi on January 23, 1937. The delegates represented the Central Trades and Labor Council of Corpus Christi, the International Longshoreman's Association, the Oil Workers Industrial Union, the Workers' Alliance of America of San Antonio, and the CTM. The Texas Agricultural Workers Organizing Committee (TWOC) emerged from this conference, and it would spearhead the strike actions in the lower Río Grande Valley of Texas. The delegates passed resolutions for a minimum wage for farm workers, a union wage scale on all government work relief projects, the admission of Tejanos into the AFL, broader cooperation with labor unions in Mexico, and solidarity with the struggle of the Spanish loyalists "against the fascist rebels" in Spain. An expression of Popular Front activism that showed the delegates identified with the antifascist cause, this last resolution was tabled over concern that it would discredit the TWOC as communist.[14]

In late June, Tejano cotton pickers in the lower Río Grande Valley represented by TWOC demanded that area growers pay them a wage of one dollar per hundred pounds of cotton. The cotton growers, organized as the Tri-County Vegetable Producers' Association, refused to bargain, and this rebuff sparked the launching of a series of strikes throughout the south Texas cotton-growing region. The rising tempo of solidarity was a testimony to the validity of TWOC's judgment that Tejanos were ready for organizing. Because of the spreading labor conflict, strikebreakers were brought in to smash the TWOC union drive. TWOC apparently succeeded in preventing workers from Mexico from crossing the border to break the strike, because the scabs were black cotton pickers brought in from Waco. Given the militancy marking the cotton strike, the panicky blacks were warned by Tejano strikers that they would be "shot if they picked cotton." The walkouts persuaded growers to accede to a wage increase in a few cotton-growing areas. TWOC was soon absorbed into the newly founded UCAPAWA, which had entered the fields to recharter locals at Laredo and Corpus Christi. It organized new locals in the lower Río Grande Valley and brought 5,000 workers into the CIO. (This figure would be significantly higher if it included the spouses, children, and extended family members who made up the majority of the pickers.)[15]

However, reflecting the international union's shift in policy, UCAPAWA turned to organizing the packing and processing plants and began withdrawing organizers and scarce resources from the Texas agricultural fields. Tejano farm workers remained without union protection for the same reasons as elsewhere—the economic recession building anew, the inability of low-wage farm workers to pay their membership dues, the seasonal and migratory nature of their work, and the entrenched antilabor hostility the UCAPAWA encountered in Texas from Anglo farmers convinced that Reds and foreign aliens dominated the union. The AFL Fruit and Vegetable Workers' Union No. 20363, an interracial packing shed workers' union, was the sole labor organization remaining in the lower Río Grande Valley. It established a wage standard for packing shed workers by staging wildcat strikes. Huge car caravans carried the protest against antiunionism and the prorating of produce shipments to other areas. The latter practice had eliminated 8,000 packing shed jobs and threatened the potential loss of 5,000 to 6,000 additional jobs. By the end of 1938, all farm worker union activity ceased in the lower Río Grande Valley. The problems intrinsic to organizing seasonal and migratory workers, as well as competition from a surplus of nonunion farm workers, prevailed throughout the Valley, the Winter Garden area, and the El Paso district and extended beyond Texas to New Mexico and Arizona. Part of the problem with the labor market was that in 1938 Congress passed a second AAA, which reinstated production controls and reduced cotton acreage by 43 percent. Relief once more became a key issue. Despite the cessation of organizing in the agricultural fields of southwest and south Texas, the labor struggles had emboldened the Tejanos. Moreover, participation in the campaigns of the CIO, the Workers' Alliance of America, and the Popular Front had honed their skills in political activism.[16]

The union drive by Tejanos now shifted to the city of San Antonio. The city was a focal point for pecan shelling and other sweatshop work that employed thousands of Tejanos, many of them drawn to the city from central and south Texas. Here the largest and most dramatic labor upheaval in an agriculture-allied industry involving Spanish-speaking workers unfolded in late January 1938. Over 1,000 picketers would be arrested and jailed by San Antonio police during the thirty-seven-day strike. The pecan shellers' strike capped a wave of Tejano organizing, but it also helped compel a rightward turn against organized labor in Texas.[17]

A POWER TO BE RECKONED WITH: EMMA TENAYUCA, LA PASIONARIA

Grassroots activism by Mexican American women brought them to the forefront of the labor struggles of the Depression era as rank-and-file organizers and as strike leaders. Such acts of solidarity transformed their lives and consciousness, just as gender, racial/ethnic, and class identities in turn shaped the various working-class movements that unfolded among the Mexican American population.[18] As workers and strike leaders, Manuela Solís Sager, Minnie Rendón, Juana Sánchez, and other Tejanas played a prominent role in the Depression-era union effort in San Antonio. A key Tejana activist was Emma Tenayuca. She had a magnetic personality and possessed extraordinary organizing abilities honed during years of active struggle on behalf of San Antonio's Mexican community. Under the banners of the Unemployed Councils and the Workers' Alliance of America, Tenayuca helped Mexicans organize hunger marches, protests, and demonstrations to gain relief, obtain jobs on public works, and fight against racial injustice and harassment by the INS. Tenayuca is best known as a leader of the 1938 pecan shellers' strike, an event that was also a mass civil rights movement. With over 10,000 participants, it was the largest labor strike in San Antonio history and the most massive community-based strike waged by the nation's Mexican Americans in the 1930s. In calling for equal pay for equal work, the Tejana also sought the restructuring of the workplace on the basis of racial and gender equity. Emma Tenayuca's efforts thus shared a common purpose with those of women of diverse backgrounds during the 1930s whose heritage of struggle is being chronicled by historians.[19]

As Tenayuca grew in the belief that the workplace would require radical revision to achieve equality, she joined a small group of Mexican Americans who turned to the Communist Party. She belonged to communist-led organizations, married an avowed communist, and joined the party in 1937, only to leave disillusioned two years later, following the signing of the Nazi-Soviet pact. Marxism was especially suited to Tenayuca's own intellectual identification as a communist; she co-authored a polemic for the Communist Party on Mexicans and the national question and ran for office as a party candidate. She never advertised her membership, nor did she recruit Mexicans to join the party. The impassioned crusader's motivations were bound less by propagandizing Marxist ideology than by a strong attachment to her working-class community, whose miserable plight saddened and angered her. According to Tenayuca, she joined the party because no one but the communists expressed the least interest in helping San Antonio's dispossessed Mexicans.[20]

Tenayuca was not without enemies. San Antonio's middle-class Mexican American community did not appreciate the Tejana's aggressive pursuit of labor and civil rights for workers or her challenge of the city's long-established racial caste system. Driven by a blind obsession with anticommunism, San Antonio's city bosses and the Catholic Church roundly condemned Emma Tenayuca and launched a Red-baiting campaign to discredit her. What they feared most was that Tenayuca was undermining their authority by instilling confidence in the city's Mexican workers, telling them that they alone could determine their own destiny, that empowerment could come about through mass action. The threat of communism would play a central role in the San Antonio pecan shellers' strike. Communist subversion became a shibboleth that would alter public perception of the strikers and their cause and thus inhibit potential strike support. It would divert action away from the strike issues toward fighting the strike's negative aspects, which the public dreaded. Feared and loathed, communism became the pretext for San Antonio city officials and police to unleash a torrent of violence against the strike and its leaders. Undaunted by the fierce diatribes targeting her, the strong-willed Tenayuca remained firm in her commitment to gaining social justice for Mexicans through collective self-organization.[21]

Several factors coalesced to make Emma Tenayuca a dedicated and persistent organizer and advocate of Mexican workers in the 1930s and the era's most celebrated Mexican American champion of labor and civil rights. Her strong commitment to rectifying injustice was the result of a deep-rooted Catholicism merged with a strong Tejano identity. Radicalism later supplied the added dimension of class conflict to this worldview.[22]

One of eleven children born in San Antonio to poor working-class Tejanos, Emma Tenayuca was raised by her maternal grandparents. A devout Catholic, Tenayuca's grandfather was an important force in shaping her social consciousness. Tenayuca grew up in a household of daily masses, weekly confessions, and complete silence during meals that always began with prayers. However, the patriarch taught Tenayuca that Catholicism also meant embracing the practice of championing the cause of the poor.[23] It was from her grandfather that Tenayuca learned of her rich family history. On the maternal side, the Tenayuca family could trace its origins to the Spanish who settled northwestern Louisiana in the seventeenth century and later helped colonize San Antonio. Native Americans made up the family's paternal side, a lineage readily evident in Tenayuca's dark complexion. Early in her life the granddaughter was imbued with tremendous pride in her mestiza heritage.[24]

Tenayuca's grandfather informed her too about the evils of Anglo oppression through accounts of the Ku Klux Klan and the racial violence that swept Texas in the early twentieth century. But these misfortunes were counterpoised with tales of Tejano bravery that inspired resistance against Anglo domination. Her grandfather recounted the story of Gregorio Cortez, emphasizing the morality of Gregorio's actions in defense of his rights against the forces of racial and class oppression. On weekends, the elderly Tejano would take the child to San Antonio's Milam Park, also called Plaza de Zacate, a popular political and social gathering spot. It was here that the young Tejana was first exposed to a range of ideas and the everyday experiences of the Mexican worker. Radicals and intellectuals of divergent political persuasions used Milam Park to present their points of view to the groups of people who collected there. It was common practice for these men, usually hoping to procure work from labor contractors, to recount their experiences of abuse at the hands of Anglo farmers. Tenayuca listened intently to their stories of tragedy and despair, as attentively as she did to the speech making of the agitators.[25]

The intellectual appeal of radicalism began to characterize Tenayuca's political development, an attraction piqued through books. The Tejana had an insatiable passion for reading: "I was reading books at a very early age. I cannot remember a time when I could not read. My grandfather would come home from work, go to the porch, sit down on the rocker, and read the paper to me. I would play hooky from school and go to the library and read." In high school the adolescent's social consciousness was honed by a few of her teachers, who encouraged this bright Mexican American student and introduced her to progressive writers and intellectuals. The works of Émile Zola elicited her compassion for the reality of human suffering. The materialism of Darwin's *The Origin of Species* made an impact on Tenayuca. The avid reader absorbed Charles and Mary Beard's sweeping history *The Rise of American Civilization*, as well as Charles Beard's *An Economic Interpretation of the U.S. Constitution*, his retrospective exposé of America's founding fathers. The writings of English socialists Beatrice and Sidney Webb, particularly their pioneering *History of Trade Unionism*, appealed to Tenayuca's growing interest in how, throughout modern history workers attempted to redress their social and economic grievances. The teenager was especially influenced by the playwright Henrik Ibsen, whose works dramatize how women struggle to achieve social and psychological liberation from the "doll house" constraints of their domestic roles as wives and mothers.

Young Emma Tenayuca embraced the values of her grandfather. His moral lessons that repudiated the notion of Anglo Texan superiority and Tejano inferiority remained with her throughout the years. Tenayuca never forgot her grandfather's advice: "Just remember this, Emma, you have been here a long time. You have deeper roots than the Anglos." Memories and collective traditions thus held a strong resonance for Tenayuca, shaping her perceptions of Tejano history and influencing how she responded to unfolding events that would soon call her to action. Like her grandfather's historical and moral lessons, the allure of the power of ideas stayed with Tenayuca. Direct action through organizing would soon fill out her education, and the young Tejana's forceful and dynamic personality would make her a power to be reckoned with.[26]

"She's Nothing but a Damned Communist": Emma Tenayuca's Work in the Unemployed Councils and the Workers' Alliance of America

Organizing San Antonio's Spanish-speaking labor force proved a gargantuan endeavor for Emma Tenayuca. Forty percent of the nation's Mexicans resided in Texas, and large numbers lived in the cities. The Spanish-speaking population consisted of Tejanos and Mexican nationals. The latter, either longtime Texas residents or recent arrivals, assimilated the culture and language of the Tejanos, so that to Anglos, differences between the two became imperceptible. However, the vulnerability of Mexican nationals to abuse and exploitation irrevocably influenced the fate of this population mixture then, as it continues to do now. They gained no sympathy from middle-class Mexican Americans indifferent to their plight, or from organized labor and its rank-and-file membership. As with blacks, total exclusion, confinement to segregated locals, and racially prescribed employment quotas characterized the treatment Mexicans received. Nor did the Texas AFL recognize the huge army of Mexican farm workers as a wage-earning class. Representing nearly half of the state's 236,201 gainfully employed Tejanos, Tejano farm workers were overwhelmingly locked by old-time Texas racism into seasonal migration patterns. The Texas Farm Placement Service controlled the intrastate and interstate movement of Tejano migratory workers, handling, organizing, and routing laborers from farm to farm, season to season. Another problem the Spanish-speaking faced was decentralized New Deal programs controlled locally by employers, unions, and city officials. Discriminatory New Deal legislation that acquiesced to the demands of large-scale commercial farmers penalized Mexicans and contributed to the pervasive poverty.[27]

Tens of thousands of desperately poor and job-hungry Tejanos left Texas on labor contracts through a virtual underground railroad that flowed to other farms and urban centers in the Southwest, the Plains States, and the Midwest. The Tejano farm laborers came from rural counties where the widespread unemployment was as high as 84 percent. Without work and destitute, migrant farm laborers converged on cities like San Antonio to seek relief or work from New Deal programs and thereby increased the number of Mexicans in the local labor force. Yet much of the New Deal legislation overlooked this huge and exploited segment of the American working class. Government relief programs in the cities became a revolving door for needy migrant farm workers. Mexicans could not count on receiving aid; residency or citizenship requirements usually disqualified the migrants, though blatant racial discrimination was the motive for denying them relief. Sympathetic to local farmers, WPA program directors released Mexicans from work relief usually at the beginning of harvest season.[28]

Along with the rural culture that Mexican migrant workers duplicated in San Antonio, Jim Crowism prevailed in the city. Semi-industrial firms and skilled labor had established patterns of Anglo and Mexican work. This entrenched dual wage labor market had cheated Mexican workers out of their pay for almost fifty years.[29] Gender-based discriminatory patterns compounded the sweatshop conditions of the factories. Mostly young and single, Mexican and Tejana women made up 79 percent of San Antonio's low-paid garment, cigar, and pecan-shelling labor force. New Deal wage and hour legislation essentially ignored women. One-fourth of the NRA codes adopted a lower wage rate for women. Just as women earned less than men, minority women earned even less than white women. Occupational segregation along racial and gender lines, combined with San Antonio's discriminatory work relief program policies, would decide the nature of the subsequent labor struggles.[30]

Given the exploitation and inequality of Tejanas in society and in the workplace, it is not surprising that they would be at the forefront of the labor demonstrations and daily picketing in 1930s San Antonio. Emma Tenayuca and a small group of labor and community activists took up the cause of the beleaguered Mexicans. For years, a handful of dedicated men and women had been attempting to organize Mexican workers in Texas. Their importance rested not only in their organizing abilities but also in their ties to local communities. For instance, Juan Peña had spent the twenties working with south Texas Mexican coal miners and had acquired a fundamental understanding of radical labor politics. Emma Tenayuca's growing radical leanings and her challenge of the established racial and social order would have repercussions leading to her denunciation as a communist by city officials as well as attacks on her by the middle-class Mexican American community.[31]

As noted, Tenayuca's first encounter with labor organizing occurred in 1933, when several hundred San Antonio women cigar workers walked out of the Finck Cigar Company, demanding increased pay, better working conditions, and union recognition. She saw the police swiftly break up the picket lines and arrest their adversaries, hauling the protesting women to jail in paddy wagons deftly dubbed "Black Marías" for the prostitutes who earned their living near the Plaza. Prostitution was part of the vice perpetuated by poverty from which San Antonio police profited. Sixteen-year-old Emma Tenayuca went to jail with the strikers the second time police arrested them for protesting against discriminatory wage rates and bad working conditions. The Tejana high school student had joined the labor movement. The following year, Tenayuca helped organize Mexican garment workers when the women struck Dorothy Frocks, an infant and children's wear company. Impressed with Tenayuca's leadership abilities, Tejana workingwomen in their newfound militancy now looked to her for leadership, and she complied. Tenayuca's visible and active presence and her refusal to be intimidated soon earned her a reputation on the West Side as a devoted organizer, and she often heard, "Here comes the little girl who confronts men," when she walked down the working-class streets.[32]

The ILGWU launched another drive to organize San Antonio's infants' garment workers in the spring of 1938. The main worker grievance was homework. Embroidery workers affiliated with Local 180 struck the Shirlee Frock Company and set up pickets around the factory. Fifty strikers were arrested. A court injunction against the ILGWU restricted picketing to no more than three persons and prohibited the use of banners. The marked militancy of the Mexican infant wear workers impressed ILGWU leaders Myrle Zappone and Rebecca Taylor. According to Zappone, "the Mexican workers really stick during trouble. The workers say that they cannot attend meetings but they will come out if a strike is called." The extent of the rank-and-file militancy visible during the Texas Infants Dress Company strike was noted by the *Houston Chronicle*:

> Violence flared in the Texas Infants Dress Co. strike here Thursday afternoon when two young women employees were set upon and beaten. Mrs. Nieves Carrillo, 35, suffered the loss of three teeth, face bruises, and her clothing torn. Mrs. Josefa Alvarez, 39, received bruises and scratches and clothing was torn. The attack in which three other women were the aggressors took place several blocks from the factory as the two victims were returning from lunch, according to J. Nedler, Manager of the factory.[33]

After three months, the Shirlee Frock Company signed a contract. It recognized the union shop and increased wages to twenty cents per hour. The ILGWU strike against the Texas Infants Dress Company resulted in an NLRB ruling favorable to the ILGWU. The contract signed between the union and management recognized the ILGWU as the bargaining agent and set a minimum wage of twenty cents an hour. Three other companies signed similar contracts establishing ILGWU Local 347 as the bargaining agent. Apparently the ILGWU had invested both time and money in support of the garment workers of San Antonio, knowing that the union movement would fail if it relied only on the local garment workers, who could ill afford the cost of a sustained organizing drive because of their low wages. Rebecca Taylor remarked: "The ILGWU in San Antonio is really the only militant union among the Mexican workers. It had the backing of a powerful and wealthy International. No union can survive and do anything on the wages of the Mexican workers."[34]

Recently graduated from Breckinridge High School, Emma Tenayuca played a leading role in forming locals of the ILGWU in San Antonio, despite repeatedly hearing ILGWU organizers make disparaging remarks about the Mexican women. Tenayuca worked with W. H. Ernst and Myrle Zappone, who were well-liked and respected local women labor activists. However, Tenayuca and ILGWU representative Rebecca Taylor had countless disagreements. Tenayuca disliked Taylor because this daughter of wealthy Texans did little work on behalf of the needleworkers, and because Taylor openly expressed her contempt for Mexicans.[35]

Another important undertaking for Emma Tenayuca was battling the repressive political machine of Mayor C. K. Quinn and Chief of Police Owen W. Kilday that ran San Antonio. Poll taxes and citizenship requirements had disenfranchised most of the city's Mexicans, and by buying what remained of the Mexican vote, the political machine maintained its power. Quinn and Kilday colluded with employers in the exploitation and oppression of Mexicans. Fearing Mexican empowerment with the arrival of the labor movement, these city bosses employed force, violence, and Red-baiting to break any strike threat.[36]

Much of this hostility was directed at Emma Tenayuca, who was advocating community action in her determination to do something about the urban poverty in San Antonio's West Side. Here, compressed into a four-square-mile area, two-thirds of the city's 100,000 Tejanos lived in the nadir of wretchedness. Tenayuca's hometown had the worst slums in the United States and, because of rampant disease and malnutrition, the nation's highest tuberculosis and infant mortality rates. The continued influx of migrant families compounded the problems of overcrowding, poor health, and misery. Clearly, San Antonio's Mexican heritage existed only for tourist consumption. The Tejana teenager earnestly began her work with the West Side's voiceless and powerless Mexicans through the Unemployed Councils. As an Unemployed Council relief worker, Emma Tenayuca promptly introduced jobless Tejanos to organized social and economic protest.[37]

In 1935, as the secretary of the West Side Unemployed Council, Tenayuca held mass meetings to protest the elimination of thousands of Mexican families from the city's relief rolls. The next year she set up chapters of the Workers' Alliance of America following the merger of the Unemployed Councils with this organization. The Tejana activist devoted much of her time to the Workers' Alliance, eventually being elected the general secretary of at least ten chapters in San Antonio. Emphasizing issues pertinent to women and their families, Tenayuca appealed to the working-class Mexicans and Mexican Americans to join the progressive organization to ensure equitable distribution of WPA job and wage assignments and to improve the quality of food relief. Speaking for the Workers' Alliance, Tenayuca explicitly called for a revision of minimum wage guidelines to fifty cents an hour. A higher WPA wage scale existed for Anglos; while Mexicans averaged $21 per month, WPA wages for Anglos ranged as high as $75 a month. As noted, gender complicated this problem of wage disparity. Tenayuca helped Mexicans formulate other demands, such as the restoration of WPA projects and a thirty-hour workweek for unskilled labor. Mexicans also demanded that children of all relief recipients be furnished with clothing, school supplies, and free school lunches.[38]

Tenayuca launched a letter-writing and telegram campaign aimed at New Deal officials in Washington, cleverly timed to coincide with congressional appropriation decisions in June, and the Workers' Alliance activist completely immersed herself in the door-to-door, street-by-street organizing. At the instigation of the Workers' Alliance, a mass movement of working-class protest was emerging on San Antonio's West Side. Tenayuca affirmed this fomenting of the Mexican masses:

> There was a feeling here in San Antonio of activism. We built up an organization of workers that were out of work. Every day of the week we got them food, help, work. We would take the sons of workers over eighteen to the Tree Army [Civilian Conservation Corps] or the WPA to learn some kind of trade. We would take those who just came in from outside San Antonio to the WPA. We took Mexicans who couldn't speak English to the relief office. If they didn't get what they wanted, we would return.[39]

The small and frail Tejana sacrificed her health for the poverty-stricken Mexicans of the West Side. Without much sleep or food to sustain her, Tenayuca suffered from nervous exhaustion and became seriously ill with tuberculosis. Despite her failing health, Tenayuca daily confronted the San Antonio police force and the INS to protest their harsh suppression of workers' rights. Employers used the police and the INS to intimidate Mexican WPA workers and to discourage them from joining the Workers' Alliance.[40]

Figure 3.A. Emma Tenayuca exemplified the new leadership of the 1930s. Emma Tenayuca with other Tejanos protesting alleged beatings by U.S. Border Patrol, Federal Building, San Antonio, Texas, February 23, 1937. Enrique Perez, on Tenayuca's right, claims to be one of those beaten. (L-1540—Courtesy of the Institute of Texan Cultures at UTSA).

At the risk of confinement and deportation, Mexican workers nevertheless persisted in their organizing activities. Many were veterans of previous attempts to organize the pecan sheds or else had relatives who had taken part in the cigar and garment workers' strikes. Still others, like James and María Solís Sager, had participated in strikes in the Río Grande Valley called by the Texas Agricultural Workers Organizing Committee. Tenayuca made sure that undocumented Mexican workers would not be singled out for special harassment.[41]

Knowing she would face intimidation and arrest, Emma Tenayuca staged marches and demonstrations for the Workers' Alliance of America to protest the repatriation of Mexican-born workers engaged in union activities. This was a major accomplishment, given the scope of the repatriation program begun in Texas in 1928. Over one-fourth of the estimated half-million Mexicans repatriated during the Great Depression were from the Lone Star State, and nearly 10,000 of the repatriations after

1933 were concentrated in southwestern states like Texas with sizable Mexican populations. Through rousing speeches Tenayuca instilled confidence in the Mexicans, prodding them to organize. She repeatedly told them: "Even though you are not U.S. citizens, you have the right to join the union." Tenayuca worked to eliminate strikebreaking by Mexican nationals and led the campaign to unionize the pecan shellers. She left a lasting impression on Mexican workers, men and women who were not accustomed to seeing either a Mexican or a woman confronting the police over violations of civil rights.[42]

In 1937, Emma Tenayuca was appointed to the National Executive Committee of the Workers' Alliance, where she served with African American Frances Duty, the leader of the Harlem Workers' Alliance. The two appointments exemplified the attempts at multiracial solidarity by the Workers' Alliance and by the Communist-led mass-based movements. In June 1937, Tenayuca attended the Workers' Alliance convention in Milwaukee, where the Tejana supported a bill for relief work and a resolution against war and fascism. Clifford Odets's play *Waiting for Lefty* was staged for the delegates, and Tenayuca attended this agitprop theater performance about the New York taxi strike, which conveyed the emotion of actual participation in America's unfolding class struggle. It was at the Workers' Alliance convention that Tenayuca learned, probably from Mountain States delegates, of the bad treatment of Mexicans in Colorado, where the governor's declaration of martial law had led to the roundup and arrest of Mexican aliens and Mexican Americans. Tenayuca's thinking about class struggle was shifting as she rode the train home from the Workers' Alliance convention, and it was to connect the plight of San Antonio's Mexicans to that of other American workers and to international events.[43]

Under the dedicated leadership of twenty-year-old Emma Tenayuca, the Workers' Alliance of San Antonio now numbered fifteen city branches with 3,000 members, making it one of the strongest in the country. The Tejana's call for WPA relief workers to stage sit-ins and mass demonstrations against WPA cutbacks and racist relief policies created trouble for her with city officials. They were outraged that evil communism now exerted its influence on Emma Tenayuca's thinking, as was reflected increasingly in the tone of her organizational activities. Red-baiting became a potent and racist weapon in Texas and in San Antonio, as it seriously undermined community activism and labor insurgency. It was a tactic effectively used to isolate Tenayuca from the workers. Moreover, anticommunism became a weapon that city officials could use to repress Mexicans, thereby gaining public favor and winning votes.[44]

The Texas Communist Party was quite small. Nevertheless, communists and communist sympathizers from the National Maritime Union,

Locals 227 and 336 of the Oil Workers Industrial Union, the all-Tejano Local 412 of Mine-Mill of Laredo, and the Texas labor movement exerted considerable control over the Texas State CIO Council from its formation in 1937 until the German invasion of the Soviet Union in the summer of 1941. Communists had been active in San Antonio since 1930. In 1937, there were 409 members, and by the following year membership had grown to only 500, essentially a smattering of college students, professionals, workers in CIO locals, and poor and jobless Tejanos and blacks. Forty communists were active in San Antonio. Jewish immigrants formed the mostly ethnic membership of the party in this city. (Tenayuca stated that the communist meetings she attended were often conducted in Yiddish, until the presence of non-Jewish members was recognized.) In 1937, Tenayuca joined the Communist Party and married fellow communist Homer Brooks, whose influence drew her deeper into the party. The Tejana would be ostracized because of her political affiliation and for crossing the acknowledged social barrier of race through her marriage to Homer Brooks. Known in local Communist Party circles as the "Blue-eyed Boy," Brooks had established a reputation as an indefatigable organizer. The party had sent him to Texas as part of its southern strategy to recruit and support new members. Homer Brooks's effectiveness was confirmed when he was appointed secretary of the Texas Communist Party.[45]

Emma Tenayuca and other Workers' Alliance organizers continued to stage protests against relief conditions and the abuse of Mexican-born workers. A considerable degree of apprehension now gripped the political leadership of San Antonio; city officials feared that the Workers' Alliance headed by the notorious rabble-rouser Emma Tenayuca posed a genuine challenge to domestic peace. Suspecting that communist agitators were inciting Mexicans to revolt, Police Chief Owen Kilday stepped up his attacks on the Workers' Alliance. On June 29, 1937, Kilday led a police raid on the Workers' Alliance hall. Police armed with axes wrecked the meeting place, confiscated literature, and arrested Tenayuca and five Workers' Alliance grievance committee members on charges of unlawful assembly and disturbing the peace. When hundreds of angry Alliance members protested the arrests, Kilday seized the opportunity to smear Tenayuca as a communist subversive. The police chief boasted that the material captured in the police raid "just proves my former contention that the Tenayuca woman is a paid agitator sent here to stir up trouble among the ignorant Mexican workers." The presiding judge, W. W. McCrory, had little sympathy for Tenayuca and added his voice to the condemnation of the Tejana radical plotting revolution. When Tenayuca's attorney presented her petition for release from jail, the judge angrily shouted back at him: "She belongs in jail, let her stay there. She's been raising too much hell around here anyhow.... She's nothing but a damned Communist and ought to be sent to Russia." Released from jail and ever defiant, Tenayuca swore she would continue her activities on behalf of the Mexicans by visiting the WPA offices again. Her next opportunity would come during the pecan shellers' strike.[46]

"THE CIO DOESN'T EXIST HERE": THE 1938 PECAN SHELLERS' STRIKE

Forty percent of the nation's pecans came from Texas. The Southern Pecan Company, owned by "Pecan King" Julius Seligmann, shelled 15 million pounds of pecans a year, valued at more than $1 million. The machine shelling of pecans was phased out in 1926, when the process was converted to less expensive handwork. Working on a contract basis under sweatshop conditions in sheds that had poor ventilation and lighting and lacked inside flush toilets and running water, approximately 12,000 Tejanos shelled pecans during the season that ran from November to March. Women made up over 90 percent of this poorly paid and highly seasonal workforce. The pecan shelling was performed in 400 work sheds scattered throughout the West Side's working-class neighborhoods. A Mexican family earned five to six cents per pound for shelled pecans and averaged $1 to $4 for a fifty-one-hour workweek, or $192 annually, the lowest wages in the nation. Pay was frequently in food; the impoverished workers of the Southern Pecan Shelling Company received meager allotments of coffee, flour, rice, or beans for their week's work, drawn from the company commissary. With the onset of the Depression, the already abysmally low wages of pecan shellers plummeted further, from $2 per week to sixteen cents per week. Discriminatory New Deal policies multiplied the severe problems workers faced. San Antonio's pecan-shelling industry was considered an agricultural enterprise; therefore, employers like Julius Seligmann refused to recognize government codes that fixed pay scales at a higher rate. The local labor force mushroomed with the arrival of jobless farm workers desperate for work. Out of work, Mexicans had no alternative but relief.[47]

San Antonio's Mexican pecan shellers first walked out in 1934 during the wave of ILGWU organizing in the city to protest low wages, but the strike was settled through arbitration. The issues of meager wages and unfair labor practices remained unresolved for almost four years. A wage reduction coupled with the economic recession of 1937 seriously worsened the shellers' plight. Across Texas, relief rolls dropped precipitously—from 1.2 million to 46,616—and the first to be discontinued were Mexican clients. A workers' tempest was brewing in San Antonio's West

Side as the sentiment for change became widespread. The organizational groundwork for the upcoming battle had been put in place by Emma Tenayuca and other key Workers' Alliance members and by the chartering of the Texas Pecan Shelling Workers Union by UCAPAWA. Hard lessons had been learned from the previous strikes. Only through collective action, Emma Tenayuca exhorted, would the workers achieve victory, and she urged them to walk out. Militancy spread quickly through the crowds of pecan shellers; their ranks increased with the steady arrival of migrant families being pushed out of the Río Grande Valley by low wages and crops destroyed by an early frost.[48]

On Monday, January 31, 1938, between 6,000 and 8,000 workers from 170 of the small pecan-shelling plants walked out in a spontaneous protest against a 15 percent pay cut, bad working conditions, and the notorious homework. Linked by the strong bonds of kinship and community, the pecan shellers collectively prepared to challenge employer abuse through picketing and demonstrations. Each confrontation swelled the size of the crowds, producing fear of a mass uprising. Tenayuca was a major voice calling for the walkout, convincing the pecan shellers that it was in their best interest to strike to gain higher pay and better working conditions. The workers responded and joined the picket lines. Many were Workers' Alliance members; unfailing in their support of the popular and capable community organizer, they unanimously elected Tenayuca honorary strike leader. Tenayuca's foes thought otherwise. The police quickly arrested the Tejana and several UCAPAWA organizers on charges of communist agitation.[49]

While Tenayuca sat in jail, demonstrations took place at nearby parks, including downtown Milam Plaza, and workers on the West Side held meetings in lots next to the pecan-shelling sheds. Women formed the majority of strikers, just as they composed a significant proportion of the membership of the Workers' Alliance. The strike brought many women out of their homes for the first time in their lives as active participants in a labor struggle. Adapting to their new role as strikers, the empowered women persuaded husbands and children to come to the rallies so they could be educated about the issues. The strike's Mexican leadership reflected a diverse range of men and women activists that included various *mutualistas*, ex-Magónistas, socialists, and communists. Stirred to action, these ardent crusaders gave the strike a voice Mexican workers could identify with. The organizers were not outsiders—like Emma Tenayuca, they were Mexicans and Tejanos from the local West Side barrio and included María Solís Sager, Minnie Rendón, and Willie González. The Mexican and Tejano leaders all but called for a class war as the labor situation intensified in San Antonio. Support for the striking pecan shell-

Figure 3.B. Emma Tenayuca joined the Communist Party in the thirties because it sought to eliminate racial barriers. Emma Tenayuca addressing a rally on the steps of the San Antonio City Hall, San Antonio, Texas, 1938. (L-1541—Courtesy of the Institute of Texan Cultures at UTSA).

ers also came from across the border, from Vicente Lombardo Toledano's Confederación de Trabajadores Mexicanos.[50]

The Mexican Communist Party was prodding the CPUSA to take up the problems of Mexican workers within its borders. Mexico's Communist Party had similarly pushed the CTM to take the initiative in a joint organization effort with the CIO. The CTM had supported the militant labor uprisings in south Texas, and its union work extended outside the Southwest. A CTM delegation had attended a May Day celebration held in Nuevo Laredo to commemorate both the Chicago Haymarket martyrs and U.S. recognition of Mexico's recent oil expropriation policies. An estimated 5,000 Mexicans met representatives of labor organizations on the international bridge linking Nuevo Laredo and Laredo. During the celebration, the Mexican confederation publicly praised the efforts of Tejano workers to establish their own branch of the CTM. As noted, the CTM trained Mexican American labor organizers at its El Colegio de

Obreros. CTM members helped educate their ill-informed American counterparts about the plight of Mexicans, lecturing them about doing more to benefit the growing Spanish-speaking population. In 1940, Mexican delegates attended the Second Congress of the CTM, held in San Antonio. One of the guests was Gilfredo Serna, a leader from the Nuevo Laredo CTM, which had close relations with Texas labor organizations. The following year the Mexican CTM also sent a representative to the Third Congress of the CTM, held in Austin. The CTM was concerned with the welfare of its Mexican American compatriots, who invariably lost jobs to Anglo workers and were dropped from relief rolls. More important, the CTM cooperated with CIO locals along the border to curtail further immigration from Mexico.[51]

The pecan sheller labor disturbance amplified the already strong anti-Mexican sentiment in San Antonio. The purportedly large communist element involved was particularly distressing to Anglo and Mexican American class interests and to the Catholic Church. The city's two biggest newspapers, the *San Antonio Light* and the *San Antonio Express*, assailed anyone who lent support to the strike. The timid and relatively weak middle-class Mexican American establishment was represented by the conservative League of United Latin American Citizens. This self-serving, "loyal and patriotic" Mexican American organization sympathized with the pecan shellers' deplorable working conditions and dismal wages but, along with the Mexican Chamber of Commerce and the Catholic archbishop of San Antonio, condemned the strike because of its Red leadership. LULAC unfortunately supported the repatriation campaigns by the U.S. Border Patrol and called for the suppression of the pecan shellers' strike by the police. The Catholic Church's involvement in the strike grew out of its paternalism toward Mexicans but was ultimately driven by the fanatical desire to battle the communist influences threatening to seize the union drive's leadership and objectives. While embracing labor's cause, the Catholic Church also vilified the CIO for allowing godless communists into its leadership ranks.[52]

By 1938, the Catholic Church, through the auspices of the archbishop, was advocating strong adherence to the principles of Americanism, Catholicism, and an extreme brand of anticommunism. At the end of the first week of the strike, the church's focus was on control of the strike by communists. Atheistic communism posed a very real threat, considering the fate of the church in Mexico and the civil war in Spain. The Catholic Church would assure the well-being of its Mexican flock by endeavoring to prevent the spread of communism among its Spanish-speaking parishioners, who numbered 100,000 souls in San Antonio. The church was determined not to let Mexicans fall for the Red menace's "lying promises that through communism all their ills will come to an end and an earthly

paradise will be established for them." In addition to battling communism, priests worried about the erosion of their paternalistic influence and
control over Mexican Catholics. The interference of a Mexican woman,
an admitted communist, in the entrenched patriarchal power structure
particularly appalled the good fathers. Beyond offering a prayer that living conditions would improve for the pecan shellers, the church's involv-
ment in the strike consisted of efforts to dislodge dangerous radicals like
Emma Tenayuca, to stifle her voice in the community, and to restore the
church's power over the Mexican parishioners' lives. Like LULAC, the
church would not support the strike until its leaders signed a statement
renouncing communism. Every effort therefore was made to discourage
the workers from joining the Red union UCAPAWA, including smearing
the jailed Emma Tenayuca.[53] These harsh sentiments were shared by a
small group of Mexican Catholics who resented Tenayuca for overstep-
ping the traditional boundary governing the behavior of Mexicans—not
to challenge the rule of discrimination. The men viciously denounced the
Tejana radical in the pages of their Catholic newspaper, *La Voz*. They
angrily warned their readers:

> In the midst of this community exists a woman by the name of Emma
> Tenayuca who wants to spread disorder and hatred. This woman has
> all the appearances of a communist. . . . Don't give your names to her
> when she comes around to solicit them. Warn people when she comes
> around. Mrs. Tenayuca de Brooks is not a Mexican, she is a Rusofile
> [*sic*], sold out to Russia, communist. If she were a Mexican she would
> not be doing this type of work.[54]

Tenayuca's grandfather had taught her that it was her moral duty to
fight against racial and class injustice, and in this respect the Tejana social
activist disagreed with the sheepish LULAC and its accommodationist
politics. Given her great affection for San Antonio's poor Mexicans and
the selfless work she did on their behalf, it was the church and the West
Side's devout Mexican Catholics, and not Emma Tenayuca, who clearly
had forgotten Jesus Christ's teachings.

The police released Tenayuca, and she resumed her work with the strikers. The San Antonio branch of the progressive Women's International
League for Peace and Freedom (WILPF) had supported Tenayuca's work
among the city's West Side Mexicans before the strike and now set up
soup kitchens and declared a nationwide protest against the excessive
police violence. Formerly the Women's Peace Party, a pacifist group opposed to war and militarism founded in 1915, WILPF attempted to solicit
funds for the strikers, but the San Antonio Vigilance Committee stopped
the campaign. Such actions by WILPF obviously posed a threat to class
interests in San Antonio. Field representatives of the national CIO had

taken an interest in the strike, as had those of UCAPAWA who arrived in San Antonio several months earlier. The CIO took charge as soon as its field representatives entered the local scene, even though they were promptly arrested by San Antonio police. The UCAPAWA unionists who helped in the strike included Clyde Johnson, James Sager, and John Beasley, veteran labor organizers of the union drives by, respectively, black workers in the South, Mexican onion workers in south Texas, and Mexican beet workers in Colorado. Rank-and-file leadership remained in the hands of local West Side Mexicans, who had already been organized by Emma Tenayuca's Workers' Alliance. UCAPAWA moved to settle the labor dispute through arbitration. Meanwhile, the strike spread.[55]

Predictably, the Texas AFL and its locals disapproved of the picketing by Mexicans and in various labor newspapers branded the CIO leadership as communist agitators. The CTM's efforts the previous year to gain agreement from the AFL state federation for the admission of Mexicans to local affiliates had apparently been ignored. UCAPAWA and the CPUSA's open practice of racial unity within union organizing was strongly looked down upon and resisted in Texas, which, as noted, displayed many of the South's Jim Crow habits of race hatred and discrimination.[56] Most of organized labor's criticism of and contempt for radical agitation was then directed at Emma Tenayuca, who was bringing the race issue out into the open by calling for the unionization of Mexicans. Typical of the indictments was the following excerpt from the *Houston Labor Journal*: "These . . . mostly Mexican [workers] were organized into a CIO local of the cannery workers by the communistic organizer Emma Tenayuca. . . . This is another incident of a communist as a leader of what is supposed to be an American labor union."[57]

In Texas, race would undermine gender alliances between most Anglo and Mexican women. In its efforts to crush the communist plot, the Texas AFL had an ally in Rebecca Taylor of the International Ladies' Garment Workers' Union. The bigoted ILGWU leader, though a fellow Texan, had little rapport with San Antonio's Mexicana workers. She remained outspoken in her criticism of Tenayuca's radical beliefs, thereby fueling organized labor's suspicions regarding Tenayuca's actual intentions. Rebecca Taylor's indictment of Emma Tenayuca, on the other hand, further alienated the Mexican pecan shellers, who, deeply devoted to and protective of their community leader, became even more wary of the Anglo ILGWU representative, who they rightly believed was a stooge for the police. Concerned with UCAPAWA's communist ties and needing to regain and align public support, the Texas State CIO Council sent its own representatives to San Antonio to stay apprised of developments and provide assistance. This move reflected the new measure of labor strategy as the CIO expanded. Collective bargaining was replacing the militancy of confrontation and the wide scope of issues that characterized the early strikes Emma Tenayuca had been a part of. This shift would ultimately affect the Tejana's capacity and effectiveness as a female community organizer.[58]

Homer Brooks, who had taken initial control of strike operations, did not hide his Communist Party affiliation. In his distinct role as a party functionary, Brooks's primary concern was forming and maintaining cells. According to one former strike participant, the dogmatic Brooks "would give the pecan shellers . . . lectures on the Communist party . . . and the great things the Party had done in Russia. . . . There would be a meeting in the morning . . . at eight o'clock, and Brooks would still be lecturing at eleven o'clock with no strike business having transpired."[59] Brooks caused considerable consternation among the strikers when he removed all the strike leaders who had not officially identified with the Communist Party by signing a card and agreeing to come to the meetings. Brooks's marriage to Emma Tenayuca had no doubt gained him access to the West Side Mexican community. Privately, Tenayuca did not hide her disapproval of her husband's zealousness, which, despite reflecting her own radical tendencies, went against her dictates of how the strike should progress. The veteran Tejana organizer remained confident, however, that Mexican workers would dismiss much of her husband's communist propaganda in favor of issues that applied directly to their concerns.[60]

Political conflicts within the Communist Party periodically surfaced and in many instances lacked resolution and produced discord. Subservience to party directives and discipline prevailed. Notwithstanding UCAPAWA president Donald Henderson's own communist membership, the progressive federation dictated that its continued support was conditional on Emma Tenayuca (as well as other communists) not participating further in strike activities because too much attention had been focused on her open ties to communism. Tenayuca remembered that she was infuriated by this demand: "I organized that strike, led it, and then Don Henderson came in, a left winger. I was never consulted. I was given a paper to sign removing myself from the leadership of the strike so workers could get support of the people here." Headstrong, Tenayuca still held daily meetings, produced and distributed circulars, and sent strikers to picket lines.[61]

Big city politics did not maintain neutrality in the strike, as Chief of Police Kilday carried on a relentless campaign of harassment. In fact, Kilday was using the communist issue to break the strike. At the request of employers, city police kept the pecan-shelling plants open and protected those few workers who crossed the picket lines. Kilday repeatedly refused the striking pecan shellers the right to picket and remained firm in labeling the strike as an illegal action. Ever vigilant and believing he was protecting the West Side from a communist takeover, Kilday boosted morale among his forces with venomous anticommunist exhortations. On at least six occasions during the pecan shellers' walkout, strikers had confrontations with San Antonio police officers and more than a hundred firemen who served as an auxiliary police force. What unfolded in San Antonio was an unusual Mexican and Anglo confrontation—a 1930s version of the proverbial Mexican standoff.[62]

Following Emma Tenayuca's instructions, picket captains told the pecan shellers not to make eye contact with the hated police, and they ordered those strikers sick with tuberculosis not to spit. Both of these acts could be construed as violations of city ordinances and would result in arrests under this state of martial law. The picketers instead devised methods of resistance that exploited weaknesses in police surveillance and enforcement, including blowing out the tires of police cars by throwing tacks on the streets and vandalizing shipments of unshelled pecans. Police intensified the brutality to diffuse the working-class protest and break up their trade union organization. The strikers were warned by police, "The CIO doesn't exist here!" "You should not belong to an organization that tries to do anything for labor!" Men, women, and children were run down, dragged, clubbed, and kicked by hostile police, many officers armed with three-foot-long axe handles, in keeping with the notorious Texas style of justice when dealing with "bad Meskins." The police teargassed picketers on eight separate occasions, sending women and children running, their shrieks piercing the smoke-filled air. Police officers arrested hundreds of strikers without a warrant, charging them with obstructing sidewalks, drunkenness, and vagrancy, and dragged them off to jail. The INS joined in the fray and began arresting Mexicans. The government dragnet stopped only when the Mexican consul filed a formal protest. Women strikers went to jail accompanied by their children, who were also arrested in the sweeps. Because of rampant hunger, some shellers willingly went to jail to be fed. Once in jail, the strikers had their CIO buttons taken away, thrown to the floor, and stepped on by the jailers. When the incarcerated strikers protested against the overcrowded conditions, jail keepers turned fire hoses on them. Such acts of cruelty failed to break the strikers' spirits. At night, the jailed but jubilant strikers sang Spanish renditions of "We Shall Not Be Moved" and "Solidarity," and Mexican labor songs also poured out from the jails.[63]

Emma Tenayuca devoted much time and effort to helping feed the families of the jailed strikers, even after the latter were released. Tenayuca remained adamant about the union; repeatedly explaining to the Mexicans how their lives could be improved through unionization, she stuck to her message of direct action through organizing. San Antonio's West Side Mexicans filled the streets to hear Tenayuca angrily rail against the Southern Pecan Shelling Company and the city bosses, the open-air meetings drawing an average attendance of 5,000 pecan shellers.[64]

News that the pecan shellers' strike had assumed the dimensions of a popular uprising reached the capitol in Austin. The governor warned that he would call in the Texas Rangers and possibly the National Guard to restore order in San Antonio. The Texas Industrial Commission began public hearings of the strikers' grievances. At issue was the possible violation of civil rights as witness after witness testified before the commission about full-scale police repression. The police continued to blame the Workers' Alliance of America and Emma Tenayuca for the labor disturbance.[65]

In early 1938, Local 172 was recognized as the sole bargaining agent for the pecan workers. As a result of the strike, pecan workers gained a closed shop, wage increases, a checkoff system, and a grievance committee. However, the passage of the Fair Labor Standards Act resulted in a minimum wage of twenty-five cents per hour and the unemployment of 7,000 pecan workers. The UCAPAWA at first blamed this problem on the firings that took place after unionization. The cause, however, was the Fair Labor Standards Act, which provided for the minimum wage, prompting the pecan industry to return to mechanization. During this time, Local 172 was trying to force the smaller companies to comply with the Fair Labor Standards Act. The union picketed the Sunshine Pecan Shelling Company, the Ernesto Moran Company, and the Victor Ramirez plant, small firms that contracted with the Southern Pecan Shelling Company. To undermine Local 172, the Southern Pecan Shelling Company also tried to reestablish its company's union. No longer was off-season employment in the pecan-shelling sheds available to the stricken migrant farm workers in San Antonio. Moreover, because of their low wages, shellers who lost their jobs did not receive benefits under the Texas Unemployment Compensation Act. On November 29, 1939, with Christmas fast approaching, an unemployed Mexican pecan sheller sent the following request for aid on behalf of several dozen of his fellow jobless workers to the Works Progress Administration Headquarters in Washington, D.C.: "We the undersigned native-born citizens of the United States respectfully request that a week's work on WPA be given to us [so] that we may be able to give our families a decent meal on Christmas Eve. We are without employment since the shutdown of the pecan shelleries on the 24th of October. Altho [sic] we applied for unemployment benefits shortly after the shutdown of the shelleries, our claims were disapproved [because] our wages were so small that we were not entitled to the benefits under the Texas Unemployment Compensation Act." Famished, these men and women had to rely on charity from the CIO and the Catholic Church.[66]

The Southern Pecan Shelling Company was also conducting a union-busting campaign in the plants. In October 1939, company president Julius Seligmann signed a new contract with Local 172, raising wages to thirty cents an hour. However, Seligmann began hiring nonunion workers and later discharged sixty-nine union workers from two shops. This action prompted a walkout by 300 workers on November 8. Mayor Maury Maverick was asked to mediate, and the mayor's office soon resolved the strike in the union's favor. All workers who had walked out were to be reinstated; of the fired workers, the local believed it would be able to get about half rehired. The problem of speedups was essential to any future contracts, as Fair Labor Standards Act minimum production rates would help prevent speedups. In 1940, new contracts were signed containing the added provisions for the rehiring of the discharged workers and for morning and afternoon rest periods. The Southern Pecan Shelling Company remodeled its plant and installed new machinery, which increased production, prompting Local 172 to go on strike in 1941 for a wage increase. Picket lines went up on October 8. The union made its last offer of a two-and-one-half-cent increase until the company records could be audited to determine whether a nickel raise was feasible. The Southern Pecan Shelling Company rejected this offer, but the strike's final settlement granted the compromise increase to the workers.[67]

Despite the hardships and short-term strike gains and the waning of mass protest, Emma Tenayuca helped Mexicans achieve a sense of unparalleled confidence and group pride as racial minorities. Her efforts brought Tejana workers to the forefront of the demonstrations, marches, and picketing, as well as bringing the issues of wages, relief services, and civil rights to the attention of the public. At the beginning of the pecan shellers' walkout, just fifty women were union members. By the end of the strike, Tenayuca had helped increase their number in the pecan shellers' union to 10,000.[68] An important goal besides union organizing remained for Emma Tenayuca: to expound the communist philosophy of class struggle and its relation to the Mexicans of the Southwest. During the height of the pecan shellers' strike, Tenayuca and husband Homer Brooks had formulated and written a treatise on Mexicans and the question of nationalism. They provided the first discussion of the historical relationship of Mexican nationals to the Mexican American experience and how their shared, though distinct, commonalties shaped the social and cultural identity of the Spanish-speaking community of the Southwest.[69]

EDUCATING THE PARTY: EMMA TENAYUCA PENS "THE MEXICAN QUESTION IN THE SOUTHWEST"

As party members or sympathizers, Mexican Americans provided leadership for the jobless by heading marches on city halls; calling for an end to racial discrimination; engaging in union drives, land disputes, and relief bureau sit-ins; and rallying against discrimination in WPA cutbacks and New Deal programs. In the late 1930s, the CPUSA altered its organizing strategy from work among the unemployed to trade unionism, which placed a few Mexican Americans in positions as officers of some unions. The party's tactics likewise changed from mass confrontation and protest to electoral politics. This policy shift would cause Tenayuca to seek national office on the Communist Party ticket. She was the only Mexican American who held this distinction in the 1930s.[70]

In 1938, the Texas Communist Party, at its state convention in Houston, nominated Emma Tenayuca as its candidate for the U.S. Congress from San Antonio. The party nominated Homer Brooks as its candidate for governor, and the lieutenant governor's nomination went to black civil rights activist Cecil B. Robinet from Houston. This doomed multiracial ticket reflected the party leadership's advocacy of racial equality; however, it was nothing more than a symbolic gesture in the context of old Anglo Texan prejudice, a method of emphasizing the party's stance on race.[71]

Emma Tenayuca put practice into theory in 1939, when she co-authored, with Homer Brooks, "The Mexican Question in the Southwest." The polemic was valuable because the party had passed no resolutions regarding the right of Mexicans as an oppressed nation to self-determination. The Tenayuca-Brooks article was the first analysis of the issue of Mexican nationhood produced by a Mexican American party member. Not since 1915, when the irredentism program, El Plan de San Diego, was drawn up, had a member of the Spanish-speaking community of the Southwest raised the issue of nationhood in a radical form.[72]

"The Mexican Question in the Southwest" was conceived and written in a span of two weeks during the height of the pecan shellers' strike and was based on Tenayuca's interpretation of the Marxist concept of national minorities. It also reflected her extensive reading in Texas history and the firsthand knowledge she had gained of the experiences of the Tejano residents of Texas. With precision and clarity, Tenayuca and Brooks stated that the Southwest's Mexican Americans and Mexican nationals did not constitute a separate nation because they lacked "territorial and economic community," but they had faced the treatment "of a conquered people." Instead, Tenayuca and Brooks argued that the Spanish-speaking of the Southwest were one people who represented an oppressed working class, sharing a common history, culture, and language. Mexican Americans were a conquered population, the result of the Mexican War in the nineteenth century. Mexican nationals had entered the United States and served as exploited, unskilled workers. Racial, cultural, and political discrimination indissolubly bound all Mexicans. Nonetheless, according to Brooks and Tenayuca, the Spanish-speaking people of the Southwest did not represent an "oppressed national group" within the United States. Nor did Mexican Americans constitute a border segment of the nation of Mexico. Rather, the two communists argued that Mexican Americans and Mexicans historically had evolved separate communities in the Southwest. Though declaring Mexicans a separate ethnic group that had been exploited as such, Tenayuca and Brooks explicitly added that the distinct Spanish-speaking communities were interconnected through a shared economic life and were linked to the Anglo working-class populations of the Southwest as a result of the region's economic and political integration with the rest of the United States. Liberation for Mexicans could come only through connection of their struggle with a wider movement, essentially with "the labor and democratic forces in the Anglo-American population." This would require that the party mandate consider the language and culture as well as the day-to-day needs of this oppressed racial minority and that it include eliminating the dual wage labor system, preventing confiscation of small landholdings, promoting bilingualism in the public schools, and eradicating Jim Crow segregation (connected to the "Negro" struggle) and political repression through a revision of government regulations regarding citizenship.[73]

Moreover, Tenayuca and Brooks emphasized the parallels to inter-American economic relations, arguing that "the treatment accorded Mexicans is a carryover to the United States of Wall Street's imperialist exploitation of Latin America." The two left-wing activists asserted that "The task now is to build the democratic front among the Mexican masses through unifying them on the basis of specific needs and in support of the social and economic measures of the New Deal." As "a significant beginning in this direction," Tenayuca and Brooks applauded the "First Congress of the Mexican and Spanish-American People."[74]

The Tenayuca-Brooks article was printed in the *Communist*, a journal devoted principally to addressing the finer theoretical points of party strategy for an intellectual audience well versed in Marxist philosophy. It is doubtful that large numbers of Mexicans had access to Tenayuca and Brooks's important formulations or that Tenayuca had articulated these tenets to the working masses of San Antonio. Probably the aim of "The Mexican Question in the Southwest" was to educate the party about the Spanish-speaking of the Southwest, to explain the importance of expanding the work of the Communist Party in the direction of a Popular Front definition of an oppressed national minority who were an integral part of the American working classes. During this Popular Front period, the Communist Party was careful to avoid sectarianism as it promoted its "unity against fascism." It therefore undertook extra efforts to improve and expand its influence and membership among mostly second-

generation Americans, like Mexican Americans, to rally support for Soviet Russia as war loomed over Europe.[75]

"PUSHING BACK THE RED TIDE": THE DOWNFALL
OF EMMA TENAYUCA

Tenayuca's fate was inextricably tied to national Communist Party policy.
The party's declining militancy, its emphasis on international relations,
and its efforts to become part of the lobbying and electoral mainstream
placed many of the local issues the Tejana had embraced in the background. On August 25, 1939, the Texas Communist Party planned to
hold its state convention in San Antonio. A staunch believer in civil rights,
Maury Maverick, the new city mayor, gave Emma Tenayuca permission
to use the city auditorium on behalf of the Communist Party. Tenayuca
and Maverick were friends, and she was giving behind-the-scenes support
to his reelection. Local 172 had campaigned for Maverick because it
viewed his victory as a victory for the pecan workers. The Catholic archbishop immediately filed a statement protesting the city's decision to agree
to "a bold and brazen harangue of Communism from the platform of our
auditorium." Other area churches and veterans' groups registered their
own strong protests against the upcoming conference. In the wake of the
anticommunist hysteria in San Antonio, Tenayuca and fellow party member and Texan Elizabeth Benson decided not to hold the meeting. Homer
Brooks, recently returned from the party's district headquarters in Houston, decided otherwise. The timing could not have been worse. A near riot
ensued that night at San Antonio's Municipal Auditorium as the Texas
Communist Party convened its meeting. A furious, rock-throwing mob of
5,000 stopped the talk. Acting in the name of Americanism, the unruly
crowd destroyed public property and battled police on the pretext that
they were defending the Constitution against a Moscow conspiracy. As
the angry swarm wrecked the auditorium, police escorted Emma Tenayuca, Homer Brooks, and the rest of the rally participants out of the building. That night the "one hundred percent Americanism" of San Antonio's
citizens pushed back the red tide of communism. The ousted city machine
used this highly controversial event to regain control of San Antonio and
to finally bring about the downfall of Emma Tenayuca.[76]

What proved most destructive to the Tejana's credibility was the announcement that the Soviet Union and Nazi Germany had signed a nonag-
gression pact, ushering in the German invasion of Poland and the start of
World War II. Homer Brooks, in keeping with his autocratic tendencies,
never showed Tenayuca and other party members the telegram from the
CPUSA's National Executive Committee announcing the signing of the

pact and the start of the war. Tenayuca learned of the Nazi-Soviet pact from the newspapers. Like many devoted American communists who had consistently spoken out against the spread of fascism, Tenayuca was stunned by the news. "It was a very peculiar situation. I think every communist in the country was confused because a few days earlier [Earl] Browder had said Stalin would never do anything like that." It took the disenchanted Tejana several weeks to recover from the betrayal.[77]

Meanwhile, Tenayuca and Brooks separated. Homer Brooks was eventually arrested for draft evasion. When the Soviet Union entered the war, the National Executive Committee of the Communist Party expelled Brooks. Disillusioned, Tenayuca quit the party. More important, she could not uphold the party's stance that World War II was an imperialist conflict because one of her brothers was in the army and tens of thousands of Tejanos were entering the military. Tenayuca found herself isolated and without friends. Ostracized for her recent activities, Tenayuca was unable to find work in San Antonio. A Jewish garment manufacturer of U.S. Army officer uniforms who had sympathized with Tenayuca's community work finally gave her a job as a secretary and bookkeeper.[78]

Emma Tenayuca, like other party members, had trusted that Soviet leaders knew what they were doing when they dictated what was best for American communists. The Tejana learned the hard lesson that Marxist doctrine and unwavering allegiance to party principles counted more than promoting the welfare of Mexican workers. The actions of her ex-husband, Homer Brooks, emphasized this quandary. Tenayuca had been subjected to condemnation by city officials, church leaders, and members of the San Antonio Mexican community for the left-wing views she espoused. It was a cruel blow to Tenayuca's dreams of the progress Mexicans could make with her help.[79] Emma Tenayuca's legacy is that she challenged an important enterprise, the power structure of San Antonio city government, called for equal pay for equal work in an era of wage differentials, and articulated the integral issue of Mexican American identity. Tenayuca never lost her courage or convictions. The fearless Tejana became a key catalyst for subsequent worker actions by Mexicans in Texas and the rest of the Southwest.

With the exception of the aforementioned activity in 1937 in the Río Grande Valley and the subsequent pecan shellers' strike in San Antonio, UCAPAWA organizing in Texas virtually ceased. Organizing agricultural unions was no longer a UCAPAWA priority. UCAPAWA's failure in Texas was attributed to the scattering of the migrant workers, the fact that many of the organizers feared suppression and deportation, and widespread antiunionism.[80] Meanwhile, the protracted struggle for union recognition continued among Spanish-speaking beet workers in Colorado.

Left Behind: UCAPAWA and Colorado's Mexican Sugar Beet Workers

In February 1935, delegates from twenty-five beet worker locals representing workers in Colorado, Nebraska, Montana, Wyoming, and South Dakota met in Fort Lupton, Colorado. The major issues for debate were wages, contracts, working conditions, and the formation of a national farm worker organization. Learning of the union drive, the sugar companies immediately put up opposition. This included seeking help from the Immigration and Naturalization Service to apprehend and punish Mexican beet workers. Federal agents soon launched a sweep of the farms and towns to round up dissident workers.[81] Despite the crackdown, organizing by sugar beet workers in the Mountain States continued on and off, scoring more losses than victories, and culminated in another convention in Denver in July 1937, from which emerged UCAPAWA. The goals of the Colorado workers were generally economic—wages of twenty-five dollars per acre, bonuses, guaranteed wage payments, and nonwithholding of wages. Attention was also devoted to the right to union negotiations, nondiscrimination in federal work relief hiring and employment, worker education, and adequate housing, drinking water, and garden plots.[82] Organizers kept up with pending legislation before Congress related to the sugar industry. In July 1937, Isaac Durán, president of the Agricultural Workers Union of Scottsbluff, Nebraska, sent a letter to President Roosevelt, urging him to sign the Sugar Bill. Duran informed the president that if sugar beet workers did not get this bill, it would put 7,000 beet laborers in the area out of work, and a large percentage of them would be forced to go on relief. The Mexican American unionist ended his letter by stating, "We have confidence in you that you wish to help the laboring class."[83]

About 12,300 sugar beet workers belonged to the UCAPAWA, most of them from the Mountain States. It was not an auspicious time for organizing; conditions for waging strikes were no longer favorable, as they had been at the beginning of the decade. A main impediment to unionism was the tremendous labor surplus in beet-growing areas. To prevent growers from further flooding the beet fields with excess labor by bringing out-of-state jobless workers into Colorado, UCAPAWA got the Workers' Alliance of America and La Liga Obrera de Habla Español to picket labor recruiting offices in New Mexico and west Texas and to persuade workers not to take the scab jobs. UCAPAWA was also prepared to prevent workers from northern Colorado from migrating to the Wyoming and Montana beet fields and to delay the layoffs of WPA relief workers that took place at the start of the beet harvests. UCAPAWA got support from the

Colorado State AFL, headed by Frank Hefferly from the UMWA. Hefferly, on the advice of John L. Lewis, ignored AFL president William Green, who instructed him to kick the CIO out of Colorado. Hefferly had also been contacted by the National Beet Growers Association (NBGA) about starting a rival union but refused. UCAPAWA's plans ran into further problems. Only a handful of growers agreed to negotiate directly with UCAPAWA while growers' associations stood firm against any talks. The main deterrent to collective bargaining was the Department of Agriculture, which now set minimum wages for beet work. UCAPAWA could only exert influence on wages indirectly by enforcing wage standards set by the agriculture secretary and by appearing at the public hearings held under the Sugar Act. The NBGA warned workers not to appear at the government hearings to testify, and it put more direct pressure on the Mexican American unionists by threatening to resort to intimidation and violence. The combative behavior of the Spanish-speaking beet workers had apparently aroused considerable anger: farmers were being deputized and given guns and ammunition. A last-minute settlement averted these preparations for civil war in the beet fields.[84]

In 1939, there were about 93,100 contract sugar beet laborers employed in the United States, and Mexican Americans made up over half (57 percent) of this beet labor force. The Sugar Act raised the per acre rate to about twenty-one dollars, but this was still two dollars below the pre-Depression rate. Moreover, the restrictions on child labor stipulated in the Sugar Act reduced a beet family's total earnings by one-third. The Sugar Act essentially penalized families because it did not compensate for the money lost through the elimination of child labor. Furthermore, Mexican American beet workers with CIO affiliation were refused contracts; the NBGA brought in over 1,000 workers from Texas, Arizona, and California as replacements; and the WPA forced Mexican Americans off work relief and into the beet fields regardless of their experience with farm work. In an attempt to stop this last policy, workers from Denver's Workers' Alliance of America and the UCAPAWA organized as the Spanish Defense Council (SDC). Protesting this policy, the SDC accused the Great Western Sugar Company of colluding with the WPA and the Colorado Employment Service in creating a condition of forced labor in the beet fields, since Great Western determined WPA job placement. In light of the general anti-Mexican environment in Colorado, the SDC also protested against the racial divisions in the state.[85]

In the Midwest, the sugar companies countered the activism of beet workers by recruiting additional workers from south Texas. This further enlarged the reserve beet labor force, cut wages to half their 1936 levels, and created animosities among Spanish-speaking workers thrown into competition for scarce relief. Organizing was hindered by the defeat of collective bargaining rights legislation for farm workers. As Devra Weber correctly notes, the federal government now dealt with farm workers by including them in legislation that initiated inquiries into working and living conditions. The war in Europe halted further legislative action on behalf of farm workers, and as a result their plight remained unchanged.[86]

The geographic center of Mexican American labor struggle shifted to Southern California, specifically to Los Angeles, since that city now had the largest Mexican population in the United States.

Shifting Gears: UCAPAWA Organizes Cannery and Food Processing Workers in California

The organization of California's migratory workers was imperative because they were an integral part of the state's highly integrated agricultural industries. The lessons of the recent past dictated that the agricultural union had to be industry-wide and statewide in scale to battle the powerful employer associations. The AFL built on the initial work of left-wing unionists from the National Committee for Unity of Agricultural and Rural Workers, which began unifying local farm labor unions to align them with organized workers of allied processing industries. State AFL participation in organizing activities in California was largely confined to granting union charters. By 1937, sixty thousand workers in California were covered by AFL-negotiated contracts.[87]

Organizational drives by California agricultural workers continued into 1936, but as the workers increased their activities, the growers stepped up their own efforts to suppress them. Four thousand Mexicans walked out of the orange orchards and packing plants outside Santa Ana in Orange County, but after seven weeks growers broke the strike by bringing in scab labor from Los Angeles. Mexican, Filipino, and Japanese American celery workers walked off the farms in Los Angeles and received assistance from truck drivers belonging to Chauffeurs and Truck Drivers Union Local 208, who refused to haul the produce. Raising the specter of class conflict, the strike triggered a reign of terror involving 1,500 deputy sheriffs, special guards, and the infamous Red Squad.[88]

Many Mexican families still left Los Angeles each year to harvest crops, but changes in relief guidelines were constricting the annual peregrinations. The WPA's Division of Social Research reported that 11,000 Mexican families in Los Angeles with two or more members received relief in 1936. California's Republican governor, Frank Merriman, reversed this by changing the eligibility requirements for assistance from the State Relief Administration (SRA). Under what was christened the "no work, no eat" policy, the governor directed that all persons fit for work, irrespective of experience, be removed from SRA relief if they refused farm work. Workers who stayed in Los Angeles during the off-season were cut from the relief rolls at harvest time and forced to take jobs in agriculture.[89]

In the recession year 1937, sixteen strikes involving 4,000 workers took place in California. UCAPAWA tripled the number of locals to 400, which included locals chartered by the Southern Tenant Farmers Union. As UCAPAWA shifted perceptively in the direction of organizing packing shed and cannery workers, it cut its organizing force to twenty-eight full-time organizers and as a result many UCAPAWA locals were run locally. In 1938, ten thousand pickers struck the San Joaquin Valley cotton district but lost. With an estimated 60,000 members, UCAPAWA was involved in a dozen of the forty agricultural strikes in 1938, including the one by Tejano pecan shellers in San Antonio, Texas. The following year, labor organizing in California intensified. Strike actions and work stoppages by farm workers unfolded throughout the Southwest as well. However, the course of the farm labor movement shifted inexorably in favor of the growers' associations.[90]

Having faced off with the Associated Farmers, the National Sugar Beet Association, and the National Canners Association, all steadfastly opposed to unionization, the CIO formally abandoned the organization of agricultural workers and now made the organizing of the cannery and food processing workers a matter of priority. The difficulties in organizing farm workers in California illustrated the great challenge. According to historian Cletus Daniel, the Associated Farmers furnished growers with a powerful weapon to fight unionism. The growers, the business community, the general public, and law enforcement agencies, it was observed, "seemingly rise as a body in opposition." The arrival of Anglo migrants from Oklahoma and Arkansas, combined with unemployment, led to deep wage cuts. Moreover, the influx of this white labor with its strong racist views failed to sustain interracial solidarity and further complicated the problems an existing labor surplus had created. Finally, the exclusion of agricultural workers from NLRA provisions allowed California growers to use antiunion schemes that were banned in other industries. Attention from organized labor focused more and more on unionizing the state's cannery and food processing workers.[91]

In Los Angeles, the California Sanitation Canning Company (Cal San) canned a variety of fruits and vegetables over a seven-month season with a workforce of 400 people. The majority of the cannery workers were Mexican women, who were paid on a piece-rate basis and averaged half the wages paid to Cal San's male workers. Arbitrary discharges for speaking Spanish and other abuses contributed to bad feelings inside the plant.[92] In 1937, Cal San workers were chartered as AFL No. 21,138, but dissatisfaction with the AFL led the cannery workers to seek assistance from the

CIO. In July 1939, after a three-week organizing drive led by veteran party member and UCAPAWA international vice president Dorothy Ray Healey, the workers were chartered as UCAPAWA Local 75. Left-wing labor activists like Healey were successful because they embraced the Popular Front viewpoint and represented themselves as links to ethnic communities and as steadfast advocates of racial equality. Healey was assisted by a core group of college students and Young Communist League members who worked in the plant during the summer and were actively involved in organizing. Notwithstanding, the organizing was borne by Cal San's Mexican women cannery workers dissatisfied with low wages and tired of ethnic and gender abuse. Contract negotiations broke down in August, and all but 30 of Cal San's 400 employees walked out. Organized into various committees, the workers began picketing. As the strike intensified, they received aid from community members, including several East Los Angeles grocers who had donated money to found the Congress of Spanish-Speaking Peoples (Peoples' Congress). The strikers demanded a wage increase, elimination of the piece-rate system, union recognition, and the dismissal of almost all the plant supervisors. The strikers knew they were taking a considerable risk because only one UCAPAWA local had won a contract.[93] Nonetheless, the strikers remained determined to achieve their goals and extended their activities by employing a secondary boycott of Cal San products. The Teamsters Union initially stated that it would honor the strike, but many of its members crossed the picket lines. This betrayal angered several women strikers, who retaliated by climbing onto the Cal San loading platforms and "depantsing" the Teamster truck drivers.[94]

Local 75 filed grievances with the NLRB against Cal San for refusing to bargain in good faith. The NLRB upheld these grievances, further raising the strikers' morale. Yet the strike, the secondary boycott, and favorable NLRB decisions failed to bring Cal San to the bargaining table. Deadlocked, the cannery workers initiated a twenty-four-hour picket by children at the homes of owners George and Joseph Shapiro. Caving in to community pressure, the Shapiros agreed to meet with Local 75's negotiating team, and this ended the strike. Three months later, Cal San signed a contract with Local 75. This victory allowed UCAPAWA to establish a foothold in the Los Angeles fruit and vegetable canning industry. Consolidation of Local 75 followed. At poststrike meetings, Dorothy Healey outlined election procedures and general union bylaws. The cannery workers who had led the strike were elected to every major post. UCAPAWA organizers Luke Hinman and Ted Rasmussen, who began an organizing drive at the California Walnut Growers' Association plant, replaced Healey. In late 1940, UCAPAWA representative Luisa Moreno took charge of Local 75.[95]

UCAPAWA's success in organizing Cal San was due to several factors. In addition to bad working conditions, low wages, and oppressive supervisors, the pro-union climate being nurtured by the CIO labor movement in Los Angeles influenced Cal San's workers to take action. New Deal labor legislation, the Public Contracts Act, and the California minimum wage laws also contributed to the rise of Local 75. Dorothy Healey played a critical role in the initial successes of Local 75, while Luisa Moreno's leadership extended the organizing drive to other food processing plants. The recruitment of minority workers and the promotion of local leadership by Healey and Moreno reflected the practice of democratic trade unionism. It was the creation of this solid nucleus of organizers and the involvement of workers in building UCAPAWA Local 75 that ultimately accounted for its success.[96]

Following the "March Inland" strategy of ILWU president Harry Bridges, and as part of the offensive by labor, UCAPAWA began a major union campaign in the food processing plants of Southern California in 1941. Women cannery workers were encouraged to take a leading role in unionization (women would hold more than 40 percent of all UCAPAWA shop steward positions). With aid from Cal San Local 75, Luisa Moreno, the newly elected vice president of the national UCAPAWA and the nation's leading Latina labor organizer, consolidated Local 92 at the California Walnut Growers' Association's two sorting plants, which employed a workforce of 500 women. The stimulus for the escalation in organizing came primarily from the workers, who had been carrying on a resistance movement inside the sorting plants against despotic supervisors. Previous employee agitation had twice forced management to shut down the sorting plants. The march inland was underway. Led by Moreno, Local 75 members initiated a union drive at the Royal Packing Company, the Glaser Nut Company, and Mission Pack. This action led to the formation of Local 3, the second-largest UCAPAWA union.[97] UCAPAWA Local 2 of Fullerton, the Citrus Workers Organizing Committee in the Riverside-Redlands area, and UCAPAWA Local 64 of San Diego made concrete gains. At Val Vita, California's largest cannery, the mostly female Mexican workforce was paid substandard wages and exploited by plant supervisors. Worker dissent triggered harsh reprisals. The repeated violence prompted protests from several local Spanish-speaking community organizations and the Mexican consul. An NLRB election in the fall of 1942 brought victory to Val Vita workers. In the meantime, workers at the Van Camp Seafood Company in San Diego organized Local 64 in May 1939 and one year later signed a contract, becoming one of California's leading UCAPAWA locals. Victory had not come easily. Union members faced an onslaught by the Ku Klux Klan, battling for white supremacy, and Red-baiting by conservative Spanish-speaking elements, since many Van Camp Seafood workers belonged to the Peoples' Congress. UCAPAWA international president Donald Henderson, who was also one of the founders of the Peoples' Congress, noted the importance this union placed on popularizing the conditions of black and Mexican American workers and organizing them as a way to improve their social and economic situation.[98] At UCAPAWA's second international conference, Henderson declared that the "International Office was sufficiently concerned with the conditions facing . . . the Negro people and the Mexican and Spanish American peoples." Henderson observed that both minority groups were deprived of civil rights, exploited to the point of starvation, kept in decayed housing, denied educational opportunities, and, in Henderson's view, "blocked from their own cultural development."[99]

Mexican women workers proved dedicated labor activists in the Southern California CIO drives. They represented their locals and were involved in the CIO's grassroots movement to register workers in support of Roosevelt and pro-union candidates on the Democratic Party ticket. Framing its appeal in ethnic terms complemented by New Deal rhetoric, the CIO held up the notion that political coalitions should include ethnic Americans of all nationalities.[100]

COLLECTIVE ACTION: MEXICAN AMERICAN CIO
UNIONISTS ORGANIZE LOS ANGELES

California Mexicans were being integrated into manufacturing jobs in the state's industries. According to a WPA survey, over three-fourths (77.5 percent) of Mexican male workers in Los Angeles worked at unskilled or semiskilled jobs, while more than four-fifths (85.4 percent) of the city's Mexican females held unskilled jobs. The WPA survey noted the concentration of this wage worker population in certain neighborhoods. Half lived in the Central, Boyle, and Belvedere districts, and the remainder lived in the Elysian, Vermont, Harbor, and Compton areas. Mexicans employed principally as farm laborers lived further out of the city limits in West Covina, Whittier, and Pomona.[101]

The CIO union movement was well under way in Los Angeles, and it took place in conjunction with an escalation of the larger CIO insurgency. The Los Angeles Industrial Council was set up as the central coordinating body for various CIO unions in the Los Angeles area. There were about 22,500 dues-paying CIO members, though as many as 50,000 workers claimed CIO affiliation. With a membership of 3,000, the ILGWU was a principal union and had established a closed shop in the making of ladies' dresses, coats, and other garments. The International Longshoremen's and Warehousemen's Union (ILWU), organized for warehousemen and truck drivers, was undertaking a major organizing drive of the wholesale drug companies. The Los Angeles drug industry prospered during the Depression through expansion into the big discount and high-volume drugstores. Consequently, drug industry workers now put in three times more hours on the job but received inadequate compensation. The paternalistic drug companies fired workers involved in union activities. Because of poor wages, the drug industry workers employed by Brunswig began organizing and joined the ILWU as Local 26 in the fall of 1937. The Steel Workers Organizing Committee (SWOC) was organizing various steel plants and had gained considerable strength. Making up the majority of workers in several foundries, Mexican Americans were elected as presidents of SWOC lodges at Continental Can, Bethlehem Steel, and Utility Steel and filed grievances on behalf of their membership for nonpromotion.[102] In December 1937, the CIO chartered the United Furniture Workers of America (UFWA), an action that brought furniture workers affiliated with AFL locals into its fold. Mexican Americans belonging to AFL upholsterers' and carpenters' locals endorsed the change to the CIO. In February 1938, members of AFL Carpenters' Local 1561 led by Ernest Marsh, Frank Lopez, Manuel García, and Oscar Castro voted to join the CIO-affiliated UFWA Local 576, despite attempts by AFL officials to stop this move through a year-long campaign of Red-baiting. Membership in Local 576 grew rapidly, and so did its militancy. Despite competition from the Teamsters Union, favored by Los Angeles employers, between 1937 and 1940 Mexican American workers from ILWU Local 26 organized the hardwire, paper, and waste material industries and the malling warehouses. In addition, Local 26 helped the CIO organize furniture plants, die-casting plants, molding plants, and metal-fabricating plants, as well as assisting affiliated unions in organizing clothing, oil, auto, electrical, mining, and rubber workers. By 1941, Local 26 had over 6,000 members. Its newly elected president, Bert Corona, signed twenty-six union contracts prior to his induction into the army in 1943. ILWU Local 26, UFWA Local 576, and UE Local 1421, all predominantly Mexican in membership, became three of the most active locals in the Los Angeles CIO Industrial Union Council.[103] The example of the union movement in Los Angeles demonstrates that most of the CIO advances, including those of UCAPAWA, occurred within an urban frame of reference. Nonetheless, in the 1930s Mexican Americans as a working people had forged a framework for collective action through the CIO.

The devastating events of the Great Depression ushered in important political and social developments and pressed Mexican Americans to join the CIO union movement. The CIO's organization of the basic industries brought in thousands of Spanish-speaking industrial workers, who benefited enormously from union membership. The CIO industrial unions and some AFL craft unions integrated Mexicans into the new multiethnic union movement. Time and again, Mexican American men and women proved their organizing abilities, determination, and commitment to labor's cause. Collective action brought higher wages and the promise of civil rights. This was an important development for first- and second-generation Mexican Americans, who sought integration into American life. They believed John L. Lewis and other labor leaders who asserted that the labor movement stood "for equality of treatment, opportunity, and participation irrespective of creed, color, or nationality."[104]

In response to the labor movement's gathering force, a new generation of Spanish-speaking leaders arose and mobilized Mexican workers behind the CIO. For example, in South Chicago, Refugio Martínez of the Packinghouse Workers Organizing Committee (PWOC), working through the Left-led Vincent Toledano Club, brought many Mexican meatpackers into PWOC. Indicative of the activities coordinated with the international struggle against fascism, an important Spanish-speaking organization was El Frente Popular Mexicano (the Mexican Popular Front). With ties to Mexico's CTM and with its goal the "social and economic betterment of the working classes," El Frente Popular was active in the Chicago labor movement and embraced issues pertinent to Mexican rank-and-file union members. Like Chicago's Guadalupe Marshall, Mexican women with roots in the working class participated in this democratic worker activism, with young women especially taking an active role in working for labor and civil rights.[105] In San Antonio, Emma Tenayuca, the leading Tejano labor and community activist, was the architect of victory in the pecan shellers' strike. Through her example and her writings, Tenayuca underscored the fact that consciousness could serve to mobilize class awareness among Mexicans in their struggles against the iron grip of oppression.

By the late 1930s, the CIO was reluctant or unwilling to confront racism in the workplace. As the Third Period line gave way to the Popular Front, communists likewise abandoned rank-and-file militancy and the commitment to fighting racism in favor of accommodation with the CIO. With Hitler's invasion of Russia, the party called on Mexican Americans to support the opening of a second front in Europe and to subordinate their demands for integration of the defense industries to aid the success of the war effort. As a consequence, Mexican Americans would fight against both employers and the unions for advancement.

The CIO drives and Popular Front activities nevertheless continued to occupy America's Spanish-speaking working classes as the decade of the 1930s ended. In 1938, Mexican American progressives joined together and with assistance from the party formed the Congress of Spanish-Speaking Peoples. The CIO industrial unionism movement influenced the Peoples' Congress, which recognized its importance for Mexican

American workers. The Peoples' Congress therefore made its highest priorities the support of industrial unionism, winning over the Mexican American people to the CIO, and bringing antiracist issues into the labor movement. The ongoing exposure to and immersion in unionism, combined with progressive politics shaped by major events at home and in Europe, were transformative. As an American people, Mexican American workers were prepared to carry on their struggles into the World War II years as supporters of civil rights, foes of fascism, and advocates of racial justice.

Advocates of Racial Democracy: Mexican American Workers Fight for Labor and Civil Rights in the Early World War II Years

> The CIO must do more than verbally protest this segregation. It must militantly fight against its practice.
> —ISADOR ARMENTA, ILWU Local 26

> We must keep away the terror of the laboring class, Fascism and Nazism.
> —JOSÉ JACOBS, Tejano labor and civil rights activist

THE COLOR LINE that separated racial minorities politically, socially, and economically from the rest of Americans was breached in the summer of 1941 by A. Philip Randolph and other black labor and civil rights leaders in their planned mass march on Washington, D.C., to protest discrimination in the defense industry and in the armed services. President Franklin D. Roosevelt yielded to this daring show of black defiance and signed Executive Order 8802, which set up the Fair Employment Practices Committee (FEPC) in order to maximize the use of manpower and productivity to facilitate the American war effort. The formation of the FEPC stirred Mexican Americans to secure their share of the jobs being created through rapid war mobilization. In principle, the FEPC assured that all workers would participate fully in the defense industries without the burden of discrimination based on race, creed, color, or national origin. In reality, the FEPC was underfunded, it lacked autonomy, and its enforcement authority remained weak and vague. Mexican American blue-collar workers in the end received far less from the FEPC than black workers, because federal action to remedy the inequities Mexican Americans suffered was linked to American foreign policy initiatives regarding Latin America. Specifically, public hearings on job and wage discrimination against Mexican American workers were canceled because of the government's fear that the finding of widespread discrimination would jeopardize its Good Neighbor Policy, the foundation of the wartime alliance of the United States with other nations of the Western Hemisphere. Of particular concern was the Bracero program, the contract labor program the United States was negotiating with Mexico. Because of foreign policy concerns, the U.S. government never fully addressed nor challenged the long-lived and extensive inequality in employment experienced by Mexican American workers in the Southwest.[1]

The restrictions on immigration imposed in the 1920s, along with the drawn-out hardships of the Great Depression, altered the makeup of the American working classes. For the same reasons that contributed to the growth of workplace and community activism among other men and women whose parents were foreign-born immigrants, Mexican Americans were taking on larger and more distinctive roles in rank-and-file and neighborhood militancy. They were educated, spoke English, voted, and contributed to the victories of Roosevelt and the CIO in the 1930s. Moreover, these second-generation American workers forming the new CIO working class did not back down from disagreements with their employers; they were more receptive to the call for unionism; and they engaged in alliances across ethnic and racial lines. Many CIO activists identified strongly with the labor and civil rights concerns of Mexican Americans. As advocates of racial democracy, they were guided by the principle that only a united working class in partnership with the federal government would overcome racial intolerance. Most important, the unionists fully understood that Mexican Americans were critical to union success in industries with racially mixed labor forces and where Mexicans represented the majority of workers. The CIO filed complaints of discrimination on behalf of Mexican Americans in its negotiations with employers, labor boards, and the federal government. CIO unions brought about worker understanding of federal standards and policies and of grievances arising from infringement of these measures. Unlike black workers, Mexican Americans did not have a national civil rights organization such as the Urban League that could serve as an alternative for organizational activity. This is important, given that legislation in Texas and California made labor organizing in these two states more difficult. Various newly created civil rights organizations therefore assisted Mexican Americans in reporting complaints of discrimination and in filing complaints of their own. Like black workers, Mexican workers transformed CIO membership drives and gained power in the course of refashioning them. In providing the CIO with lessons about the common relationship of labor and civil rights, Mexicans assured that the CIO's rhetoric against discrimination was matched with action.[2]

This chapter will take up the organizing campaign by the International Mine, Mill and Smelter Workers Union (hereafter referred to as Mine-Mill) of nonferrous metals workers in the Southwest, with a special focus on the four-year (1939–43) union drive in El Paso, Texas. The nonferrous metals industry suffered from oversupply and depressed prices, which resulted in cutbacks in production and employment. Disagreements among the copper industry operators prevented agreement on a fair NRA code. In the Southwest, acute unemployment and widespread deprivation now overshadowed long-existing wage differentials between this mining region and other regions. Against this backdrop and in the prevailing open-shop atmosphere, unionism in the nonferrous metals industry was nonexistent. For most of the 1930s, Mine-Mill was at a low ebb and membership declined. However, the collective bargaining provisions of the NIRA and the short-lived copper code buoyed Mine-Mill organizers, AFL representatives, and workers to restore provisional local unions at some southwestern mines and metal-processing refineries. Several obstacles stood in the way. The Mine-Mill union locals could not battle the oppression alone; the national organization was embroiled in infighting and in disputes with the AFL over industrial unionism, and it was in desperate search of financial security.[3]

Mexicans and Mexican Americans made up 50 to 60 percent of the 15,000 workers employed by Phelps Dodge, Nevada Consolidated, Anaconda, and the American Smelting and Refining Company, the employers that dominated the copper industry's mining camps and smelter towns in the Southwest. The miners and smelter workers were confined to common laborer positions with the lowest job classifications and wage scales, and the men lacked seniority provisions. Outside the workplace, the miners and smelter workers and their families faced persistent social and economic discrimination. There was little optimism that a successful labor movement headed by Mine-Mill could arise in the southwestern copper industry. The workforce was dispersed over a wide area in Arizona, New Mexico, and west Texas, insulated in most instances from other labor groups and employment opportunities, and subordinated to business and agricultural interests. Mine-Mill's efforts soon began to bear fruit. Tracing its origins to the old Western Federation of Miners, Mine-Mill possessed a history of rank-and-file militancy and solidarity that was embraced by the Southwest region's Spanish-speaking miners and smelter workers. Mine-Mill's brand of interracial unionism proved especially effective in cross-border alliances to build its locals because it drew on the long-standing conflict between aggrieved Spanish-speaking workers and the mining companies. Even in remote areas more subject to company domination and far removed from the emerging cross-border linkages, workers maintained a degree of solidarity. In the Clifton-Morenci area of Arizona, in Silver City, New Mexico, and elsewhere, bitter memories of the World War I strike repression remained vivid. Mine-Mill tapped a core of activism among Spanish-speaking miners, who also resented the social discrimination that mirrored the larger racial climate of the Southwest region.[4]

This chapter also considers the subject of the formation of the Congress of Spanish-Speaking Peoples (hereafter referred to as the Peoples' Congress). This Mexican American labor and civil rights organization was part of the Popular Front coalition of communists, socialists, and democratic segments in pursuit of common interests, namely, social reforms and alliances in support of the Soviet Union following the shift away from the "class against class" sectarianism that marked the Third Period. Many Anglo participants in the Popular Front were outspoken racial liberalists who worked diligently for the betterment of Mexicans. As war unfolded in Europe and Martin Dies's House Un-American Activities Committee hearings into subversive activity cast a pall over progressive causes in the United States, the Peoples' Congress defended the labor and civil rights of the Mexican and Mexican American people. A special focus of this chapter will be the antifascist struggle waged by the Peoples' Congress and its Popular Front allies against La Union Nacional Sinarquista. The clash between the Peoples' Congress and the Sinarquista elements, one of the high points in the history of Mexican Americans in the early World War II years, took place in Los Angeles. Los Angeles became a virtual ideological battleground, with fascism and communism locked in a struggle for the hearts and minds of the Mexicans of the city, as well as those of the Southwest and Midwest.

Executive Order 8802 and wartime labor needs promised new opportunities for the Spanish-speaking and black workers of the city of Los Angeles, but as will be seen in the final section of this chapter, they would have to fight for these opportunities because of job discrimination. In 1940, Mexicans made up nearly 10 percent of the 2,785,643 residents of Los Angeles County. Along with the widespread employer discrimination that marked this period of growing racial unrest, restrictions based on legal U.S. residency also barred an untold number of Mexican workers from wartime jobs. Job openings came about through a joint push by the CIO and community organizations promoting interracialism. Although Los Angeles's Mexican blue-collar workers belonged to AFL affiliates, they were especially active in CIO union locals, which were organizing through the Los Angeles CIO Industrial Union Council. Headed by Philip "Slim" Connelly, the Los Angeles CIO Industrial Union was a chief organization of the urban Popular Front. The Industrial Union Councils, as Michael Denning notes, organized strikes and other collective actions, partook in political campaigns, and favored civil rights and social democracy. Despite the new opportunities ushered in by the multiracial brand of industrial unionism spearheaded by the CIO unions, Mexican Americans and blacks were excluded from semiskilled and skilled work in the initial CIO contracts.[5]

Reports by various government branches nonetheless revealed that sufficient evidence existed for the claims that profascist propaganda exploited the persistent discrimination against Mexicans, blacks, and other minorities. The Minorities Group Service Commission of the Office of Production Management (OPM) conducted a survey of racial and ethnic discrimination in war industry centers. It concluded that because of ongoing employer discrimination, factories converting to war production discharged their black employees and that those war defense employers with closed shops refused to hire blacks and Mexicans, in many instances discouraging these workers from seeking employment at all. Moreover, government-funded vocational training schools were closed to minorities or admitted only those applicants with job offers. Guy T. Nunn, OPM Minorities Group Service Commission spokesman, stated that if blacks and Mexicans were hired in the aircraft plants in proportion to their numbers in the area, they would have 35,000 jobs. Instead, these two minority groups held just 1,500 jobs between them. As World War II unfolded, the CIO and the Communist Party exhorted their members to rally behind the war effort. These two ardent champions of civil rights now took on the role of custodians of patriotism. The CIO committed itself to its no-strike pledge for the duration of the war. The Communist Party endorsed this move. The CIO was no longer willing to push its white members in the direction of racial harmony, and after the signing of the Nazi-Soviet pact in 1939, the party was more straightforward on the matter of civil rights, for it abandoned work on behalf of racial equality at home. Meanwhile, blacks and Mexican Americans faced an escalation of racism and an onslaught of violence.[6]

INCLUSIVE UNIONISM: THE CASE OF MINE-MILL AND MEXICAN AMERICAN MINERS AND SMELTER WORKERS

Mine-Mill consisted of six chartered locals in Montana, Utah, Colorado, and California. None of these locals had established bargaining rights for its rank-and-file membership. In early August 1934, Mine-Mill won a strike in Montana against the Anaconda Copper Company, and it established additional local unions in Utah. At this time, Mine-Mill began a gradual expansion into the southwestern mining and processing centers in the face of a hostile antiunion environment. Mine-Mill was going to organize Mexican American mine workers employed in this mining region, much of it located in remote mountainous areas. This kind of ethnic and working-class isolation, as one scholar has noted, engendered unity and militancy even as it made possible social control. The besieged miners had organized in response to the mine operators' forming company unions to sidestep the NRA, as well as the long-standing grievances of low pay, perilous working conditions, and a very poor living environment.[7]

Historians have described the power wielded by the western mining companies. State and local governments were allied with the hard-rock companies. State legislators and mining industry heads served on government boards together and developed tax, welfare, and law enforcement policies favoring the metals industry. At the local level, the sheriff's departments, assisted by the state police and U.S. Immigration Bureau agents, controlled labor strife, immigration troubles, and actions by radicals. Many county deputy sheriffs were on the company payroll as guards; some peace officers had criminal records or were under indictment for committing serious offenses. These hired thugs mistreated union men and often beat them when making arrests. The western mining companies collected information on the union through a system of paid informers. Despite the NLRA ruling that forbade employer interference in the legitimate union campaigning of workers, these spies attended union meetings and reported on speeches and deliberations. The success of the infiltrators depended on whether or not the miners had a secrecy network of their own to protect against spies. Following a general pattern of surveillance, the western mining companies intercepted union telegrams, opened private mail, searched the homes of miners for incriminating documents, pressured miners whose relatives made trouble through the union, and likely contacted state agencies for information on unidentified vehicles or strangers on the streets. Moreover, the western mine companies exchanged information on union activity and obtained the criminal records of labor leaders for use against them. In essence, labor disputes were defeated before they started because the metals industry exercised total control. Still, the miners could not stand the hard conditions, and they walked out of the mines and smelters.[8] The collective effort on the part of Mexican mine workers to gain higher wages, improved working conditions, and union recognition fell to El Paso's Spanish-speaking smelter and metal refinery workers.

America's contribution to the war effort in Europe accelerated the union drive at home. Growing defense production boosted copper prices, labor demands, and soon wages as the United States mobilized for war and developed its defense program. Mine-Mill began a nationwide campaign to organize the workers of the dominant corporations, the brass-fabricating plants, the copper mines, and smelters of the "Big Five"— Anaconda, ASARCO, American Metals, Phelps Dodge, and Kennicott. With defense production expanding in the western mining areas, Mine-Mill president Reid Robinson encouraged the organizing drive and the extension of the union into southwestern copper. Like other Left-led CIO unions, Mine-Mill utilized Mexican Americans in its union movement.

For example, Leo Ortiz and Arturo Mata were full-time Mine-Mill staff members. Mata was from Morenci, Arizona, and was active in labor and civil rights organizations. During the World War I strikes, Mata had been deported to Mexico with his father, a labor leader. Humberto Silex, Ceferino Anchondo, Joe Chávez, and Juan Peña became organizers for Mine-Mill in El Paso. Mine-Mill leadership at this time also underwent a leftward shift because radicals from the CIO and the Communist Party were aiding in the organizing drive. Mine-Mill grew stronger as CIO contributions poured in and as membership rolls expanded.[9]

"A Society without Classes": Mine-Mill and CTM Undertake an Organizing Drive in El Paso

Mine-Mill leaders understood that mass unionization in the Southwest region would be impossible without the successful organization of Mexican American workers. In El Paso, cross-border relations between American and Mexican unions were facilitated by the urban industrial nexus of the Queen City and Ciudad Juárez. Organizing the area's workers nevertheless presented an imposing task. AFL organizer Clementino Idar had realized fifteen years earlier that it would be utterly futile to organize El Paso labor unless the workers in Ciudad Juárez were organized first. Racism kept most Mexicans out of the unions because very few Anglos broke racial ranks to promote biracial unionism. Mexicans who joined unions during strikes were blacklisted. El Paso's existing AFL affiliates had small numbers of Spanish-speaking members, and because racism permeated every aspect of society, these men probably belonged to segregated AFL locals. Labor activists questioned this craft-union connection with its solid anti-Mexican and antiradical tradition. Recognizing the need for a wider and more progressive base of support among the Spanish-speaking populations on both sides of the border, the Mine-Mill unionists turned to the Confederación de Trabajadores Mexicanos for assistance in stirring El Paso's smelter workers to action. In 1937, Mine-Mill sent a letter to the CTM promising assistance in its fight with ASARCO and alerting it to the likelihood of Mine-Mill's own strike throughout the Southwest. Mine-Mill's organizing drives along the Texas border got support from militant Tejano smelter workers from Laredo. In July, Juan Peña and the other Tejano foundry workers employed at Laredo's Antimony Foundry had organized as La Union de Trabajadores de la Fundición de Antimonio (the Foundry Workers Union) with help from the CIO, the Mexican consul, and the newly established CTM branch across the border in Nuevo Laredo. The members of the Foundry Workers Union voted for CIO affiliation and became Mine-Mill Local 422. Similar joint actions in local organizing by American and Mexican organizers were taking place elsewhere in Texas and in California.[10]

Mexican Americans and Mexicans made up the majority of the production and maintenance workers at the El Paso ASARCO smelter and at the Phelps Dodge refinery, where, like other Spanish-speaking mining and smelting workers, they faced both class and racial oppression. In the late 1930s, the mines and mills were integrated enough to remind Mexicans that white coworkers could easily take their jobs and segregated enough to cause whites to realize that their advantage could be taken away by the CIO. Eighty percent of ASARCO's 500 employees were Mexican Americans or Mexican nationals who belonged to an AFL-affiliated local. The men were low-wage common laborers, and the handful holding semiskilled positions were not paid for what the work entailed. All the men put in ten-hour days and seven-day weeks with no vacations. The work was dirty and hard. The men incurred a high incidence of burns, falls, and other job site injuries; the extensive discrimination included segregated bathrooms and showers; and the ASARCO workers were forced to buy supplies at the company store. Many workers and their families lived in Smeltertown, inhabiting dilapidated houses with poor sanitation located on company-leased land. Most of the men could not afford to live in the recently built New Deal housing projects in El Paso's South Side working-class neighborhoods, where the majority of the city's Mexican residents lived as second-class citizens. Space in this federal housing project was open only to applicants who were U.S. citizens; however, a combination of high rents and racism kept most Mexicans out. In a demonstration of the entrenched and rampant anti-Mexican sentiment, 500 El Paso "citizens" sent a petition to President Roosevelt requesting that the federal government deport Mexicans because they were exhausting available relief.[11]

Though aware of the persistent discrimination in the copper industry, Mine-Mill had difficulty resolving this problem because rather than concentrating on this issue, the union concerned itself instead with building a broad-based membership, winning economic benefits, and achieving industry-wide organization. In its drive to increase union membership, Mine-Mill was recruiting Anglo Texans at the same time that it was bringing Mexicans into its ranks. Any collaboration by Anglo Texans with Mexicans would offend Texas racial convention and moreover would mean equality in pay and work. Anglo Texan and Mexican workers lacked a base for cooperation and mutual respect, and this fact affected the dynamics of race and labor at the mines and inside the metal-processing plants. In its efforts to circumvent New Deal labor legislation and prevent CIO organizing, ASARCO encouraged a company union with AFL affiliation, the Smelter Workers Union. Anglo craft workers who controlled the Metal Trades Council also held control over the Smelter

Workers Union and were aided by obliging plant supervisors. At Phelps Dodge discrimination was rampant. Mexicans worked mostly as common laborers, performing hard and dangerous work for less pay than Anglos received. Those who sustained serious, debilitating injuries on the job were discharged and denied pensions. Like the ASARCO employees, Phelps Dodge workers were required to purchase their supplies from a company store, and the segregated bathrooms, showers, and lunchroom facilities served as daily reminders that the company bestowed a higher status on Anglo workers. The Phelps Dodge Refinery did not have a company union. Organizing the Spanish-speaking workers at ASARCO and Phelps Dodge proved troublesome because a large number of the workers were Mexican aliens and because intimidation and coercion by companies, local authorities, and the INS remained widespread.[12]

Nevertheless, initial contacts between the CIO and the workers at ASARCO and Phelps Dodge in El Paso were made in late 1938 with the arrival of a Packinghouse Workers Organizing Committee representative from Denver. Because the CIO was challenging a move by the AFL's Amalgamated Meat Cutters to unionize the meat industry, this PWOC official was in the Queen City to begin the organization of the local Peyton meatpacking plant. Humberto Silex and other ASARCO smelter workers met with the PWOC organizer and told him they wanted a union. It was explained that Mine-Mill was sending a representative to help them unionize. Two months later, veteran CIO organizer James Robinson arrived in El Paso. Robinson met with Silex and informed him that Mine-Mill would undertake an organizing drive in El Paso. Mine-Mill contacted the CTM in Ciudad Juárez for help organizing El Paso smelters, and the Mexican labor federation assigned two organizers to the task. Mine-Mill also got support from the Mexican consul in El Paso, Colonel Manuel Esparza. Unlike his predecessor, who helped deport Mexicans during and after the Gallup strike, Esparza was strongly committed to the labor reform policies of President Lázaro Cárdenas. A foundation for labor mobilization in El Paso was developing within a wide social network. The informational meetings held in Smeltertown and in El Paso's Mexican working-class neighborhoods soon brought new members into both ASARCO Local 509 and Phelps Dodge Local 501. Additional workers joined as word spread of the union drive. American-born Tejanos were the main union participants, and they would not be cowed by threats of deportation.[13]

In the membership drives, labor activists sought out union-minded men, making contact with prospective recruits on the job, in their homes, and in recreation halls; the organizers also persuaded others to abandon AFL-affiliated labor unions for the CIO. Once a union base was built and an NLRB election scheduled, Mine-Mill next sought to initiate a concerted union campaign. The organizational groundwork by rank-and-file committees in the smelters and refineries ensured votes for unionization. Important publicity for the CIO movement culture and tactics included parades and appearances and speeches by Mine-Mill union leaders. One lingering task that worried Mine-Mill organizers was getting Mexican nationals employed by ASARCO and Phelps Dodge to unionize. These men at first shied away from Mine-Mill. Years of repeated antiunion warnings from the company and steady harassment by the INS had made them fearful. Mine-Mill overcame this problem and persuaded the Mexicans to unionize by relying on its Spanish-speaking unionists, the Mexican consul, and the CTM.[14]

By 1940, Mine-Mill's prospects began to improve. It had made considerable headway in its national organizing drive, largely as a result of the widespread acceptance of the NLRA and the solvency of the nonferrous metals industry due to the growth of production to fill defense orders. Mine-Mill increased membership by 20 percent, and in the following year of nationwide strike actions, the union experienced a 58 percent increase. By June of 1941, Mine-Mill had 50,000 members, and those numbers would climb to 97,000 by 1944. In El Paso, many ASARCO and Phelps Dodge workers had been brought into the respective locals, but Mine-Mill faced some competition from the AFL in signing up workers and considerable opposition from company officials. Determined to break Mine-Mill's organizing drive, ASARCO began discharging workers who signed union cards, with foremen singling out known or suspected leaders for dismissal. El Paso County Sheriff Chris P. Fox, a longtime adversary of unionism who considered the CIO as synonymous with radicalism and who had never respected Mexicans, lent support to ASARCO. So did officials from the INS and other federal government officials who were growing concerned about the alliances being forged in the Southwest between the progressive Peoples' Congress, pro-Cárdenas Mexican consuls, and the CTM. Put off by the contentious spirit of Mexican working-class conflict, Fox and his deputies scared workers away from the union meetings, while immigration agents harassed the workers and threatened them with deportation if they joined Mine-Mill. Bending to Mexican American grassroots pressure and to formal requests by Mexican consular officials concerned about the problem of discrimination against the region's Spanish-speaking residents, the U.S. State Department made a confidential investigation of this matter. In his report, U.S. Consul General William Blocker stated that complaints of discrimination were exaggerated, emphasizing that the real problem of discrimination was caused by the championing of the "lower strata" of Mexicans by manipulative Mexican American organizations. Blocker fixed the blame squarely on the Peoples' Congress, accusing that organization of developing a strong following among working-class Mexicans with the aid of Mexican consuls and the CTM. Blocker charged that the Peoples' Congress "seized the opportunity" of using the Good Neighbor Policy "to force special recognition of social privileges." Moreover, Blocker added that the CTM's call for *"una sociedad sin clases"* (a society without classes) formed an integral part of the Mexican government's "uplift of the Mexican people at home and abroad."[15]

TEXAS SHOWDOWN: THE CIO ON TRIAL IN EL PASO

What proved harmful to union organizing and civil liberties in El Paso and along the Texas border at this time was the so-called "little Red Scare" of 1939–41, the highly publicized and scurrilous Un-American Activities Committee hearings on communist activities and propaganda chaired by the ultraconservative Texas Democratic congressman Martin Dies. In the context of this demagoguery, which explicitly linked communism with the CIO and with Mexican nationals, Red-baiting became another glaring antiunion tactic that Mine-Mill faced in El Paso. Rather than battling the fascist threat posed by the Sinarquistas who set up headquarters in El Paso, Sheriff Fox, a rabid adversary of communism, chose instead to spearhead the local Red Scare. In early March 1940, Fox arrested six organizers. One of these men possessed CIO application cards and membership literature. The sheriff seized this incriminating evidence and turned it over to immigration officials; government confiscation of the union material flushed out the workers connected with the CIO. Frightened by the mop-up operation of Sheriff Fox, many other workers came forward and told the sheriff they had not signed the union cards. Meanwhile, the labor organizers were put in the El Paso County jail, held without bond, and charged with spreading communist propaganda in the Queen City. The sheriff had received information on the CIO from a labor spy employed at ASARCO. The company mole revealed that a communist agitator had written to Mexican Communist Party officials in Ciudad Juárez urging "hands across the border" collaboration with their counterparts in El Paso and emphasizing that El Paso CIO unions would eventually become part of the international communist movement. Seething with anger over this revelation of communist conspiracy and disregarding the deference owed to a diplomatic official, Fox went after Mexican Consul Esparza. Fox lashed out at Consul Esparza, charging him with supporting the CTM, the CIO, and the newly formed Peoples' Congress, which were all part of the alleged subversive inter-American "communist movement." The sheriff went to the U.S. consular officials in El Paso and warned them that Esparza had links to both the PCM and the CPUSA and was acting on behalf of these revolutionary organizations. Ever vigilant, the sheriff contacted the Un-American Activities Committee about the possible communist threat in the El Paso area. Congressman Martin Dies, a fellow Texan who sat tall in the saddle against both pernicious communism and black and brown aspirations for equality, responded by dispatching HUAC investigators to El Paso to assess the communist menace. Labor organizer Humberto Silex was investigated, as was Juan Peña.[16]

Sheriff Fox and Acting El Paso County Attorney W. H. Fryer, who shared the sheriff's conviction that the CIO was a tool of the communists, requested a court of inquiry and subpoenaed thirteen persons, including the six arrested unionists. Three of the men were CIO organizers; one of these had been charged with distributing union and CPUSA materials and with recruiting workers into both organizations. The lone CTM organizer was accused of being a party member. Evidence implicated the other men arrested; one was a party member and the second a communist sympathizer. During his testimony, Sheriff Fox stated categorically that communists were distributing subversive literature and that the newly founded El Paso branch of the Congress of Spanish-Speaking Peoples had been formed "to instill in Mexican aliens living in the United States . . . the principles of the Mexican Communist form of government." Fox denounced the CIO for authorizing one of its organizers to participate as a party representative in the "May Day communist celebration" held across the border in Ciudad Juárez the previous year. The Red-hunter bragged that his office had seized a large cache of revolutionary literature.[17] One by one, the remaining subpoenaed witnesses broke down under questioning and testified about the possible link between CIO organizing and the Communist Party in El Paso. Afterwards, attorney W. H. Fryer remarked: "To my mind, the hearing . . . establishes the fact that when you scratch the hide of a CIO member you find a Communist." These observations were echoed in comments by the presiding judge. After the court of inquiry finished its deliberations, the judge concluded that communism needed to be "wiped out" in El Paso. The judge ordered the release of the three agitators arrested in the dragnet but detained the others for further investigation.[18]

The CIO strenuously protested the arrests ordered by Sheriff Fox and accused the peace officer of Red-baiting and violating the civil rights of two of the men jailed. In its account, the CIO stated that the men had been arrested without warrant or formal charges, fingerprinted, and placed in jail incommunicado for several days. Furthermore, during their incarceration the men were subjected to physical coercion, to "third degree methods in an attempt to extort information of a connection between the local CIO and the Communist Party." CIO officials deemed Fox's action a witch hunt, which it obviously was—a Red Scare aimed at stopping labor organizing along the border. The incident was not entirely at an end: Texas Communist Party secretary Homer Brooks weighed in with his own views. Brooks openly admitted that one of the men arrested was a communist. However, Brooks correctly pointed out that what was at issue was not the party's legal right to assist in the labor movement but the blatant violation of the civil rights of workers by the El Paso County sheriff in his attempts to intimidate the men and stop them from engaging in union organizing.[19]

Mine-Mill requested and obtained NLRB hearings concerning antiunionism at ASARCO and Phelps Dodge. The hearings revealed widespread labor violations at the Phelps Dodge metal refinery. Using labor spies, Phelps Dodge fired union member employees who attempted to sign up fellow workers; meanwhile, the company tried to set up an AFL union and pressured employees to support it. The hearings further disclosed that the El Paso Farmers and Merchants Association had mobilized antilabor sentiment in the Texas border area, had colluded with the mine companies to prevent the CIO from organizing in the city, and had actively participated in the drive to oust communists and radicals. In February 1941, the NLRB ruled in favor of Mine-Mill. The board ordered Phelps Dodge to cease making its employees join the company union and to reinstate three of its workers fired for union activities. In the wake of this victory, Mine-Mill filed grievances against ASARCO. However, the NLRB ruled in favor of the smelter company and recognized the AFL affiliate as the bargaining agent: Mine-Mill at this time seldom secured exclusive bargaining rights.[20]

THE PUSH BY MEXICAN AMERICAN CIO UNIONISTS FOR LABOR AND CIVIL RIGHTS CONTINUES

Mine-Mill gained strength during World War II because of the wartime urgency to expand metal production. This occurred despite many rank-and-file members' abandonment of mine work for better-paying and less hazardous work in West Coast defense plants and shipyards and despite the fact that single male workers were being drafted. Nevertheless, Mine-Mill continued organizing, for it believed that improved working conditions and a higher wage scale could only increase output, reduce turnover and absenteeism, and prevent strikes in the nonferrous metals industry. The war and the national spirit of unity inspired Mine-Mill to push for union representation and—as with other left-wing CIO-affiliated unions, such as the UCAPAWA and the UE—for equality for racial minority workmen. However, like the Left-led unions, Mine-

Mill avoided risking shop floor conflict over race if it might jeopardize production. The CIO at this time did not want to anger its Anglo rank-and-file members, many of them first-time union members and new to interracial unionism, by pushing too hard for racial reform and thus jeopardizing war production. Mine-Mill's commitment to racial equality would be achieved through the efforts of its Mexican American rank and file and labor leaders, who sought further assistance from the union's international office in Denver in securing union recognition. Dual wage rates, job misclassifications, the absence of job upgrading, and work in segregated "Mexican gangs" remained widespread throughout the copper industry. Concern over foreign relations issues blocked the push by Spanish-speaking CIO unionists for racial equality in the mines and smelters of the Southwest. In the spring of 1942, Mexican American workers from the National Maritime Union, the progressive locals of the Oil Workers Industrial Union, and the UCAPAWA convinced FEPC officials that rampant discrimination justified a public hearing to expose the problem and take remedial action. The FEPC hearings were scheduled to take place in El Paso but were canceled. U.S. government officials feared that any adverse publicity regarding racism against Mexicans in the Southwest would jeopardize America's Latin American Good Neighbor Policy—specifically, the successful negotiation of the contract labor program with Mexico, which was well aware of the disenfranchisement of Mexicans in the United States. Union activities did not stop in the El Paso border area. Mine-Mill field representative Harry Hafner, Humberto Silex, and other union members worked to secure an NLRB election at the Phelps Dodge refinery. These unionists had little trouble convincing the rank and file at Phelps Dodge of the significance of a union election; the aggrieved workers knew it was the first stage in ending the long-standing discriminatory wage differentials based on a dual wage system. Mine-Mill's struggle for labor and social equality remained within a Popular Front framework; the union utilized its links with its counterparts in Mexico to create and promote antifascist working-class internationalism. Mine-Mill Local 501 president Antonio Salcido confirmed that the struggle for labor and social equality by Mine-Mill was being fought within this frame of reference. The Tejano labor leader wrote, "Here in the Southwest, the victory of the Phelps Dodge workers under the CIO banner will be a blow in the face of all the fascist-minded employers who utilize racial and national discrimination as a means of paying starvation wages."[21]

Mine-Mill organizers at Phelps Dodge were stymied in their efforts to gain an NLRB election. The Mine-Mill locals could not come up with union dues, and Silex was discharged for his increasingly militant activities as a union organizer. With help from other Spanish-speaking union organizers, Silex had brought many workers into the union, including more than one hundred women and black workers hired by Phelps Dodge to replace the Tejano workers drafted for military service. Unlike Anglos, these Tejanos newly inducted into military service did not hold skilled jobs and thus did not qualify for job deferments that would have spared them from the draft. As will be shown in the next chapter, biased, indiscriminate military conscription of Mexican Americans spread to epidemic proportions during World War II, and so did protest by Mexican Americans angrily opposed to this form of aggression against them. In late May 1942, Mine-Mill Local 501 at Phelps Dodge petitioned the NLRB for an election, which it won in late June. Local 501 also succeeded in gaining union recognition for workers at the El Paso Brick Company, which made bricks for the blast furnaces of the area smelters. This indicates that the CIO-mounted campaign very likely won backing where Mexican workers had no union affiliation. The next goal for Mine-Mill Locals 501 and 509 was to secure initial contracts. Mine-Mill started an organizing drive at the ASARCO smelter in July 1942. As a way to stave off Mine-Mill's efforts, ASARCO supported the AFL company union by giving its members a fifty-cent pay increase. Mine-Mill continued to organize the plant; it held meetings at Smeltertown, and union representatives also visited workers at their homes in Ciudad Juárez. By late 1942, more than a third of ASARCO's 600 workers had signed up with Local 509. Mine-Mill succeeded in winning another NLRB election in early March 1943.[22]

Unable to get initial contracts with either Phelps Dodge or ASARCO, Mine-Mill Locals 501 and 509 appealed to federal regulatory agencies to rectify their grievances. Having secured the appointment of union members Leo Ortiz and Ceferino Anchondo to the War Manpower Commission, Mine-Mill successfully appealed to this federal body, as well as to the director of the Labor Department's Conciliation Service, and as a result won additional cases for its members. This was done amidst charges by Anglo workers that Mine-Mill was a "Mexican union," despite the fact that Mine-Mill had also won cases for its Anglo members. Mexican Americans were attempting interracial solidarity at a time when the Anglo rank and file made no effort to get Arizona's Spanish-speaking into defense-related work nor to protest the state's meager record on this issue.[23]

After more than a year of negotiations, Mine-Mill Local 509 got Phelps Dodge to agree to contract negotiations and, soon thereafter, ASARCO smelter workers in Local 509 secured a contract. The Phelps Dodge contract recognized Local 501 as the sole bargaining agent for the plant's

Figure 4.A. Mexican American metal workers in El Paso conducted a successful organizing campaign, increased membership in Mine-Mill Locals, and secured NLRB-sanctioned elections. Jubilant Local 509 members, October 11, 1943. (6x553, Courtesy of the Archives, University of Colorado at Boulder Libraries).

production and maintenance workers and moreover approved a nondiscriminatory clause stating, "There shall be no discrimination against any employee because of race, creed, color or national origin." ASARCO workers won a forty-hour workweek, time and a half for overtime work, an automatic wage increase of eleven and one-quarter cents an hour, a one-week paid vacation, and most important, seniority with regard to advancement, retention, and reemployment. The contract also stipulated that ASARCO would not discriminate against Mine-Mill and provided for a checkoff to ensure that the union received dues from its members. Published in both English and Spanish, the one-year contracts eliminated the company stores and the separate bathroom and shower facilities at both the smelter and the refinery. The latter improvement gained a modicum of dignity for the Spanish-speaking workers who had endured years of shame using the separate facilities.[24]

By 1943, largely through the efforts of its Mexican unionists, the union's fortunes improved, for it began making major election inroads into craft- and company-union territory. For example, in the El Paso area, Mine-Mill eventually eliminated the nine-year craft-union domination at

ASARCO; the union won additional victories at the Phelps Dodge refinery and secured a closed-shop contract at Laredo. Mine-Mill shared representation of Nevada Consolidated production workers in Silver City, New Mexico, with the AFL; it won sole bargaining rights in the smaller mining and smelter operations in the area; and it obtained representation rights for workers at the Phelps Dodge open-pit mining and smelter operation at Morenci, Arizona. The copper producers continued to resist unionization, and discrimination against Mexicans, which remained rife at mines and smelters, delayed contract negotiations. In the meantime, an exodus of Spanish-speaking miners to West Coast war mobilization centers, as well as the elimination of these workers through the draft, was leading to a manpower shortage in copper mining and processing, and this in turn threatened war production. The copper companies began to seriously contemplate bringing in braceros from Mexico. These contracted workers could work in the smelters and mines at much lower rates than union workers, since the U.S. government set their meager wages.[25]

As we have seen, Mine-Mill's successful organizational strategy in the El Paso area rested in part with the cross-border collaboration between American CIO union activists and those from the CTM in Mexico, despite an onslaught of Red-baiting. With America's entry into the war, followed by that of Mexico, the two labor movements opened a united Popular Front offensive along the Texas border, placing workers' rights in an international context of working-class solidarity and the fight against fascism worldwide. For example, with support from the CIO, the AFL, and the CTM, Mine-Mill organized the 1942 El Paso Labor Day observance as an international worker commemoration. This huge, joint Labor Day expression of Popular Front culture demonstrated organized labor's commitment to defeating the Axis powers and to preventing the profascist Sinarquistas from making further headway in El Paso and along the lower Río Grande Valley. Local 501 president Rodolfo Ingle and Local 509 president Humberto Silex addressed a workers' meeting in Ciudad Juárez to express international solidarity against Nazi fascism. Addressing the spirited gathering in Spanish, Silex asserted: "The workers of North America are united with our working brothers in Mexico in the great fight that humanity wages against its greatest enemy, international fascism." On July 4, another Mine-Mill international Labor Day tribute featured as a keynote speaker CTM labor leader Vicente Lombardo Toledano, who now headed the anti-Axis Confederación de Trabajadores de América Latina (Latin American Confederation of Labor or CATL).[26] We now turn to the fortunes of Mexican American war workers in Los Angeles, California, in the context of the Popular Front, heightened racial tensions, and the rapid expansion of federal authority during World War II.

Figure 4.B. Mine-Mill's organizing drives in El Paso, Texas, gained support from the CTM across the border in Cuidad Juárez. Mine Mill Locals 509 and 501 and other CIO locals joined a parade of 10,000 workers in Cuidad Juárez, Mexico. (WFM Local 509, box 553, Courtesy of Archives, University of Colorado Boulder Libraries).

Getting a Foot in the Door: Mexican American CIO Unionists Enter Los Angeles War Defense Industries

In 1940, more than a fourth of the American population consisted of first- and second-generation immigrants. Concerned about any disruption of America's war mobilization, officials from the U.S. Justice Department and other federal government agencies focused on the matter of discrimination because it might make aliens and the larger ethnic community vulnerable to fifth-column propaganda and recruitment. To prevent the kind of anti-immigrant sentiment that had accompanied World War I and the postwar Red Scare, as well as guarantee workers the right to organize, the Justice Department created a Civil Rights section in 1939. Furthermore, to better monitor and control foreign alien activity, President Roosevelt in June 1940 transferred the Immigration and Naturalization Service (INS) from the Labor Department to the Justice Department, which also housed the FBI. Congress also passed the Alien Registration Act and the National Defense Act. A response to Axis activity, the Alien Registration Act required all aliens to be fingerprinted, carry identification cards, and file a sworn statement of their associations and membership in political organizations. The National Defense Act ordered the exclusion of aliens from certain defense jobs. However, this action inadvertently produced an immediate increase in anti-ethnic bias that was clearly racist. Plant managers restricted hiring to those job applicants with nonforeign names and appearances. For example, companies in Southern California recruited Anglo Texans as new hires because they "looked American" and thus did not have to prove U.S. citizenship. In thwarting a fifth column, federal intervention produced reports showing considerable discrimination against aliens, naturalized citizens, and second-generation Americans with foreign names. Defense industry employers were dismissing aliens and turning them down for employment, despite the government's request to these employers that they provide equal job opportunities to the foreign-born. This included Mexicans, who, along with blacks, confronted a new wave of racism in the form of housing discrimination and police violence reflecting the deep-seated racial sentiments of white America. This upsurge of racial intolerance denied Mexicans and blacks the labor and civil rights through which they could attain empowerment and improve their material circumstances. Yet preventing racial violence and discrimination was not a central part of state intervention at this time. In their struggle for labor and civil rights, minorities in progressive CIO unions like the UFWA, UE, and ILWU therefore made community activism a fundamental part of their war-supporting activities.[27]

At its 1941 convention, the CIO denounced discriminatory hiring practices as a "direct attack against our nation's policy to build democracy in our fight against Hitlerism." This CIO egalitarianism came about because black and Mexican American CIO union activists, joined by progressive Anglos, continued to press the national union in the direction of racial equality. Upon the insistence of its growing number of black members, the CIO at its 1942 convention formed the Committee Against Racial Discrimination (CARD). CARD rallied support for the FEPC and promoted the inclusion in contracts of antidiscrimination clauses. CARD's policy, however, was to shun direct involvement in local racial disputes. Instead, CARD encouraged CIO-affiliated unions, the Industrial Union Councils, and union locals to establish their own anti-discrimination committees.[28]

In California, CIO unions like the UAW, UE, and UCAPAWA with large racial minority memberships were closely intertwined with the powerful ILWU, headed by Harry Bridges. Bridges served as director of West Coast CIO, the center of the California Popular Front. The "march inland" strategy of Bridges sought to organize the mostly Mexican and Filipino warehousing, packing shed, food processing, and agricultural workers through UCAPAWA. At state CIO conventions and at Industrial Union Council meetings, Spanish-speaking union activists took the lead in educating their fellow union members about conditions affecting Mexican workers, many of whom were permanent U.S. residents or nonnaturalized or else could not speak English. As a result, and with support from Harry Bridges, the Committee to Aid Mexican Workers (CAMW) was organized in Los Angeles in 1939 within ILWU Local 26. The CAMW raised money to sponsor citizenship classes and to print Spanish-language materials to educate Mexican workers about their rights and the importance of unionization. The CAMW's major tasks were to eliminate the dual wage structure, end the exclusion of Mexicans from factory jobs, including skilled work, and mobilize them against other forms of workplace discrimination and bigotry in society at large. In addition, the CAMW, with the newly formed Congress of Spanish-Speaking Peoples as a partner, supported labor actions by Mexican workers in Orange, Riverside, Ventura, and San Joaquin Counties, as well as work stoppages by Spanish-speaking Santa Fe Railroad workers and miners and smelter workers in Arizona and New Mexico. The striking miners and their families faced the usual array of repressive tactics: attacks by vigilantes and police, threats and deportations by INS agents, the shutting off of utilities, and evictions. The CAMW appealed to California unions to support the strikers with donations of food and money. These various undertakings did not arouse direct assistance from the California CIO. Like the FEPC, this labor body focused its attention on eliminating discrimination against blacks, even though Mexicans made up the largest group of minority CIO members.[29] Collectively, Mexican American CIO unionists continued to insist that social justice was as important as labor rights and called for a united front in this direction.

Despite signs of CIO intransigence, Mexican Americans increased their pressure on the CIO to take action. Working through the Los Angeles CIO Industrial Union Council, Mexican American unionists set up committees whose specific purpose was to address the discrimination faced by the city's Spanish-speaking residents. Reconstituted in November 1941, the CAMW was chaired by ILWU Local 26 president Bert Corona and included rank-and-file members from this union local as well as from UFWA Local 576, USWA Local 2172, UE Local 1421, the Transport Workers' Union, and the UCAPAWA. All of the union representatives belonged to the Peoples' Congress, with UE member Rosendo Rivera serving as president of this labor and civil rights organization.[30] With assistance from the California CIO Anti-Discrimination Committee (ADC) and the Peoples' Congress, the CAMW scheduled a conference for December 7, 1941, on the "plight of Spanish-Americans" in Southern California. Mexican American and Mexican workers packed the CIO hall to hear about gaining greater participation in union affairs, fighting against job and relief

Figure 4.C. Mexican American women helped the burgeoning CIO drive in Southern California. Garment workers with picket signs, San Fernando, California, 1943. The picketers' signs read: "We want a union," and "We want a free country too." (00002239—Shades of L.A. Archives, Courtesy of Los Angeles Public Library).

discrimination, helping Spanish-speaking workers to learn English, and encouraging them to become naturalized citizens so they could secure defense industry employment and better defend themselves against discrimination. Carey McWilliams, head of the California State Division of Housing and Immigration, and UCAPAWA official Luisa Moreno were scheduled as the main speakers. Before it started, however, the conference was canceled by the news that the Japanese had attacked Pearl Harbor. The next day the United States declared war on Japan.[31]

During this time, there would be considerable cooperation between black and Mexican American CIO unionists and community members in Los Angeles to combat social and economic oppression and to aggressively pursue employment in the burgeoning aircraft and shipbuilding industries. A few months before the FEPC hearings scheduled for Los Angeles, the ADC was involved in a campaign to stop the exclusion of blacks from employment in Southern California's war industries. This action came about following the announcement by a government official that just 1,000 jobs would be reserved for black workers in defense plants and shipyards. The recently formed Los Angeles Negro Victory Committee (established in April 1941) notified the War Manpower Commission, the president, and senators and congressmen from California that the war effort was being hurt by their failure to utilize full manpower. Black Assemblyman Augustus Hawkins and ILWU Local 26 president Bert Corona addressed a joint ADC-United Autoworkers Union meeting to protest anti-black and anti-Mexican discrimination in the defense industry, grievances that would be taken to the FEPC. However, in the case of the aggrieved Mexicans, only two witnesses gave testimony during the two-day FEPC hearings. Los Angeles CIO Industrial Union Council secretary Philip "Slim" Connelly complained that the CIO was given just ten days to collect information and prepare affidavits of job discrimination against Mexicans. Connelly further noted that the reason Spanish-speaking workers were reluctant to testify about discrimination was that they feared being "eternally black-listed" by their employers.[32] The Congress of Spanish-Speaking Peoples would soon emerge as a pivotal force to defend the labor and civil rights of Mexican Americans as well as to address the broader national issue of Mexican American inequality in the United States.

ALLIES OF LABOR: THE POPULAR FRONT OF THE CONGRESS OF SPANISH-SPEAKING PEOPLES

The founding of the Peoples' Congress represented another turning point in Mexican American history as the decade of the 1930s ended. Unlike

LULAC, the Peoples' Congress as a Popular Front organization embraced the CIO's new rhetoric of class and thus acknowledged a common bond with working-class Mexicans. The Peoples' Congress undermined what little political leadership LULAC provided in the Mexican community. As its name indicated, the Peoples' Congress was designed to appeal to the majority of this Spanish-speaking population, and it easily outstripped LULAC in solidifying a united front in the push for labor and civil rights for Mexicans. Like the National Negro Congress, founded in 1936, the Peoples' Congress represented a broad coalition of Mexican American organizations and of Spanish-speaking unionists committed to labor and civil rights and to the Popular Front struggle against fascism abroad and at home. As it did in the creation of the National Negro Congress, the Communist Party played an important, though not commanding, role in the formation of the Peoples' Congress. Because Mexicans belonged to the CIO, had links to the labor movement, and supported a pro-labor agenda, leading figures of the CIO pushed its affiliates to back this Spanish-speaking labor and civil rights organization. Harry Bridges, ILWU president and CIO West Coast regional director, Donald Henderson, president of the UCAPAWA, and Reid Robinson of Mine-Mill supported the Peoples' Congress because they sought to build an all-embracing Popular Front civic culture among the large and growing Mexican American CIO rank and file. The New Deal had not remedied the problems of economic need among Mexican Americans. Therefore, the program of the Peoples' Congress would address the economic and social inequality faced by nearly two million Mexican American and Mexican people caused by the lack of relief assistance, housing, health care, education, and employment. The goals of workers in regard to labor and civil rights and fighting the rise of fascism changed in August 1939 with the signing of the Nazi-Soviet pact. The Peoples' Congress stayed preoccupied with the world calamity as it accommodated and prodded the CIO on the issue of racial justice.[33]

UCAPAWA organizer Luisa Moreno, a rising figure in the American labor movement who became a leading national voice against the civil rights violations that threatened the Mexican population, was behind the formation of a national Spanish-speaking organization invested in labor issues and social democracy. Moreno traveled through the Southwest to build bridges in the Mexican community in an effort to gain broad-based support for a national Spanish-speaking organization from trade unionists, the Workers' Alliance of America, and progressive fraternal organizations now consolidated as large national bodies. Everywhere Moreno's message was the same: only through a concerted effort would conditions improve for Mexican Americans and Mexicans, whose problems differed slightly, as both groups faced workplace discrimination and inequality in society at large. For the Spanish-speaking people to advance, Moreno stressed, they needed the assistance of a broad alliance of all the progressive elements inside and outside the labor movement. Contact with the CIO labor organizations was especially crucial. The goals of the Peoples' Congress therefore remained within the framework established by the national CIO leadership: to maintain and strengthen the New Deal social agenda, to wipe out unemployment through New Deal relief programs, and to carry forth the organizing drives set in motion in 1936 and 1937.[34] Like its counterpart, the National Negro Congress, the Peoples' Congress advised Mexican Americans to join the CIO because interracial unionism was the best vehicle for extending democracy to Mexican Americans.

The main labor unions aiding in the formation of the Peoples' Congress were the CIO's UCAPAWA and Mine-Mill, though some input came from progressive AFL affiliates like the Sawmill Workers Union of New Mexico. Swept up by the politics of international class solidarity, the Peoples' Congress requested and received support from Mexico's labor movement. Again, this outreach was in keeping with the national CIO's point of view that the first line of resistance against the rise of fascist and totalitarian movements in the Western Hemisphere was Latin America and the building up of the trade union movement there. Moreno established contact with the Congreso de Unificación de las Cámaras de Trabajadores (Unification Congress of Workers Chambers) meeting in Dallas, and the Confederation of Mexican Organizations, which met in Port Arthur, Texas, voted to support the formation of the Peoples' Congress. Contact was also established with the Texas State CIO Council. This Left-led labor body assured Moreno that it would cooperate in any program of the Peoples' Congress for the advancement of the Mexican American people. The planning of the Peoples' Congress inaugural conference abruptly came up against stumbling blocks that resulted in a temporary setback. The initial conference was originally coordinated through committee work in San Antonio, but in the latter part of 1938, the location of the convention was switched to Albuquerque. No doubt, the right-wing backlash produced by the pecan shellers' strike, which equated the CIO with radicalism, and Congressman Martin Dies's "little Red Scare," as well as the absence of viable mainstream Mexican American organizational leadership in Texas caused the organizers to look elsewhere for support.[35]

The choice of Albuquerque as the site of the first Peoples' Congress convention came about through an agreement between Luisa Moreno and professors Arturo L. Campa and George I. Sánchez of the University of New Mexico. However, this agreement was premature. Moreno's primary antagonist became Campa, who tried to obstruct her efforts. Unfortunately, Moreno had failed to fully sound him out. Congressman Martin Dies sent an investigator from HUAC to El Paso, and he relayed information about the Peoples' Congress to certain New Mexico LULAC leaders, who began to complain. They then contacted Campa and told the professor the Peoples' Congress was a "communist sponsored affair," a radical separatist organization whose purpose was to incite Mexicans to riot and rebellion in order to reclaim the Southwest and return the region to Mexico. Learning that the Peoples' Congress was a communist front organization, Campa refused to participate. These LULAC representatives also pressured Sánchez to rescind his support of the Peoples' Congress. Undaunted, Luisa Moreno persisted in her efforts and quickly organized a new Peoples' Congress committee to identify individuals to replace Campa and Sánchez, and this time Moreno made certain they would be more sensitive to the interests and concerns of the Spanish-speaking working classes and all progressive strata. The new committee consisted of three New Mexico state legislative representatives, all whom shared Moreno's views and were spokesmen for this viewpoint: state representative for San Miguel County John J. Fernández chaired the committee, state representative for Río Arriba County Ralph Gallegos served as secretary, and state representative for Bernalillo County Elias Gonzales was treasurer. All three elected officials were pro-union; Fernández was a Mine-Mill union leader, while Gonzales headed the powerful Sawmill Workers Union and had done organizational work in New Mexico, Arizona, and Colorado, over which his union held jurisdiction. Furthermore, the endorsement of the Peoples' Congress by La Liga Obrera de Habla Español provided it with considerable grassroots support from politicized Spanish-speaking farmers, farm workers, and miners throughout New Mexico and Colorado.[36] The Peoples' Congress got support from Mexican Americans in Colorado, Arizona, Kansas, and Chicago, centers of union activism by Mexican Americans belonging to Mine-Mill, the Packinghouse Workers Organizing Committee, and the Steel Workers Organizing Committee. An untold number of these blue-collar workers belonged to El Frente Popular Mexicano and other Popular Front organizations. The Peoples' Congress gained the most support in California because of strong backing from the state CIO office, Mexican American CIO unionists, and an active Popular Front movement. An executive chair of the Peoples' Congress was elected following a meeting held in Los Angeles on December 4, 1938, attended by eighty-eight delegates representing seventy-three organizations with a total membership of over 70,000. Most of these organizations were from Southern California, where the majority of the state's Spanish-speaking population resided and where a Popular Front culture thrived.[37]

Mexican Americans in Los Angeles who were active in the Popular Front were transformed by its democratic culture, which stressed the themes of labor rights, antifascism, anti-imperialism, and racial justice. They attended the weekly Sixth Street Town Meeting to hear various speakers address New Deal and CIO issues. Meetings on Republican Spain, on Latin America, against Hitler, and on defending Jews in Nazi Germany were well attended by Mexican Americans. The League Against War and Fascism, the Committee in Support of Republican Spain, and other left-wing organizations, which appealed to and received support from numerous ethnic groups in the city whose members either belonged to the Communist Party or were socialists, sponsored these gatherings. The Sunday town forum at the Grace Methodist Episcopal Church in East Los Angeles, led by Methodist Bishop Harry F. Ward, drew Mexican American audiences because Bishop Ward embraced social progressivism; he was a fervent peace and civil rights advocate committed to educating people about the threat posed by Hitlerism and fascism and about the racial injustice blacks faced in the South.[38]

The Communist Party helped promote and advance the cause of the Spanish-speaking working people of the Southwest. Many Spanish-speaking workers were receptive toward the party, even though large numbers never became members. The party was very active in the Spanish-speaking working-class neighborhoods of Los Angeles, where it had built a strong relationship with progressive Mexican American activists. Four hundred and thirty-five Mexicans belonged to the party in Los Angeles and were active through the El Sereno Club, the Mexican Concentration Club, the North Hollywood Branch, and the 13th Congressional District of the Los Angeles County Communist Party. These men and women distributed communist literature, including the *People's World*, and sponsored new members; some held low-level positions in the party. Party members who joined the Peoples' Congress later belonged to or were active in La Asociación Nacional México-Americana, the Civil Rights Congress, and the East Side Branch of the Los Angeles Committee for the Protection of the Foreign Born. Some Mexican American men and women who led CIO locals were party members or fellow travelers who had learned or honed their organizing and leadership skills in the party. These activists belonged to the Workers' Alliance of America and supported political causes such as the Committee in Support of Republican Spain. Mexican Americans were deeply affected by the rise of fascism in Italy and Germany, where it smashed labor unions and committed unspeakable atrocities against minorities. Unknown numbers of Mexican American party members and labor activists made a stand against fascism by volunteering to fight in the International Brigades in Spain. For example, Nick Ramírez went to Spain via Mexico as a member of that country's Benito Juárez Brigade. The son of a Jewish mother and a Mexican American father, he had been named Nicolas Lenin Ramírez in honor of the famous Russian revolutionary.[39]

As a Popular Front organization, the Peoples' Congress attracted many communists and party supporters as members, and while a few were open about their party membership, most remained silent on this issue. Communists took credit for setting up the Peoples' Congress, but its spokespersons cautiously stressed that their organization had not been "captured" by an outside group and that there was no Communist Party or socialist representation on any of its committees. Peoples' Congress spokespersons defused such suspicions by stating that the party's interest in and support of their organization were similar to its interest in and support of other progressive labor and civil rights movements. Furthermore, in light of the presence of Sinarquista agitators spewing out a reactionary brand of Mexican nationalism, the Peoples' Congress was opposed to a national minority problem viewpoint and other nationalist tendencies, as these could generate divisiveness among its mixed membership of Mexican Americans and Mexicans. The Popular Front national objectives of the Peoples' Congress were in line with those of the New Deal: it was planned as an initial step in the development of widespread debate among the Spanish-speaking people and the larger progressive movement in an effort to incorporate into American life and citizenship Mexican Americans and Mexican nationals victimized by racial and economic inequality. In this context, and because of its large female membership, the Peoples' Congress adopted an enlightened position on the question of gender inequality. The outreach efforts of the Peoples' Congress, based on mass organization representing the interests of all social groups, included the concerns of women who, young and old, were fervently dedicated to the struggle against the oppression of the Mexican American people.[40]

Women constituted 25 percent of the American workforce. They made up from 6.5 to 50 percent of the low-wage workforce employed in auto work, electrical appliances, garment making, needle trades, meatpacking, and agricultural work, and they were also represented in the white-collar and retail trades. Moreover, the wives and daughters of male workers played critical roles in the era's strike actions as members of women's auxiliaries and community organizations. Both the ILGWU and the UCAPAWA were formed through women's activism. However, the CIO's focus on the male-dominated core industries marginalized the concerns of women workers. Nevertheless, scholars note that the CIO organized women workers and afforded them opportunity and recognition; as a result it was by far the most inclusive force the labor movement had produced in over a half century. For its part, the Communist Party did not address the woman issue, but it recruited women and put the more advanced women members in positions of leadership, where they easily demonstrated their militancy and effectiveness. Women made up nearly a third of the Peoples' Congress membership. They were UCAPAWA and ILGWU rank-and-file members and civil rights activists, many of them class-conscious and militant individuals in leadership positions; others had been exposed to progressive movements; some were simply moved by the sense of urgency to free Mexicans from the yoke of racial oppression.[41] Because of the prominence of women, the Peoples' Congress put forward a resolution at its second California state convention that it "carry out a program of organization and education of the Mexican women . . . that it support and work for women's equality, so that she may receive equal wages, enjoy the same rights as men . . . and use her vote for the defense of the Mexican and Spanish American people, and of American democracy."[42]

The platform of the Peoples' Congress affirmed that the labor movement was an ally and the principal vehicle for the organization of Spanish-speaking people. Peoples' Congress members were urged to affiliate with their respective union locals. Reflecting the alliance of the Popular Front with Roosevelt's Democratic Party, the Peoples' Congress also stressed the crucial importance of political participation in movements aligned with Labor's Non-Partisan League, a multiunion organization that supported and campaigned for progressive candidates running for public office. The Peoples' Congress was particularly invested in the full political mobilization of the Mexican people. In Los Angeles, many Mexican Americans lived outside the city limits and thus could not participate in city elections, and because of the redrawing of county supervisory districts and assembly districts, Anglo voters outnumbered Mexican Americans. The Peoples' Congress was especially interested in organizing Mexican Americans living in New Mexico and south Texas, where they formed majorities in many counties. A long-standing problem in these two southwestern regions was the control maintained over Mexicans by local political bosses, both Anglo and Spanish-speaking, who used them as pawns. In Texas, the Peoples' Congress, with support from the Texas State CIO Council, helped West Side San Antonio Tejanos elect Maury Maverick to office and demanded the abolition of the poll tax and greater civil rights for Tejanos. Though short of money, the Peoples' Congress sent invitations to popular political figures to serve as convention speakers to emphasize the organization's American base. These included pro-CIO and pro–New Deal American Labor Party congressman Vito Marcantonio of New York and Democratic congressman Maury Maverick of Texas; an invitation to address the convention was also extended to Eleanor Roosevelt.[43] Because progressive organizations were playing a growing role in California's Democratic Party and because Mexicans had supported their political campaigns, the Peoples' Congress received support from California liberal Democrats like newly elected Governor Culbert Olson, State Attorney Robert Kenny, State Housing and Immigration Director Carey

McWilliams, Los Angeles County Supervisor John Anson Ford, and Los Angeles Mayor Fletcher Bowron.[44]

The Peoples' Congress successfully built a broad base of unity. Support came from individuals and progressive organizations, including the Workers' Alliance of America, the American League for Peace and Democracy, the Women's International League for Peace and Freedom, and a faction of left-wing Hollywood artists and writers from the Screen Actors Guild. This last group's involvement came about because Peoples' Congress member Josefina Fierro de Bright, who was married to screenwriter John Bright, and other Peoples' Congress members had begun building support among Hollywood progressives. These individuals advocated and promoted social justice through labor-sponsored weekly radio shows, and they supported union boycotts and other pro-labor causes. For example, the John Steinbeck Committee to Aid Agricultural Organization arranged conferences between government officials and migrants, planned fundraising events, and collected and transported food, while the Motion Picture Guild, in addition to contributing money and entertaining workers at migrant camps, screened trade-union films. On the eve of World War II, Hollywood studio employees were mobilized into a mass labor and Popular Front movement that recognized racial equality. The alliance of the Peoples' Congress with this Hollywood faction was essential to the Mexican American struggle for racial justice in Los Angeles.[45]

In late April 1939, over 130 Spanish-speaking and Anglo representatives from labor, community, and religious organizations attended the first national convention of the Peoples' Congress in Los Angeles. Forums addressed labor issues, education, health care, police violence, and citizenship and naturalization. With their main concern the expansion of Mexican American membership in the CIO, labor representatives in the Peoples' Congress renewed their commitment to assist the various CIO union organizing drives. They called for a Spanish-language version of the *CIO News*, which would aid in the organization and education of Mexicans about the singular importance of unionization and other pro-labor activities and would also serve to keep the attention of the CIO focused on the problems of job discrimination and racism among its minority Spanish-speaking rank and file. The various resolutions adopted by the convention included support for the extension of the NLRA to agricultural and domestic workers, relief for unemployed workers, minimum wage revisions, and affordable housing. Regarding the last, the Peoples' Congress called for congressional investigation of the awful living conditions of the Spanish-speaking population. For example, the completion of the Alazán and Apache Courts in San Antonio's blighted West Side provided 1,180 housing units, amidst loud protests by the city's Anglos that Tejanos would ruin any new housing built for them. Nonetheless, the poorest Tejano West Side slum dwellers still remained without housing. Accustomed to paying fifty cents to one dollar a week for rent, many impoverished Tejanos could not afford to pay $8.75 to $12 a month for the new rentals. Only 5,000 Tejanos were rehoused; 50,000 Spanish-speaking San Antonio residents still lived in substandard houses and shanties. Some of the Tejanos displaced by construction of federal housing hauled away salvaged boards and sheets of tin and built new shack towns outside the city limits that were more crowded and unhealthy than the old ones.[46]

The cutting off of state relief to Mexican families whose main bread-winner was a nonnaturalized citizen was an issue taken up by the Peoples' Congress. CTM representative Adolfo Orive Alba expressed concern about California legislation that would halt relief to Mexican families. The California State Relief Administration (SRA) was coming under criticism by right-wing Democrats and Republicans for practicing "state socialism," that is, extending rather than reducing state relief. At issue was granting public aid to recently arrived white Dust Bowl migrants and recertifying Mexican families headed by an alien for welfare aid. Reactionary politicians also charged that communists and other subversives from the Workers' Alliance of America or the progressive State, County and Municipal Workers of America union had infiltrated the SRA. The Peoples' Congress organized a car caravan from Los Angeles to Sacramento to persuade Governor Culbert Olson to veto the legislative bill that would have denied relief payments to aliens in California who had not yet become U.S. citizens. Olson vetoed the bill.[47]

Prejudice against Mexican American youth was another key issue of increasing concern. In the early war years, the Peoples' Congress became deeply involved in combating police violence against Spanish-speaking youth. With labor and community groups, it helped organize the Sleepy Lagoon Defense Committee to help defend seventeen Mexican American youths wrongly convicted of murder. To emphasize unity among Mexican Americans and Mexicans in light of the ongoing deportations, a major resolution called for the defense of the Mexican immigrant from harassment by the INS and the Border Patrol. The Peoples' Congress in this regard counseled aliens about immigration and naturalization issues.[48]

Another important resolution adopted dealt with fascism. The Peoples' Congress called on the Mexican people to give their active support to Republican Spain, condemned the fascist powers for supporting General Franco, and criticized the Roosevelt administration for its blockade against Spain and for its weak protest against Hitler and Mussolini's providing Franco with arms and munitions. That the Peoples' Congress embraced international issues is indicated by its resolution on the Spanish Civil War and by its forging alliances with pro-Cárdenista officials. The convention's session on U.S.-Mexico relations, led by left-wing Hollywood screenwriters John Bright and his brother-in-law Robert Tasker, gained support for Mexican President Lázaro Cárdenas's recent expropriation of American and foreign oil. The Peoples' Congress organized a protest march of nearly 9,000 people in downtown Los Angeles to oppose possible American intervention in Mexico to get back the oil concessions.[49]

The Nazi invasion of the Soviet Union in June 1941 and the subsequent Anglo-Soviet pact produced an international realignment that suddenly brought the beliefs of individual Mexican Americans into greater harmony with American patriotism. The Soviet Union was now acclaimed by Western democracies as the advance guard in the struggle against fascism. With the Communist Party, the Left-led CIO unions and Popular Front organizations now deemed Hitlerism the chief foe. The Peoples' Congress initially endorsed the national CIO policy of unanimous opposition to defense mobilization as well as to America's participation in World War II as a solution to the difficulties the CIO confronted. Now the Peoples' Congress supported America's war effort against the Axis powers because it believed unity of the Spanish-speaking community behind the war effort was imperative. The start of the war momentarily halted the civil rights activities of the Peoples' Congress because it threw its support behind the no-strike pledge of labor and the Communist Party. This progressive organization shifted its concerns to the promotion of wartime unity against fascism. In 1942, it organized a major rally in Los Angeles to show that it backed national unity in the international struggle against fascism. In this context, the Peoples' Congress was actively involved in undermining attempts by the Sinarquistas to gain a following among America's Spanish-speaking people. The strong presence of the CIO within the Mexican community, in terms of leadership and rank-and-file support for the labor movement with an antifascist message, hindered the Sinarquistas in sending out their ultranationalist message that filled Mexicans with false hope and in recruiting new supporters for the fascist cause.[50]

Suppressing Fascism: Mexican Americans Battle the Sinarquistas

La Union Nacional Sinarquista (the National Union of Sinarchistas) was founded in Guanajuato, Mexico, on May 23, 1937, and was the forerunner of El Centro Anti-Communista (The Anti-Communist Center). It is uncertain whether La Union Nacional Sinarquista was part of a global strategy to achieve fascist ends, but one of the three founders of La Union was the Nazi agent Hellmuth Oskar Schrieter. Though an accurate tally of total membership in the fascist Mexican organization is not available, the number was reported to be 600,000, and most of La Union's activities were confined to the Mexican states of Guanajuato and Sinaloa. Staunchly anticommunist, La Union Nacional Sinarquista was at first pro-Catholic; its bylaws forbade anyone who was not a Catholic to join. It advocated nonviolence and was against the use of revolutionary tactics to attain its goals. La Union Nacional Sinarquista came to exercise considerable influence in the Southwest and Midwest and was perceived by its Popular Front adversaries and the U.S. government as quite a serious domestic threat. The racial discrimination Mexican Americans encountered indirectly resulted in notoriety for this right-wing movement. Because they were looking for an audience for their fascist views, the Sinarquistas sought to exploit this condition of inequality to advance the fascist cause.[51]

The ultimate goal of the Sinarquistas was the extension of *Sinarquismo* abroad. They sought to recruit Mexicans to their cause, form local committees, and carry out a host of other activities, though always avoiding public spectacles. Headquartered in El Paso, the American Sinarquista movement was set up much like that in Mexico; stateside, it had regional committees, municipal committees, and rural subcommittees. The last were formed to centralize leadership at the local level. The Sinarquistas had two American regional committees, one in El Paso and another in Los Angeles. The one in El Paso had five municipal committees: in addition to the one in El Paso, municipal committees were established in Mission, Edinburg, and McAllen in the lower Río Grande Valley and in Laredo. The Los Angeles Sinarquista Regional Committee controlled twenty municipal committees, and plans called for additional municipal committees in Fresno, Oxnard, Santa Paula, Santa Ana, and Colton. In addition, branch chapters of the American Sinarquistas were planned for Phoenix and Nogales, Arizona; there was a Sinarquista municipal committee in Indiana Harbor, Indiana, and another was being established in Milwaukee, Wisconsin; and the Sinarquistas also had a presence in Chicago. The American Sinarquista organization was registered with the U.S. State Department under the McCormack Act and with the U.S. Justice Department in accordance with the terms of the Foreign Agents Registration Act.[52] Therefore, it is unlikely that the Sinarquistas carried on espionage or other subversive activities in the United States, for to do so would only have called attention to them. Moreover, because all the Mexican consular officials in the United States were Cárdenista loyalists, there was no close relationship between the Sinarquistas and these Mexican diplomatic officials.

Sinarquista activities in the Southwest anticipated scenarios that unfolded in Germany as the Nazis rose to power. The pro-Mexicanism of the Sinarquista movement espoused a radical nationalism to appeal to the sentiments of Mexicans in the United States for their Mexican homeland.

Its weekly newspaper, *El Sinarquista*, became the medium for the dissemination of Sinarquista propaganda among the Mexican community. The Sinarquistas conjured up nostalgic, mystical visions of the glorious Mexican past, and their articles promoted identity with the ancestral homeland of Mexico. *El Sinarquista* constantly touted the glories of colonial Mexico and pointed out to its readers that the destruction of Spanish power in Mexico was the result of an American Masonic-Protestant conspiracy. The Sinarquistas presented the fantasy of a new Spanish empire, El Gran Imperio Sinarquistas, whose capital city, "Sinacropolis," was to be built on the plains of west Texas. The newspaper's other themes struck a familiar and shrill fascist and anti-Semitic tone: Jews, Bolshevists, Masons, and international bankers centered in Washington controlled "Democracy." It is especially interesting in this connection that the Sinarquistas warned that this cabal was attempting to dominate the Western Hemisphere without regard to Latin Americans. To put an anti-Anglo agenda in motion, the movement alleged that the Anglo world was corrupt, godless, and immoral and that it granted rights only to the moneyed class. Because the Sinarquistas now had close ties to the Roman Catholic Church, the Spanish Civil War intensified the involvement of the church in the movement, and as a result Catholicism became linked with fascism.[53]

Mexico's International Anti-Sinarchist Committee in Defense of Democracy investigated the subversive activities of members of La Union Nacional Sinarquista, including allegations of espionage. It denounced Sinarchism as a ruse initiated "by Nazi and Falangist Spaniards with the help and direction of the clergy." Other charges made against the Sinarquistas were that the movement was controlled and financed by Axis money, that it was making a concerted effort to sabotage the allied war effort of Mexico and the United States, and that there were 50,000 members of La Union Nacional Sinarquista in California. This number was drastically inflated, as there were no more than 500 Sinarquistas in Los Angeles, but it was a necessary piece of antifascist propaganda.[54] Nevertheless, these profascist exploiters were going to revive and intensify a radical Mexican identity among the Mexican population in the United States and possibly provoke violence, in accordance with the master plan of Sinarquismo.

The efforts of the Peoples' Congress to stave off Sinarquista activity received assistance from antifascist authorities from Mexico who belonged to the International Anti-Sinarchist Committee in Defense of Democracy. This antifascist organization had established local communities in the Southwest and Midwest. On October 12, 1942, the president of the International Anti-Sinarchist Committee in Defense of Democracy of Mexico visited Los Angeles. He was Alfredo Díaz Escobar, a Mexican congressman from the state of Queretaro, a Sinarquista stronghold. Escobar visited Southern California to encourage the formation of additional local committees of his antifascist organization in the United States. Escobar had direct contact with American Communist Party members and CIO activists in California, such as civil rights activist Josefina Fierro de Bright of the Peoples' Congress, a widely respected community leader. Through a series of speeches, Escobar warned his audiences in Los Angeles that the Sinarquistas were in league with the Spanish Falange and the Nazis. The confrontations between anti- and pro-Sinarquista factions heated up and caught the attention of federal agencies. More interested in investigating communists than fascists, these federal agencies nevertheless soon began their investigations of Sinarquista activities.[55]

The communist parties of the United States and Mexico, under orders from the Soviet Union, spearheaded the attacks on La Union Nacional Sinarquista. This circumstance was underlined in a U.S. Justice Department field investigator's report. The same report went on to remark that American and Mexican communist elements "have been tenaciously conspiring to form a current of anti-Sinarchist opinion in the United States."[56] For example, the June 30, 1942, issue of the CPUSA's western region newspaper *People's World* featured an article accusing the Nazis of disseminating propaganda in the southwestern United States in an effort to undermine U.S.-Mexico relations by stimulating friction and promoting disunity between the two nations. Titled "Southern California Is Fascist Target," the article avowed: "Piped from Berlin through Spain to Mexico, and thence northward, a flood of Nazi propaganda . . . is pouring unchecked over the Southwestern states." The article specifically went on to warn that "Sinarchist propaganda . . . is . . . effective among the tens of thousands of Mexicans . . . whose long-standing . . . grievances make easy sailing for trained agitators to crystallize discontent and promote disunity. Behind this whole mess . . . is Adolph Hitler."[57] Continuing its exposé of Sinarquista activity in the Southwest, the party's national newspaper the *Daily Worker* carried an article on November 2, 1942, on the pro-Nazi Sinarchist activities in the lower Río Grande Valley of Texas. The article explained that Sinarquistas were holding "open as well as secret meetings" and distributing Nazi-inspired propaganda from Franco's Spain transshipped from Berlin. Using the occasion to highlight the Rome-Berlin Axis, the article added that members of the Spanish-Speaking Caballeros de Colón (Knights of Columbus) in Texas were actively cooperating with the Sinarquistas in the lower Río Grande Valley.[58]

During his visit to Los Angeles, Alfredo Díaz Escobar, the head of Mexico's International Anti-Sinarchist Committee in Defense of Democracy, had accused the Sinarquistas of attempting to convert Mexican American youth into ardent fascists by instilling hatred in them for Anglos and of furnishing money to the youth gangs to stir violence against the Spanish-speaking community. In light of the Sleepy Lagoon murder trial, a serious civil rights case, this was an important revelation of fascist complicity.[59]

LABOR, THE LEFT, AND SLEEPY LAGOON

In August 1942, the arrest and conviction of seventeen Mexican American youths on murder charges outraged the Mexican community and the Left. The so-called Sleepy Lagoon defendants became the West Coast complement of the earlier Scottsboro campaign. Like Scottsboro, the protest campaign built around the Sleepy Lagoon defendants mobilized mass support. The Sleepy Lagoon Defense Committee (SLDC) became the major vehicle uniting activists from the Peoples' Congress, Left-led progressive unions, and other Popular Front allies in a two-year defense campaign. The CIO's participation in the SLDC indicated an extension of labor struggles grounded in community matters, as three of the convicted Mexican Americans were furniture workers. Headed by Armando Davila and with many Spanish-speaking members, the UFWA was one of the most militant CIO unions in the city. Overlapping this extended struggle was the fight to fend off alarmist rumors of a "Mexican crime wave" that was purportedly sweeping Southern California and that climaxed in the Zoot Suit Riots of June 1943.[60]

The SLDC brought together activists from the CIO, the Peoples' Congress, and the Communist Party.[61] A coalition across class, racial, and ethnic lines, the SLDC got support from a wide range of minority leftists and liberals. The racist events surrounding the Sleepy Lagoon affair aroused outrage in these individuals. For example, Filipino American writer Carlos Bulosan helped the SLDC rally support in the Filipino community. Another key supporter was Charlota Bass, publisher of the black newspaper *California Eagle*, an influential voice within the black community, and an extremely outspoken Los Angeles progressive. The *California Eagle* was one of the first Los Angeles newspapers to publicize the racist nature of the Sleepy Lagoon case. Together, these racial minority activists argued repeatedly that social, educational, and employment discrimination, and not the Mexican's alleged genetic and cultural inferiority, contributed to delinquency in the Mexican American population.[62]

At this time of heightened racial tensions in the city of Los Angeles, Mexican American local union officials focused on how to aid the Sleepy Lagoon defendants. Accordingly, in August 1942 the CIO sponsored a Mexican Workers' Trade Union conference, where the participants made the following demands: that the Mexican government protest the conduct of the trial, including the district attorney's biased prosecution; that the Los Angeles Police Department and County Sheriff's Office stop the "unwarranted round-ups and arrests of Mexican youth"; and that the press curtail unfavorable coverage of the trial. The Los Angeles press fed its readership one-sided news accounts. This glaring instance of press bias was the beginning of the anti-Mexican sentiment the *Los Angeles Times* and other city newspapers whipped up in their sensationalist coverage of the Los Angeles Zoot Suit Riots. Scholars have concluded that such overheated press and radio coverage created a climate of fear and reprisal as the term "zoot-suiters" with all its negative overtones replaced "Mexicans." Readers assumed that the Mexican zoot-suiter was an immoral and deviant pariah strongly inclined to criminality, gangsterism, and even draft dodging. Conference participants also requested that the CIO officially endorse and join the SLDC, that the Los Angeles CIO Industrial Union Council establish a Mexican workers' committee and urge local unions to reach out to Spanish-speaking workers, and that a plan be implemented to prevent the Sinarquistas from exploiting the Sleepy Lagoon case so as to undermine the Los Angeles Mexican community's support of the war effort.[63]

With many members active in the Peoples' Congress, the ILWU played a main role in building a broad base of support for the Sleepy Lagoon defendants. Growing incensed over the excessive violence perpetrated against young Mexican Americans by local law enforcement officials, the union loudly condemned the Los Angeles police for their indiscriminate "mass jailings, unnecessary arrests and beatings of Mexican youth," declaring that such "iron-handed methods will only create a worse and more bitter feeling among the Mexican people." ILWU Local 29 warehouse workers circulated a petition demanding more recreational facilities, training schools, and jobs for unemployed Spanish-speaking youth. In addition, Local 29, ILWU Local 26, and UFWA Local 576 condemned the Sinarquistas as an antiunion hate group with links to international fascism. These CIO locals called for a federal investigation of a group of Mexican individuals "who call themselves the Sinarquista Union, preaching fascism . . . the disruption of our trade unions and hatred against the American people and government." In November, a Mexican Workers Committee was set up, led by Luisa Moreno and Revels Cayton, to initiate a multifold plan of action. The goals were to develop an educational program to solicit support for the SLDC, coordinate efforts to end racism against Mexicans within unions, and launch a CIO membership drive in the Spanish-speaking working-class neighborhoods.[64]

Meanwhile, the Communist Party made a determined effort to link the murder trial of the Sleepy Lagoon defendants with influences from the "Axis-controlled Sinarquistas." Alleging that the sinister fascist organization was provoking the Mexican population of Los Angeles with right-

Figure 4.D. The arrest and conviction on murder charges of seventeen Mexican American youths outraged CIO unionists and California Popular Front members. Arraignment of Sleepy Lagoon murder suspects, 1942. (00019388—*Herald Examiner* Photograph Collection, Courtesy of Los Angeles Public Library).

wing propaganda, the Citizens' Committee for the Defense of Mexican American Youth once again demanded an investigation of La Union Nacional Sinarquista by the Joint Fact-Finding Committee on Un-American Activities in California, the state's "little HUAC," headed by State Senator Jack B. Tenney. The harbinger of the postwar HUAC investigations, the blacklist, and the national CIO's purge of the Left-led unions, the decade-long Tenney Committee hearings began in July 1941. Senator Tenney invited several Citizens' Committee members to furnish evidence to substantiate their charges. These individuals failed to respond. Their uncooperative behavior of course raised suspicions in Tenney, who then subpoenaed them. The Citizens' Committee members eventually complied, for they knew that failure to do so would result in legal action against them.[65]

Actually, individual members of the civil rights defense committee had sent telegrams and letters in which they stated that they would not testify, asserting that all the information gathered by Senator Tenney's committee was going to be turned over to federal agencies. Moreover, the Office of War Information (OWI) had warned that the hearings would create additional unrest between Mexican Americans and Anglos and thus generate adverse publicity detrimental to the war effort. The telegram CIO official Philip Connelly wired to Senator Tenney's committee clearly revealed these reservations:

> I understand . . . that the FBI is conducting official inquiry therefore I believe it inadvisable . . . to respond to your invitation to participate in public hearings. . . . *Sinarquistas* and other fascist elements might well utilize publicity attended [*sic*] to your proposed hearing to stir up additional unrest . . . between Mexican-Americans and Anglo-Americans who must be thoroughly united in order to effectively win the war.[66]

The first of the three Citizens' Committee members subpoenaed by Senator Tenney was Mrs. LaRue McCormick, a Los Angeles civil rights activist and Communist Party member. Careful to provide no incriminating information, McCormick under oath pleaded ignorance of any factual information regarding the Sinarquistas, saying that any statements made by her regarding the Sinarquista movement were based solely "upon her own intuition and conviction." California State CIO president Philip Connelly, like McCormick, admitted under questioning that he did not know of "evidence to substantiate the charge the Union Nacional Sinarquista [was] a subversive organization controlled by the Hitler regime." The testimony of the third witness, Los Angeles CIO Industrial Union Council representative Oscar Fuss, resembled that of the previous two witnesses; Fuss had no information proving the Sinarquistas were subversive. Upon completion of its hearings, the Tenney Committee issued a statement declaring the charges made by the Citizens' Committee and Communist Party members "devoid of truth and without foundation."[67]

Guy T. Nunn, an outspoken field representative of the Minorities Group Service Commission, Office of Production Management (OPM), gave important testimony to the Los Angeles grand jury investigating the Sleepy Lagoon murders. Nunn was aware of the threat that fascist propaganda posed. He testified that he had received numerous complaints from Spanish-speaking communities throughout the Southwest of increased discrimination, which right-wing groups in Mexico and Latin America were exploiting to their advantage. "Certain elements in the Latin-American press," Nunn warned, "capitalized on these events in order to harm inter-American cooperation." Overall, Nunn's testimony challenged the arguments of the prosecution and the media about supposed Mexican criminality. Nunn basically substantiated the argument already made repeatedly by CIO activists and community spokesmen—that it was destitution and congested slum conditions, not juvenile crime, that set apart the

Spanish-speaking minority.[68] Nunn then focused on the consequences of long-term employment discrimination for Mexican workers, particularly their racialization as an inferior cultural group:

> The major afflictions of the Spanish-speaking minority stem from the basic types of employment to which this group has been confined by a combination of historical coincidence, deliberate design on the part of certain employing classes, and gross neglect or short-sightedness on the part of many community and government agencies.[69]

The U.S. Justice Department reconfirmed its initial report by concluding that the actual purpose of the Citizens' Committee for the Defense of Mexican American Youth was to show that the Sinarquistas in California were engaged in fifth-column activities, specifically in spreading hate and mistrust toward the U.S. government among Mexicans residing in the country. Aware that the root of support for Sinarquismo lay in Mexicans' Catholic traditions, party officials had instructed the Citizens' Committee in their attacks on La Union Nacional Sinarquista to demonstrate that the right-wing organization was "using the role of religion in order to further its fascist purposes." In exposing this Rome-Berlin Axis, however, the Citizens' Committee was careful to avoid alienating the Mexican people on religious grounds. The party had an interest in this antifascist campaign. It was part of the party's strategy to win Mexicans to its cause by gaining their vote in order to elect the party's candidate, LaRue McCormick, to the California Senate. According to the Justice Department, Local 26 of the ILWU had passed a resolution calling for the prosecution of the Sinarquista elements in California, directly charging Sinarquista agents with responsibility for the crimes allegedly committed by the city's Mexican American youth. In November 1942, at the request of its Spanish-speaking members, the Los Angeles CIO Industrial Union Council had undertaken a study of the Sinarquista influence in America. This resulted in the passage of a resolution stating that the Sinarquistas were an "evil influence among Mexican workers in the United States." Furthermore, the Sinarquistas were sabotaging Mexican American support of the war effort. Fascist agents were telling the Mexican people in the United States not to enlist in war activities such as the Civilian Defense and the Red Cross and not to purchase war bonds because the "Mexican people have nothing to gain from an Allied victory." This Axis propaganda stressed that the war would take an unfairly large toll on the lives of Spanish-speaking people because the armies of Uncle Sam "are made up of colored peoples—black and brown—considered as inferiors by the Anglo Saxons who always looked down upon them." This was another invention of Sinarquista propaganda but nonetheless potent, given the rise in the number of Mexicans being drafted or else volunteering for military service because they could not get paying jobs. The statement would certainly ring true in future wars.[70]

The FBI's Division of Surveys reached the same conclusion. In 1943, the year that Hitler took office in Germany and racist protofascist activity increased in the United States, President Roosevelt instructed the bureau to undertake the investigation of racist or "Anti-American activities" with any "possible connection with official representation of the German government in the United States." The FBI saw Sinarquista propaganda quite correctly as an attempt by this organization's agitators to spread hatred of Anglos and divert the attention of the Spanish-speaking population away from the war effort. Its activities thus resembled divisive schemes used by similar fascist groups to sabotage the war effort. The FBI observed, "Hatred of Americans is whipped up by publicizing discrimination against Mexicans in Defense jobs and social life. This discrimination, Sinarquistas say, proves that the U.S. is not a democracy and that the Mexicans have nothing to fight for on the American side, but everything to gain by a fascist victory."[71]

That La Union Sinarquista Nacional was spreading propaganda about the Communist Party taking control of the Mexican government was deemed especially unpropitious by government investigators, because the United States now counted on the Soviet Union as its ally in the war against the Axis powers and was reaching out to Mexico through its Good Neighbor Policy. Also disturbing were the attacks by the Sinarquistas on the newly implemented Mexican contract labor program. The Sinarquista movement instilled fear in Mexican nationals by warning that they would be conscripted to serve in the U.S. Army. Action by the U.S. Office of Censorship finally brought about the downfall of the Sinarquista movement in the United States. This federal agency stopped the distribution of the organization's newspaper *El Sinarquista*, since its pages disseminated right-wing nationalistic and anti-Democratic propaganda critical of both Mexico and the United States.[72]

The Sinarquista movement eventually waned. Although boosted by profascist Catholic priests, the Hearst press, Charles Lindbergh, and the American Firsters, the Sinarquista movement failed to gain a strong following in the Los Angeles Mexican community or among the ranks of the city's Spanish-speaking working classes. Propaganda presenting racial discrimination as the end result of a "democratic government . . . a thousand times more dangerous than a dictatorship like Hitler's or Mussolini's" was thwarted by activists with a strong Popular Front antiracist message. These labor and left-wing activists fused their work for social and economic equality with the Popular Front goal of defeating international fascism and with the goals of Roosevelt's Good Neighbor Policy. "They [the Sinarquistas] were windbags, more than anything," recalled

Mexican American activist José Gastelum. Help also came from Vicente Lombardo Toledano, the head of the Latin American Confederation of Labor, to generate support for the war effort by the city's Mexicans. Josefina Fierro de Bright succinctly surmised that the Spanish-speaking people lacked understanding "as to the meaning of democracy because they have not had the opportunity to be part of it." From de Bright's point of view, the Sinarquista propagandists and agitators capitalized on the persistent discrimination against Mexicans and "use[d] all of this to deviate us from the road to Victory." However, such distortions fell on deaf ears. In a rising spirit of American patriotism, the Spanish-speaking community was rallying behind the nation's war against the Axis powers. The Sinarquistas soon faded from governmental and public view with America's growing involvement in the war effort. This fact likewise signaled the imminent demise of the Congress of Spanish-Speaking Peoples. World War II thinned the ranks of this organization as members volunteered for military service or were drafted. As will be noted, McCarthyism would later silence former members of the Peoples' Congress, particularly the more leftist labor element belonging to the Communist Party.[73]

In the meantime, Los Angeles CIO leader Philip "Slim" Connelly urged State Attorney General Robert W. Kenney to push for the release of the "Sleepy Lagoon youth." Labor unions throughout California donated to the Sleepy Lagoon cause, and the national CIO passed a resolution supporting the Sleepy Lagoon defendants at its sixth convention. Three years would pass before the appeals court ruled to drop charges against the defendants, freeing the jailed youths. The struggle for their release had been a united effort on the part of progressive labor, civic, and religious groups. As the war spread, the CIO ADC, the Peoples' Congress, and other civil rights groups pressed on in a campaign for national unity against the Axis powers.[74]

Mexican American Unionists Press On to End Discrimination

The Committee to Aid Mexican Workers continued to press the issue of flagrant job discrimination by the Los Angeles office of the U.S. Employment Service. Following the mass rally held by the Los Angeles Negro Victory Committee in early April 1942, the California CIO ADC met with USES officials to plan ways of eliminating discriminatory practices in the employment services of this federal agency. This meeting came about because the Los Angeles USES office had implied that black women were not interested in defense work, adding to the insult by stating that the women would be more suitable as domestics and cooks. As an example of the ability of the black church to marshal protest, the Reverend

Clayton D. Russell mobilized the city's black community. Blacks fell into step behind Reverend Russell because he was an influential clergyman to whom they looked for leadership. Black workers in particular knew that in addition to convening rallies, Reverend Russell would keep them apprised of strikes and negotiations. Revealing the degree of concern over their exclusion from defense jobs, angry black women crowded into the first-floor offices of the USES as negotiations took place upstairs with government officials; meanwhile, the WMC dispatched investigators to Los Angeles to assess the overall situation and submit a report on the USES's activities. This direct action involving both black and Mexican American labor and community activists forced the USES out of its lethargy. It agreed to investigate and remedy all complaints by unions, community organizations, civic groups, and churches regarding discrimination against Negroes, Mexicans, and other minority groups in carrying out its work; to eliminate the practice of specifying the race, color, and creed of job applicants; and to organize its own antidiscrimination committees for northern and Southern California. By exerting pressure on the USES and the FEPC, the ADC and Mexican American CIO unionists immediately obtained jobs for several hundred blacks and Mexicans. These two minority groups continued to monitor the enforcement of Executive Order 8802, which would be achieved only through considerable public pressure. The Negro Victory Committee in this regard set up a system of informers; this spy network was made up of blacks in the USES offices, the police department, the unions, and the war industries who reported on instances of racial discrimination against blacks and Mexicans.[75]

Because of the persistent and widespread discrimination in government vocational training programs operating in the city of Los Angeles, only a small number of Mexicans had been trained for war industry employment relative to their percentage of the total population. The factor accounting for this was racial prejudice. For example, the East Side Chamber of Commerce publicized a contract between the Neighborhood Youth Administration (NYA) and the California State Relief Administration for aircraft mechanical training. The NYA certified only white youth for this training. In cooperation with progressive black ministers and the Peoples' Congress, California CIO ADC secretary Revels Cayton from the Marine Cooks and Stewards Union went before the Los Angeles Board of Education in May 1942 to lobby for "immediate classes" in welding, aircraft sheet metal, riveting, ship fitting, and expanded machine shop at various high schools in the black and Mexican communities. The black veteran trade unionist and Communist Party stalwart demanded that "Negro and Mexican teachers, advisers, fieldworkers, clerks, and other staff be hired to help integrate the two minority groups in defense [work] training" and that "defense classes be opened for women." By June, blacks and Mexi-

cans were enrolled in aircraft, welding, and other national defense training classes. Continued inaction on the part of the Board of Education
pushed the Negro Victory Committee in August 1942 to mobilize mass
action. It staged a march on the Los Angeles Board of Education to demand war industries job training for black women. As a result of this
grassroots pressure, the Board of Education called a special session to
consider these demands, at which time it was revealed that the Board of
Education would not open training centers in the mixed black and Mexican communities but would instead place these centers in outlying all-
white areas, where there was considerable bigotry toward blacks and
Mexicans. For example, one training center was located in Inglewood, a
hotbed of Ku Klux Klan activity, and another training center was placed
in Glendale, where because of the city's "sunset laws," police routinely
stopped blacks who were on the city's streets after 6:00 P.M. Afterwards,
defense training schools were opened in the city's black and Mexican
communities. When the ADC conducted a job registration campaign in
the minority neighborhoods, it received 4,000 applications. In the meantime, the CIO continued its union drives to organize the defense industries
in Los Angeles and the rest of Southern California. Progressive unions like
the ILWU dispatched its organizers to target for unionization industries
employing Mexican, black, and women workers, such as the Los Angeles
shoe industry, the plants of North American and Vultee Aircraft, the Los
Angeles Municipal Railway, the electrical plants, and tunnel, cement, oil,
rubber, and chemical works.[76]

An important target for unionization was the Los Angeles Municipal
Railway because it operated all the city's streetcars and buses. Blacks and
Mexicans relied heavily on this public transportation. Several hundred
streetcars were not in operation, and the idea arose that these streetcars
could be used to transport black and Mexican war workers to their jobs
in the defense plants. After holding a series of successful war bond rallies
in Pershing Square to publicize its battle with the Los Angeles Railway
System, the Negro Victory Committee contacted the AFL. The black
grassroots organization told the AFL local it would support its efforts to
win higher wages and job upgrading for its members employed by the
Los Angeles Railway System if the local agreed to support the committee's
efforts in return. CIO Mexican American activists endorsed this strategy.
In addition, the ILWU aided campaigns by Mine-Mill to organize tunnel
workers at Trona, Tehachapi, the San Jacinto Tunnel, and Monolith Cement; these union activists also helped organize oil and rubber workers
and technicians in the chemical industry. Mexican American trade unionists were achieving some success in eliminating racial discrimination in
defense work and in expanding job opportunities in the war industries.
The unionists would have to fight on two fronts because the problems the

Mexican community faced in Los Angeles were being amplified by the increased racial tensions World War II was creating at home.[77]

Federal official Nunn recommended a national program to integrate racial minority workers into the U.S. economy. Nunn emphasized that the war effort demanded "the economic rehabilitation of Mexicans and other minorities," but he cynically pointed out that "Only the draft to date has shown no bias against Mexicans." Nunn wisely warned that the United States needed to take the "lessons of interracial democracy" to heart or it would lose the war. Six months after Nunn's testimony, the Zoot Suit Riots reinforced the necessity of such lessons. Latin American allies questioned the wisdom of U.S. official policy regarding race relations. Harsh criticism of American race relations poured out from Mexico after the outbreak of the Los Angeles riots. For instance, one university official addressing protesting students at a Mexico City university told his audience that President Roosevelt's liberal attitude unfortunately freed him from all responsibility for the racial violence. Expressing little reservation in criticizing America's racism, the university students called on the United States to launch "a widespread press and radio campaign [to] make the North American public realize that the people of Mexico, mostly of mixed Indian and Spanish blood, can not fight in this war with enthusiasm side by side with a country that harbors racial prejudice."[78]

The Los Angeles Zoot Suit Riots represented a degree of violent racial turmoil not seen in America's cities since the post–World War I years. Scholars conclude that preventing race-related violence and discrimination was never a central part of the Roosevelt administration's war on crime. In addition to penetrating organized labor, newspapers, educational institutions, and the armed forces, the FBI infiltrated youth groups in its ongoing investigations of fascist and anti-American activities. However, notwithstanding pressure from the Justice Department, the FBI under J. Edgar Hoover failed to investigate the practices of the nation's local police forces. The growing confrontations between the Los Angeles Police Department and Mexican Americans, combined with glaring misreporting by city newspapers, precipitated the large-scale rioting that unfolded in June 1943. Containing outbreaks of domestic racism was not one of the national problems that could be solved by central planning and control in America's mobilization for war.[79]

The California State CIO did not have the same success in bringing Mexican Americans into the trade unions that it did with blacks because it did not extend the same kind of concentrated effort. The state CIO essentially conceded that it had failed to carry out a "solid" trade union program among Spanish-speaking workers, adding that a "strong and aggressive" community movement among the Mexican people was lacking. Moreover, the CIO Anti-Discrimination Committee admitted that it had failed to "weed out" the influence of a small but intensely active group of "Fascist-minded Mexicans," who opposed the CIO program through their Sinarquista Union. The ADC concluded, however, that the great majority of Mexicans were not profascist or seditious and whole-heartedly backed the "joint war effort of the United Nations."[80] During the war years, the CIO focused on enforcing and improving contracts in addition to organizing new workers. As we have seen in the case of Mine-Mill, Mexican workers did not immediately win jobs in all-Anglo work-places, nor did Mexicans working in industries with racially mixed work-forces win the higher-paid jobs monopolized by Anglos. Yet no one can deny that the wage increases the CIO won for Mexicans, as with black workers, kept hundreds of them off public and private relief lists and put money in the hands of Mexican workers. Together with black workers, Mexicans were elemental to the success of CIO industrial unionism. Moreover, these two racial minority groups pushed the CIO to back the larger issue of civil rights. For the remainder of the World War II years, Mexican Americans continued their push for labor rights with demands that called for civil rights.[81]

The Lie of "America's Greatest Generation": Mexican Americans Fight against Prejudice, Intolerance, and Hatred during World War II

> I will not characterize any group of people by its less desirable members. Every race is composed of all kinds of individuals; you can be sure you are wrong when you say, "They are all alike."
> —*Commandments of Race Relations*, Detroit Y.M.C.A.

> I swear to the Lord
> I still can't see
> Why Democracy means
> Everybody but me.
>
> —LANGSTON HUGHES

WITH THE START of World War II the federal government committed the nation to total victory. The numerous social and economic problems faced by the Spanish-speaking hampered their participation in the war effort because their overall economic and social status had not measurably improved since the Great Depression. As hostilities mounted in Europe and the Pacific, the Mexican American population remained overwhelmingly working-class in composition, and they still faced the dilemma of great inequality. They were affected to a disproportionate degree by malnutrition and disease, housing conditions for them were the worst in the nation, and illiteracy was extensive. In sum, Mexican Americans remained outside the larger American society. Government officials concluded that the nearly two million U.S. citizens of Mexican descent were the most oppressed and destitute minorities in the United States. The federal government would not intervene on behalf of blacks or Mexican Americans, the nation's most highly visible disadvantaged groups. The White House appeared to ignore the rapidly escalating racial tensions in America, which climaxed in a wave of race riots in the late spring of 1943. On the labor front, Mexican American workers used the wartime FEPC to press for employment gains, despite the fact that this government agency lacked significant enforcement powers of its own. Mexican Americans thus found themselves the last hired for defense work; discriminated against in federal job training programs, they worked at the lowest-paying jobs. Economic disparity impeded their opportunities for advancement. Denied deferments owing to their concentration in agriculture and in unskilled defense industry work, the Spanish-speaking were drafted and voluntarily enlisted in dramatically increasing numbers.[1]

Wartime experiences offered new opportunities as the manpower requirements of both war industries and the military increased. However, the impact of the war rapidly changed the pattern of race relations in America and created a volatile social climate as rationing, shortages, overcrowding, long workweeks without recreation, uneasiness over new jobs, and relocations to other cities produced outbreaks of violent racial conflict. Specifically, the flow of workers into America's industrial cities created tensions and produced clashes as competition for jobs and housing intensified. Using race as a mechanism of exclusion, war industries employers prevented racial minority workers from making employment gains, while the unyielding attitudes of whites increased racial strife at the workplace. Whites also put up resistance to fair housing and enforced racial covenants through the courts to bar the entrance of blacks and Mexicans into areas outside the central cities. Federal agencies launched investigations of racial discrimination as the United States created a network of surveillance and screening plans to target trouble areas for ameliorative and police action. Within this context of war mobilization and escalating racial turmoil, Mexican Americans persevered in demanding advancement.[2]

Los Angeles was booming in the 1940s. The city was bound by dramatic economic change, and the effects of migration had an exacting impact on available housing. The war workers' acute need for housing was a serious problem in this West Coast war mobilization center, but so was discrimination in housing. Mexican Americans could not choose where they could live. Good rental housing was unavailable to them, and they found it impossible to purchase housing outside segregated areas. Housing discrimination resulted in the segregation of Mexican Americans in areas marked by substandard living conditions. As policy scholars have shown, the federal government aided this housing discrimination through financial and construction practices that produced minority concentration in central cities and white homogeneity in outlying areas. Economic disparity reduced the housing choices for Mexican Americans, and housing segregation in turn relegated this minority group to schools with scant resources, a situation that, when combined with racism, produced a lethal outbreak of juvenile delinquency.

Beginning in 1942 and over the next twenty-two years, approximately five million Mexican nationals were brought into the United States for seasonal employment in agriculture, with the majority of the contract laborers being shipped to work in Texas, Arizona, and California. Mexican nationals imported into the country by the U.S. government as part of its newly implemented farm labor program through the auspices of the Good Neighbor Policy replaced those Mexican American residents who depended on farm work for their livelihood. The presence of contract labor imported from Mexico, along with *mojados* illegally crossing the border, conspired to depress wages and encourage poor working conditions, and once again it confounded for Anglos the identity of Mexican Americans.

Racial discrimination impaired national unity, lowered morale, and hurt America's war effort at home and overseas. This situation produced considerable dissatisfaction with federal policies among the Spanish-speaking population. A disgruntled Mexican American revealed the disappointment over the shortcomings of the federal government in the matter of discrimination when, in July 1943, he told a representative from the Division of Inter-American Activities of the Office of the Coordinator of Inter-American Affairs:

> The "No Mexicans Allowed" idea has extended to such places as churches and to such events as July Fourth celebrations—even to the extent of the exclusion of war veterans from patriotic rallies and festivals. These discriminatory practices weigh heavily not only upon the total Spanish-speaking population but . . . [also upon] the Spanish-speaking soldiers, their relatives and friends. I have heard of numerous cases where soldiers in uniform . . . have been refused services in such places as barbershops and restaurants.[3]

In light of the nationwide outbreak of racial conflict and the potential ability of Axis propaganda to exploit the issue of racism, numerous official and private institutions and organizations began to express more interest in the plight of America's Spanish-speaking peoples, especially the living standards, wages, and manpower mobilization of this racial minority group. Another matter of concern was the overall relation of the Spanish-speaking to America's war effort—that is, how certain measures or policies involving the Spanish-speaking population would affect public morale, discrimination, housing, educational standards, social work, delinquency, recruitment for the armed services, propaganda and information, labor relations, and inter-American relations. With the exception of the highly criticized FEPC, the chief vehicle for the wartime initiative in civil rights, and the poorly funded Office of the Coordinator of Inter-American Affairs (OCIAA), no coordinated national effort existed to assist the Spanish-speaking in resolving problems of discrimination or to address the relation of this minority group to the war effort.[4]

This chapter argues that the federal government failed to take a stand to protect the rights of America's racial minorities or to enforce the policies adopted to assure their full participation in the war effort. Unresponsive to the realities of race relations in the Southwest, the government was not overtly committed to the matter of full equality, particularly the elimination of racial barriers preventing the hiring and upgrading of Mexican Americans in use by firms with defense contracts containing nondiscrimination clauses. Increasingly dissatisfied with the racial barriers blocking their advancement, Mexican Americans began to voice their need for equality more vigorously. Certain so-called intergroup conflict associations surfaced at the local level to join existing organizations like the Mexican American Movement to agitate for social justice. However, despite the increase in racial prejudice against the Spanish-speaking, national Mexican American civil rights organizations remained nonexistent. Having filled this void successfully in the 1930s, labor unions continued to serve as the main vehicles for the development of Mexican American leadership and as a following for that leadership in the fight against social injustice during the war years. Through contact with and engagement in trade unionism, Mexican Americans articulated their demands for civil rights and pressed the CIO to take a hard line against intolerance.[5]

Eternal Victims of Race Hatred: The Predicament of Tejanos

The basic dilemma of racism, poverty, and lack of education faced by Mexicans in the Southwest remained especially appalling in Texas. In the World War II years, Texas had the highest concentration of Mexicans in the nation, nearly one million. Tejanos lived in all parts of Texas; however, the largest concentrations remained in the lower Río Grande Valley and central Texas. Agriculture was the leading economy in the state, and Tejanos remained dependent for their livelihood on the fruit, vegetable, and cotton harvests. Race relations stayed virtually unchanged in both rural and urban areas. The political and economic elite of Texas consisted of Anglos. These conservative Anglos controlled the Texas economy and sought to control governmental machinery locally, in the state, and in Congress. Order was imposed through the long-standing practice of suppression. Deeply racist, the Anglo elite wanted to ensure the economic dependence and political impotence of Tejanos where they formed majority populations. As with the strict regulation of blacks in other states in the South, state laws, mores, customs, and traditions in Texas controlled how Tejanos worked, ate, slept, rode, drank, were entertained, conversed, and even were buried.[6]

The out-migration of thousands of Tejanos from rural areas to the cities continued. Spurred by employment opportunities at military installations like the Kelly Army Air Base, many migrated to San Antonio. Yet persistent misery, want, unemployment, and the inability to break out of this circle of poverty were the grim facts of life for Tejano residents of San Antonio. A survey of San Antonio in 1943 revealed that the city's 100,000 Tejano residents had larger families, smaller houses, and less income than the city's blacks. San Antonio's Tejanos lived as "rootless, semi-urbanized workers," Carey McWilliams noted, since many remained confined to agricultural work. The lack of job skills combined with entrenched and widespread discrimination kept the majority of Tejanos segregated in the West Side, in the most crowded and deteriorating housing in San Antonio. Over half (56 percent) inhabited substandard homes; Tejanos accounted for nearly three-fourths (72 percent) of the city's tuberculosis deaths, and they had the nation's highest infant mortality rates. Living under these circumstances promoted an extreme alienation of Tejanos from the larger American society. Attending schools in such a dismal environment moreover undermined the motivation to learn and resulted in high dropout rates. A study of the 1942–43 Texas school year revealed that a little over half (53 percent) of the state's Tejano children were enrolled or attended school on a regular basis. More than 3,000 Tejano children—and possibly as many as 10,000—were not enrolled in San Antonio's public schools. In fact, large numbers of the city's Tejano youth never graduated from high school. Lacking job skills, Tejanos wound up unemployed, and deprivation led to the development of criminal activities. Because Anglo police embodied the constant threat of discrimination, intimidation, and violence, Tejanos accounted for over half (55 percent) of all juvenile arrests in the city. Illiteracy among San Antonio Tejanos stood at over 15 percent. The segregation of San Antonio's Tejanos, like that of blacks, extended from housing to public transportation, waiting rooms, bathrooms, theaters, and restaurants. Socially and economically, the status of Tejanos remained far below that of the Anglo population of Texas, an unreconstructed, segregationist, and antiunion state. United by their racism, Anglo employers and workers had nearly locked Tejanos out of industrial employment, and little help came from the federal government. Despite the job boom created by wartime production in Texas, less than 5 percent of Tejanos held jobs in war-related industries.[7]

As the value of farm production tripled during World War II, the wartime needs of the Texas cotton economy presented cotton growers with new opportunities for profits. Cotton growers therefore attempted to hoard Tejano farm workers, who had not lost their economic value because tens of thousands of them could be hired for next to nothing in wages, increasing the profit margin. Texas farmers received help from government officials in extending the color bar to Tejanos to keep them out of vocational training programs and the war industries. Between 100,000 and 150,000 Tejanos continued to follow the crops through Texas, spilling into the Midwest, the Plains States, and the Pacific Northwest. The migrant workers in every respect remained exploited, poor, socially fragmented, and for the most part invisible to the rest of America. In the 1930s, New Deal agencies such as the Farm Security Administration attempted to improve migrant workers' dreadful living conditions but met considerable resistance from Anglo growers, who feared that if Tejanos achieved better living conditions, they would soon expect higher wages. As we have seen, Tejanos organized against grower exploitation and abuse by joining unions, but this increasing militancy was stopped by a combination of intimidation, violent reprisals, and the decision by the UCAPAWA to abandon the organization of farm workers. When the federal government intervened, it did so on the side of the growers and singled out labor activists for investigation and deportation.[8]

In the World War II years, Tejanos fell victim to the all-white local draft boards, microcosms of inordinate Anglo political power and authority, bigotry, and cultural customs. Employed mainly as migrant workers or farmhands, Tejanos could not claim deferment on this basis, even though the passage of the Tydings Amendment in November 1942 exempted agricultural workers from the draft. Moreover, a nondiscriminatory provision in the Selective Service Act of 1940 specified, "In the selection and training of men under this Act, there would be no discrimination against any person on account of race and color." Yet complaints submitted by Tejanos to the U.S. War Department stated that Anglo draft boards were sending thousands of Tejanos off for duty on the war front so that they would be killed. These accusations were substantiated by the fact that Tejanos made up nearly three-fourths of the war casualties from south Texas.[9]

The total number of Tejanos available for farm work actually declined after 1937 as a result of interstate migration to farm and nonfarm defense work out of state and the passage of the Alien Registration Law and the Selective Service Act. War mobilization presented Tejano migrant workers and Texas farmers with a new set of opportunities as well as problems. With their men in military uniform, Tejano migrant families now had to fend for themselves, and tire and gasoline rationing and the procurement of special permits hampered travel and caused other hardships. Texas farmers, on the other hand, were being asked to produce over a third (37.5 percent) more crops for the war effort but with a significantly reduced labor force. Unlike other southwestern ranchers and growers, Texas farmers could not allege shortages of domestic labor and import contract labor from Mexico because the persistent mistreatment of Tejanos had excluded Texas from participation in the new program. The contract labor program shunned Texas, and given the nation's vital war material needs, maximizing the productivity of the available Tejano farm labor force to lessen manpower shortages became a priority for the state's agricultural interests, particularly the cotton growers. In 1943, the U.S. Employment Service and the War Manpower Commission ceded power to local Texas authorities for the regulation of rural manpower in the state. Through a contract with these two federal agencies, the Texas A&M College Extension Service took charge of routing and placing migrant workers. It did this through the Texas Farm Labor Program (TFLP), whose other purpose was human relations—specifically, to relieve race tensions by educating local farmers and communities about the value of Tejano farm workers in facilitating the state's cotton crop harvests. This joint venture utilized federal monies and know-how without disturbing the existing economic order in Texas, which rested on a distinct and advantageous system of race relations.[10]

Through its county agents, the Texas A&M College Extension Service provided Tejano migrants with information on crops, working conditions, and rest stations with cooking and bathing facilities, and it explained to recalcitrant Anglo farmers and businessmen the necessity of welcoming the itinerants in the local communities. Discontinuing its initial contract with the USES, the extension service took over full operation of the TFLP, which, along with its other services, continued its educational work to acquaint the public with the need for migratory workers. While carefully explaining that racial discrimination threatened the vital Texas cotton harvest, the extension service simultaneously stressed that managing race relations was not, in itself, part of its program.[11]

Despite the statewide publicity campaign launched by the TFLP, prejudice against Tejanos prevailed throughout Texas. Predictably, neither the state's Good Neighbor Commission nor the passage of the "Caucasian Race" resolution in May 1943 reduced prejudice. The latter was a nonbinding law that affirmed the right of all Caucasians within the state—and Tejanos were considered Caucasian—to equal treatment in public places. Theaters, restaurants, swimming pools, public parks, barbershops, and other facilities in Texas were nevertheless closed to Tejanos. In El Paso, Anglo hostility toward the city's 60,000 Spanish-speaking residents flourished, despite the president's call for wartime unity. In the town of Del Río in southwest Texas, Tejanos made up almost two-thirds (65 percent) of the population, but they were segregated in all facets of life. The local draft board had emptied the town of military-age Tejano males. Like all the other local draft boards in Texas, the Del Rio draft board was all-Anglo in composition, because to allow Tejanos on the draft boards would give them power over Anglo draftees. Tejanos represented 90 percent of Del Rio's draftees, notwithstanding rejections based on poor health and low education. While a discriminatory deferment standard was applied to Tejanos, Del Rio Anglos secured the much-valued deferments because the draft board listed them in essential occupations such as stock-raising and wool-marketing activities management.[12]

In the Gulf Coast cotton-growing area of Wharton County and in the west Texas cotton district in Cochran County, the courthouses had separate bathroom facilities for "Colored and Mexicans and Whites." In Fort Worth, Anglo, Tejano, and black residents had to use different doors at the courthouse to pick up their government ration books. (A sign on the courthouse read: "Whites use the East Door, Mexicans and Negroes use West door.") Tejanos were even segregated in Catholic parishes, and some Catholic churches would not permit marriages or baptisms of Tejanos, despite their being overwhelmingly of the Catholic faith. Segregation followed Tejanos to their graves, for at many public and private cemeteries in Texas, Tejanos were buried in areas separate from Anglos or denied interment altogether. Officials of the town of Paducah in the west Texas cotton district apparently took this matter to an incomparable level of racial loathing: local Tejanos were buried in the city dump.[13]

Tejanos could not sue Anglos; they were denied this right by local juries or else withdrew their complaints after being intimidated by local authorities. Tejanos could not vote in many Texas counties, and if they tried to vote they were driven away with threats. In Wharton, Brazoria, Fort Bend, and Matagorda Counties in southeast Texas, the so-called White Man's Union prevented Tejanos from voting in the Democratic primary elections. Where Tejanos were allowed to vote, deceitful Anglo political bosses monitored them at the polling booths to make certain they voted for handpicked candidates and programs. Fighting for one's country mattered little in Texas if the GI was Tejano or black. More than 250,000 Tejanos served in the armed forces, representing 57 percent of the nation's Spanish-speaking servicemen and women, yet every opportunity was found to discriminate against Tejano GIs. Back home from the war front, Tejano servicemen confronted open hostility from Anglo merchants and brutality at the hands of police and townsfolk. As with black servicemen in the South, the army failed to protect Tejano servicemen who went off military bases in Texas, where they were harassed, beaten, and robbed by Anglos. Spanish-speaking and black GIs were segregated to movie theater balconies and were not allowed to wait for buses inside the bus stations owing to strict Texas laws and customs regarding racial mingling. In south Texas, the fear of racial fraternization also resulted in the exclusion of female relatives of these Tejano servicemen from participation in USO and other home front activities in support of America's war effort. Maintaining a resolute demarcation along color lines was more important.[14]

Anglo race hatred had already been demonstrated in Texarkana, Texas, with the lynching of Willie Vinson, and talk of the rape of a white woman by a black man in Beaumont, Texas, set off a rampage by revenge-seeking whites through the black districts that resulted in the killing of two blacks and the injuring of hundreds of others. Racism's vices spilled over into the labor movement, reflecting the previously noted rightward shift of Texas politics toward antiunionism. Yet from the outset, entrenched racism was an important factor in restricting opportunities for Tejano workers. Universally, Anglos refused to work with either Mexicans or blacks, and as a result employers shied away from integrating their workforce. The general feeling among Anglos was that their jobs would be degraded by the admission of Tejanos or blacks to defense employment. Despite the national CIO's embrace of racial equality and the fact that the Texas State CIO Council in 1942 went on record opposing discrimination against Tejanos in public places, in the armed forces, and in Texas war industries, union affiliates in the state, along with their Anglo rank-and-file membership, remained extremely unfriendly to Tejano workers and vigorously resisted their efforts to attain equal opportunities. Many dissident locals either did not grant membership to Tejanos because Anglo workers failed to perceive Tejanos as their equals, accepted them with restrictions on equal pay and seniority rights, or made sure Tejanos, along with black workers, remained confined to unskilled and menial jobs. For example, Tejano employees of the Humble Oil Company and the Shell Oil Company in east Texas were paid ten to thirteen cents less per hour than Anglo workers and were repeatedly denied promotions to semiskilled and skilled positions. In their defense, the oil companies argued that their Anglo employees resisted the promotion of Tejanos. Yet the policy of the oil companies was to deny Tejanos job upgrades and to maintain work site segregation, including separate bathrooms, drinking fountains, eating facilities, and bus transportation to and from work. Frustrated by the lingering racism and the lack of job opportunities in their home state, some Tejanos escaped by migrating north.[15]

By 1940 over 60,000 Tejanos had migrated to the Great Lakes region; as Dionicio Valdés has pointed out, many of those heading north had lost their WPA jobs, or else Anglos had pushed them out of wage-protected packing shed and cannery work. Many of the Anglos who were hired over Tejanos for defense work had been brought into Texas from outside the state, a practice the Texas State CIO Council was aware of as early as 1938. In that year the State CIO Council passed a resolution introduced by Gaspar Virgilio of Oil Workers Industrial Union Local 228 to protest the practice by large industrial employers of encouraging the influx of Anglos from other states to depress wages and increase work hours. The Tejanos who left for the Midwest were being recruited by northern beet farmers resupplying their labor force, which had been depleted by the departure of farm workers to the area war production centers. Many Tejanos followed suit: one in four Tejano males between the ages of twenty-one and thirty-five eventually left the migrant stream and entered midwestern war production centers for higher pay and more regular work.[16]

The nation's expanding war economy intersected with the ongoing urbanization of Mexican Americans, blacks, and whites. In this context, rural Tejanos enlarged the North's older Spanish-speaking blue-collar neighborhoods or entered new working-class sectors in other manufacturing cities. Michigan foundries like those in Ecorse, Wyandotte, River Rouge, and Pontiac recruited thousands of Tejanos; about 4,000 Mexican Americans in Chicago's Stockyards district were employed in area meat-packing plants; and in South Chicago the number of Mexicans who toiled in the area steel mills reached 10,000 by 1945. Still, job expansion failed to reach Mexican Americans because of the primacy of skilled labor needs, widespread employment discrimination, and exclusionary defense contracts that did not cover new hires. The Great Depression had severely restricted the skills that minority job applicants had to offer, and management's preference for white labor had dislodged minorities from construction and other traditional jobs that now flourished alongside other war-related employment. A 1941 Social Security Board survey found that half (51 percent) of the anticipated openings in defense plants were closed to nonwhite applicants. For the Mexican Americans fortunate enough to partake in defense work opportunities, earnings undeniably increased, but not to the extent of white workers' earnings because of discriminatory job clustering in low-wage and unskilled aircraft, packinghouse, steel mill, foundry, auto, mining, rail yard, and service work. The story of opportunity and inequality was the same for Mexican American women defense workers.[17]

"WORKING OVERTIME ON THE RIVETING MACHINE": MEXICAN AMERICAN WOMEN WAR WORKERS

The war production boom provided new opportunities for Mexican American women. Like their black counterparts, rural Spanish-speaking women tended to forgo farm and domestic work, since they now received money from male relatives in military service or from those working in war production centers. However, with the departure of husbands and brothers to war, first single, then married Mexican American women entered defense work and became their families' primary breadwinners. In the Midwest, about 5,000 Mexican women worked in defense plants at jobs ranging from riveting to munitions. Most of these female workers were young and single, but after 1943, married, divorced, and elderly women (some as old as seventy-five) entered the ranks of defense plant employment. Many were recently arrived Tejanas who had fled Jim Crow-ism in Texas. Despite federal intervention to eliminate racial and gender inequality in defense work, Mexican American women war workers suf-fered workplace discrimination. They often were assigned to work along-side black women, because white women steadfastly refused to work with blacks, or else were hired into low-paying, low-status, and dangerous jobs in the place of black women.[18]

Mexican American women defense workers put in sixteen-hour days for months at a time in various war industries. They made up almost 40 percent of munitions workers engaged in the production of bombs, fuses, bullets, shell casings, mines, grenades, rifles, machine guns, artillery, and rocket launchers for Kansas Ordnance, Parsons Ordnance, Hastings Am-munition Depot, Lake City Ordnance, and other armaments producers. Most were assigned to low-paying and quite dangerous jobs in lieu of black women, who were denied this work. Small numbers worked in the steel mills of U.S. Steel, Bethlehem Steel, Great Lakes Steel, Inland Steel, and Youngstown Steel. Performing the same jobs as the men, these women steel workers were assigned to the rolling mills, blast furnaces, and open hearths, and worked as crane operators, welders, and riveters. Large num-bers worked for the Burlington and Santa Fe Railroads as well as for the rail lines of some steel companies, such as Inland Steel. The women held jobs as section hands replacing ties and rails; they were roundhouse me-chanics and train dispatchers; they loaded and unloaded boxcars of war materials and heavy chunks of ice for the air-conditioning system during the summer; others were employed as waitresses and tellers in the railroad lunch rooms and ticket offices. During winter, many of these women rail-road workers toiled in freezing weather, clearing the tracks of snow for the troop and supply trains. The Armour, Swift, Wilson, Morrell, and Cudahy meat companies employed many Mexican American women as trimmers, butchers, and packers and in the production of C and K rations. The women labored under harsh conditions all day inside the meatpack-ing plants and in loading refrigeration cars. Constantly sick from colds and the flu, they endured freezing temperatures along with the terrible stench of dead animals.[19]

Mexican American women war workers made the high production quotas because they believed they were making direct contributions on behalf of so many Mexican American males in the military. Such was the case of South Saint Paul's Mexican women packinghouse workers. They kept up production because they thought they were helping feed 790 of their men fighting overseas. Mexican American women in CIO locals par-ticipated in numerous home front activities; part of the CIO's strategy during the early war years to fight worker apathy was to boost morale through meetings, literature, blood and war bond drives, and other activities in support of the war. In Southern California, Mexican American cannery workers at Continental Can raised over $21,000 during a war bond drive, while the workers at Cal San increased their production of spinach as part of the "Food for Victory" campaign. Women workers at the California Walnut plant belonging to UCAPAWA Local 3 donated one day's wages to the American Red Cross and sponsored successful blood drives. In Texas, Tejanas in CIO locals purchased war bonds and stamps, raised funds for the Red Cross, donated blood, took part in the United War Chest Campaign, and worked with the national CIO War Relief Committee in the state. Many Mexican American women war workers had entered the labor force before the start of World War II, and like other women, they would seek to retain their jobs once the war ended. As strikers in the postwar years, they would bravely hold the line to improve wages and working conditions.[20]

FLEEING POVERTY: THE CASE OF THE SPANISH-SPEAKING OF NEW MEXICO

High draft and volunteer rates, out-migration, and participation in federal vocational job training programs were native New Mexicans' options for dealing with the lack of work opportunities at home. The Office of War Information reported that New Mexico's Spanish-speaking residents represented over 40 percent of the state's population. Mostly American citizens, they were nevertheless victims of persistent and widespread discrimination and economic deprivation and had little protection against the legally and economically powerful Anglos who dominated in the state. In the case of rural Spanish-speaking New Mexicans, access to communally held land shrank to two acres per family as Anglo newcomers and absentee owners obtained titles to these lands, often through unscrupulous methods. These factors, along with the loss of water rights to Anglos developing corporate farming in the river valleys, caused overpopulation, poor housing and sanitation, hunger, and poverty. During the Great Depression, the poor job prospects of New Mexico's Spanish-speaking farmers attracted the attention of various federal government agencies. However, because New Deal programs were being phased out or cut back, Spanish-speaking farming families continued to lose their lands at a rapid pace. Consequently, over half were forced to migrate to search for work, and many others were drafted or volunteered for military service.[21]

Discriminated against in nearly all facets of their lives and with the twin curse of underemployment and unemployment, Spanish-speaking New

Mexicans assumed a greater role in the war effort overseas as draftees and voluntarily enlistees. It was a widespread practice for the state's Anglo-dominated draft boards to induct large numbers of Spanish-speaking males into military service. Despite protests, local draft board officers defended this conscription of Mexican American males, claiming it was necessary to preserve the more valuable Anglo manpower, because employers were not about to substitute Mexican for Anglo labor. To raise their families out of abject poverty, thousands of Spanish-speaking New Mexicans joined the New Mexico National Guard prior to the war. These units were activated when America declared war on the Axis powers. As a result, Spanish-speaking New Mexicans accounted for a fourth of the 5,600 besieged New Mexico National Guardsmen at Bataan and Corregidor in the Philippines and with other Mexican Americans suffered the highest casualties of all of America's minority groups. Many of New Mexico's Spanish-speaking GIs stationed overseas came from impoverished backgrounds, and as they died in record numbers on the battlefront, some of these GIs wrote to elected officials to express concern about their parents' plight back home. For example, one New Mexican family, descendants of the first settlers of New Mexico, lost a son at Bataan, and a second son was reported missing in action in the Pacific. The week this family was notified that their second son was shot down and missing, their third son, a college graduate, was denied work by three different employers. In the proverbial slap in the face, all the employers told him, "We don't hire Mexicans."[22]

As a result of the worsening economic and social conditions, northern New Mexico's Spanish-speaking male residents increased their migration rates to levels higher than those of the Depression years, while many others were drafted or volunteered for military service. Forty-five percent of New Mexican males between the ages of fifteen and sixty-five left to search for work or entered military service. The wartime sojourners followed the same trajectory as earlier migrants; however, more men were traveling farther in search of work. The need to find work also drew disenfranchised families and more married and young women into the migration streams from southern New Mexico, where loss of farmland was even greater. Notwithstanding, Spanish-speaking families from all of New Mexico's counties took part in the exodus.[23]

Migration patterns replicated those of Mexican Americans who had left New Mexico previously. Letters and visits from relatives and friends spoke of new opportunities and reinforced the decision to migrate, the destination, and the kind of work sought. Men tended to enter new occupations in groups. For example, most of the men from Dona Ana County went to California to seek defense jobs, while those from northern Sandoval County sought work in Arizona, Nevada, Utah, and Colorado. Further north in Taos County, almost all the Spanish-speaking population migrated to Colorado, Utah, or Wyoming. The 18,416 residents (all native-born) of San Miguel County in the north central part of the state represented the largest part of the exodus out of New Mexico, migrating to Arizona or else to Colorado. And the Selective Service continued to draw men away; one in four Spanish-speaking New Mexicans was now in military service.[24]

Unlike the Mexican Americans of Texas and California, thousands of native New Mexicans were prepared for entrance into war work by various federal training programs, which also got them off relief. This came about through the intervention of Democratic Senator Dennis Chávez and Spanish-speaking representatives in the state legislature. Chávez had pushed for the FEPC and for the inclusion of farm workers in the NLRA and the Social Security Act. The federal vocational training programs, in combination with the needs of the out-of-state wartime economy, dramatically increased opportunities for native New Mexican wage earners. Training programs like Santa Fe County's Vocational Trade and Industrial Education Project resembled earlier programs, implemented during the New Deal years, which had been converted to train residents for defense jobs out of state. Upon completing their training, both male and female Spanish-speaking New Mexicans were channeled into war work as riveters, airplane mechanics, electric welders, and machinists and into airplane construction and fabrication in Arizona and California. In 1941, the National Youth Administration provided job training to more than one million rural youth and channeled them into war industries. However, only about 2,500 young men in New Mexico, representing less than a tenth of the state's unemployed residents between the ages of eighteen and twenty-four, qualified to participate in this federal program. Still, Spanish-speaking New Mexicans from the most impoverished families on federal relief made up three-fourths of NYA program enrollees. The required physical examinations revealed the extent of their poverty. Two-thirds of the Mexican American enrollees had never been to a doctor, while four-fifths had never had dental care. In addition to the NYA, the War Production Training programs offered job skills to 5,000 rural New Mexico residents, 70 percent of them Mexican American men and women. Over an eighteen-month period, the trainees received instruction in machine tooling, arc welding, and aircraft sheet metal work in preparation for jobs in West Coast wartime industries. Despite this defense work training, Spanish-speaking New Mexicans who applied for defense work faced discrimination in job placement by the USES and the WMC, which deferred to the racial prejudices of their representatives and employers.[25]

Illiteracy remained a problem in New Mexico, especially among the youth. Of 69,000 state residents between the ages of eighteen and twenty-four, only 3,743 (a mere 5 percent) were enrolled in schools. Like their parents, unemployed native New Mexican youth opted to leave the state to search for defense work opportunities. However, the lack of both a nominal public education and vocational training limited the job prospects for many of these young men and women. The Civilian Conservation Corps provided literacy classes to about 3,500 Spanish-speaking males, and like the 1960s Job Corps program, it prepared 600 of these males, who had been previously rejected for military duty, for enlistment.[26]

Other federal programs aided the integration of New Mexico's Spanish-speaking residents into the national war effort and instilled in them a sense of the importance of a united effort to defeat the Axis powers. War Information Centers educated native New Mexicans about food production, and conservation, and rationing. The Institute of the Air broadcasted a radio program in adult education for Spanish-speaking residents in the remote villages of Mora, Guadalupe, and San Miguel Counties. Airing on Sunday afternoons, the radio broadcasts focused on sanitation, health practices, soil use and conservation, and citizenship and gave its listeners information about available government services. The Taos County Project provided programs on soil conservation and soil rehabilitation; the Cooperative Health Association served the health needs of low-income families; another government project established a county library and visual education program in both English and Spanish by means of a traveling bookmobile. Through this last project, local residents acquired information about rural electrification, road construction, and the proper recording of property deeds (a valuable service, given that many were losing their lands). In addition, the bookmobile program sold war stamps and war bonds and kept rural residents informed about the war. Albuquerque's Barelas Community Center trained Mexican Americans in civic leadership, provided home front civil defense training, distributed war-related information, and offered services to Spanish-speaking military personnel and their dependents. The problems of Mexican Americans in New Mexico would surface in similar ways in Colorado but would not gain complete resolution.[27]

REMAINING SEPARATE AND UNEQUAL: COLORADO'S MEXICAN AMERICANS

Colorado's Mexican American population resided in three main concentrations in the state—in the San Luis and Arkansas River Valleys, in Denver, and in northern Colorado—and were engaged primarily in agricultural work and coal mining. Thirty thousand Mexican Americans lived in Denver, many of them recent arrivals, because the state's Spanish-speaking residents continued to leave outlying farms and farm labor camps for urban centers. Almost all of Denver's Mexican Americans were poor and suffered high infant mortality rates, and there was an active effort to keep Mexican Americans out of white neighborhoods and put them in segregated public housing projects.[28]

Mexican Americans were considered inferior to whites in Colorado, and the racism and substandard schools pushed many of these minorities out. Of 5,000 Mexican Americans enrolled in Denver's public schools, only 400 attended high school, and many dropped out before graduating. Lacking job opportunities and facing family economic need, high school–age Mexican American males left school in large numbers to volunteer for military service prior to the national draft and thereafter made up a considerable number of the draftees from Colorado. To reduce the high dropout rate, federal vocational training programs and job counseling and placement were made available to prepare young Mexican American men and women for wartime employment. This came about only after Mexican Americans prodded the government to make Denver school officials implement these programs to combat discrimination. Mindful of the impact of prejudice against Mexican Americans on the success of the Good Neighbor Policy, the OCIAA's Joint Committee on Spanish-Anglo War Activities sponsored adult education night classes in various communities in southern Colorado to increase the inclusion of Mexican Americans in local Civil Defense Council work and other home front activities. Another OCIAA project to combat prejudice against Mexican Americans was educating Colorado's Anglo population about the numerous contributions of the Spanish-speaking people to the war effort. Likewise, the University of Denver and the University of Wyoming both held OCIAA-funded Inter-American Workshops to study the problems faced by Mexican Americans and to highlight their contributions to the larger society.[29]

Colorado's Mexican Americans experienced considerable discrimination in obtaining defense work and once on the job were segregated from Anglos in low-wage, menial work. For instance, Mexican Americans made up just 3 percent of the 9,000 employees on one Colorado war defense project, and all worked as common laborers. While the Anglos enjoyed heated barracks and a mess hall located on the project site, the Mexican American defense workers had no housing and consequently commuted to work daily over mountain roads from their homes over twenty miles away. The WMC intervened. The Mexican Americans were issued tents, but these were placed outside the main camp. The tents had no floors or stoves, nor were bathing and other facilities provided to the men. The WMC made only nominal efforts in the matter of equal opportunity on the job. War industry managers in the end passed up Spanish-speaking workers, regardless of their education and skill, in favor of less qualified Anglos and upgraded Anglos while segregating Mexican Americans in the jobs with lower pay.[30]

Through training or on-the-job experience, Colorado Mexican Americans in fact qualified for such skilled work as construction machine operation and truck driving, but they were put on pick-and-shovel jobs while Anglo workers recruited out of state got the better jobs that paid more. Employers frequently promoted Anglos who were not as well qualified as Mexican Americans. Rather than hire local Mexican Americans, defense employers recruited Anglos from Kansas, Missouri, and Arkansas to fill jobs that should have gone to the state's Spanish-speaking residents. Assigned as instructors to these out-of-state Anglo hires, Mexican Americans remained on the "Mexican wage scale" while the Anglo trainees received the higher, "white" pay rate. Once an Anglo trainee learned the job, he was promoted to even higher-paying work. Moreover, the exemption from military service expired for the Mexican American trainers, while the Anglos, who were now skilled workers, were exempt from war service. Angered by this double standard, Mexican Americans individually and through their local organizations pushed the federal government for more forceful involvement. Employment discrimination in defense work improved somewhat only after government intervention, first by the USES, then by the WMC, which, after its own investigation, finally turned the matter over to the FEPC.[31]

The federal government's attempts to maintain harmonious race relations on the Colorado home front, including taking action to quell discrimination, came about only because Mexican Americans pushed the government to respond. Justice Department and State Department officials were primarily concerned about complaints of racism from Mexican Americans because the situation was having an impact on wartime morale and, if not remedied, could prove detrimental to United States–Latin America relations. Federal intervention failed to resolve the problem of discrimination in Colorado, which was particularly evident in the low numbers of Mexican Americans employed in defense work. Only after the relocation of Japanese Americans to the Mountain States and the arrival of large numbers of blacks in the region in search of work did Colorado's war industries make efforts to hire Mexican Americans. Mexican Americans, however, were given jobs for cosmetic purposes—to cover up discrimination against the other two racial groups so employers could show that they were complying with Executive Order 9346. Passed in May 1943, Executive Order 9346 created a new FEPC and transferred it from the WMC to the Executive Department. As we have seen, inequality was rampant in Texas, the Midwest, New Mexico, and Colorado, and it remained so in Arizona.[32]

"Stolid and Stunned, Brother to the Ox": The Mexican Copper Miners of Arizona

Mexican Americans made up 30 percent of Arizona's population. Twelve thousand lived in Tucson, representing 40 percent of that city's residents. The majority of Tucson's Spanish-speaking population lived in downtown neighborhoods, where Mexican residents experienced widespread discrimination. The Southern Pacific Railroad was Tucson's largest employer. Sixty-five percent of its 2,500 employees were Mexican, and all held unskilled jobs. Constitutional provisions, ritual, and collective bargaining power, as well as the fact that FEPC hearings on unfair practices in railroad employment had been postponed, encouraged the railroad to stonewall on promotions of Mexicans to skilled positions. The railroad used the supposed incompetency of Mexicans and the barrier of language to justify its policies, which barred Mexicans, along with blacks, from skilled track work. The promotion of Mexican railroad workers was effectively stopped by Rule 54 of the Shop Craft Agreement that went into force on April 18, 1942. Because voluntary enlistments and the draft were drawing away more and more of the Southern Pacific Railroad's Mexican American section hands, a number of Mexican American women took jobs with this rail line; others enlisted in the Women's Army Auxiliary Corps (WAACS) or in the women's auxiliary of the Marine Corps (WAVES). One-fourth of the 4,000 workers at Consolidated Vultee Aircraft Corporation were Mexican American, many of them recent arrivals from Colorado and New Mexico, though the Mexicans of Arizona remained confined to farm work and mining. Mexicans represented nearly two-thirds (60 percent) of the workforce on the farms and ranches around Tucson, and they made up half of the workforce in mining. Like Mexican American railroad workers, Mexican copper miners lacked political influence at the top levels of their union, Mine-Mill, and this resulted in the union's failure to act to end discrimination in the copper mining industry. Systematically denied promotions and job upgrades, the copper miners remained frozen in common labor or semiskilled positions, and they lacked wage parity with Anglos.[33]

In the mining town of Douglas, Mexicans made up over half (59 percent) of the 1,080 employees of the Copper Queen Smelter owned by the Phelps Dodge Corporation. They were segregated from Anglos, and all but thirty of the Mexicans worked at low-wage jobs above ground at the last "white camp" in the West. Mexicans represented 45 percent of the workforce of the mines Phelps Dodge operated in the Bisbee mining district. Bisbee's Mexican copper miners worked in all the jobs held by whites and earned the prevailing union scale. This was a recent occurrence; previously, the local mines had relegated their Mexican workers to blasting and loading ore, work so dangerous it produced injury and death rates three times higher than those for Anglo miners. Following the pattern of strict housing segregation found throughout the Southwest mining region, Mexicans inhabited dilapidated miners' huts in the canyons, where they were exposed to the annual flash floods, while Anglo miners, accorded higher status owing to their race, lived in boardinghouses and miners' cabins close to the mines.[34]

In the Clifton-Morenci mining area north of Tucson, Mexican copper miners and smelter workers employed by Phelps Dodge were segregated in their work and endured extensive job discrimination, particularly exclusion from apprenticeship programs. The "Mexican boys" who were in the AFL affiliate were put in a separate AFL union, the Federated Labor Union. As a result, the CIO focused on them for organization, and in 1942 they were certified as Morenci Miners Local 616, a Mine-Mill union. However, with encouragement from Phelps Dodge, twelve all-Anglo AFL craft unions split the representation territory of Clifton-Morenci copper miners, thereby giving an advantage to Phelps Dodge in contract negotiations. In the Miami and Globe mining area north of Tucson, the majority of Mexicans worked as laborers for the Inspiration Copper, Miami Copper, and Castle Dome Mining Companies. Because of the unfair wage scale and lack of job promotions, CIO labor organizers also targeted these men for unionization. However, organizing proved dangerously challenging owing to the power wielded by Miami's chief of police, who instilled great fear in the miners. The brother of the employment manager of the Inspiration Copper Company, the police chief already had six notches on his gun—he had killed six Mexican Americans. As a result of such obstacles to unionization and job advancement, the Spanish-speaking miners were overrepresented in the military draft because the local draft board granted deferments only to skilled mining employees, virtually all of them Anglo.[35]

Individually and in groups, Mexican American copper miners filed reports of discrimination with the FEPC. When FEPC field representatives questioned management about allegations of discrimination, personnel officials replied that many jobs in the copper mines are traditionally white, that Anglos would not work with Mexicans, or that the AFL-affiliated unions refused to accept Mexicans into the skilled crafts. In some cases, placing actual blame for discrimination proved difficult, since discrimination was facilitated by preferential government treatment of the AFL in its competition with the CIO to unionize the copper industry. In

1943, Congress approved a measure that overrode NLRB rulings invalidating so-called backdoor AFL contracts. This measure trapped tens of thousands of workers in the AFL's racist and undemocratic metalworkers' unions and jeopardized Mine-Mill's presence in war production facilities. For example, in the mining operations of Nevada Consolidated in Hurley, New Mexico, the upgrading of Mexican Americans from the labor gangs to skilled or semiskilled positions required taking them out of the CIO and placing them in AFL unions.[36] Nevada Consolidated had a contract with Mine-Mill Locals 63 and 69, which contained a provision that workers shall not be discriminated against "because of race, creed, color, or national origin." However, Nevada Consolidated also had a contract with the Chino AFL Metal Trades Council, which contained the same nondiscrimination clause, except for the term "national origin." In Arizona, the contract between the Phelps Dodge smelter in Douglas and Mine-Mill did not contain a provision against unequal treatment, but it had a clause providing for promotion on the basis of merit and seniority. The rest of the Phelps Dodge operations had contracts with AFL unions, all of which had a nondiscrimination clause, but this clause did not cover national origin. Enforcing these contract provisions of course was another matter because of the stiff resistance of Anglos.[37]

Altogether, Mexicans made up 60 percent of the 15,000 men employed in Arizona's mines, and almost all of them held common labor or semiskilled positions. Because of discrimination, the Spanish-speaking copper miners filed 150 separate complaints with the FEPC. Mexican copper miners would have filed more job discrimination charges against their employers, but they feared retaliation or else adverse reaction from Anglo miners desirous of maintaining their feelings of racial superiority. Mexicans employed in other Arizona war defense industries were not immune to discrimination, and they also filed complaints with this federal agency. Although some of the workers were not American-born citizens, they were legal residents, were war veterans, or had American-born children who had been called up for military service. Workplace discrimination prevailed mostly in areas without union representation. Nevertheless, the unions were too weak to provide full protection, or they faced hard-core resistance by white miners, and in light of its national policy on the matter of wartime unity, Mine-Mill made little effort to challenge the industry's discriminatory practices. A strong antidiscrimination movement during contract negotiations was years away. The requests for help from the federal government through the FEPC went unanswered. As noted, the FEPC was reluctant to hold hearings on the mistreatment of Mexicans and to make public the evidence it gathered because doing so would jeopardize America's Good Neighbor Policy relations with Latin America.[38]

Spanish-speaking copper miners alleged three kinds of workplace discrimination. Some miners were paid lower wages than Anglos for the same work. Others trained Anglos for better, higher-paying jobs, despite company policy dictating that new hires must start on the labor gangs and work their way up. As a further insult, the Anglos received higher pay as trainees than Mexican Americans who remained on a labor gang at the same wage rate. Still other copper miners were never upgraded from the low-paying "Mexican jobs" to better-paying jobs. The classification of mine jobs by which racial group did the work, rather than by job description, indicates how profoundly the racialization of work shaped the Mexican copper miner's world. The Mexicans had little faith in the possibility of improving their lot. The aggrieved miners had essentially given up waiting for job advancement, for they "knew there was no use for a Mexican asking for a promotion." Their protests about being employed as common laborers for ten, twenty, and even thirty years without a job promotion went unanswered.[39]

The FEPC field investigators concluded that a pattern of social and economic discrimination against Mexican Americans prevailed at mining sites in Arizona and throughout the Southwest that included total separation in the pay lines and in the use of bathroom and recreational facilities. According to FEPC field investigators, there was a widespread belief among employers that Mexicans were second-rate workers: that they were physically inferior to Anglos and thus not as productive at work, incapable of assuming responsibility, not sufficiently intelligent to use additional pay wisely, and lacking in the mentality necessary for advancement. Because of growing manpower shortages, the copper industry wanted to import contract labor from Mexico to work the mines and thereby drive the costs of labor down further. The federal government rejected this request; the glaring discrimination against Mexican Americans, if made public, would no doubt embarrass the United States.[40]

The FEPC field representatives confirmed the consensus among Mexican American mine workers that because of discrimination they did not have an equal chance for job advancement. Furthermore, discrimination had lowered the morale of the men. This low morale provided fertile ground for subversive propaganda by communists and fascists, both of whom found the Mexicans' desire to be "good Americans" laughable. The Mexican American copper miners had been discriminated against for so long that they held no hope of ever moving out of the common laborer positions, regardless of their efforts. According to the FEPC investigators, the men had become "A thing that grieves not and that never hopes. Stolid and stunned, a brother to the ox." World War II did not destroy the color line in the mining industry. California, fast becoming the center for the nation's Spanish-speaking population, had its own unique challenges.[41]

"Dirty, Noisy, and Lawless": The Further Segregation of Mexican Americans in Wartime Los Angeles

Approximately 457,900 Mexicans resided in California in 1940, and American-born citizens predominated (just a third of this population was foreign-born). Although Mexicans lived throughout the state, the largest numbers lived in Southern California, concentrated mainly in the working-class neighborhoods of Los Angeles and San Diego. Regardless of citizenship status, Mexicans were victims of pervasive discrimination; they occupied the lowest social, economic, and political rungs and essentially remained outside the American mainstream.[42] Mexican contract labor being imported into California by growers was beginning to displace many Mexican Americans from citrus, grape, and other agricultural crop work, as well as railroad maintenance and repair work. Notwithstanding, as defense production increased manpower needs, Mexican Americans began leaving the migrant stream for Los Angeles because of the attractive job prospects in defense work. The city's industrial area was one of the nation's most prosperous and rapidly changing manufacturing regions, its growth fueled by the newly built branch plants of the large corporations and the ongoing industrial diversification of national, regional, and local markets converted to war production. The promise of well-paying jobs brought tens of thousands of Mexican Americans from Texas, New Mexico, Colorado, and Arizona down U.S. Route 66 to California. These men and women formed part of the huge migration to Los Angeles defense industries that included about 54,000 job-hungry blacks from the South. Between 1940 and 1943, the black population of the nation's ten western states doubled. An estimated 3,500 blacks arrived each month in Los Angeles, so that by 1944 the city's black population stood at 134,519, a 75 percent increase over the 1940 figure. The rising expectations of war work in Los Angeles set whites against blacks and Mexicans as the city was swept up in tensions over employment, housing shortages, crime, and the overall social disorder generated by the expansion of Southern California war production.[43]

Approximately 315,000 Mexicans lived in Los Angeles County, and they were concentrated throughout the metropolitan district, making the Spanish-speaking population density second to that of Mexico City. Most lived in poverty and urban squalor. The average annual income of a Mexican family was $790, far below the minimum standard of $1,310 (for a family of five). Discrimination by landlords, homeowners, and real estate agents was pervasive. The fact that landlords refused to rent to Mexicans, coupled with restrictive covenants, excluded Mexicans from most city neighborhoods. This, along with the acute housing shortage, accounted for the high-density population levels in Mexican working-class quarters like the Belvedere barrio, which had the distinction of being the worst slum on the Pacific Coast with the highest number of relief cases, delinquencies, and other social problems. The incoming Mexican Americans crowded into Belvedere, Boyle Heights, and other working-class neighborhoods that were becoming predominantly Spanish-speaking as Anglos emigrated out for fear of being swallowed up by the invasion of Mexicans. The residents of these areas, whose boundaries expanded with the huge population influx, absorbed the growth by doubling up. A 1941 survey of Los Angeles housing confirmed that Mexicans had the worst housing problems.[44]

The CIO linked the housing issue closely with other civil rights issues, such as job training, employment, better schools, and voter registration. Because of the acute housing shortage and the racial housing covenants in force in much of Los Angeles, the CIO CARD worked to get public housing for Mexicans. Prior to the start of the war, CIO labor actions stirred the Spanish-speaking community to demand better housing, and as a result of this grassroots pressure, some low-income housing projects were built. However, as scholars have made abundantly clear, federal housing policy at this time effectively linked race prejudice to the structure of property values and the housing market in American urban areas. Quota restrictions were in place to keep blacks and Mexicans out of certain areas of Los Angeles, even when housing was available. Furthermore, the housing construction companies, engaged in one of the biggest federally assisted building programs in the United States, would not lift the quota restrictions for fear that Mexicans, who greatly outnumbered blacks, would flood the area and engulf Anglos.[45]

Believing they would be eligible to apply for the government housing project planned by the Los Angeles Housing Authority, thousands of Mexican workers gave up their homes in areas targeted for housing construction. Many were non-U.S. citizens. However, upon completion of the housing project, only war workers who were U.S. citizens were permitted to move in. In an effort reminiscent of the militant actions against evictions by the Unemployment Councils in the early 1930s, Mexican American union leaders, with help from the CIO, organized the displaced workers and their families, moved them into the housing projects at Ramona Gardens, and got some of the families to picket the Los Angeles Housing Authority to demand more federal housing. This tenant organizing coincided with the ongoing CIO drives in the warehouse industry. ILWU Local 26 therefore brought the housing issue before the Los Angeles CIO Industrial Union Council. The local did this by introducing a resolution calling for an amendment to the Federal Housing Authority Act that would permit "allied and friendly aliens" to occupy government housing projects. Adopting Local 26's resolution, the Los Angeles CIO Industrial Union Council petitioned the city's Federal Housing Authority. Thereafter, nonnaturalized

Figure 5.A. Mexican American CIO trade unionists like those in the International Longshoremen's and Warehousemen's Union joined the fight by the CIO CARD to break down racial barriers in Los Angeles. Union members outside the ILWU office, Wilmington, California, September 25, 1943. (00040632—SPNB, Courtesy of Los Angeles Public Library).

Mexican workers were admitted into the Ramona Garden federal housing project, as well as Aliso Village, Estrada Courts, and Pico Gardens. One serious problem with this federal housing that had long-range implications was that locating public housing in barrios increased the residential segregation of Mexicans. Many of these public housing projects were at great distances from the war production plants located in outlying areas. As a result, absenteeism was quite high among Spanish-speaking war workers, who were affected by the costs of limited access to adequate housing. One employer noted that absenteeism among his Mexican American workers corresponded to the distance these workers traveled from their homes to the plant, adding that minorities found "it difficult to obtain housing" and "therefore live the farthest away." All workers in Los Angeles who lived great distances from factories showed elevated rates of absenteeism, but the absentee rates were highest for the city's Spanish-speaking war workers because of the segregation.[46]

White Los Angelenos were developing a siege mentality regarding the significant multiracial presence in the city, and events during the war era were clearly beginning to set the pattern for the postwar years. Two serious issues were restrictive covenants and, as the CIO's Luisa Moreno had warned, the rise of anti-Semitism. The California State CIO urged Governor Earl Warren to counter actions that were "sabotaging the war effort," such as the distribution of circulars in Los Angeles opposing housing construction for black war workers and the exclusion of Jews and blacks from neighborhoods where housing projects were planned. No blacks lived in any of the housing projects in Los Angeles County, and most of the housing projects in Southern California excluded them.[47]

The use of restrictive covenants and the development of protective associations to stop black and Mexican infiltration into new neighborhoods were increasing rapidly. One example of white homeowners' attempts to stop minorities who strayed across the color line took place in February 1942, when the Alex Bernal family decided to purchase a home in a white neighborhood in Fullerton, California. A racial covenant was used to bar the entrance of this Mexican family. Three Anglo residents used a 1923 deed restriction to bring suit against the Bernals, charging that they were "Mexicans, persons other than the Caucasian race." Concern over the possibility that land values would decline elicited Anglo stereotyping of Mexicans and their social values throughout the formal examination by the court. During the four-day trial, a stream of plaintiff's witnesses testified that Mexicans were "dirty, noisy and lawless," and therefore Mr. and Mrs. Bernal and their two young daughters should not be allowed into the neighborhood. Talk of unity and racial harmony in the matter of housing frequently fell on deaf ears within labor's ranks, as evidenced in 1943 when AFL and CIO shipyard workers circulated a petition to remove four black families from a San Pedro housing project. With help from the CIO Maritime Committee, Marine and Shipbuilding Workers Union Local 9, the representative local union, stepped in to quell this dissidence. Local 9 firmly resolved that any member violating the union's constitutional provision for racial equality would be expelled and denied work.[48]

"IT's THE AMERICAN WAY": THE RACIAL ASSAULT AGAINST MEXICANS IN LOS ANGELES

The Mexicans of Los Angeles at this time in general had little contact with public officials and organizations. Mexican American youth, on the other hand, had far greater exposure to things American. These urban youth confronted discrimination on a daily basis, with the schools playing a profoundly damaging role. The public schools for Mexicans were horribly inferior to those for whites, and Mexican school children learned of their inferior standing at an early age because many teachers were racist. Widespread discrimination clearly affected the lives of all Mexicans in Southern California, and if left unchecked, it was potentially detrimental to American race relations and the nation's international relations as well.[49] With one in ten Mexicans in Los Angeles County between the ages of six and seventeen (about 36,410) and with few youth intervention programs in place, almost every family in the city's Mexican neighborhoods had juvenile problems. As is still the case today, there was an undeclared war between Mexican American youth and the police. The youth were the victims of excessive police force in the form of beatings, harassment, frisking and searching, false arrests, and insulting language. There was great mistrust of the police, who were viewed as enemy combatants. Community police relations were nonexistent, and with little proficiency in English, Mexican community residents rightfully feared that any contact with police could increase the risk of serious confrontation.[50]

The eruption of gang warfare in Los Angeles was part of the wave of clashes between rival youth gangs that took place nationwide between May 25 and June 22, 1943. Integrating their racial and ethnic identities into their group association and attire, the city's self-styled pachucos waged one form of protest against the constricting pressures of economic, political, and social discrimination. Pachucos captured the nation's attention in early June 1943 during an outbreak of strife that took on the dimensions of organized race warfare, the Zoot Suit Riots. The riots were characteristic of anti-Mexican violence in the city. Sensationalist reporting by the city's newspapers precipitated the battle that pitted Mexican Americans against mobs of Anglo GIs and civilians. By accentuating spurious yet constant stereotypes of Mexicans, Los Angeles newspapers were the main culprits in creating a climate that conditioned Anglos to reject Mexicans and encouraged them to commit acts of terror and violence against this minority group. Mobs of more than 1,000 white attackers, mainly sailors and soldiers, roamed the city and specifically targeted for attack groups of Mexican American as well as black zoot-suiters. Like the local Mississippi newspapers that reported the planned lynching of a black two days beforehand, the Los Angeles newspapers perpetuated an unhealthy attitude of mass prejudice. The press immediately picked up the story of the riots and for six days reported the physical assaults as headline news. Through mop-up operations, local authorities and military police quickly suppressed the fights between angry servicemen and resentful zoot-suiters. Nonetheless, batches of rowdy and drunken soldiers and sailors continued their sporadic raiding of nightspots and movie

Figure 5.B. The pachucos believed servicemen attacked them solely because they were Mexicans wearing zoot suits and thus felt justified in defending themselves. Police lineup of Mexican women in connection with the zoot suit gang wars, 1942. (00019405—*Herald Examiner* Photograph Collection, Courtesy of Los Angeles Public Library).

theaters in search of more victims. Shouting racial slurs and drinking liquor to build up their courage, some servicemen using weighted ropes or clubs as weapons, the GIs assaulted Mexicans and tore the clothes off some of their victims. The soldiers and sailors spared no Mexican, also assaulting women and children. The Zoot Suit Riots had the effect of victimizing not just the immediate target, the pachucos, but every member of the group that the immediate target represented. After nearly a week of mayhem, the rioting stopped when the U.S. Navy declared the city of Los Angeles off-limits.[51]

Given the incendiary nature of these race riots and the rumors of impending racial violence, public officials in America's large cities began taking precautions to avert racial disorder. The cities quickly reinforced local police forces, instituted curfews, set up interracial committees, canceled leave for servicemen, and banned the sale of liquor. In Los Angeles, amidst charges by left-wing newspapers and organizations that the eruptions of violence were "race riots," the Los Angeles Committee for American Unity was set up to focus on the alleged problems of Mexicans in the city. This working group submitted a report to a committee appointed by California Governor Earl Warren to inquire into the situation. The report noted that the riots were not the result of a serious crime wave by zoot suit gangsters, that the number and severity of crimes committed by pachucos had been grossly exaggerated, and that there was no proof that Mexican youth gangs had actually committed these crimes. The city's newspapers were blamed for using race-coded language to criminalize the Mexican and black zoot-suiters, who were victims of a systematic pattern of violent repression by white police. This was an unbiased report that actually revealed the truth behind the riots. A barrage of hate-filled, negative, and irresponsible reporting by the racist Los Angeles Hearst newspapers the *Examiner* and the *Herald Express* and by Harry Chandler's *Los Angeles Times* created a climate in which Anglos seized on the racially contentious words and images and were motivated by their racism to attack Mexican Americans. By now the press associated Mexican males and females with indolence, sex crimes, knifings, other gang-induced violence, and drugs. According to the newspapers, this criminal behavior accounted for the Mexicans' high rates of poverty, relief need, and incarceration. Local radio stations contributed to the racist incitement by broadcasting indiscriminate and repeated racial slurs against Mexicans. Dubbing Mexicans' "lazy, syphilitic, and tubercular" and using other racially charged epithets, the local radio stations likewise called for good old vigilante justice to cure the alleged epidemic of Mexican juvenile delinquency. Concluding that the housing shortages, restrictive covenants, and racial discrimination were at the root of juvenile delinquency, the Los Angeles Committee for American Unity called for "an inter-racial committee composed of community leaders and with representatives from the Chamber of Commerce, AFL, CIO, Church, Social Agencies, and all minority groups."[52]

CIO president Philip Murray wrote to President Roosevelt, urging him to mobilize the OWI, the OCIAA, and the War and Navy Departments to launch educational campaigns "to eradicate the misconceptions and prejudices" that had led to the events in Los Angeles. At the 1943 CIO state convention held in Los Angeles, Harry Bridges addressed the police brutality that victimized the city's racial minorities. In the Hollenbeck, Watts, and other Mexican districts there were repeated acts of police brutality, intimidation, verbal abuse, and disregard for the civil rights of the residents, noted Bridges. He added that police officers cooperated in furthering hatred of Mexicans by brutalizing and harassing them and making false arrests. State CIO president Philip Connelly added his voice to the protest, but he placed blame for the racial violence at the feet of labor for ignoring the obvious signs of the brutalization of Mexican Americans by law officials. Connelly told the convention delegates that the Zoot Suit Riots "resulted because we in the labor movement failed to recognize the importance of the Sleepy Lagoon case as a trial balloon to see how far people of this country would stand for Gestapo methods." The CIO state convention attendees concluded by declaring that discrimination must be met "with community forces, under union leadership." That August, the CIO's Minorities Committee held a conference on racial and national unity in San Francisco, which was attended by over 1,200 people and featured Harry Bridges and Paul Robeson as speakers. Calling discrimination "Hitler's secret weapon," Bridges once again charged that "Hearst made the riots in Los Angeles."[53]

The Roosevelt administration paid close attention to the racial disturbance in Los Angeles because of the wartime atmosphere and because it occurred in a major war production center. The FBI reported that owing to the lack of manpower and facilities, the Los Angeles Police Department could not control about thirty "Mexican youth gangs" with 750 members who were under eighteen years of age.[54] However, the bureau's report supported the conclusion of the various interracial committees and the CIO that serious Mexican crime was not on the rise. Of the city's approximately 45,000 Mexicans between the ages of sixteen and twenty, only 1,400, or a little over 3 percent, had been arrested during the past year for various street crimes. Furthermore, nearly all the Mexican American gang members who were eighteen years old or older had been rejected by the army or had been discharged from the service after their induction. A medical officer from the Selective Service assigned to the Los Angeles U.S. Army induction station had investigated those young men arrested by the police. According to the medical officer, the young men did not have a higher rejection rate for military service than other nationalities. Rather, most of the Mexican inductees had been rejected because they were in poor health—many suffered from tuberculosis due to their bad living conditions—or were deemed unfit for military service because of a prior criminal conviction or a lack of education. After May 1941 all draftees had to demonstrate reading and writing competency at the fourth-grade level. Through its Special Training Center, the U.S. Army salvaged those Mexican Americans classified as illiterate. Its eight- to twelve-week intensive remedial classes brought the recruits up to the fourth-grade level of literacy. Moreover, government investigators noted that local draft boards in the city had become more lenient in their classification of Mexican American youth, including those who were legal U.S. resident aliens, since larger numbers of them were being ordered to report for induction. Representing a disproportionate share of the draftees from Los Angeles, by war's end Mexican Americans made up 20 percent of the Los Angelenos killed in action, although they accounted for 10 percent of the city's total population. Instead of being locked up in jails and prisons, the large population of supposedly incorrigible Mexican Americans was dealt with through induction into military service.[55]

GETTING THE UNION INVOLVED AGAINST
DISCRIMINATION IN LOS ANGELES

Like blacks, the Mexican Americans of Los Angeles were basically excluded from defense work up to the year 1942 because labor shortages supposedly were not yet sufficiently serious to make jobs available to them. The early restrictions on foreign-born job applicants notwithstanding, discrimination played a large part in the continued exclusion of Mexican Americans from defense work. One government report noted that for the first year and a half of the war defense mobilization, discrimination by local Los Angeles industries had produced a high rejection rate for Mexican American job applicants, and some industries got around Executive Order 8802 by making token hires. Many companies holding war contracts, like Vultee Aircraft, simply bypassed Mexicans in hiring. North American Aircraft stipulated that it would hire only U.S. citizens with "American names" and excluded Mexicans, Asians, and Jews. In the case of Jewish job applicants, those with a foreign cast faired poorly in getting defense work because of the fear that they were either strong unionists or radicals. Employers also feared that hiring Mexican Americans and blacks could potentially disrupt war production by triggering hate strikes. Mexican American women were playing a larger role in the war effort as defense workers, but like their fathers, uncles, husbands, and brothers, the women also faced discrimination. Those who had taken job training courses and graduated at the top of their class were passed over for employment in favor of less-qualified Anglo women. Despite federal rules, Mexican American women earned about two-thirds of what men earned doing the same work, and they joined black women in the worst job assignments.[56] The same racial discrimination characterized San Diego's defense plants.

Some war defense employers resorted to at-the-gate hiring when the USES rejected their requests for Anglo workers. Local USES branches in fact tacitly cooperated with defense industry employers in perpetuating discrimination, despite assumptions to the contrary. Fewer than a dozen Mexican Americans participated on the interviewing staffs of the USES offices and other government employment agencies, a fact substantiated by Dr. Will Alexander of the WMC's Minority Groups branch on his visit to the West Coast. That many vocational training centers were located far from Mexican and black residential areas made it difficult for members of these two minority groups to attend the classes, and those training facilities that opened near minority residential districts did so only after considerable community action. Though minority hires by the defense industries increased, complaints of discrimination continued.[57]

The CIO responded to numerous complaints about job discrimination. However, the initiative to combat racial bias in defense work came from Mexican American rank-and-file members, who were growing more assertive in their demands for advancement. They pressured labor organizations to lobby city and federal officials and to outline avenues for action against racial intolerance. The many appeals for integration of Spanish-speaking workers into the war effort through hiring and job upgrading, including improving opportunities for youth, pushed the State CIO Council to establish the Minorities Committee. Twenty-three CIO international and local union representatives were appointed to the Minorities Committee, which was divided into southern and northern California divisions. However, only five of the Minorities Committee members were Mexican, three of them representing Southern California, where most of the state's Mexicans resided. This omission reflected the state CIO's continuing neglect of the problems of Spanish-speaking rank-and-file members.[58]

Despite the bitter resistance put up by Anglo employers and workers, Mexican American CIO unionists remained active in the ongoing drives to open job training programs to minorities and to hire more of them through recruitment campaigns. As defense production peaked in 1943, the campaign bore fruit. Minority placements in job training programs, in factory and military base construction, in steel production, and in aircraft assembly and shipbuilding increased by two and a half times over the previous year. The aircraft industry was now hiring minorities at all skill levels. About 12 percent of all Lockheed aircraft employees were Mexican American, with women making up 80 percent of the company's Mexican American employees working in detailed assembly, general assembly, and riveting work. The California Shipbuilding Corporation made a concerted effort to hire Mexican Americans, and by 1944 this defense employer counted 1,300 as employees. Nearly 58,000 Mexican Americans were at work in other war industries. The growing numbers of Mexican Americans in defense work, however, could not make up for years of unemployment, and underemployment, and discrimination continued to dictate hiring policies.[59]

By the fall of 1944, there were signs that Southern California's booming war economy had crested and was slowing down, and once again unemployment would fall the hardest on Mexican Americans and blacks. In August, Los Angeles County reported a one-year employment decline of

Figure 5.C. The CIO, in conjunction with the WMC and the FEPC, gained employment for Mexican Americans in war industries. Mexican American, Negro, and white women sewing parachutes at Pacific Parachute Company, San Diego, California, 1942. Note the FEPC sign hanging above them. (FSA/OWI-J61177—Courtesy of Library of Congress).

52,200 manufacturing jobs; a 10 to 15 percent decline was expected in aircraft industries employment, and similar reductions were expected in shipbuilding. Officials estimated that 100,000 workers in Los Angeles County and possibly 1.2 million workers in the state would be affected by the eventual conversion to a peacetime economy. Because aircraft assembly, shipbuilding, and ship repair employed the most Mexican Americans and blacks during the war, these two racial minorities were expected to experience the most strain from readjustment. As we shall see, they would be the first workers fired and, regardless of qualifications, the last hired in the peacetime economy.[60]

The push for labor rights served as the impetus for a Mexican American civil rights front to combat poor housing, exclusion from public housing, wanton police brutality, and other abuses. Because of the absence of effective Mexican American civil rights organizations, campaigns for civil rights continued to be carried out by Mexican American CIO unionists and the Peoples' Congress. CIO unions in California claimed thousands of Spanish-speaking members. At the end of 1942, 15,000 Mexican Americans in Los Angeles County belonged to the CIO. Sixty-five were full-time CIO business agents, union officials, or shop stewards. Mexican Americans headed the ILWU, the USWA, and the Ship Scalers' Union, participated on the Shipyard Workers' Union executive board, and organized for the Laundry Workers Union. By 1944, Mexican Americans made up half of the UFWA in Los Angeles and a third of the ILGWU's membership in Southern California. Like their black counterparts, Mexican Americans had gained confidence and strength as citizens through their experience voting in NLRB elections, their election to CIO local union offices and committees, and their activities as organizers. These Mexican American union leaders and union activists remained in the front ranks of the fight for civil rights that would accelerate in the postwar years.[61]

FOCUSING GOVERNMENT EFFORTS ON RACIAL INEQUALITY

In the wake of the bloody race riots of late spring 1943, scores of progressive organizations across the nation, led by the American Council on Race Relations through the support of the Julius Rosenwald Fund, undertook the promotion of interracialism. By the end of 1943, over one hundred local, state, and national race relations commissions had been established. Interracialism became the main approach of the civil rights movement on the home front. However, beyond heightening public awareness of racism, increasing the lines of communication between the white and minority communities, and setting up training sessions on human relations for police departments, most of the committees failed to improve race relations. The committees that sponsored interracialism produced more committees, more surveys, more reports, and then disappeared. What was needed was a focus at the national level on policy issues that addressed the pandemic race sickness in America.[62]

In this context, larger efforts were being made to improve conditions for Los Angeles Mexican Americans. The city established a five-year community development program; Mayor Fletcher Bowron appointed a Committee for Home Front Unity; provisions outlawing discrimination in employment were included in municipal, county, and state codes; Mexican Americans were hired into the Los Angeles County Probation Department; and special job classifications were established with fluency in Spanish as a requirement. Reflecting national trends whereby intergroup relations agencies worked to resolve interracial conflict, twelve interracial committees were formed in Los Angeles County. With few exceptions, working-class Mexican organizations did not exist, and blue-collar Mexicans tended not to participate in this organizational activity, even though Mexican workers, through their respective union affiliates, spearheaded efforts to foster racial tolerance and understanding in Los Angeles. Anglos formed the majority on the various interracial unity councils and Mayor's Committees. The small number of minorities on these councils and committees were selected on the basis of a class background that reflected that of the Anglo representatives.[63]

The sad fact was that Mexican Americans overall had no voice in any branch of Los Angeles city government in matters of city services or other decisions directly affecting them. There were no Mexican Americans on the mayor's two dozen commissions dealing with matters pertaining to police, fire protection, civil service, public works, and health and social services. The Los Angeles City and County Civil Service Commission reported in 1944 that only 2.5 percent of Mexican Americans held civil service jobs, though this minority group made up 10 percent of the city's population. The Los Angeles Police Department was no friend to the city's Spanish-speaking population. Interestingly, in an effort to reduce police brutality directed at Mexicans, police officers from Local 665 of the Police Employees Union in 1944 launched a campaign through the Los Angeles Central Labor Council and the Los Angeles City and County Civil Service Commission calling for the immediate hiring of one hundred Mexican American policemen and ten Spanish-speaking policewomen. Local 665 pointed out that fewer than a dozen Mexican Americans were on the city's police force, and there were no Mexican American women police officers. The local union correctly argued that Spanish-speaking police officers could achieve far better results in dealing with juvenile delinquency and adult crime detection than any "greater number of so-called Anglo-Saxon policemen." Although a cohesive force in the city's Mexican neighborhoods, the organization of the community by Mexican American labor and civil rights activists had not reached the level of demanding such rights.[64]

Field investigators from various federal agencies concluded that it was imperative that the Mexican Americans of Los Angeles be fully integrated into the war effort. This "war-imposed necessity" had to go beyond the various committees appointed by city Mayor Bowron and the Los Angeles County Board of Supervisors, because alone they would be unable to put sufficient public pressure on elected officials and employers who were either indifferent or resistant to racial equality in order to improve the dismal social conditions of the city's Spanish-speaking residents. The investigators all agreed that local interracial citizen committees could help remedy the problem of discrimination by staging public meetings to draw attention to the causative factors underlying the recent racial disturbances and mobilize pressure to implement change. They all concluded that there was a need for greater federal involvement. The government must make the citizens of Los Angeles aware that American citizens elsewhere did not condone the repressive manner in which the city handled minority group relations, including such simplistic measures as banning the wearing of zoot suits and warning zoot-suiters to leave town. Federal investigators thought such ameliorative activities would prove valuable in radio propaganda broadcasts to Latin American countries. This last point indicates that Mexican American–related civil rights issues were viewed in the context of the international interests of the United States, particularly to its Good Neighbor Policy initiatives in Latin America.[65]

In response to numerous appeals to address the subject of discrimination against the Spanish-speaking of the Southwest, the OCIAA finally allocated funds and assigned personnel to address this pressing domestic issue, with special attention given to Los Angeles. This decision to focus government efforts on Los Angeles angered FEPC official Lawrence Cramer; after he had spent months collecting data on cases of discrimination in Texas, the State Department informed Cramer that the scheduled FEPC hearings in El Paso would not take place. The shift of federal attention toward discrimination in Los Angeles and away from discrimination in Texas was explained by the unique political cultures of the two areas. More important, public hearings in El Paso would further embarrass the United States, since they would reveal that discrimination against Mexican Americans was not confined to the Pacific Coast but was of epidemic proportions throughout the Southwest.[66]

Following the OCIAA meetings, Josephina Fierro de Bright and husband John Bright wrote a "Prospectus for the OCIAA on the Mexican Americans of the Southwestern United States." Reiterating the underlying philosophy of the Good Neighbor Policy to address these domestic troubles, the Brights alluded to the awareness among Latin Americans of the great racial discord in America. They outlined the causes for the failure of Mexicans to assimilate into the larger American culture and give unanimous support for the war. They once again asserted that discrimination was the "most influential factor of all" in explaining why "the Mexican-Americans . . . continued to ignore the war."[67]

However, the OCIAA had its critics. One of the more acerbic critics was longtime activist Carey McWilliams. He alleged that the agency was more interested in conducting publicity campaigns with its limited funds than in helping to reduce discrimination against Mexican Americans. The OCIAA had not coordinated its endeavors with local community members, according to McWilliams, and was acting "as though it wanted to frustrate any real efforts on the part of the Spanish-speaking people to improve their lot." Limited by its budget, the OCIAA in fact did very little to assist the Mexican American community of Los Angeles. At a time when the United States sought to extend its influence over Latin America through the Good Neighbor Policy, Congress seemed to sabotage some of this agency's programs. For the 1943–44 fiscal year, Congress appropriated the OCIAA only a fourth of the operating funds it had requested.[68]

The serious and plentiful civil rights violations against Mexican Americans were damaging relations between Mexico and the United States just as both countries were attempting to implement a Mexican guest worker program. However, the Mexican contract labor program had the effect of exacerbating the problems of economic and social inequality for Mexican Americans. The Southwest region was flooded with cheap labor, a development that eventually canceled out all of the accomplishments of Mexican Americans on the labor and civil rights fronts. Specifically, it caused considerable difficulties for Mexican Americans seeking to gain their right to American citizenship.

The Beginnings of the Mexican Contract Labor Program

During World War II, a short-term solution to farm labor shortages led to the importation of contract labor from Mexico. These temporary workers provided American agribusiness interests, as well as some railroad companies, with a cheap and abundant labor source. Powerful independent farmers' associations and the American Farm Bureau Federation soon took control of the bracero contracts and grossly inflated labor needs.[69]

There was no shortage of farm workers on the eve of World War II, and wages for these workers had actually fallen. According to a 1941 U.S. Bureau of Agricultural Economics report, more than 1.5 million farm workers could leave agriculture without jeopardizing the nation's farm production. However, farmers began to circulate rumors of labor shortages out of a supposed fear that ample numbers of workers would be unavailable at harvest time. As the government reported, growers were accustomed to a "great oversupply of workers" and thus had "come to consider this over-supply as the normal supply, and to deem any reduction in the surplus supply as a shortage."[70]

With the bonanza of government subsidies dangling before them, Texas cotton farmers, acting through the Texas Farm Bureau Federation and the Nueces County Agricultural Association, contacted Congressman Richard M. Kleberg about a possible labor shortage for the state's cotton crop harvest. The congressman, whose district extended from Corpus Christi to San Antonio, was empathetic to their needs because of his own economic interests. Kleberg's family owned the huge King Ranch and controlled Corpus Christi and adjacent counties, a completely segregated

Figure 5.D. Braceros brought to the Arkansas Valley, Colorado, Nebraska, and Minnesota by the FSA to harvest and process sugar beets, 1943. Pro-grower interests pressured the U.S. Department of Agriculture to replace domestic farm workers with contract labor from Mexico. (FSA 8e01495—Courtesy of Library of Congress).

area. Kleberg hired Tejanos but was not the least interested in protecting their rights. The farmers' associations warned the congressman that labor shortages would have dire effects on the cotton harvests extending from west Texas south into the lower Río Grande Valley. As previously noted, the shortage of farm labor in Texas had come about because both the National Defense and Selective Service Acts were drawing heavily and unfairly on the area Tejano labor. Also, many Tejanos were fleeing Jim Crow injustice, specifically, the use of the color bar to exclude them from wartime employment. The Texas farmers beseeched Congressman Kleberg to urge President Roosevelt to bring in seasonal labor from Mexico under the auspices of the president's Good Neighbor Policy. Cotton growers in the El Paso area and in Arizona apparently could not wait for the federal government. Resorting to their practice of running "wets" across the border, these cotton farmers hired private labor contractors to induce more than 1,500 job-starved Mexican nationals to cross into Texas with offers of ten dollars per worker.[71]

Department of Agriculture officials became suspicious of these doomsday reports warning of labor shortages in Texas; such reports were generally false, as sufficient numbers of workers were always available for the various fruit and vegetable harvests in the Southwest. By seeking imported workers from Mexico the Texas farmers sought to maintain the cheap labor pool in the Lone Star State and drive down the already draconian wages for farm work. Without effective organizations to raise a protest sufficient to get the attention of the federal government, Tejanos resorted to seeking help with their plight at home from Mexican officials. The Mexican government looked askance at the plan by Texas farmers to import workers from Mexico. Because of long-held concern about the starvation wages, terrible working conditions, and abuse endured by Tejano farm workers in the state, Mexico did not believe the best interests of its citizens would be served if they went to work in Texas.[72]

The Department of Agriculture refuted the reports of labor shortages in Texas and in the nation as a whole: the shortages were actually the result of the overall increase in available nonfarm jobs in manufacturing, transportation, and service work as the labor demands for war industries production accelerated. Furthermore, the expanded nonfarm job market due to the war effort had raised wages, making it harder for farmers to obtain workers—that is, at wages farmers were willing to pay for this labor. A report by the Twentieth Century Fund noted that two million workers would not qualify for defense-related employment owing to the location of this work and their lack of necessary job skills. The report also documented that a large portion of this labor reserve was located in the nation's southern states, such as Texas. The Lone Star State had a sufficient supply of workers employed on various government-funded work relief projects, and in addition, a large number of the state's idle workers were actually waiting for the cotton harvest season to begin. Armed with this data, President Roosevelt contacted Congressman Kleberg and reminded him that many individuals on government relief in his home state were farm workers. The president therefore recommended that "it would be both economically and socially desirable" to give these workers the first chance at jobs in the cotton harvest in south Texas. The president reminded the Texas congressman that sufficient numbers of these workers could be obtained through the offices of the Texas Farm Placement Service, a state agency established in 1933 for the specific purpose of assisting farmers in securing farmhands and of guiding these workers to areas of labor demand. With the help of this state agency, south Texas farmers could obtain workers from among the thousands of underemployed family laborers, from relief rolls, and from urban centers.[73]

President Roosevelt was not in favor of importing labor from Mexico until all sources of domestic labor had been exhausted. Also, the president was concerned that a contract labor program would provoke substantial opposition from jobless Americans and labor groups, opposition that would be directed at the governments of the U.S. and Mexico. However, a far more important reason was the desire of the United States government to maintain strong relations with Mexico. As noted, Mexican government officials were acutely aware of the impoverished working and living conditions among Tejano workers. Only when Mexico's guest workers were guaranteed a minimum wage, adequate living conditions, and transportation to and from their homes in Mexico would the Mexican government endorse the proposed contract labor program.[74]

In 1942, the demand for agricultural workers increased as growers throughout the West expanded their production of crops over 1941 levels. Because the draft, voluntary enlistments, and well-paying war production jobs continued to draw away large numbers of Mexican American workers from rural areas, more and more farmers began seeking alternative sources of labor. U.S. Agriculture Secretary Claude R. Wickard believed that the world crisis produced by the war required greater food production and therefore developed and promoted farm policies and programs to expand American farm output in order to feed the nation and its allies abroad. Wickard left for Mexico City to attend an inter-American conference on agriculture, but he would also use the occasion to begin negotiating with the Mexican government on a farm labor importation program to be placed under the Farm Security Administration (FSA).[75]

As the United States prepared to negotiate a guest worker program with Mexico, various U.S. government agencies were brought together to address the problems that might arise from the importation of large numbers of workers from Mexico. The issues of man-hours, minimum wage standards, discrimination, and the placement and distribution of the workers in the United States were never fully addressed by American officials or the Mexican government. Consequently, the problem of American growers reducing wage standards and increasing work hours, as well as the related matter of farm labor exploitation by means of private recruiting, company stores, and noncompliance with contracts, remained unresolved. One additional difficult issue was the task of informing American trade unions about the proposed Mexican contract labor program.[76]

Most American labor union officials believed that Mexican nationals would abandon farm work and take nonfarm jobs away from American citizens. In response, several CIO unions passed resolutions urging elected officials to prevent the contracting of Mexican labor during the period of conversion to war production. Disliking the idea of Mexican immigration and acting in apparent deference to organized labor, which had supported them at election time with votes, the Los Angeles County Board of Supervisors on March 31, 1942, asked California's governor to oppose plans to bring upwards of 50,000 Mexican contract laborers into the state. Despite protests by organized labor, the first Mexican guest workers arrived in California for the beet harvest.[77]

Problems arose within a week as additional guest workers arrived from Mexico. The Mexican laborers staged numerous work stoppages over their dissatisfaction with beet work, while other contract laborers walked off their jobs and got farm work that paid as much in one day as one week of sugar beet work. Some beet growers "pirated" the Mexican contract laborers with offers of hourly pay because the men could not understand the tonnage-based pay scheme and because an hourly wage scale prevailed on the area farms. Meanwhile, cotton growers in Arizona contacted federal government officials about bringing contract labor from Mexico into the state to harvest the cotton crop. As in California, Arizona cotton growers and government officials failed to agree on the issue of hourly wage rates for the Mexican workers.[78]

In light of potential Nazi propaganda, the U.S. government had to address the problem of discrimination against imported Mexican contract laborers. As previously noted, the subversive campaign of the Sinarquista movement in Mexico included propagandizing at screening centers in Mexico among prospective Mexican farmhands being sent to work in the United States. In an effort to alienate Mexican workers through misinformation, the Sinarquistas were telling the men that once they were in the United States, they would be drafted into the American army to fight overseas as conscripted soldiers.[79]

American labor representatives recognized the serious impact the Mexican contract labor program would have on domestic farm workers in terms of undermining wage levels. California UCAPAWA organizer Elizabeth Sasuly testified before a U.S. Senate committee that bringing Mexican braceros into the Imperial Valley had led to a 25 percent drop in wages in the area. Mexican Americans, most likely those in the labor movement, soon added their voices to these protests. Contact at this time between Mexican contract laborers and local Mexican Americans in California was often unfriendly. The Mexican Americans called the workers from Mexico scabs, told them they were being exploited for lower wages than local labor received, and prophetically added that they would remain in the state to take the jobs of local Spanish-speaking workers.[80] Mexican Americans were especially concerned that racial discrimination against them would only intensify in response to the added presence of Mexican nationals. One Mexican American from Wilmar, California, astutely summed up the great need to educate Anglos on the matter of discrimination, which had turned the Mexican American into "a moral, economic, and social delinquent," before braceros were allowed to enter the country:

> Before . . . another million Mexican peons [are brought] to labor and sweat in the back breaking toil required to harvest American cotton in Texas and elsewhere, the citizens of those agricultural communities should be educated to remove from their mental make-up all traces of anti-Mexican prejudice, intolerance and hatred. They could much better serve "National defense" in this manner than by opening the gates for more victims to enter and be exploited.[81]

No Freedom from Fear: The Federal Government, Race Relations, and Mexican Americans

At the start of World War II, one-third of the U.S. population consisted of various ethnic and racial minorities. Twenty-three percent of the American population was made up of first-generation foreign-born individuals and the sons and daughters of foreign-born parents. Sixteen percent of Americans spoke a language other than English. Ten percent of the national population was African American. Yet despite universal racial tensions, white Americans were opposed to racial change. More than half of all whites interviewed by the Office of War Information in the summer of 1942 believed there should be separate schools, separate restaurants, and separate neighborhoods for the different races. These widespread feelings may have partly provided the rationale for national legislative inaction on the matter of race relations. However, the expression of racial tensions as open conflict was becoming commonplace. It increased to dangerous levels, and as we have seen, in late spring 1943 the time bomb of race exploded in a series of race riots. Following the race riots in Los Angeles, Detroit, Harlem, and elsewhere, the Social Science Institute at Fisk University reported 242 additional racial conflicts in forty-seven cities.[82]

In 1943, a black sociology professor at Atlanta University remarked that four fears, and not the president's "Four Freedoms," dominated America's black population: the fear of physical violence in the form of lynching and race riots, the fear of additional discrimination, the fear of appeasement—that is, the giving of minor racial concessions to prevent major change—and the fear that fascism would destroy democratic rights.[83] The nation's nearly two million Mexicans shared similar trepidations. For them, racial violence was a daily reality; they were still held down by social and economic discrimination; they had made only marginal gains in employment and in the improvement of low wages and bad working conditions; they had gained few benefits from the New Deal and not many opportunities from the wartime economy; and they had been the targets of a campaign by Sinarquista forces to win them over to the fascist cause. Fear and uncertainty gripped Mexican Americans as the United States committed itself to winning the war. They could not count on the federal government to take an active hand in matters that concerned them. Having responded reluctantly to the FEPC, Roosevelt failed to address the plight of Mexican Americans through government intervention. To do so would further expose racism against the Spanish-speaking people on a national and international scale and thus jeopardize the successful achievement of favorable international relations through the Good Neighbor Policy.

Field investigators from various offices in and out of government warned that further outbreaks of racial unrest could be expected and that therefore the Roosevelt administration had to be prodded to take action on a national scale. Edwin R. Embree of the Julius Rosenwald Fund recommended that the president establish a commission on race relations to advise him on how the government could improve matters. Other proposals for a committee on race relations were suggested, but the president would not change his position. Instead, Roosevelt appointed Jonathan Daniels to collect information from government departments and from the virtually powerless FEPC (dubbed by one civil rights scholar as "the Wailing Wall of minorities") on existing racial tensions and how they were going to fight them. The Roosevelt administration refused to accept that the nationwide outbreak of racial strife was the result of endemic racism. A major reason for this inaction was that the president was preoccupied with the war; more important, he was to a great extent dependent upon the phalanx of conservative Southern Dixiecrats for his planned postwar foreign policy. The 1942 congressional elections had increased Roosevelt's reliance on Southern Democrats, who persuaded the president to weaken the FEPC and hold up action on all racial issues. Roosevelt's cautious outlook and inaction on the matter of race were definitely motivated by politics. Just as he had not pressed earlier for an anti-lynching bill, the president was following the custom of other successful politicians by not meddling with states' rights to control racial issues.[84]

Many officials within the Roosevelt administration believed that the solution of America's race problem required top government priority and that it had to be part of the measures the nation was taking in mobilizing for war. No doubt, reducing mounting racial unrest at home would have an impact on America's allies and, more important, would deprive Axis propaganda of one of its effective anti-American arguments. Several of the newly created federal departments and agencies dealt with problems of discrimination, but they had no specific programs or responsibilities in this regard and lacked the power to enforce the president's executive order. No single federal government agency dealt directly with the civil rights problems of America's minorities. The Interior Department proposed that the president establish an Office of Race Relations with Cabinet standing to coordinate and develop programs of action to ameliorate racial strife. An initial step proposed in this direction was for the president to appoint a national committee to investigate the racial difficulties. Interestingly, the list of names submitted to serve on this committee contained no individuals from racial minority groups. Another plan proposed was for a special unit to be set up in the Office of War Mobilization to investigate areas of racial tension and assist in implementing remedial action before a situation led to civil breakdown. A possible government office selection for this purpose was the U.S. Justice Department. Its Organization and Propaganda Analysis Section was collecting and analyzing information concerning the various nationality, racial, and minority political groups, as well as enemy agencies and propaganda. This agency could be merged with the War Mobilization Unit, since the latter dealt with racial tensions better than previous government methods employed. Also suggested was a national campaign by government and labor leaders, elected officials, and celebrities. This "just say no to racism" campaign could educate Americans about the problems of racism and unite them by emphasizing that prejudice was un-American.[85] Given the upcoming national election, the president's advisers for public relations unfortunately put all these proposals for a governmental race relations committee on hold, including plans to have Congress investigate the racial disorders.[86]

The War Department reported that discrimination in employment, housing, education, recreation, and military service was widespread throughout the United States, but some advances were being made to forestall further racial disturbances. For instance, civic and religious agencies in Los Angeles and other large California cities were making progress against discrimination in housing, employment, and recreation. Yet discrimination against Mexican Americans persisted, particularly in Texas. For example, on April 30, 1943, Kerr City, Texas, demonstrated its own version of Southern-style justice when a Texas Ranger and the county sheriff together savagely whipped, beat, and tortured eight Tejanos and one black to procure confessions in a murder case. Numerous instances of blatant racial violence went unreported. The list of discriminatory cases from Texas included segregation of Tejanos in the public schools; segregation of Tejanos by refusal to sell them real estate in restricted Anglo areas; exclusion of Tejanos from public parks built with federal monies; refusal of service in restaurants to Spanish-speaking military personnel; intimidation through threats that "Mexicans" who refused to work at starvation wages would be drafted; evidence that in some Texas counties where the population was 50 percent Anglo and 50 percent Tejano, 95 percent of the draftees were Tejano; refusal to permit citizens of Mexican descent to participate in democratic primaries; denial of the right of Tejanos to serve on juries; and the issuance of substandard insurance policies to Tejanos.[87] Thus in Texas, collective defiance by whites was greatest against any threat to the privileges their whiteness bestowed upon them.

"They Just Don't Get It": Fighting Racism within Labor's Ranks

Organized labor protested loudly against the wave of racial unrest in America, particularly the confrontations over jobs. On July 8, 1943, at its executive board meeting in Washington, D.C., the CIO issued a resolution to abolish racial discrimination because it was seriously imperiling the war effort. American workers were called upon to wage an all-out attack on racial intolerance on a daily basis. Sharply condemning mob hatred and violence against black citizens and other racial minorities, the CIO Executive Board asked President Roosevelt to order government agencies to make a full investigation of the racial unrest, giving special attention to the activities of Axis agents among racial groups. Calling for a nationwide program to prevent racial tensions, the CIO asked the federal government to recognize the discriminatory conditions that had led to the race riots and to implement a program to eliminate these causative factors. The CIO recommended that various federal agencies give full support to the president's FEPC and that the president give a national radio broadcast outlining the causes of racial strife and the remedies the government would undertake to alleviate the crisis. Once again, the CIO expressed solidarity with all its fellow workers and renewed its vow to fight racial discrimination as a necessary part of the common battle against America's enemies. For Mexican Americans this support was important. Democratic unionism would mean an end to racial inequality in local union activities, and it would spontaneously facilitate a process of change not only on the shop floor but also in the working-class neighborhoods. Specifically, union activism could expedite the process of assimilation into American life. This is why Mexican Americans agitated loudly to gain employment in the war industries by ending the racist hiring policies of employers and the racism of Anglo workers.[88]

The problems Mexican American workers faced during World War II unfolded in the context of workplace discrimination exacerbated by the wartime national emergency. White workers, most of them part of the second wave of job hires, expressed disdain over the increase of black employment in defense work, which represented a 150 percent expansion between 1942 and 1944 in the basic war industries. More than 1.25 million blacks worked in war industries, 300,000 of them women. Blacks now made up from 5 to 13 percent of the workforce in aircraft, military vehicles, shipbuilding, steel, and munitions. Although only 1.1 percent of all strikes between July 1943 and December 1944 involved racial issues, twenty-five of these work stoppages, involving 181,791 workers at a loss of 185,581 man-days, occurred in important war production plants. They were caused by alleged discriminatory employment policies or practices and acts of white worker racism and black worker resistance to this racism. Stiff opposition from white workers to the hiring and upgrading of blacks caused nine work stoppages affecting 84,698 workers at a loss of 44,130 man-days. These numbers included white UAW members in Detroit; white male and female shipyard workers in Mobile, Alabama, led by the League of White Supremacy, who organized to put a stop to the FEPC upgrading of black workers; and white steel workers in Gary, Indiana. The growing militancy of black workers over demotions, unfair promotions of white workers, and discriminatory workplace conditions resulted in eleven work stoppages involving 74,974 workers at a loss of 18,974 man-days. In 1943, the Labor Department's Industrial Relations Division reported that fifty strikes lasting more than a day had occurred over racial issues. These strikes, some of them hate strikes, involved 64,907 employees and resulted in the loss of 221,239 man-days of work. Triggering these strikes were the hiring of blacks in previously all-white departments, the upgrading of blacks to semiskilled and skilled occupations, and protests by black workers against racist treatment. The Labor Department reported that racial discord was long-standing at some industrial plants.[89]

Overshadowing the campaign for national unity behind the war effort was the stubborn racist resistance to the president's policy of equal opportunity. Employers refused or were reluctant to hire minorities, and unions experienced considerable opposition from their Anglo membership to providing assistance to minorities with hiring and job upgrading. In California, the CIO Minorities Committee continued to push the federal government to implement nondiscrimination programs in the WMC and in the USES by working closely with the FEPC and civic organizations. The CIO Minorities Committee continued to demand that the state of California establish its own FEPC and, in light of the fact that the KKK had opened a headquarters in Los Angeles and was also quite active in the San Diego area, that affirmative steps be taken to halt the growing racism and anti-Semitism in Southern California.[90]

However, important changes were afoot in America that influenced how labor carried out its policies to achieve social equality for its minority rank and file. In the 1942 election the antilabor Republican Party won forty-forty House and nine Senate seats, regaining more power than it had lost in 1932 and 1936. The soft coal strike in the spring of 1943 deepened antiunion sentiment across the country and immediately gave rise to antiunion legislation. In June 1943, Congress passed the War Labor Disputes, or Smith-Connally, Act. It ordered a thirty-day cooling-off period, allowed government takeover of military production plants threatened by labor disputes, banned strikes and strike support in federally run facilities, and curbed the political activities of unions. The law had little effect on the CIO, as it was committed to the no-strike pledge and political mobilization in support of Roosevelt. Nonetheless, an antilabor environment had been spawned in America. By the end of 1943, the CIO Minorities Committee countered racist and anti-Semitic attacks by changing its focus from antidiscrimination activities to a campaign for racial unity on behalf of the war effort. The tenor of political mobilization shifted in response to the progressive defeat in 1942, the result of low voter registration and voter turnout in industrial districts, as well as obstacles like the Smith-Connally Act. CIO Minorities Committee chair Revels Cayton now urged his committee to coordinate its efforts with the CIO Political Action Committee (PAC) in uniting California's 225,000 black voters with Mexican Americans and all people of color to build an enthusiastic "spirit of liberation . . . which will spread to white workers as well."[91]

The vehicle for CIO political activity during the 1930s had been Labor's Non-Partisan League, but because of the quarrels between Sidney Hillman and John L. Lewis, it was replaced by the CIO PAC. The CIO PAC worked directly with Roosevelt and the Democratic Party's liberal wing to advance the agenda of industrial unionism. In this respect, the CIO PAC mobilized its union members; it directed affiliated unions to build local CIO PAC bodies by concentrating on voter registration, voter turnout, and the distribution of political literature. The CIO PAC especially made appeals to women and minorities. The CIO had gained considerable prestige among the Spanish-speaking of Los Angeles because of its union organizing drives, its support for the push for war industries training programs for minorities, and its defense of the victims of the Sleepy Lagoon and zoot suit cases. The CIO PAC now turned to the Mexican community, 130,000 of them registered voters, to urge them to participate earnestly in its campaign for another Roosevelt victory.[92]

In August 1944, the CIO PAC, with the assistance of the CIO Minorities Committee and with Mexican American unionists at the forefront, mobilized Spanish-speaking workers and their families into a broad coalition to reelect Roosevelt and put down the basis for a rejuvenated postwar New Deal. Mexican American and other CIO union members were being moved toward a more pluralistic understanding of labor's goals in support of national unity. To halt prejudice against women and minorities was to insist upon more social equality in the form of an abolition of the poll tax, aggressive voter registration drives, and an expanded economy through a union movement that provided well-paying jobs for all Americans. Working through their respective union locals and through the Los Angeles CIO Council, Mexican American labor focused on community issues in conjunction with civil rights organizations. A major project was establishing a California FEPC. With assistance from the FEPC's Spanish-speaking division and civil rights groups, Mexican American CIO members led by Jaime González of the USWA began organizing in late 1944 to support the Hawkins Bill to set up a state FEPC. Assemblyman Gus Hawkins had written to Spanish-speaking leaders for support of his own legislative bill for a California FEPC, which would cover all employees, employment agencies, and labor organizations in the state.[93]

The shift in the CIO's national policies to reflect those of the Democratic Party included support for establishing friendly U.S. relations with its Latin American allies. Additional assistance to America's Spanish-speaking citizens was related to the promotion of Roosevelt's Good Neighbor policies because they were serving as a direct link in achieving and maintaining amicable relations with Latin American countries.[94] In this regard and because of concern over the discrimination experienced by the great numbers of Mexican Americans in military service, the OCIAA as a result of input by Mexican Americans made the following recommendations to the War Department: eliminate the term "Mexican" from all military records; station Spanish-speaking noncommissioned officers at military centers with Spanish-speaking enlistees; assign military officers to duty in the Southwest and brief them in matters pertaining to inter-American affairs; recruit Mexican Americans into the American Red Cross, the USO, and other organizations working with the Spanish-speaking in the military; and instruct the Navy Relief and the Army Emergency Relief offices to produce bilingual information on allowances for dependents, maternity care, and other issues relevant to Mexican American servicemen and their families. In addition, the OCIAA produced a pamphlet on the contribution of America's Spanish-speaking minorities to the war effort as a way to bolster morale among this group making significant sacrifices at the battlefront. The OCIAA distributed 600,000 copies of the pamphlet, targeting cities with large Mexican populations like Los Angeles, Denver, and Chicago.[95]

When America entered World War II, the Spanish-speaking people of the Southwest and the Midwest remained dependent upon New Deal agencies to bolster their standard of living. Before they were phased out, the WPA, the NYA, the CCC, the FSA, and other New Deal programs directly benefited Mexican American families and introduced them to the

New Deal ethos. The fact that so many Mexican Americans relied on New Deal government assistance had made them in a sense "intermittent wards" of the state.[96] Racial discrimination shaped the attitudes of Mexican Americans toward the war. A longtime economically underprivileged segment of the American working classes, Mexican Americans wanted to secure well-paying jobs in war industries and military construction projects to attain material rewards. Those who did attain material success did so largely as CIO unionists. In this regard, the president's Executive Order 8802 on nondiscrimination in defense work spurred Mexican Americans at the grassroots level to fight discrimination in employment. During the war, Mexican American membership in the CIO increased and brought with it good pay and regular employment. Prodded by America's fight against Nazism and its adherents' claim to racial superiority and by federal intervention in combating racial injustice at home, Mexican Americans wanted to claim full rights as citizens in the larger American society.[97]

Because of the homegrown racism in the United States, widespread inequality remained a barrier against the concerted efforts of Mexican American citizens to rally to the defense of the nation. They were denied employment in war industries and access to decent housing, and police violated their civil rights. Racial bigotry against Spanish-speaking GIs was creating a state of low-morale among both Mexican American military personnel and civilians. Poverty, underemployment, and the lack of job opportunities outside low-wage agriculture pushed up volunteer rates among Mexican Americans. The Institute of Ethnic Affairs at the end of World War II confirmed the fact that the vast majority of the Mexican American draftees and voluntary enlistees were poor, uneducated, blue-collar, or unemployed. This agency reported that prior to their induction into the armed forces, the Mexican Americans who won the Congressional Medal of Honor were all poorly educated, physically malnourished, and of working-class backgrounds: bellboys, farmhands, kitchen help, and common laborers. The high percentage of Mexican American voluntary enlistments undeniably evidenced their patriotism, their desire to do something for the war effort. Because Mexican Americans were woefully underrepresented on draft boards, discrimination by local Selective Service boards accounted for the high Mexican American draft rates. The Anglo-dominated local Selective Service boards tended to give fewer deferments to Mexican Americans. A biased classification system was in place in Texas with regard to the second draft registration. The common practice in Selective Service records throughout the Southwest and Midwest was to use the term "Mexican" for American citizens. This became, in the hands of a draft board, a racial epithet that implied inferiority and decreased the chances that the inductee would receive a deferment. In sum, Anglo society had condemned Mexican Americans to starvation wages, inferior housing, and disease, but it expected them to defend American freedoms overseas.[98]

Deep-seated racial tensions continued to plague the United States. In the Southwest, Anglos for their part seemed to take for granted a racial superiority and established practices that segregated, disenfranchised, and ostracized Mexican Americans. Various government reports all showed that the eleven million Anglos in the Southwest, many of them recent arrivals from other regions of the United States, were keenly color-conscious and actively practiced discrimination. They would not live or work with Mexicans.[99] Thinking in terms of racial segregation, the region's Anglos had become "Southwestern Bourbons," in the process imposing their racist views of cultural matters upon the rest of American society. A change of attitude would not bring Mexican Americans and Anglos closer together within the same community, but as we have seen, it was widely believed by government officials and private individuals that it would at least unify the American community in the war effort. Racial tolerance would increase manpower through integration, and the benefits of this growth would redound to the advantage of the Anglo. This was something the Mexican Americans and their progressive supporters knew and understood.

Labor Rights Are Civil Rights: The Emergence of the Mexican American Civil Rights Struggle

> [A] large number of devoted leaders are needed within the group of Spanish-speaking people within the United States if the people are to take an active part in the development of genuine democracy.
>
> —ROBERT C. JONES

> We feel that good Americans have been imposed upon by minority groups pleading their alien cause as an American ideal.
>
> —WE THE MOTHERS MOBILIZE FOR AMERICA, INC., Los Angeles

I was welding some material together for a part of a tank when all of a sudden I noticed lots of commotion on the work floor as women were hugging and crying. I turned off my torch gun and heard the company whistle tooting and tooting. One of my friends ran up to me and told me that the war was over. I [sat] down on a workbench, [placed] my hands over my face, and [cried]. All of the emotion, which had been locked up for all these four years, was released. All I could think of was that our boys would be finally coming home to be reunited with their families.[1]

World War II had finally ended. For several days Mexican Americans in the Southwest and Midwest streamed into local churches to rejoice and give thanks for the safe return of their kin. Many of the parishioners, however, did their praying in segregated sections of the Catholic churches. This was an initial indication that the innumerable wartime contributions of Mexican Americans on the battlefields of Europe and the Pacific and in the defense plants and shipyards had not eliminated discrimination. For Mexican Americans, social and economic inequality still persisted, and they all knew this was unfair.[2]

Many Mexican American World War II veterans expressed resentment at having played such a prominent role as Americans overseas only to go back to living as outsiders again. Contemporary observers confirmed this general feeling of bitterness. The editor of *Speakers Magazine*, Stuart Banes, wrote: "All through Texas, New Mexico, Colorado, Arizona, and California, it is the same story. [Mexican Americans] have returned home only to be put in their place—that place being of course, on the bottom rung of the Southwest's social and economic ladder."[3]

The hard-won economic, social, and political gains Mexican Americans had made during the war years were being swiftly reversed, and there was a general indifference to their plight. In the absence of a federal FEPC, which ended in June 1946, and with discrimination in hiring increasing, Mexican Americans were victims of a swelling backlash against racial change that meant deteriorating conditions for the growing Spanish-speaking population.[4]

Undeterred by such defeats and setbacks, Mexican American unionists and union leaders continued to contest job and wage discrimination by employers and to demand seniority provisions in their struggle to achieve economic parity with other American workingmen and thus attain first-class citizenship. Unions had broken down the barriers to economic and racial equality, and Mexican Americans still held out hope that unionism would provide advancement.[5] The World War II years likewise had been a turning point for Mexican American women, an apprenticeship in waging resistance against biased employers and unions. Though both Anglo and Mexican American male union activists paid little attention to women's issues, Mexican American working-class women carried on the fight against degrading racial and sexual discrimination and for equal pay for equal work, paid maternity leaves, a higher minimum wage, and greater job opportunities. Spanish-speaking women had gained social and economic independence during the war years, and they had been further politicized through grassroots community activism. They too demanded full citizenship. As a Mexican American woman defense worker recalled: "We women didn't want to turn the clock back . . . regarding the social positions of women before the war. . . . We didn't want to give up this experience simply because the war ended. We, too, wanted to be first-class citizens in our communities."[6]

As it did for blacks, the postwar environment shaped the politics of social change for Mexican Americans. Wartime service and sacrifices, the experience with racism at home and overseas, and the rising expectations for social, racial, and economic equality, along with the growing urbanization of the Spanish-speaking population, set the stage for a new era in civil rights. Mexican Americans began to press for changes in their communities by forming and strengthening new and old alliances with labor and with progressive civil rights organizations. The movement focused on the need for better jobs, an end to police brutality, access to housing and education, and representation in government.[7]

This chapter provides an examination and discussion of the Mexican American struggle for equality after World War II. This struggle began as large-scale participation in postwar strikes for higher wages. Mexican

Americans similarly engaged in the fight to make the FEPC permanent and to keep or gain jobs during the conversion to a peacetime economy. They campaigned and voted for state FEPC ballot initiatives in the face of discrimination in hiring, job training, and job upgrading. In the climate of renewed racism, Mexican Americans led community-based struggles for economic, political, and social equality as they fought against the increase in employer discrimination and the Anglo rank-and-file racial backlash. Mexican American labor activists fought to repeal the Taft-Hartley Act as the right-wing attack heated up against labor and civil rights activism. The participation in local, state, and national politics will also be assessed, with a focus on voter education and registration; and I show that Mexican Americans expressed growing concern about direct competition for jobs and housing as a result of the Bracero contract labor program and the *mojado* influx, which also brought increased racial tensions and fragmentation. The choices made and the strategies utilized by Mexican Americans in their campaigns for economic and social justice were constrained and eventually stalled, though not defeated, by the circumstances of the anticommunist and anti-alien reaction, growing CIO autocratic rule, and a resurgent racism. These factors momentarily served to keep Mexican Americans in their place and rendered them virtually invisible until the emergence of the modern Chicano protest movement.

EXPRESSIONS OF THE MEXICAN AMERICAN UNION MOVEMENT AND ITS REPRESSION

Side by side with Anglo and black workers, Mexican Americans engaged in the dramatic wave of demonstrations and strike actions of the early postwar era to protest workforce reductions and to win higher wages. This was shown plainly in 1946, in a near general strike in basic industry, when the CIO's Big Three—UAW, Steelworkers, and UE—struck major manufacturing employers to recover ground lost during World War II. The strike produced a turnout of Mexican American CIO unionists on the picket lines and further organizing in response to the call by the CIO Councils, an action that brought additional numbers of Mexican Americans into the CIO and local union leadership. UE shut down General Electric, Westinghouse, and numerous other electrical and machinery manufacturers to demand an hourly wage increase of 18.5 cents. In Los Angeles, UE Local 1421 won a representation election at U.S. Electrical Motors in 1945. However, in the next year, when contract negotiations stalled, the workers walked out. Vast picket lines of unionists, many of them World War II veterans wearing their uniforms, marched up and down Slauson Avenue and were soon teargassed and clubbed. CIO leaders Slim Connelly and Jim Daugherty, Jess Armenta from ILWU Local 26, and Frank Lopez from the UE were gassed, arrested, and fined $500 each for violating an antipicketing order.[8]

In the metals industries of the Southwest and Mountain States, Mexican Americans constituted nearly half the workforce and made up 15 percent of the membership of the independent International Union of Mine, Mill and Smelter Workers, and many served as leaders of their locals. Clearly, the Spanish-speaking miners and metal refinery workers, inured to years of hardship before the union era, respected and supported their union. Just as it registered black voters in Alabama and fought segregation in the North, Mine-Mill championed the civil rights cause of the downtrodden and underprivileged Mexican American workmen and eventually succeeded in helping these rank-and-file unionists break the so-called "Mexican wage scale," the notorious two-tiered wage system. This progressive union's campaign included pressuring the government for equal job opportunities. Mine-Mill was able to obtain National Labor Relations Board hearings concerning antiunion conditions, and the union remedied grievances and won compensation on behalf of its Mexican American members through appeals to the director of conciliation of the Department of Labor. Once again, it was rank-and-file Mexican Americans who pushed the union in the direction of action.

In March 1946, 1,100 workers in El Paso belonging to Mine-Mill Local 509 and Local 501 walked out over a dispute regarding low wages and bad working conditions. The work stoppage in El Paso was part of the larger strike action by Mine-Mill against the nation's eighteen ASARCO plants to demand industry-wide bargaining. In an example of past and present coalition-building with allies in Mexico, Mine-Mill gained strength through cross-border solidarity with the Confederación de Trabajadores Mexicanos. The Mexican labor federation donated money and promised that workers from Mexico would not cross into El Paso to scab. A CIO Relief Committee and a Citizens Committee were quickly established to support the strike. The Relief Committee set up soup kitchens at CIO headquarters and at Smeltertown, while the Citizens Committee made donations of food and money. The latter committee was made up of members of union groups such as United Bakery Workers Local 1145 and Tejano, black, and progressive Anglo El Paso community members, including housewives. All of them were fully aware of the broader implications of the strike and came to the assistance of the strikers despite strong pressure from El Paso reactionary elements. Indeed, the strike issues were of immense importance and the potential gains wide-ranging. They would have a direct bearing on the wage situation of Spanish-speaking workers in El Paso, who represented 60 percent of the city's workforce, and were bound up as well with the future of the Spanish-speaking working classes of the Southwest, who made up a large portion of the region's wage earners. More important, because El Paso's ASARCO and Phelps Dodge plants paid lower wages in Texas than in New Mexico, Arizona, Utah, and Nevada, the successful outcome of the strike meant the opportunity for a further organizational drive in the region to improve the overall living conditions of the Spanish-speaking community.[9]

Humberto Silex once more played a leading role in labor ferment. Born in 1903 in Managua, Nicaragua, Humberto Silex had been a permanent U.S. resident since 1921. He received an honorable discharge from the U.S. Army in 1922 and came to El Paso in 1933, after working in Missouri, Illinois, and Texas. From the beginning, Silex had been associated with the labor movement in El Paso and was acknowledged as a truly exceptional labor leader. Silex was responsible for establishing Local 509, the first CIO local in El Paso, but because of his organizational work he was singled out by ASARCO and discharged for union activity in July 1940. The NLRB reinstated him with back pay. Silex quickly rose through the ranks of Local 509; in 1942 he was elected secretary and treasurer; in 1943 and 1944 he was selected president of this local; and in 1945 Silex became national representative and organizer for Mine-Mill District 2, which covered Texas, New Mexico, Arizona, Utah, and Nevada. In 1946, Silex was the primary force in maintaining the spirit and morale of the workers in their victorious strike against ASARCO and Phelps Dodge.[10]

Strike leader Silex went to Cuidad Juárez as the representative of El Paso's CIO unions and the main speaker at the May Day celebration held there jointly by the CIO and the CTM. Silex led 500 Mine-Mill members from El Paso in a huge march with 10,000 Mexican CTM members as an expression of international solidarity, which included a call for United Nations unity and action against repression of the people of Spain by General Francisco Franco. Silex possessed a valid alien resident card, which he used when he crossed into Mexico. In fact, Silex had just been issued a new card, which was valid through August 1946.[11]

Waged over four months, the strike by Mine-Mill Local 509 at the ASARCO smelter and by Local 501 at the Phelps Dodge plant was bitter. In addition to Red-baiting, INS agents on several occasions questioned strikers on the picket line about their citizenship status. Most of the strikers interrogated were legal U.S. residents. Humberto Silex, as a leader, became politically suspect and therefore vulnerable to intimidation and deportation by the INS. On June 6, 1946, INS agents arrested Silex near the El Paso Phelps Dodge refinery on the charge of aggravated assault and because of a half-hour visit he made across the border.[12]

Silex claimed the INS was attempting to deport him because of his union activity for the CIO, including leading the present strike. During his deportation hearing before the INS, Silex was never questioned about the crime he was charged with. Instead, all the questions were about Silex's union activities and his alleged membership in the American and Mexican Communist parties. Since the start of deportation proceedings against Silex, many of the strikers had felt uneasy; the men were very fearful of the INS menace, which was impeding union activity. Union officials were concerned that Silex's deportation would trigger a concerted deportation campaign against other union members who were resident aliens.[13] Silex's numerous supporters across the nation believed this union leader's deportation would have serious and far-reaching repercussions for the CIO union movement in El Paso, in Texas, and in other areas of the Southwest. They therefore argued forcefully against his deportation and urged their locals to adopt resolutions, sign petitions, and contact their respective congressional officials and the INS on his behalf. Silex finally won his case for citizenship in the federal district court in Texas.[14]

Among Mexican American women, though postwar life was marked by the twin fetters of female subordination and domesticity for many, the unions remained the most important organization in the lives of those who were blue-collar workers. Once again, Mexican American women proved they were strong union supporters and the best organizers. The United Packinghouse Workers of America (UPWA) was a union leader in defending the rights of racial minority and women workers. With its official symbol a pair of clasped black and white hands, the UPWA fought for plantwide seniority and urged locals to set up their own civil rights committees to address nondiscriminatory hiring and promotion, the insertion of articles or invention clauses in all union contracts, the integration of locker rooms, the location of eating and drinking establishments near the packing plants, and other civil rights issues. Though the UPWA did not fully address issues pertinent to the female rank and file, Mexican American women remained loyal unionists. During the 1948 packinghouse strike, at which time employers attempted but failed to defeat the UPWA by dividing the workers on the racial issue, Mexican Americans were among the tens of thousands of rank-and-file members who walked out to demand a wage increase. Fearless in the face of locally implemented antilabor injunctions and the deployment of National Guard troops, Mexican American women packinghouse workers in Saint Paul and Newport, Minnesota, stood in solidarity with their fellow workers during the three-month-long strike. They were radicalized along class lines. In addition to making signs, preparing food and coffee, and providing medical care for workers hurt in the strike, the women held the line at the key confrontations and drew the community together by organizing their families and neighbors to fight for the union. In Denver,

Mexican American female packinghouse workers belonging to UPWA Local 21 similarly demonstrated defiance on the picket line. Angered by the inequities and determined to hold their ground, some of the militant women lay down on the railroad tracks to prevent the company from moving meat products.[15]

MEXICAN AMERICANS FIGHT FOR AN FEPC BILL

Throughout the postwar years, Mexican American working men and women time and again fell into step in fully demonstrating their unwavering commitment to economic and social advancement. The labor activists among them correctly concluded that government intervention at the federal and state level was still required to push employers and Anglo workers toward the idea of equality. Mexican Americans kept apprised of legislation before Congress that was beneficial to the Spanish-speaking population, the most important being the Full Employment bill and the FEPC bill, and they stayed apprised of the status of pending state FEPC legislation.[16] These bills would provide Mexican Americans with timely access to the jobs they deserved while providing a practical solution to the ongoing crisis of employment discrimination.

In the absence of a national FEPC and faced with a Democratic administration that was at best lukewarm on the matter of civil rights, black and Mexican American workers, joined by their sympathetic Anglo allies, launched major campaigns for an FEPC at the state level. Although most of these FEPC laws in the southwestern states were defeated or narrowly passed, they were put on the agenda by a labor and civil rights coalition that mobilized community support on an enormous scale, anticipating the mass action efforts of the 1960s civil rights movements.

In Colorado, despite a grassroots push by blue-collar workers and civil rights organizations that included La Asociación Nacional México-Americana (ANMA), a state FEPC initiative failed to gain the necessary votes. In New Mexico, Spanish-speaking miners joined by the NAACP and other civil rights organizations aggressively pushed the New Mexico legislature to pass a state FEPC bill. The initiative passed by a slim margin, a vote of 25–24. All the Mexican American representatives in the New Mexico state legislature voted for the bill, which had been contained in committee by dissenting Anglo state legislators and a handful of "upper class" Spanish-speaking New Mexicans with whom they enjoyed cozy relations.[17]

In California, Proposition 11, a broadly backed measure that sought to eliminate discrimination on the basis of "race, color, creed or national origin," was placed on the ballot after a successful statewide signature drive. The State Federation of Labor, the California CIO, the Democratic Party,

Figure 6.A. In the postwar years, Mexican American CIO rank-and-file members joined the walkouts for job protection and higher wages. National Guard near the South Saint Paul stockyards during the 1948 meatpackers' strike. (66746—Governor Youngdahl Packinghouses Strike File, Courtesy of Minnesota Historical Society).

the NAACP, the California Council for Civic Unity, the California Communist Party, and scores of church, civil, and minority organizations provided key support and endorsed Proposition 11. Together these organizations launched a statewide campaign for immediate action on the FEPC. Because of growing opposition to Proposition 11, a drive was launched almost simultaneously to counter the right-wing attack and diffuse the situation. A coordinating committee was set up to popularize the FEPC and get out the vote for the initiative. In addition to distributing literature and holding rallies, the campaign sought free radio time and developed programs that relied on recorded interviews and statements by Catholic and protestant clergy and liberal businessmen who had previously come out for the FEPC in states where the measure had become law.[18]

Proposition 11 never recovered from being denounced by California reactionaries, however, and it went down in defeat. Progressives in the state quickly sensed the immediate dangers ahead for racial minorities, who looked for assurances that they had not been forgotten. The Executive Committee of the Council for Civic Unity of Los Angeles wrote to California Governor Earl Warren imploring him to do something to allay the growing fears among the state's minority groups, who looked upon the failure of the Proposition 11 drive as another indication of the increasing discrimination against them.[19]

"Nothing—We Shot a Mexican": Mexican Americans Fight Racism

"You will recall . . . I had received no support from Latin American groups, meaning organized groups. That is true, but explainable, for what organizations have we that are of any weight politically?" So wrote Dr. Carlos Castañeda to his friend Dr. George I. Sánchez in 1946, expressing his anguish and disappointment over the absence of a single national Mexican American organization capable of defending the Spanish-speaking people and uniting them against acts of discrimination. Other than progressive CIO locals and the Popular Front civil rights organizations, such as the earlier Congress of Spanish-Speaking Peoples, no single and unified national Mexican American organization existed to fully protect and represent Spanish-speaking residents. The Texas State CIO Council confirmed this fact, noting that it did not have an effective coalition with Tejano organizations in the state because there were no important national Mexican American civil rights organizations the national CIO could work with. To fill this vacuum, in 1949, Dr. Sánchez persuaded the state governor to create the Texas Council on Human Relations to focus on widespread segregation and discrimination against Tejanos, who, along with blacks, made up one-third of the state's population. However, the Council on Human Relations was powerless; it merely served as an advisory board to the governor. Little was done therefore to alleviate de facto discrimination and segregation problems faced by Tejanos in Texas.[20]

Renewed racial violence against minorities was rampant in the early postwar years. The backlash was starkly revealed in the growing number of racially charged incidents involving calculated police brutality, such as those in highly segregated Los Angeles, whose main targets were blacks and Mexican Americans. On the night of August 21, 1946, Los Angeles policemen clubbed to death black plasterer and union member Herman Burns, in full view of more than a dozen bystanders. The witnesses included Herman's two brothers, John and Julius Burns, who were also physically attacked by the police officers wielding nightsticks and blackjacks.[21]

Seventeen-year-old Augustine Salcido was shot through the head by a Los Angeles police officer; thirteen-year-old Eugene Montenegro, an honor student, was fatally shot in the back by a Los Angeles County deputy sheriff. The casual manner in which law officers took the lives of the city's Mexican Americans was revealed immediately after the shooting of Montenegro, when a neighbor inquiring about what had happened was told matter-of-factly by a deputy sheriff, "Nothing—we shot a Mexican." Officers from the Los Angeles Police Department and the sheriff's department routinely beat up Mexicans after arresting them. Among the numerous incidents of racist police practices was the savage beating of seven jailed Mexican American youths on Christmas Eve 1951 by twenty-two Los Angeles police officers during a wild drinking party at the Lincoln Heights police substation.[22]

The Burns, Salcido, and Montenegro murders by Los Angeles law enforcement officers were three more among hundreds of cases of brutality against blacks and Mexican Americans in the city who had not committed a crime and were not resisting arrest. They were shot or beaten simply because of the hatred toward these two racial minority groups, which the police wanted to dominate and emasculate. Racialized as lawless, blacks and Mexican Americans moreover were badgered nightly by officers of the Los Angeles Police Department as it enforced its "police curfew" on them, a crackdown copied from Jim Crow rules in Southern cities. Much as they are today, the Los Angeles Mexican American and black communities were terrified by law enforcement and were convinced that they had little or no protection from racist police and sheriff's officers.[23]

A resurgence of violence, threats, and acts of desecration against blacks, Mexican Americans, and Jews by the Ku Klux Klan unfolded in both northern and Southern California, frightening signs of the increasingly dangerous racial situation. Forty Klan-style incidents occurred in Los Angeles in which blacks were attacked and beaten, crosses were burned, Klan signs and symbols appeared in black and Mexican neighborhoods, and synagogues were defaced. Community leaders and public officials who decried these hate crimes and took an active part in the protests were threatened anonymously in the name of the Ku Klux Klan. Not one arrest was made by law enforcement officers. No Mexican American civil rights organization came forward to protest the violence.[24]

AN AMERICAN TRAGEDY!

OUR LIBERTIES — OUR LIVES ARE THREATENED

THE RECENT SLAYING OF EUGENE MONTENEGRO, A 13 YEAR OLD MEXI-CAN HONOR STUDENT IS A DIRECT THREAT TO ALL OF US!!

Eugene was shot in the back July 20, while supposedly fleeing from a house he was said to have robbed. Deputy Sheriff Hodges, who shot the boy, was acquitted by a coroners jury on a verdict of "justifiable homicide." Hodges stated the boy threatened him with a knife; an ordinary Boy Scout knife was found in the boy's left hand, he being right-handed. After the shooting a neighbor asked a nearby policeman what happened: "NOTHING," HE REPLIED, "JUST A MEXICAN GOT KILLED."

THE POLICE POLICY OF RACISM WHICH SAYS "SHOOT FIRST, INVESTIGATE LATER" WHEN THE VICTIM IS NEGRO OR MEXICAN MUST BE HALTED!

EUGENE MONTENEGRO JOINS IN BLOOD the four Negroes lynched in Georgia, the veterans shot to death by a Negro hating cop in Freeport, Long Island; the victims of the pogrom in Columbia, Tennessee. The killing of Eugene is added to the record that includes the beastly attack on Isaac Woodard, Negro veteran, whose eyes were gouged out by a policeman's billy-club in Aiken, South Carolina.

GEORGIA, FREEPORT, COLUMBIA, SOUTH CAROLINA AND LOS ANGELES—all crimes that bear a special and terrible stamp: FASCISM

HALT POLICE BRUTALITY!
WHAT CAN YOU DO?

1. Write or wire Sheriff Biscailuz and District Attorney Fred Howser, DEMAND immediate dismissal of Deputy (Trigger Happy) Hodges.

2. Demand a thorough investigation of the shooting by the grand jury.

3. Support the AYD's fight to bring about justice. Sign the petition, JOIN THE AYD.

AND CALL ALL YOUTH TO ATTEND

OPEN AIR RALLIES TO
Protest the Murder of Eugene Montenegro
SATURDAY, AUGUST 24TH

| 5:30 P.M. — Corner | 7:00 P. M. — Corner |
| BROOKLYN and BREED | BROOKLYN and FORD |

Sponsored by: AMERICAN YOUTH FOR DEMOCRACY, 408 South Spring Street, Los Angeles. In conjunction with: Elezalde Anti-discrimination Committee.

107   (over)

Figure 6.B. Civil rights organizations, in association with the CIO, protested the outbreak of police violence in Los Angeles. The American Youth for Democracy sponsored a rally to protest the murder of thirteen-year-old Mexican American honor student Eugene Montenegro. (Civil Rights Congress Collection, Box 3, Folder 11, Courtesy of Southern California Library for Social Studies and Research, Los Angeles).

Along with prejudice and low incomes, nonenforcement of fair housing, equal access, and other antidiscrimination laws became de facto barriers to minority residential mobility after the war. Restrictive covenants had been invalidated by the courts in *Shelly v. Kramer* (1948), but resourceful realtors found ingenious ways to circumvent the law, some of them blatant in their intent. Up to 1950 the National Association of Real Estate Boards Code of Ethics required realtors to keep minorities out of new neighborhoods. Minorities who sought to buy homes in white neighborhoods were refused mortgage insurance, and zoning regulations and an intentional failure to enforce state and federal housing laws encouraged and sustained racial exclusivity.[25] Federally financed urban redevelopment further increased residential segregation in America's cities. Chronic housing shortages were created by a spate of housing demolitions. Slum clearance and urban redevelopment through Title 1 of the 1949 Housing Act ushered in an unprecedented uprooting and moving of people to public housing or to already congested areas. The result of this squeezing on Mexican American living space was massive overcrowding and worsening housing conditions. Funding to private developers solidified racial lines by destroying poor or working-class communities in highly desired areas. Minorities were in for the long haul in the fight to eliminate redlining and other forms of housing discrimination that contributed to their increasing segregation from the rest of America.[26]

In Los Angeles, the CIO was the driving force behind the mobilization to combat the upsurge of racism in the city. Mexican American unionists within the Los Angeles CIO Council took the lead. In the wake of the demise of the national FEPC and with the national CIO sloughing off the issue of racial equality, over 150 delegates representing twenty-two international unions, one local industrial union, and the CIO Women's Auxiliary attended a CIO "Conference on Racial and Minority Discrimination" on August 10, 1946. The purpose of the conference was to develop a program of antidiscrimination work in the Los Angeles community and in the CIO local unions and, towards the latter goal, to reestablish the Los Angeles CIO Council Anti-Discrimination Committee. Many Mexican American union officials and rank-and-file members attending the conference served on or chaired the various panels.[27]

As the chairman of the "Community-wide Activities" panel, Isador (Jess) Armenta of ILWU Local 26 called for the establishment of an educational program on race relations for the Los Angeles Police Department and for greater representation of blacks and Mexican Americans on the city police force. On the issue of growing police harassment of racial minority youth, Armenta pointed out that police disregarded the curfew law if it involved Anglo youth, but if it involved black or Mexican American youth, the police enforced the clampdown by attacking and in some instances shooting them. Because of the high dropout rates and poor schools in the black and Mexican American sections of the city, the delegates agreed with Armenta that the CIO had to become more involved in school board elections by helping to elect members sympathetic to racial minorities and that it should assist in getting parents of minority youth to join and participate in the Parents and Teachers Association.[28]

The Mexican American union leader told union members to report all cases of racial discrimination and to mobilize community-wide protests whenever incidents of racial discrimination occurred nationally. This advice was vitally important because in the four-month period between June 1945 and September 1946, fifty-six blacks were murdered in a renewal of terror against them. Armenta recalled the brutal activities of local police and the use of National Guardsmen against blacks in Columbia, Tennessee, in February 1946, the so-called "Mink Slide Riot," America's first major race riot after World War II.[29]

The conference participants passed resolutions protesting the shooting of a Mexican American youth in the Rose Hill housing project; condemning the fate of the O'Day Short family of Fontana, California, a black family whose four members were burned to death in December 1945, the horrible result of restrictive covenants; and calling for support for the revitalization of the National Negro Congress. The conference delegates voted unanimously to take action to achieve the release of fellow worker Festus Coleman, wrongfully charged with the rape of an Anglo woman, and to send telegrams to President Truman protesting the terrorism against blacks in Columbia, Tennessee, and Freeport, New York. In the spirit of interracialism, Armenta also urged the CIO to go on record in welcoming the returning Japanese Americans interned during the war, to encourage them to participate in the CIO-PAC, and to demand justice for Japanese Americans who had lost their jobs because of charges of disloyalty filed against them in 1942. Finally, CIO members, noting no Mexican American political activity of any consequence outside of labor's ranks, agreed to put forth greater efforts to organize the Mexican community of Los Angeles into progressive organizations comparable to the city's black organizations. The delegates in essence enthusiastically embraced the spirit of one of the keynote addresses of the conference: that the best hope of achieving racial democracy in the United States rested with the CIO. The CIO could not be satisfied with merely fighting against exploitation of its rank-and-file members. Rather, the labor movement had to conduct a daily struggle for justice against every kind of oppression and exploitation.[30]

LAST HIRED, FIRST FIRED: MEXICAN AMERICAN JOB
LOSS AFTER THE WAR

Long-standing problems of discriminatory employment remained at the end of World War II as a result of unfair company hiring and layoff policies. Historian Bruce Nelson attributes this retrogression to the reaction against black migration during the war years, which profoundly altered race relations in the United States, and against the interracialism the CIO pushed on stubborn Anglo employers and employees. The discrimination against Mexican Americans represented a microcosm of national patterns of racism against minorities and women. Because of these circumstances, Mexicans Americans were denied employment or remained largely confined to the least desirable and lowest-paid work. Not only were Mexican Americans diverted from better-paid and more desirable work, but they also were dissuaded from obtaining job training.[31]

Spanish-speaking war veterans who applied to veterans' employment offices were referred to menial jobs, were advised to file for unemployment insurance because there were no job openings, or, along with blacks, were channeled into inferior training programs and in many instances discouraged from completing the training. When Navy veteran Paul Márquez of South Omaha, Nebraska, used the GI Bill to enter an apprenticeship to learn upholstering, the boss tried constantly to intimidate him into quitting, and he quit. Disillusioned, Márquez got a job in the local packinghouse. The experience of this war veteran was not uncommon. A vocational guidance specialist reported that the policy of vocational centers was to "direct minority group members into channels where they would least likely encounter prejudicial barriers." Consequently, vocational training for nearly every kind of skilled work was effectively discouraged. In Texas and in Arizona, oil companies and copper companies, oftentimes supported by racist AFL-affiliated unions, flatly denied Mexican Americans opportunities for job training and job upgrading. The consensus among Southwest employers, who had long controlled the economic and political life of their local communities, remained that "Mexicans are inferior people . . . they can not assume responsibility . . . they are not sufficiently advanced to use additional income wisely, and they . . . [are] physically inferior to Anglos and hence [do] not produce as much."[32]

Returning Mexican American female veterans also faced bleak employment prospects as employers resorted to prewar hiring policies. They could not find jobs that made use of skills gained through military service and were not entitled to the veterans' benefits available to males. Furthermore, Mexican American women blue-collar workers were laid off or fired while other workers were asked to stay on until the industries they worked for converted from wartime to peacetime production. Afterwards, they were denied unemployment benefits. Like their Anglo and black counterparts, Mexican American female workers lost their jobs as a result of separate seniority systems based on sex and race, or they faced union harassment. Those women who managed to keep their jobs were earning one-fourth (26 percent) less per week than they had during the war years.[33]

The national emergency produced by World War II forced the integration of the unions into the war effort and compelled employers to work out accommodations with the unions for the duration of the war. This adjustment included the push by unions for employers to hire racial minorities and to take into consideration their workplace grievances. The war and its aftermath represented a period of consolidation of union power, but this was soon followed by a period of containment because of growing autocratic rule. Corporations, moreover, joined by their conservative congressional allies, unleashed a propaganda campaign against organized labor. Fair employment legislation was stonewalled by conservative Republican and Southern Democratic congressmen, and many employers, lacking essential conviction on fair employment practices, readily abandoned special steps to employ racial minorities and women.[34]

At the end of the war, the aircraft industry, shipbuilding and repair facilities, and ordnance factories in California slashed production and manpower requirements by two-thirds because they had the least potential for conversion to peacetime production. As a result of "last hired, first fired" policies, racial minorities in Los Angeles County accounted for only 14,188 (5.16 percent) of the 274,163 workers employed in both manufacturing and nonmanufacturing jobs. Now more selective in their hiring practices, employers demanded highly trained, multi-skilled workers and rejected the war workers who had learned a single skill in the war emergency training classes. Most black and Mexican American job applicants had little or no industrial background and thus were at a disadvantage. Those minority workers who had become highly skilled production workers during the war could not find comparable peacetime jobs. Moreover, because of the adequate labor supply, employers were not interested in implementing any large-scale training programs.[35]

Disproportionately unemployed, though just as qualified for skilled and semiskilled jobs as Anglo workers, California's blacks and Mexican Americans were forced to take the more menial and lower-paying jobs. These did not include clerical and sales jobs because 93 percent of these jobs were still monopolized by Anglos. At the Los Angeles downtown office of the U.S. Employment Service, over 40 percent of the mostly minority applicants were forced to take service jobs. Overall, USES nonwhite job placements in Los Angeles represented an average of 18 percent of the total placements in domestic service in private households, in wholesale and retail, in apparel, in food processing, and in furniture, rubber products, and iron and steel products manufacturing.[36]

In May 1946, the USES director for Southern California told a committee made up of CIO representatives and minority group organizations that 80 to 90 percent of local employment orders likely were discriminatory. Employers in Los Angeles, like those elsewhere across the country, had drawn the color line. A survey of its field offices by the national USES in Washington, D.C., revealed that nearly 43 percent of local employer orders in the construction industry were for "whites only" and that 31 percent of local employer orders from manufacturing firms in such industries as paper, furniture, rubber, and nonferrous metals likewise drew the color line, regardless of the minority applicants' military service during the war or their qualifications in war production. The iron and steel industry generally hired blacks and Mexican Americans; after the war, however, it had a below-average record of hiring from these two minority groups and confined them to the worst and lowest-paying jobs. Furthermore, 43 percent of local employer orders in the apparel industry insisted on "whites only," even though both the CIO and AFL unions had attained nondiscrimination policies in this industry. Inequitable local employer orders were highest in the textile industry, over 66 percent. Many of the USES reports from areas with large minority populations showed that in addition to local employment orders bearing restrictions against blacks and Mexican Americans, many orders were "discriminatory in spirit." In other words, employers refused to hire minority applicants even though they were qualified for the job openings.[37] The FEPC in its final report revealed the sad truth that unfair employment practices were greater and more extensive at the end of World War II:

> The wartime gains of Negro, Mexican-American and Jewish workers are being lost through an unchecked revival of discriminatory practices. The war veterans of these minority groups today face far greater difficulties than other veterans in obtaining training and finding work. . . . Nothing short of congressional action to end employment discrimination can prevent the freezing of American workers into fixed groups, with ability and hard work of no account to those of the "wrong" race or religion.[38]

The pressing problems of discriminatory hiring, job training, and job upgrading did not stem from employer practices alone: rank-and-file Anglo workers adamantly opposed the entry of minorities into all Anglo shops and departments and blocked job upgrading for them. The trade union movement continued to be defined by the racism of white labor as solidarity by exclusion. This racism by Anglo workers who considered themselves superior to blacks and Mexican Americans undermined equality in seniority, union governance, and social relations inside and outside the workplace.

As employers one by one said no to minorities applying for employment, Anglo workers used the power gained during the previous organizing struggles to maintain and even expand their high-ranking economic position and enforce workplace inequality. On the shop floor, Anglo, black, and Mexican American union members on occasion worked together when fighting management, but this cooperation ended when minority workers raised the issue of economic and social equality within the union. A pattern of racial discrimination persisted in the union locals. Unions had opposed lynching and segregation, fought for equal pay for equal work, and supported a national FEPC, but they rarely challenged workplace discrimination. This partially accounted for the harmful racial economic imbalances that existed in America. Anglo workers dominated the union locals. Their outlook on civil rights issues, rooted in years of racial competition, conflict, and privilege, did not change in the postwar era. For Anglos, change would mean surrendering their monopoly of skilled jobs, higher pay, and better and safer working conditions to minorities who dominated the lower-wage jobs. The stiff competition for jobs after the war was a powerful incentive for defending segregation on the shop floor.[39]

Emboldened by the ameliorative cultural pluralism of the World War II era, resentful Anglos transmuted ethnicity into white entitlement. Accordingly, they attempted to stop the integration of all white departments through threats, intimidation, and harassment, as well as by advancing racist arguments to achieve Anglo unity, staging hate strikes, and resorting to workplace violence. Because of the fine line between their job consciousness and race consciousness, Anglo blue-collar workers sabotaged the hiring and promotion of Mexican Americans and blacks. Anglos especially opposed and resisted any changes to seniority systems that would jeopardize their exalted position, and they voted against union contracts that would facilitate mobility for minority workers. In the backlash, some all-Anglo locals separated from international unions, or else Anglo workmen withdrew from union activities altogether. Racial divisions in the workplace, which were put in place by employers and maintained by Anglo workers and which went unchallenged by the unions, thus limited job opportunities for Mexican Americans and blacks, and whenever certain tasks were mechanized, the result was that a disproportionate number of minorities lost their jobs.[40]

In Texas, where strong feelings of hatred toward Mexicans and blacks ran deep, the national CIO's attempts to curb discrimination provoked little support from Anglo workers or endorsement from the local unions that limited minority opportunities for employment and economic advancement. Although the laboring classes of Texas, like those of much of the South, remained without union coverage, it became readily apparent that the Anglo Texan rank and file had no intention of supporting Operation Dixie when the CIO launched it in 1946 to organize one million workers in the region. Because of widespread workplace discrimination in Texas, Tejanos, along with blacks, continued to work in separate departments and suffer the dehumanizing and humiliating abuse of drinking from separate drinking fountains and using separate bathrooms and bathing facilities. A few racially progressive union locals protested against workplace discrimination but, caving in to pressure from angry and resentful Anglo union members, nonetheless negotiated union contracts that included company-segregated job categories and work areas. The hard fact was that Anglo CIO union members adamantly refused to be educated in the matter of race relations and, as proud Texans, were determined to take a strident stance against any kind of integration. One reason was that many Anglos were recent arrivals from other parts of the South. These "cornpone whites" not only preempted job openings in Texas but also had a strong racist penchant. As newcomers to the union, they resisted any kind of racial change, for their general feeling was that too much social change had come during the war from the intrusion of the federal government, the Democratic Party, and the CIO itself. The Texas State CIO Council as a result was forced to walk the color line, satisfying the antidiscrimination policies of the national CIO while making sure it did not push employers too hard on the matter of fair employment or alienate Anglo rank-and-file members with calls for racial equality. Self-interested Anglo workers in essence maintained the color line in the workplace, which management created and reinforced. Believing that blacks and Tejanos must be kept in their place, more and more Anglo workers now embraced states' rights and soon channeled their resistance to racial change by joining the Ku Klux Klan and later the powerful White Citizens Council.[41]

In California, the FEPC would not be tolerated. The opponents of the informal alliance of labor and civil rights groups gathered their forces to defeat the FEPC initiative. These included wealthy Republican businessmen helped by their politically influential pressure groups, the Associated Farmers, the Veterans of Foreign Wars, and the Young Republicans. Not surprisingly, the actions of these conservative Anglo Republicans reflected the sentiments of many Californians who were annoyed by the excesses of government tinkering with race relations and believed that law could not force tolerance. The bogus Committee for Tolerance launched a campaign to denounce and defeat Proposition 11. By now the call for civil rights was equated with communism. The backers of the Committee for

Tolerance charged that Proposition 11 was a CIO- and communist-inspired measure and that its originators were seeking disunity and discord in America. State Senator Jack B. Tenney, chairman of the legislative committee conducting an ongoing investigation of un-American activities in California, lent his voice to the anti–Proposition 11 clamor. Adding to the wild charges about the origin and intent of the state FEPC initiative, Tenney declared, "The Communists of the United States plan to drive a wedge between the people of America, thus creating the 'revolutionary soil' demanded by Stalin for the overthrow of the republic of the United States and the establishment of the dictatorship of the proletariat."[42]

The activities of Mexican American CIO unionists for civil rights, often with full support of the city CIO Councils, reflected the sentiments neither of the nation as a whole at this time nor of the national CIO. The latter's reneging of its support for civil rights must also be seen in the context of Truman's anticommunist campaign, which prompted a rightward shift in the CIO. The national CIO strengthened its control of the rank and file by ordering inaction by all local and state CIO Councils on resolutions dealing with national and international matters, except those the national CIO endorsed. Specifically on the matter of racial equality, delegates could not be sent to national organizations not recognized by the national federation, such as the National Negro Congress and the Civil Rights Federation, nor could CIO members become involved in civil liberties and civil rights matters of local or state concern.[43] The "Big Chill" was on.

The Right-Wing Backlash against the Mexican American Struggle for Labor and Civil Rights

Further attacks on leftist elements within the CIO followed. Delegates at the California CIO state convention in December 1946 endorsed the national CIO's "resent and reject" declaration, which barred members of communist organizations from interfering in the affairs of the CIO. This was done to destroy left-wing control of unions, and it was complemented by direct actions against individual communists. In early 1947, the removal of ILWU head Harry Bridges as director of the California CIO was achieved by separating the state CIO into two divisions, northern and southern. This drive for a more vigorous purge of Communist Party members within the CIO intensified with the launching of the Truman Doctrine in March 1947. In the following year, the national CIO rescinded the charters of the California and Los Angeles CIO Councils. This action, along with raids by newly chartered rival unions, destroyed the progressive base of the left-led CIO unions and snuffed out Popular Front politics and a progressive agenda in Los Angeles that included civil rights activism. Meanwhile, the national CIO, in its offensive against left-wing elements within its ranks, targeted international unions under Communist Party control for eventual decertification. Passed in 1947 in the shadow of the Red Scare, the Taft-Hartley Act led to further splits within the CIO, which was growing less assertive in pressing for civil rights, a cause it had championed but was now prepared to abandon.[44]

Within the context of the state-sponsored corporate assault on labor, the mass blacklisting that marked the Taft-Hartley postwar years, the close association between the fight against racial discrimination and the communists, and the purge of the CIO left-led unions, Spanish-speaking unionists fighting for labor and civil rights risked being Red-baited. The federal government once again attempted to link communism with the work of CIO unionists along the U.S.-Mexico border. The Immigration and Naturalization Service and the U.S. Border Patrol tracked down, arrested, and deported those who challenged the status quo. An important weapon in squelching dissent remained—the denaturalization and deportation of union leaders suspected of being communists. Community activists and leaders also became prime targets for surveillance by the INS, the FBI, and other government agencies, often in collaborative endeavors to eventually deprive these fighters for social justice of their citizenship or legal resident permits and to deport them. Such flagrant measures stripped the Mexican American civil rights movement of its most capable activists, reinforced a vise-like control over the Mexican Americans, and undermined their attempts at unionization and community advancement. As one observer noted, it was during these years that the threat of deportation "served as a very effective weapon to keep the Mexican people as a whole in bondage. . . . As soon as a leader arises . . . deportation proceedings are immediately used to remove [them] from leadership." These deportation cases were part of a nationwide campaign to harass and intimidate union activists among the foreign-born and to create a smoke screen of Red-baiting behind which reactionaries hoped to pass antilabor legislation.[45]

For two years the federal government tried to deport labor leader Humberto Silex, but it ultimately failed because of the nationwide defense effort launched by the American Committee for the Protection of the Foreign Born, other civil rights groups, and the Mine-Mill Solidarity Committee. In its relentless and vigorous search for and arrest of Mexicans in the service of the Communist Party, the Immigration and Naturalization Service detained UFWA Local 576 member Armando Davila for deportation because of his political beliefs. Local 576 came to Davila's defense; the union body voted to contact the Civil Rights Congress to defend him.[46] A longtime Spanish-speaking labor activist tracked down, arrested, and deported by INS agents was Refugio Martínez of Chicago. Martínez was a staff member of the United Packinghouse Workers of America. During

Figure 6.C. Progressive groups championed the plight of America's racial minorities. Demonstration sponsored by the Civil Rights Congress in downtown Los Angeles against the Smith Act and the McCarran Law. (*California Eagle* Photo Collection, Folder 74, Courtesy of Southern California Library for Social Studies and Research, Los Angeles).

the late 1930s he had been a member of El Frente Popular Mexicano and the Left-led Vicente Toledano Club. Martínez was a supporter of the left-wing organization Asociación Nacional México-Americana. The police labor detail of Chicago arrested Martínez for his involvement in trade-union activity for the UPWA, which was organizing the Wilson, Armour and Swift plants in that city. A twenty-seven-year resident of the United States, Martínez was deported under the McCarran Act because he had joined the Communist Party in 1932.[47]

Labor and civil rights activist Luisa Moreno likewise fell victim to the heated contest between ideologies. In 1948, Luisa Moreno was ordered to testify against her union, the Food, Tobacco, Agricultural, and Allied Workers of America, or FTA, before the Tenney Un-American Activities Committee in San Diego. Moreno, who had strong feelings about civil liberties, refused and instead challenged the Tenney Committee's right to question her political beliefs. Soon after the hearings, the federal government issued a warrant for Moreno's deportation to Guatemala. In 1949, Immigration and Naturalization Service agents invited Moreno to testify against ILWU leader Harry Bridges. Again, Moreno refused to talk because, in her words, she did not want to become a "free woman with a mortgaged soul." INS officials blocked Moreno's attempts to become an American citizen as punishment for "her militant leadership," her contributions to the labor movement, and her fight for the full citizenship of Mexican Americans. Called to appear for a "private hearing" before the INS in Los Angeles on August 25, 1949, Luisa Moreno left the United States before the federal government could deport her.[48]

ACHIEVING MEXICAN AMERICAN CIVIL RIGHTS THROUGH THE BALLOT BOX

Mexican American political organizations lacked the necessary power to compete in the Anglo arena of politics. A shortage of expertise and money hampered the Mexican American organizations, and literacy tests and a lack of education tended to discourage Mexican Americans from political participation. Furthermore, using the gerrymandering of districts as a major weapon, Anglo politicians precluded Mexican American representation and preserved their own power. Notwithstanding these barriers— as well as the narrow confines of political activism owing to pressure on all those in the CIO to function within the Democratic Party—in factories, in union locals, and in community workshops, CIO Political Action Committees (PACs) educated Mexican American blue-collar working men and women in participatory democracy. During the war years, Mexican American union activists through the CIO PACs had worked on behalf of Democratic Party candidates and organizations to register voters, distribute literature, and bring Mexican Americans to the polls. In the early postwar years, working-class Mexican Americans once again spearheaded the drive for voting rights and in addition helped launch a third political party in America, the Independent Progressive Party.[49]

Given the growing political awareness of the Tejano population of Texas, leaders of the new Tejano civil rights organizations urged the Texas State CIO Council and the national CIO to cooperate with them to develop a program aimed at fighting for integration, health, and other issues that promoted advancement of the state's Spanish-speaking population. An important issue that would encourage progress was Tejano participation in the political process. However, Anglos would have no part of this, for they viewed Tejanos as they did blacks, as racial inferiors, and on that ground judged them unsuited for political office. Fully acknowledging the racism of its Anglo rank-and-file members, the Texas

State CIO Council recommended, in addition to more tolerance in accepting Tejanos as members in CIO locals, tolerance toward Tejano political candidates seeking office. The latter advice was deemed important because in the next twenty years Tejano workers would account for most of the labor force in south Texas. Owing to this demographic reality, the Texas State CIO Council appealed to international and local union officers in the state to train and employ Tejano union members as organizers, for this would help the CIO organize and attain political strength more rapidly. Accordingly, the Texas State CIO Council funded three Tejanos from its south Texas locals in the Corpus Christi, Río Grande Valley, and Laredo areas to attend leadership training classes at the Highlander Folk School in Monteagle, Tennessee.[50]

High on the Texas State CIO's agenda was reversing the historically low voter participation of Tejanos in those south Texas counties where they represented large populations. As in many parts of the Deep South, this resulted from the rampant prejudice of the small towns, which induced apathy, and the fact that the poll tax voting requirement kept many potential Tejano voters away from the polls. The State CIO Council was finally going to act on the advice the Congress of Spanish Speaking Peoples had given in 1939—challenge the long history of political bossism in south Texas, the ability of ranchers, farmers, and businessmen to "deliver" the Tejano bloc vote by paying the poll taxes of the local Spanish-speaking residents who were the basis of their political power. This is what took place in 1948. In that year the formidable Texas Democratic political machine delivered the Tejano vote from Duval and Jim Wells Counties to Senator Lyndon Baines Johnson. Former Peoples' Congress members and progressive CIO union activists frowned on Johnson; the "friend of the Latin American" had voted for the Taft-Hartley bill and had climbed on board the anti-Red bandwagon.[51]

In light of the growing despotism of the CIO and the rise of racism, the pursuit of equality by Mexican Americans at this time was gradually being reshaped as the rising expectations of this minority group turned into a mass grassroots movement with its own priorities, tactics, and leadership. The early postwar era witnessed efforts at voter registration as well as desegregation of housing, public facilities, and schools by Mexican Americans. Convinced that the solutions to local problems lay in political organization, newly formed Mexican American organizations encouraged Mexican Americans to vote. East of Los Angeles and in California's rural areas, Mexican Americans, many of them war veterans, with the assistance of the American Committee on Race Relations, formed Unity Leagues and launched voter registration drives to elect progressive candidates to office to deal with local problems. In New Mexico, coalitions of

Mexican Americans that included unionists from Mine-Mill locals helped to reelect U.S. Senator Dennis Chávez, while broad-based coalitions in Arizona similarly exercised their political power in four victorious campaigns for the office of state governor.[52]

By embracing numerous community issues, the Community Service Organization (CSO), an offshoot of Saul Alinsky's Back of the Yards Neighborhood Council, helped nurture a new and well-organized grassroots political movement among Mexican Americans in Los Angeles, as it did among Spanish-speaking residents in Arizona, Chicago, and the Calumet area in the Midwest. Voter registration remained a key concern. Working through the California-based CSO, Mexican Americans from Boyle Heights in East Los Angeles undertook a mass voter registration campaign to elect Edward Roybal to the Los Angeles City Council as representative from the Ninth District. The CSO failed in this initial attempt, though Roybal lost by only 300 votes. After launching a nonpartisan voter registration campaign that gained 15,000 new voters and created seventeen new precincts, Mexican American organizers aided Roybal's second bid for a seat on the Los Angeles City Council, which he won in 1949. Unquestionably, crucial to Roybal's success were the dozens of Mexican American women who did an admirable job spearheading and energizing this door-to-door organizing drive. While holding down full-time jobs and caring for their families, women during their days off work, in the evenings, or on the weekends organized meetings, made phone calls, and distributed campaign literature. In the deepening climate of McCarthyism, however, police shadowed Roybal's supporters; their homes were broken into and ransacked; the canvassers received threatening phone calls and had their car tires slashed. Fliers and posters were torn down; Mexican American voters were harassed at the voting polls with racist taunts such as "Mexicans go home" and "Aliens can't vote" or were prevented from voting altogether. [53]

In the face of this reaction, progress-minded Mexican American workers refused co-option by the Democratic Party, which had backed down from the struggle for civil rights, and they endorsed the broader social democratic vision promised by the third-party presidential campaign of Henry A. Wallace of the Independent Progressive Party (IPP). Under the banner "Amigos de Wallace," Mexican Americans from Mine-Mill, the UFWA, the FTA, and the UPWA helped organize the IPP and led the grassroots campaign in numerous Spanish-speaking communities for Henry A. Wallace and those state and local candidates running on the IPP ticket. Wallace spoke out against racism and called for integrated housing and education, and the progressive candidate from Iowa backed other issues crucial to racial minorities. Wallace's endorsement of the FEPC and the

Good Neighbor Policy was well received by Mexican Americans, who, while seeking equality in the workplace, were just as concerned with American foreign policy in Latin America; they also backed the world peace movement and opposed the Marshall Plan. Support for Wallace was strong among blue-collar Mexicans in Southern California. Large numbers of them from the left-led unions abandoned the Democratic Party for the IPP. A "Wallace for President" rally in Lincoln Park in East Los Angeles drew 10,000 Mexican Americans. Although Wallace lost the election because of persistent Red-baiting from the Democratic Party, President Truman, the media, and CIO leaders, his campaign politicized many Mexican Americans. California's Left-led unions, such as the UFWA and the UE, who supported Wallace, his integrationist stance, and his opposition to American foreign policy overseas, drew further wrath from the national CIO federation. In fact, soon after the 1948 elections, the national CIO punitively took away the charters of the California and Los Angeles CIO Councils.[54]

The Independent Progressive Party received considerable aid from La Asociación Nacional México-Americana, a left-wing organization at the forefront of the early Mexican American civil rights struggle. Founded in 1948, ANMA by 1950 had 4,000 members consisting mainly of Mine-Mill and other trade unionists, led by veteran union organizer Alfredo Montoya. Much like its black counterpart the National Negro Labor Council, ANMA was manned and led by Mexican American blue-collar workers, who threw their lot in with this and other newly formed all–Mexican American organizations because the CIO had retreated from its commitment to the fight for racial equality. Dedicated to ending discrimination by employers, advancing the cause of economic and civil rights within the union movement for Mexican Americans, and advocating women's equality, ANMA built coalitions, such as other racial and ethnic minorities and with progressive organizations, such as the Committee for the Protection of the Foreign Born, the Progressive Citizens of America, and the Civil Rights Congress. In Phoenix and Denver, ANMA joined the Civil Rights Congress in the drive for a local FEPC and in the battle to stop police brutality against Mexican Americans, blacks, and Native Americans. In Los Angeles, ANMA and the Civil Rights Congress fought police brutality against blacks and Mexican Americans, who were routinely stopped without cause, searched, and arrested on false charges. ANMA also protested the printing of racist news articles by the *Los Angeles Examiner*, which, in associating crime with blacks and Mexican Americans, blamed "rat-packs" and "pachucos" for a crime wave in that city.[55]

Although critical of the Bracero program, ANMA helped organize bracero farm workmen in strike actions and in 1951 appealed to the United

Nations Commission on Human Rights to investigate their miserable plight as the rented slaves of growers. ANMA protested the mass deportations under the McCarran-Walter Act of Mexican immigrants, permanent residents, and Mexicans who were American citizens. This progressive body encouraged an international consciousness in its work with industrial unions and workers because it recognized the crucial interrelationship between Mexican Americans and Latin Americans in the class struggle. The organization was outspoken in its criticism of U.S. intervention in Guatemala and American support of dictatorships in Latin America and the Middle East. ANMA declared solidarity with the Cuban revolutionary movement of Fidel Castro and his freedom fighters. It also sought an alliance with Puerto Rican nationalists in their struggle for an independent Puerto Rico. Concerned with bringing about social justice at home, ANMA was also part of the peace movement. It vigorously opposed the Korean War as well as worldwide nuclear proliferation through the Stockholm Peace Appeal, initiated before the Korean War by leaders from various progressive church and civic organizations. In light of the anticommunist hysteria and resulting domestic repression and stifling of dissent, ANMA came under increasing scrutiny. The House Un-American Activities Committee investigated ANMA because of its alleged subversive activities, which included criticizing American foreign policy overseas. Charging that it was a communist organization, the FBI infiltrated ANMA; its paid informants provided the FBI with membership lists and background information on its officers and members. Red-baited by the U.S. Attorney General's Office as a subversive organization with ties to the Communist Party and a pro-Soviet position, ANMA was silenced and eventually destroyed by the anticommunist crusade of the 1950s.[56]

Mexican American Workers Confront Braceros and the Wetback Tide

In the context of the postwar era's nativist consensus, the antialien prejudice and discrimination experienced by braceros and *mojados* were redirected toward Mexican Americans. This occurred simultaneously with the expansion of the Bracero program through Public Law 45 and the flood of undocumented workers across the border. Persons of Mexican descent were blamed for job loss, poor urban conditions, and every other social ill in the United States.

Mexican Americans made up the main labor force in agriculture, and everywhere their dismal plight remained unchanged: low pay for long hours of hard stoop labor by entire families who were deprived of an edu-

cation and whose abominable living conditions were unhealthful and triggered epidemics. Already hobbled in their unionizing efforts by the migratory nature of their labor and by antilabor legislation, Mexican American
farm workers faced their biggest obstacle in the form of competition from
the growing numbers of contract laborers being brought in from Mexico
and from the greater influx of mojados. A quarter million mojados entered
south Texas illegally, and an equally large number crossed into California's
Imperial Valley. These workmen from Mexico performed arduous, labor-
intensive field work at starvation pay that widened the gap between farm
and industrial wages by 60 percent. Insofar as southwestern employers
deliberately discouraged local Mexican American labor in order to use less
costly braceros, the great numbers of mojados whittled down the already
prevailing low wages even further. Unemployment and underemployment
as a result spread among the Mexican American working-class population.
In Texas, the inability to provide for their families because of the overabun-
dance of mojados in farm work—and soon in service and light factory
work—forced an exodus of tens of thousands of Tejanos from Texas to
search for work. Together with the presence of Mexican contract workers,
the alarmingly large influx of undocumented Mexican labor, particularly
in the ten-year period from 1944 to 1954 referred to as "the wetback decade," helped further foment a hostile antialien environment. As a result,
the meaning of Mexican American identity and citizenship was constantly
challenged. The bracero and mojado influx essentially confounded in the
minds of Anglos the differences of language and skin color and made the
situation for economically and socially underprivileged Mexican Americans even more hopeless.[57] "Wetback," "dirty Mexican," and other racial
slurs became more specific to Mexican Americans, easy shorthand to let
them know where they stood.

Mojados depressed the entire Texas state economy and impeded the efforts of all workers to improve their lot. Mojados became the number one
enemy of organized labor at the border. The Texas State CIO Council,
through its Latin American Affairs Committee, protested the flood of
work-starved mojados into the state, but it placed blame for the invasion
directly at the feet of Texas growers, the INS, and the U.S. Border Patrol.
"We are fighting the cheap, unorganized labor constantly," said George
Weber, executive secretary of the El Paso Labor Council, "but we must
face and recognize the inevitable. So long as the United States Government
allows the cheap labor to cross the river we are all but helpless in trying to
obtain a fair labor scale in the area." Labor leaders correctly pointed out
that the so-called wetback tide was symptomatic of an age-old cycle perpetuated by the widespread use of cheap undocumented laborers by Texas
farmers and ranchers in collusion with INS and U.S. Border officials.[58]

In California, documented and undocumented labor from Mexico likewise dislodged Mexican Americans from fruit and vegetable production and further hampered labor organizing. "[California] was flooded with braceros while we were on strike, and before and after [a] strike," recalled Ernesto Galarza, who worked tirelessly as an organizer for the National Farm Labor Union (NFLU). Galarza relied on a strategy of moving NFLU members to areas in California marked by large numbers of braceros and the greater plague of mojados, making citizen's arrests of these contraband workers, and guarding entry points along the border to prevent their reentry. Outraged, the grower-government alliance countered this tactic; time and again, mojados were immediately legalized or "dried out" by federal agents, who then put the strikebreakers to work.[59]

Foreshadowing similar attempts in the present era, the national CIO and Mexico's CTM eventually established a Border Committee in an attempt to solve the myriad problems of a labor surplus created by the flood of undocumented workers and the Bracero program.[60] Various nascent Mexican American civic organizations were also aware that the continued importation of labor from Mexico was dislocating Mexican American farm workers and contributing to the rise of nativism, which intensified the racist attacks on the Spanish-speaking population. These organizations launched a coordinated letter-writing campaign aimed at government and state officials. They contacted the U.S. Agriculture Department and requested that it provide the same type of employment guarantees accorded to braceros, as well as transportation, housing standards, and medical care, to U.S. domestic farm workers. These groups also wrote to elected state officials and urged them to pass legislation to protect domestic workers in their home states.[61]

For the time being, it seemed that a labor-led Mexican American civil rights movement had been stalled, while labor struggles, civil court suits, and electoral politics were continuously stifled by the anticommunist and antialien climate. Red-baiters feared that, as in the case of blacks, concern for the problems of Mexican Americans had been devised to further the program of the Communist Party. The endless flow of labor from across the border undermined the farm labor and civil rights movements, created enormous strains in the Mexican American community, and increased animosity toward Mexican Americans in general.

The support and promotion of progressive goals and policies did not end with the expulsion of the Left-led unions, nor did it rest with mainstream Mexican American organizations; rather, it shifted to a grassroots movement. Cudgeled by racism, Mexican Americans created civil rights organizations or transformed other organizations to make them more active. In many instances of organization, Mexican Americans still had the full support and cooperation of progressive elements within labor.[62] This soon initiated a larger mobilization by Mexican Americans for the aggressive pursuit of social change to further improve their status. Mexican American political orientation affected the choice of priorities and strategies, the language, and the ideology of the movement. The social, economic, and political environment of Texas, the Mountain States, California, and the Midwest shaped and produced a series of distinctive movements within the larger Mexican American civil rights struggle, which the union movement had nurtured and made strong.[63]

> There go my people. I must catch them, for I am their leader.
> —MAHATMA GANDHI

THE YEARS of the Great Depression represent one of the most important periods of social and economic change for the Spanish-speaking people of the Southwest, the largest concentration of Mexicans in the United States. On the eve of the Great Depression, Mexicans constituted the fundamental bulk of the low-wage workforce necessary to the economic growth of the Southwest region. Their jobs primarily were seasonal and migratory; the workers moved about as family units or as members of labor gangs and did the work that Anglos would not do. The great majority of Mexicans were agricultural workers, and in this role they had the lowest living standard of all of America's wageworkers. The scourge of sickness wreaked havoc throughout the entire population. The proximity of the border made it easy to expand and contract the supply of agricultural labor, with the result that wages could be held at extremely low levels. The main beneficiaries were the growers and other employers who used direct and imaginative means to secure labor discipline. Whether living in rural or urban settings, the politically powerless and unorganized Mexicans were universally spurned as socially inferior.[1]

The ravages of the deepening economic crisis furthered the Mexican's pervasive impoverishment. Agricultural and industrial production fell off considerably, and the specter of poverty loomed large as the prevailing racism against Mexicans intensified. The workers were scapegoated as the cause for the host of economic and social ills that plagued the region. The barriers to relief spread to include the denial of assistance and social services even to those who were American citizens and legal U.S. residents. So as not to care for these destitute workers and their families, who only wanted food, city, county, and state officials invariably implemented repatriation programs. The punitive expeditions expelled an estimated one-third of the nation's Mexican population. In the frenzy of the removals, American citizens were sent to Mexico. The existing Mexican political organizations could not defend the shaken, broken Mexican community. The mercenary motives of the U.S. Bureau of Immigration prompted little criticism or concern from the larger American society. The Great Depression proved a terrible setback for Mexican Americans; in essence, the small gains made up to the 1930s were wiped out, and economic and social advancement for a whole generation was restricted or delayed.[2]

A national labor movement emerged in the United States in the face of mass layoffs and widespread worker frustration and anger caused by the country's painful economic crisis. The New Deal labor legislation stimulated hope, and these favorable circumstances caused a rising tempo of labor activism and unity in the Southwest. The labor campaigns had the effect of facilitating new forms of self-organization and of shifting the direction of the Spanish-speaking community toward a new leadership. The labor movement represented a high-water mark of Mexican American pride and empowerment, marking an important turning point in Mexican American history, for it fundamentally changed the way Mexican Americans dealt with economic and social injustice thereafter.

As the economic troubles spread, the Communist Party sent organizers into the Southwest, where they launched the ambitious program of organizing that this region demanded. Intrepid left-wing organizers pressed for greater rights for Mexicans and helped stage protests and write petitions, and their radical pronouncements impressed the Mexicans favorably, eliciting enthusiastic support from the workers. As long as there was discontent, reasoned the prudent party members, the possibility existed of establishing cadres of Spanish-speaking adherents to carry out a revolutionary program. The Communist Party was also closely involved with the issue of racism, which it strictly opposed on principle, since racism undermined the party's struggle to obtain freedom and social justice for all. Communists also played a role in international solidarity; their strenuously antifascist struggles in the 1930s were likewise admirable.

Adopting a resolution in late 1930 to form local Agricultural Workers Unions across racial lines, communists strengthened class and ethnic solidarity among farm workers. However, the carefully planned and organized worker rebellions aroused the fury of the growers and once again were rebuffed. This affront to the power of the growers demanded punishment. Growers utilized various methods of repression, implementing brutal tactics based on the racial makeup of the labor force and its noncitizen status. The authorities defused the strikes by isolating and dividing labor leaders and then arresting them. Charged with illegal assembly in association with parades and demonstrations, the agitators were accused of taking advantage of worker dissatisfaction to carry out revolutionary activities. The Gallup coal strike provides a perfect case in point. Few Mexicans joined the Communist Party and many of the Left-led incipient strike actions of the early 1930s failed, but the insurgency helped further raise class consciousness among the Mexican working classes.

Women were integral to the Spanish-speaking union experience because many played key roles as strike participants and as dedicated and capable labor activists. In the highly exploitive industrial work environments of the Southwest, Mexican women made up a large percentage of the labor force. They organized resistance against the sweatshop conditions and the verbal and physical harassment meted out against them, fully knowing that employers would respond with discharges and the blacklist. In 1933, Mexican female garment workers in Los Angeles accounted for half the members of the International Ladies' Garment Workers' Union and were the first workers in the city to strike under the National Recovery Act.[3] Women workers also first challenged the problem of unfair labor competition from Mexicans who crossed the border into the United States to work. In the CIO union drives in the agricultural and industrial labor sectors, the militant spirit, unity, and perseverance of the women never flagged, and some made their debut as major political figures. Emma Tenayuca became a pillar of the civil rights movement in San Antonio, where the proud and assertive Tejana led the protests on behalf of the city's aggrieved pecan shellers.

Emma Tenayuca and other members of an emerging generation of activists filled a political vacuum and accomplished something remarkable— they brought Mexican Americans together into the largest labor movement ever seen in the Southwest, a movement that spilled over into the terrain of civil rights. They learned about the value of mass action, the power of the picket and the boycott, and the need for organization and discipline. Participation in local union meetings, elections, and bargaining and grievance committees imparted political skills and tactics. Mexicans found strength in one another, and awareness sharpened among them that labor and civil rights could be achieved through unionism.

Placing a premium on interracial and interethnic collaboration as a central component of unionization, the CIO served as a center and training ground for activism for thousands of Mexican Americans. More important, the trade-union movement taught Mexicans to vote as a bloc for the union ticket. Mexican Americans were empowered by the CIO union movement because it appealed to group solidarity, stressed the importance of systematic organization and self-initiative, and demonstrated a commitment to the cause of full citizenship.

Cross-border organizing remained a central concern and strengthened links between labor movements internationally. Mexican Americans and their counterparts in Mexico increasingly recognized their common interests. They saw the solutions as coming from mass struggle in communities along both sides of the U.S.-Mexico border. The hard-won victories of Mine-Mill in El Paso showed that the power of binational coalitions could be formidable. Still, the obstacles to cross-border organizing remained great.

Mexican Americans registered the greatest economic gains as a result of World War II. Many from various parts of the Southwest migrated to war industry centers in California and the Midwest and filled the need for unskilled workers. The economic, political, and demographic changes unleashed by the war had sweeping consequences. Providing new opportunities as well as challenges, the war accelerated the Mexican American pursuit of labor and civil rights objectives. The discrimination these men and women encountered in employment boosted their membership in unions and encouraged them to use their militancy to tackle unfair housing policies and other forms of injustice.

In a show of civil rights solidarity, racially progressive CIO unions adopted a specific action plan aimed at advancing the battle against racism and xenophobia in the community as a whole. The multiracial brand of CIO unionism viewed civil rights issues in the context of the international struggle against fascism. The strong presence of the CIO within the Mexican community, with its fervent Popular Front antifascist message of "*No pasarán*" ("They shall not pass"), quelled the profascist Sinarquistas in their recruitment of new members. As proponents of social justice, many Mexican American trade unionists came to the support of the Sleepy Lagoon murder defendants.

The exigencies of World War II halted the civil rights activities of the Popular Front organizations as their priorities and concerns shifted to the promotion of wartime unity against fascism. The nationwide epidemic of racial violence and unrest in 1943 was fueled mainly by competition for jobs and housing, and Mexican Americans were fighting overseas in disproportionate numbers relative to the Anglo population. These and other war-related factors led to the resumption of civil rights activism and further heightened the consciousness and pride of Mexican Americans, who were demanding a voice as Americans.

After World War II, job expansion, the experience of military service overseas, and urbanization led Mexican Americans to resume their campaign for labor and civil rights. This at first took the form of participation in nationwide strikes and the drive for a permanent FEPC. The United States after the war returned very rapidly to the standard pattern of discrimination, and in light of the resurgence of racist activity, Mexican Americans could not find work, were pushed or squeezed out of jobs, and were being excluded altogether from the social life of the nation. The danger of Soviet totalitarianism and the obsession with communism led to a purge of Left-led CIO unions, and restraints on labor activism further increased Taft-Hartley restrictions. For America's minorities, the anti-communism undermined interracial unionism, undid the civil rights–trade union alliance, and set back the fight for full citizenship because it strengthened Anglo hostility to minority demands for social, racial, and economic equality.

The political polarization of the Cold War damaged the standing of Mexican American trade unionists as labor and civil rights leaders. The

FBI and other federal institutions, now the instruments of illegal political surveillance, assiduously investigated leftists and stifled or silenced their influence. The repression virtually wiped out Mexican American leadership and discredited their civil rights cause. Nevertheless, that overlooked generation of dedicated and effective fighters for social justice forged a progressive agenda, giving life to many important civil rights causes that served as springboards for the Mexican American activism of the 1960s.[4]

The merger of the AFL and the CIO in 1955 further subdued the drive for interracial unionism. This occurred during a period that saw a significant decline in agricultural jobs and a simultaneous increase in inter- and intraregional migration of Mexican Americans to urban centers in search of work. The changes in the urban industrial setting, combined with the relocation of plants to suburban and rural areas and the process of deindustrialization, contributed to job loss for Mexican Americans. To offset labor costs, companies mechanized more rapidly, and the resulting job cuts were concentrated in unskilled positions largely held by racial minorities who lacked job seniority.[5]

Anglos enjoyed a monopoly of many of the high-paying skilled jobs because the unionization made possible by interracial solidarity now yielded greater restrictions on minority opportunities than existed previously.[6] Along with separate lists for layoffs and recalls, the separate job seniority lists provided protection against encroachment from Mexican American and black workers. Anglo workers resisted what little remained of the pro–civil rights position of unions; they viewed the promotion of racial minorities as a demand for special treatment, a sentiment fueling the "racism in reverse" clamor. They also opposed the integration of their communities, specifically, the movement of minorities into their neighborhoods and public schools.[7]

Mexican Americans continued to fight against racial segregation in public services and establishments, as well as the ongoing repression by the U.S. Border Patrol and the Texas Rangers, and they were justifiably angry with the police because they suffered disproportionately from police-inflicted abuse. This subjection to collective punishment was based on the mere fact that the police viewed Mexican Americans as inferior. It included indiscriminate searches at gunpoint, racist harangues, station house beatings, and coerced confessions.[8] The upsurge in police killings of Mexican Americans and other acts of police abuse and misconduct galvanized local protests.

Suburbanization was encouraging the growth of a racially segmented society. It confined minorities to overcrowded, deteriorating industrial working-class neighborhoods that received little in the way of city and state resources for housing, recreation, education, and health care services.[9] Mexican Americans sought housing outside overcrowded Spanish-speaking areas, but builders, realtors, and banks, in partnership with federal government agencies that applied an apartheid system of property valuation based on race, blocked their path to integration.[10] Urban renewal likewise was a catastrophe; it destroyed established Spanish-speaking neighborhoods and replaced them with high-density housing projects that became breeding grounds for violence and crime.

The growing population of young and poorly educated Mexican Americans faced a bleak future of low-wage work or else frequent unemployment that perpetuated inferiority, because the manipulation of zoning lines by local Boards of Education helped confine minorities to segregated, inferior schools. Mexican American school dropout rates remained very high for all of the Southwest, ranging from one-third to one-half; the low educational tracking and the overrepresentation of this minority group in so-called mentally retarded school groups also persisted. All these social ills intensified Mexican Americans' belief in their dependency and powerlessness.[11]

Another threat to Mexican American economic and social advancement came from across the border: the steady arrival of documented and undocumented Mexican workers in the United States. The flow of this surplus labor became institutionalized because the federal government catered to the inflated labor needs of growers. In invoking policy and practices that affected migration patterns on both sides of the U.S.-Mexico border, the U.S. Labor, Agriculture, and State Departments worked in close partnership with the lawless growers. At the same time, the Immigration and Naturalization Service, the U.S. Employment Service, and the U.S. Border Patrol participated more directly to the benefit of agricultural interests by introducing and employing tens of thousands of mojados. The rapacious coyotes reappeared to take part in the lucrative trafficking of cheap and docile labor.[12]

Mexican Americans residing along the U.S.-Mexico border were also concerned about the nearly 60,000 Mexican commuters who worked in the United States. Known as green card holders, they displaced local labor, depressed wages and working conditions, and more important, made labor organizing in the region extremely difficult. The garment factories being established along the border would soon employ many of these low-wage workers. Further, Mexicans began to move into Matamoros, Juárez, and Tijuana, the rapidly growing sister cities of American towns that served as staging areas for those waiting to cross into the United States. Congress investigated the commuter problem and the rapidly rising numbers of undocumented workers. However, nothing was really done until the U.S. Attorney General's office undertook a massive deportation effort known as "Operation Wetback" in 1954. This federal program backfired to the disadvantage of Mexican Americans. Viewed as part of the problem that demanded drastic measures, thousands were apprehended in the roundups.[13]

Together with the contract labor program that began in 1942, peaked in the late 1950s, and would continue over the next twenty-two years, the smuggling of mojados and the commuters seriously threatened the living standards, health, and education of Mexican Americans. The growing controversy over documented and undocumented workers ushered in the so-called "wetback decade" (1944–54). Because of the rise in anti-immigrant sentiment, Mexican Americans experienced significant racial hostility. The huge alien presence not only retarded social and economic advancement but also redefined Mexican American identity for years to come, because the surge of Anglo nativism branded all Mexicans as undesirable foreigners. Mexican Americans were powerless to defend themselves against the indignities that served as painful and constant reminders of what it meant to be a Mexican in America.[14] These overwhelming obstacles did not dampen the Mexican Americans' increasing resolve to fight for their rights. They turned to civil rights groups but also charted their own course and created new organizations to push forward their demands and to mobilize political power.

Throughout the 1950s, the Community Service Organization was a politically powerful organization in Spanish-speaking strongholds emphasizing direct grassroots community action and setting in motion the process that brought this minority group into the political arena. The CSO developed leadership against the problems of restrictive housing, policy brutality, segregated schools, redlined districting, and discriminatory employment. Getting Mexican Americans to register and exercise the right to vote became a primary objective. LULAC and the American GI Forum joined the campaign for civil rights, an action reflecting the steadily growing political participation of Mexican Americans. The ensuing activity built on the foundation laid by the CSO and the earlier generation of progressive-minded civil rights advocates.[15]

Mexican American political activities and influences, which differed from state to state, increased as these individuals became educated on pertinent issues, registered to vote, ran for local office, and confronted various long-standing civil rights grievances. In 1959, Mexican Americans in California founded the Mexican American Political Association (MAPA), and in the following year Tejanos formed a counterpart of the California MAPA in Texas, the pro-Democrat Mexican Americans for Political Action, as well as the Political Association of Spanish-Speaking Organizations (PASSO).[16] These emergent groups prepared the groundwork for Mexican American participation in national politics. Labor once again lent its organizational strength as well as staff and resources; much of this electoral politics initiative continued to be generated by the CIO through its Political Action Committees.

Meanwhile, the growing integrationist challenge to segregated schools, public accommodations, and voting booths by black Americans strengthened opposition to equality, because America remained plagued with deep-seated prejudice and discrimination. Despite the dynamic economic growth of the Southwest, the majority of Mexican Americans remained impoverished and uneducated. Breadwinners were frequently unable to support their families, since they were disproportionately confined to low-paying farm work in rural areas (where Mexican Americans still tended to be locked into a caste system) or to unskilled factory and service sector work with less security of employment. The lack of union representation in these job sectors impeded social and economic mobility. The resultant inequality varied, with the cruelest conditions prevailing in south Texas, followed by southern Colorado and New Mexico, where the abysmal economic and social conditions approximated those in Appalachia.[17]

Laws were not solving the growing problems of Mexican American unemployment—which by 1960 was twice that of Anglos—residential segregation and poor housing, police violence, discrimination in the courts and in the sentencing process, and substandard schooling in urban slums and rural areas. The federal government paid scant attention to Mexican Americans and took no action on the question of their inequality until late 1963. The Federal Equal Employment Opportunities Committee at this time held its first regional meeting in Los Angeles and finally recognized Mexican Americans as a minority with special issues of concern.[18]

The confrontations of the 1960s would center on issues whose origins lay in the postwar years. Leading the struggle to gain full civil rights for America's second-largest minority group was a new generation of leaders and plans. As the black civil rights movement built up national momentum, the growing movement for social action by and for Mexican Americans concentrated on mobilization. The formation of direct action organizations involved Mexican Americans in a wave of popular protests on their own behalf that would soon jolt the Southwest. Labor rights struck a responsive cord among many Mexican Americans and remained a major factor in their civil rights struggle. This was evidenced by the growing farm worker movement demanding the extension of the Farm Labor Standards and National Labor Relations Laws to farm workers and the provision of housing for migrant farm labor. Mexican American militancy in the area of civil rights deepened and expanded, as was demonstrated in the launching of a crusade in New Mexico to regain the land illegally taken away and to call attention to the failings of the U.S. Forest Service. The rejection of nonviolence as a strategy soon led to the emergence of a separatist movement because of the influence of national liberation movements worldwide whose cause Mexican Americans championed.[19]

The stirring of the Mexican American people in response to the call for civil rights would represent a watershed in the history of this second-largest minority group in the United States. The labor movement made an enormous contribution. It laid the groundwork and continued to have a profound and lasting impact as the emphasis of social action shifted from civil rights to jobs.[20]

Notes

INTRODUCTION

1. The term "Mexican" indicates people of Mexican ethnic origin, both recent Mexican immigrants and Mexican Americans, since during this time it was the preferred term of self-reference of Spanish-surnamed people of the Southwest and Midwest. The term "Mexican American" refers to people of Mexican descent who are American-born and is used to stress American citizenship. "Tejano" refers to Texas Mexicans and to Mexicans born in Mexico. The terms "Anglo" and "white" are used interchangeably and indicate persons who are not of Mexican descent.

2. On June 30, 1937, Lupe Marshall gave this testimony of that tragic day's events to the La Follette Committee investigating violations of free speech and the rights of labor. Senate Committee on Education and Labor, *Violations of Free Speech and Rights of Labor, The Chicago Memorial Day Incident*, Hearings, June 30, July 1 and 2, 1937, in *Police in America* (New York: Arno Press and New York Times, 1971), pp. 4945–48.

3. Ibid., pp. 4950–53.

4. Ibid., pp. 4941–45.

5. Ibid., pp. 5168–69; Lizabeth Cohen, *Making a New Deal: Industrial Workers in Chicago, 1919–1939* (New York: Cambridge University Press, 1990), pp. 294, 324–25, 338–39; Robert H. Zieger, *The CIO, 1935–1955* (Chapel Hill: University of North Carolina Press, 1995), pp. 54, 62. See also Daniel J. Leab, "The Memorial Day Massacre," *Midcontinent American Studies Journal* 8 (Fall 1967), pp. 3–17; Donald G. Sofchalk, "The Chicago Memorial Day Incident: An Episode in Mass Action," *Labor History* 6, no. 1 (Winter 1965), pp. 3–43.

6. Gallup Defense Bulletin, May 11, 1935, p. 2, Gallup Committee of Santa Fe, Bulletins, Fliers, Posters, Press Releases, etc., Gallup Committee of the ILD (Santa Fe Group), Folder 11, Gallup Defense Committee of the ILD, International Labor Defense Collection, 512, Colorado Historical Society, Denver, Colorado. (Hereafter referred to as GDB.)

7. Gilbert G. González, *Mexican Consuls and Labor Organizing: Imperial Politics in the American Southwest* (Austin: University of Texas Press, 1999), pp. 1–2.

8. James C. Foster, "Mexican Labor and the Southwest," in *American Labor and the Southwest: The First One Hundred Years*, ed. James C. Foster (Tucson: University of Arizona Press, 1982), pp. 160–61; Zieger, *The CIO, 1935–1955*, pp. 112–13; Cohen, *Making a New Deal*, pp. 338–39; Zaragosa Vargas, *Proletarians of the North: Mexican Industrial Workers in Detroit and the Midwest, 1917–1933* (Berkeley: University of California Press, 1993), pp. 194–99.

9. Clete Daniel, *Bitter Harvest: A History of California Farmworkers, 1870–1941* (Berkeley: University of California Press, 1981), pp. 106, 108; Lizabeth

Cohen, "Tradition and the Working Class, 1850–1950," *International Labor and Working-Class History* 42 (Fall 1992), pp. 86–87; "Mexican Radical Activities," March 18, 1936, U.S. Military Intelligence Division Files, RG 165, File 2657–G–657–186, National Archives (hereafter referred to as NA).

10. Several unpublished and published works address certain aspects of the experience of Mexican workers in the 1930s. Among the articles, monographs, and dissertations, see Luis Leobardo Arroyo, "Industrial Unionism and the Los Angeles Furniture Industry, 1918–1954" (Ph.D. diss., University of California, Los Angeles, 1979); Luis Leobardo Arroyo, "Chicano Participation in Organized Labor: The CIO in Los Angeles, 1938–1950: An Extended Research Note," *Aztlán* 6 (Summer 1975), pp. 277–303; Victor Nelson-Cisneros, "UCAPAWA Organizing Activities in Texas, 1930–1950," *Aztlán* 9 (Spring, Summer, Fall 1978), pp. 71–84; and Clementina Durón, "Mexican Women and Labor Conflict in Los Angeles: The ILGWU Dressmakers' Strike of 1933," *Aztlán* 15 (Spring 1982), pp. 145–61. The published books include Vicki L. Ruiz, *Cannery Women, Cannery Lives: Mexican Women, Unionization, and the California Food Processing Industry, 1930–1950* (Albuquerque: University of New Mexico Press, 1987); Sarah Deutsch, *No Separate Refuge: Culture, Class, and Gender on an Anglo-Hispanic Frontier in the American Southwest, 1888–1940* (New York: Oxford University Press, 1987); Devra Weber, *Dark Sweat, White Gold: California Farm Workers, Cotton, and the New Deal* (Berkeley: University of California Press, 1994); Mario T. García, *Mexican Americans: Leadership, Ideology, and Identity, 1930–1960* (New Haven: Yale University Press, 1989); George J. Sánchez, *Becoming Mexican American: Ethnicity, Culture and Identity in Chicano Los Angeles, 1900–1945* (New York: Oxford University Press, 1993); Stephen J. Pitti, *The Devil in Silicon Valley: Northern California, Race, and Mexican Americans* (Princeton, N.J.: Princeton University Press, 2003).

11. Mario Barrera, *Race and Class in the Southwest: A Theory of Racial Inequality* (Notre Dame: University of Notre Dame Press, 1979), pp. 60, 93–97; John N. Webb, *The Migratory-Casual Worker*, Works Progress Administration, Research Monograph 7 (Washington, D.C.: Government Printing Office, 1937), pp. 12–14, 71–72; Carey McWilliams, *Ill Fares the Land: Migrants and Migratory Labor in the United States* (Boston: Little, Brown, 1942), p. 114; Carey McWilliams, *North from Mexico: The Spanish-Speaking People of the United States* (Westport, Conn.: Greenwood Press, 1968), p. 185; Cindy Hahamovitch, *The Fruits of Their Labor: Atlantic Coast Farmworkers and the Making of Migrant Poverty, 1870–1945* (Chapel Hill: University of North Carolina Press, 1997), pp. 8–9; Harry Schwartz, *Seasonal Farm Labor in the United States, with Special Reference to Hired Workers in Fruit and Vegetable Production and Sugar Beet Production* (New York: Columbia University Press, 1945), pp. 5, 10–12, 14–15, 29, 32, 34; Commission on International and Interracial Factors in the Problems of Mexicans in the United States, *Report of Commission on International and Interracial Factors in the Problems of Mexicans in the United States* (n.p., 1926?), p. 23; Jacqueline Jones, *The Dispossessed: America's Underclasses from the Civil War to the Present* (New York: Basic Books, 1993), pp. 182–83.

12. Barrera, *Race and Class in the Southwest*, pp. 65, 70, 72, 79–80; Arthur F. Corwin, "Mexican Emigration History, 1900–1970: Literature and Research," *Latin American Research Review* 8 (Summer 1973), p. 11; Carey McWilliams,

Factories in the Field (Boston: Little, Brown, 1939), p. 102; McWilliams, *Ill Fares the Land*, p. 233; Mark Reisler, *By the Sweat of Their Brow: Mexican Immigrant Labor in the United States, 1900–1940* (Westport, Conn.: Greenwood Press, 1976), p. 128; Doug McAdam, *Political Process and the Development of Black Insurgency, 1930–1970* (Chicago: University of Chicago Press, 1984), p. 90. A local Anglo Texan farmer explained why Tejanos pickers were preferred over Anglo pickers: "People here don't want white pickers. They prefer Mexicans; they are content with whatever you give them. The whites want more water, etc., and are troublemakers. If there is a labor shortage they want exorbitant prices. Yes, the Mexicans do it some, but you can handle the Mexicans better; they're more subservient, if that's the word." Victor B. Nelson-Cisneros, "La clase trabajadora en Tejas, 1929–1940," *Aztlán* 6, no. 2 (Summer 1975), p. 244; Paul S. Taylor, *An American-Mexican Frontier: Nueces County Texas* (Berkeley: University of California Press, 1934), p. 130.

13. David G. Gutiérrez, *Walls and Mirrors: Mexican Americans, Mexican Immigrants and the Politics of Identity* (Berkeley: University of California Press, 1995), p. 105; Sánchez, *Becoming Mexican American*, p. 221; Vargas, *Proletarians of the North*, pp. 199–200.

14. GDB, May 18, 1935, p. 3.

15. Zieger, *The CIO, 1935–1955*, pp. 112, 122, 149, 153, 160; Nelson Lichtenstein, *Labor's War at Home: The CIO in World War II* (New York: Cambridge University Press, 1982), pp. 48, 74; Ruiz, *Cannery Women, Cannery Lives*, pp. 55–56, 79–82; Daniel Kryder, *Divided Arsenal: Race and the American State during World War II* (New York: Cambridge University Press, 2000), pp. 126–28; Michael Denning, *The Cultural Front: The Laboring of American Culture in the Twentieth Century* (New York: Verso Books, 1997), pp. 7–8.

CHAPTER ONE
WE ARE THE SALT OF THE EARTH: CONDITIONS AMONG MEXICAN
WORKERS IN THE EARLY GREAT DEPRESSION YEARS

1. Gutiérrez, *Walls and Mirrors*, p. 93; Barrera, *Race and Class in the Southwest*, pp. 93–97; Jones, *The Dispossessed*, p. 17; Statement of Ernesto Galarza, Chief of the Division of Labor and Social Information of the Pan American Union, before the Select Committee of the House of Representatives to investigate the interstate migration of destitute citizens, Gardner Jackson Papers, Box 1, AAA-1934, Franklin D. Roosevelt Presidential Library, Hyde Park, New York, p. 1. For example, one contemporary study noted that half (56.2 percent) of the Mexican population in New Mexico was under twenty years of age, and the average size of the families was 4.6 persons. The Spanish-speaking population was working-class in composition. Sigurd Johansen, "Migratory Workers in New Mexico," *Agricultural Experiment Station Bulletin* 870, March 1939; Senate Committee on Education and Labor, *Violations of Free Speech and Rights of Labor*, 76th Cong., pts. 1–3, Supplementary Hearings. May 2, 6, 7, 8, 9, 10, 13, and 14, 1940 (Washington, D.C.: Government Printing Office, 1941), pp. 21, 75, 139 (hereafter referred to as *Violations of Free Speech and Rights of Labor.*)

2. Michael K. Honey, *Southern Labor and Black Civil Rights: Organizing Memphis Workers* (Urbana: University of Illinois Press, 1993), pp. 58–59; Jones, *The Dispossessed*, p. 177; Emilio Zamora, "The Failed Promise of Wartime Opportunity for Mexicans in the Texas Oil Industry," *Southwestern Historical Quarterly* 95 (January 1992), p. 327.

3. Arthur F. Corwin and Walter A. Fogel, "Shadow Labor Force: Mexican Workers in the American Economy," in *Immigrants—and Immigrants: Perspectives on Mexican Labor Migration to the United States*, ed. Arthur F. Corwin (Westport, Conn.: Greenwood Press, 1976), pp. 257–58; U.S. Farm Security Administration, *Migrant Farm Labor: The Problem and Some Efforts to Meet It* (Washington, D.C.: U.S. Department of Agriculture, Farm Security Administration, 1941), p. 4; McWilliams, *Ill Fares the Land*, pp. 247–49; Barrera, *Race and Class in the Southwest*, pp. 75, 94. More than half the Mexicans in the Southwest resided in Texas—703,164, or 12.1 percent of the state's population—and of these 38.4 percent were foreign-born. H. T. Manuel, "The Mexican Population of Texas," *Southwestern Social Science Quarterly* 15 (June 1934), pp. 32, 38. Tejanos were beginning to settle in the High Plains area of the Texas Panhandle, where a new "cotton empire" emerged. Tejanos had moved into the state's eastern and Gulf Coast regions and replaced blacks as the most important source of labor. T. J. Cauley, "Cotton Moves West: An Account of Some of the Agricultural Changes Which Have Created a New Cotton Empire," *Texas Monthly* 3 (March 1929), pp. 338–39.

4. Neil Foley, *The White Scourge: Mexicans, Blacks, and Poor Whites in Texas Cotton Culture* (Berkeley: University of California Press, 1997), pp. 32, 63; Schwartz, *Seasonal Farm Labor in the United States*, pp. 4, 18–19, 43; Manuel, "The Mexican Population of Texas," pp. 32, 38; Barrera, *Race and Class in the Southwest*, p. 60; McWilliams, *Ill Fares the Land*, pp. 208, 218, 224; Jones, *The Dispossessed*, p. 172. Texas had the largest population of blacks of all the southwestern states, nearly eight times that of any other state in the region. In 1930, 854,964 blacks lived in Texas and represented 14.7 percent of the state's total population. Black labor had built the cotton plantation system in east Texas and along the valleys of the Colorado, Brazos, and Trinity River regions. *Violations of Free Speech and Rights of Labor*, p. 129.

5. *Violations of Free Speech and Rights of Labor*, pp. 149, 151, 159, 271; *Migrant Farm Labor*, p. 4; McWilliams, *Ill Fares the Land*, pp. 219–20, 230–31.

6. *Violations of Free Speech and Rights of Labor*, pp. 272–76; McWilliams, *Ill Fares the Land*, pp. 234–35.

7. *Violations of Free Speech and Rights of Labor*, pp. 272–76; Cauley, "Cotton Moves West," pp. 339, 347; McWilliams, *Ill Fares the Land*, p. 231.

8. *Violations of Free Speech and Rights of Labor*, pp. 148–49, 270, 275–77; McWilliams, *Ill Fares the Land*, p. 242.

9. Nelson-Cisneros, "La clase trabajadora en Tejas," pp. 244, 246; David Montejano, *Anglos and Mexicans in the Making of Texas, 1836–1986.* (Austin: University of Texas Press), p. 60; McWilliams, *Ill Fares the Land*, pp. 234, 238–39, 254; Texas State Employment Service, *Survey of Farm Placements in Texas, 1936–37*, Annual Report, p. 36; *Violations of Free Speech and Rights of Labor*, p. 169; Jones, *The Dispossessed*, pp. 107–8, 182, 184. The Texas cotton-farming

industry entailed cultivation, cotton chopping, and cotton picking. In 1929, hand cultivation paid $1.25 to $2 per day. By 1931, no doubt as a result of the mechanization of this labor process, wages for cultivation had dropped to 60 and 75 cents per day. For cotton chopping, workers earned between 60 cents and $1 per day, but by 1932 these wages had dropped to 20 to 40 cents per day as a result of the phasing out of this labor process through mechanization. Nelson-Cisneros, "La clase trabajadora en Tejas," p. 244.

10. *Violations of Free Speech and Rights of Labor*, p. 7; Jones, *The Dispossessed*, p. 174; *Migrant Farm Labor*, pp. 6–7; McWilliams, *Ill Fares the Land*, p. 243; Schwartz, *Seasonal Farm Labor in the United States*, pp. 12, 87. Brought on by poor nutrition and a lack of health care, pellagra was an especially chronic disease among Tejano migrant workers, particularly children and childbearing women. A marked characteristic of sickness among Tejanos from pellagra was its prevalence in the spring, "following the inadequate diet during the winter months." Pellagra's effects were scaly red skin, blotches, diarrhea, fatigue, and, in extreme and fateful cases, nervous disorders and insanity. Jacquelyn Dowd Hall et al., *Like a Family: The Making of a Southern Cotton Mill World* (Chapel Hill: University of North Carolina Press, 1987), p. 150. A Farm Security Administration study of 620 farm wage workers in seventeen Texas counties reported that a third gave their address as the open country. A fourth lived in towns with a population under 2,500, while less than a tenth came from cities with a population of over 25,000. *Violations of Free Speech and Rights of Labor*, pp. 143, 215, 279.

11. *Violations of Free Speech and Rights of Labor*, pp. 220–21, 230, 264, 282–83; *Migrant Farm Labor*, p. 7; McWilliams, *Ill Fares the Land*, pp. 245, 255–56; Jones, *The Dispossessed*, pp. 187, 198–99; Julie Leininger Pycior, *LBJ and Mexican Americans: The Paradox of Power* (Austin: University of Texas Press, 1997), p. 16.

12. Schwartz, *Seasonal Farm Labor in the United States*, pp. 10, 32–33; Yolanda Chávez Leyva, " 'Faithful Hard-Working Mexican Hands': Mexicana Workers during the Great Depression," *Perspectives in Mexican American Studies* 5 (1995), pp. 69–70; McWilliams, *Ill Fares the Land*, p. 243.

13. Chávez Leyva, "Faithful Hard-Working Mexican Hands," p. 64; García, *Mexican Americans*, pp. 63, 177.

14. Chávez Leyva, "Faithful Hard-Working Mexican Hands," pp. 65–67; Pierette Hondagneu-Sotelo, *Doméstica: Immigrant Workers Cleaning and Caring in the Shadows of Affluence* (Berkeley: University of California Press, 2001), p. 15. In a 1932 letter written to the editor of an El Paso newspaper, a Tejana who identified herself as "R. Luna" angrily protested that despite her skills in speaking and writing both English and Spanish fluently, she could not get work other than as a maid: "I might as well know nothing at all, and I'd be far much better off, but I do hope that the time will come when a woman like me will have her right and be able to find a job that isn't house-keeping." Chávez Leyva, "Faithful Hard-Working Mexican Hands," p. 66.

15. Chávez Leyva, "Faithful Hard-Working Mexican Hands," pp. 52–53; *Violations of Free Speech and Rights of Labor*, p. 534.

16. McWilliams, *Ill Fares the Land*, p. 243; Nelson-Cisneros, "La Clase Trabajadora en Tejas," pp. 250–51; Chávez Leyva, "Faithful Hard-Working Mexican Hands," pp. 69–70. Laredo labor activist José Jacobs noted the following about

Laredo: "We do not manufacture anything, except straw hats. We do not have what can be called an irrigation system, and cattle that was fifty years ago a good income to this section has gradually disappeared." Nelson-Cisneros, "La clase trabajadora en Tejas," p. 251.

17. Nelson-Cisneros, "La clase trabajadora en Tejas," p. 243. Labor economist Stuart Jamieson summarized the plight of Tejanos as follows: "Mexicans on the land had a social and economic status similar to that of Negroes in other sections of the South. They were a large, lowly paid racial minority, and most of them were disenfranchised by the state poll tax." Stuart Jamieson, *Labor Unionism in American Agriculture*, U.S. Department of Labor, Bureau of Labor Statistics, Bulletin No. 836 (Washington, D.C.: Government Printing Office, 1945), p. 4.

18. Webb, *The Migratory-Casual Worker*, p. 37; Schwartz, *Seasonal Farm Labor in the United States*, p. 102; Mary Romero and Eric Margolis, "Tending the Beets: Campesinas and the Great Western Sugar Company," *Revista Mujeres* 2, no. 2 (June 1985), pp. 17–20. According to a 1935 study of 946 sugar beet families, the average Spanish-speaking beet worker household contained 6.4 persons, with over half (53 percent) being under sixteen years of age. *Violations of Free Speech and Rights of Labor*, pp. 443–45. Sugar beet labor was based on family, gang, and solo labor, with family labor predominating. *Violations of Free Speech and Rights of Labor*, pp. 215, 443; Elizabeth S. Johnson, *Welfare of Families of Sugar Beet Laborers: A Study of Child Labor and Its Relation to Family, Work, Income, and Living Conditions in 1935*, U.S. Department of Labor, Children's Bureau Publication No. 247.

19. Sister Marineil Mahony, S.L., "Some Approaches to the Problems of the Mexican Migratory Beet Laborer in Colorado (1923–1933) by the Knights of Columbus Colorado Mexican Welfare Committee under the Chairmanship of Thomas F. Mahony, Longmont, Colorado" (master's thesis, University of Notre Dame, 1961), pp. 4, 30–31; McWilliams, *Ill Fares the Land*, pp. 108–15; Daniel Thomas Moreno, "Social Equality and Industrialization: A Case Study of the Colorado Beet Sugar Industry" (Ph.D. diss. University of California, Irvine, 1981), p. 63; Jamieson, *Labor Unionism in American Agriculture*, p. 233; Elizabeth S. Johnson, "Wages, Employment Conditions, and Welfare of Sugar Beet Laborers," *Monthly Labor Review* (February 1938), p. 325; Schwartz, *Seasonal Farm Labor in the United States*, p. 112; Reisler, *By the Sweat of Their Brow*, pp. 89–90; Romero and Margolis, "Tending the Beets," p. 18.

20. Deutsch, *No Separate Refuge*, pp. 128–29, 136; Schwartz, *Seasonal Farm Labor in the United States*, p. 114; Romero and Margolis, "Tending the Beets," pp. 17, 21–23. Of the 12,500 Spanish-speaking New Mexicans who secured seasonal employment out of state, between 2,500 and 3,500 migrated north for six months on sheepherding contracts; about 1,000 to 1,500 worked as track maintenance and repair workers for the Denver & Rio Grande Railroad; mines and smelters drew about 500 to 700 workers; and the potato fields of Colorado's San Luis Valley drew 300 to 500 for the one-month harvest season. Deutsch, *No Separate Refuge*, p. 129.

21. Johnson, "Wages, Employment Conditions, and Welfare of Sugar Beet Laborers," pp. 322, 324–25; Deutsch, *No Separate Refuge*, p. 150; Reisler, *By the Sweat of Their Brow*, pp. 87–88; Mahony, "Some Approaches to the Problems of

the Mexican Migratory Beet Laborer in Colorado," p. 5; McWilliams, *Ill Fares the Land*, p. 110; Webb, *The Migratory-Casual Worker*, p. 39; Schwartz, *Seasonal Farm Labor in the United States*, p. 105.

22. *Violations of Free Speech and Rights of Labor*, pp. 441–45, 447; Deutsch, *No Separate Refuge*, pp. 137–38; Mahony, "Some Approaches to the Problems of the Mexican Migratory Beet Laborer in Colorado," p. 34; Moreno, "Social Equality and Industrialization," pp. 71–72; Lorena Hickok, Denver, Colorado, to Harry L. Hopkins, Federal Emergency Relief Administrator, Washington, D.C., June 17, 1934, Lorena Hickok Papers, Box 11 (May–August 1934), Franklin D. Roosevelt Presidential Library, Hyde Park, New York, p. 5; Johnson, "Wages, Employment, and Welfare," p. 327. Contract labor made up 35 percent of the total cost of producing one acre of sugar beets. Since 1938 the rate of payment listed in the contract was established by the secretary of agriculture under the Sugar Act provisions. In Ohio, Michigan, Indiana, Wisconsin, Minnesota, and Iowa, sugar beet workers were paid by check by the sugar company, and the amount was charged against the account of the farmer. *Violations of Free Speech and Rights of Labor*, p. 445.

23. Mahony, "Some Approaches to the Problems of the Mexican Migratory Beet Laborer in Colorado," pp. 24, 34; Moreno, "Social Equality and Industrialization," pp. 71–72; Lorena Hickok, Denver, Colorado, to Harry L. Hopkins, Federal Emergency Relief Administrator, Washington, D.C., June 17, 1934, Lorena Hickok Papers, Box 11 (May–August 1934), Franklin D. Roosevelt Presidential Library, Hyde Park, New York, p. 4; Johnson, "Wages, Employment Conditions, and Welfare of Sugar Beet Laborers," pp. 327–28; *Violations of Free Speech and Rights of Labor*, pp. 441, 445–47; Schwartz, *Seasonal Farm Labor in the United States*, pp. 105–6.

24. *Violations of Free Speech and Rights of Labor*, pp. 448–51; Schwartz, *Seasonal Farm Labor in the United States*, p. 103; Romero and Margolis, "Tending the Beets," p. 17. One-tenth of the beet workers worked more than fourteen hours during thinning. Beet workers earned $4 per day for the thinning season and $5 per day for the beet harvest. Of the 300 laborers interviewed in 1939, 10 percent reported that they did not procure other agricultural work during the year. Ninety percent received about four weeks' employment in other agricultural work on the sugar beet farm or on another farm. *Violations of Free Speech and Rights of Labor*, p. 448.

25. *Violations of Free Speech and Rights of Labor*, pp. 148, 441–42; Deutsch, *No Separate Refuge*, pp. 130–31; Schwartz, *Seasonal Farm Labor in the United States*, pp. 103–4; Romero and Margolis, "Tending the Beets," p. 20.

26. Mahony, "Some Approaches to the Problems of the Mexican Migratory Beet Laborer in Colorado," pp. 37–38; Johnson, "Wages, Employment, and Welfare," pp. 328, 330; Deutsch, *No Separate Refuge*, pp. 130, 140; Romero and Margolis, "Tending the Beets," pp. 21, 23.

27. Romero and Margolis, "Tending the Beets," pp. 24–25; *Report of Commission on International and Interracial Factors in the Problems of Mexicans in the United States*, p. 22; Jones, *The Dispossessed*, p. 196; Mahony, "Some Approaches to the Problems of the Mexican Migratory Beet Laborer in Colorado," pp. 38–40; Johnson, "Wages, Employment Conditions, and Welfare," pp. 329–

30; Sara A. Brown, *Denver and Farm Labor Families* (New York: National Child Labor Committee, 1925), p. 1; Deutsch, *No Separate Refuge*, pp. 139–42; Ruth Scandrett, Denver, Colorado, to Mrs. Beyer, Agricultural Adjustment Administration, Washington, D.C., October 1, 1934, Gardner Jackson Papers, Box 1, AAA-1934, Franklin D. Roosevelt Presidential Library, Hyde Park, New York, p. 3. These school officials, however, neglected to state one obvious advantage of this exclusion—a school district saved money by not educating migrant children. Mexican beet families did make efforts to keep their children in school, even though in most cases their children did not begin school until November, when the beet harvest season ended, or were absent in the springtime, when the beet season began. A Mexican American beet worker told New Deal field representative Lorena Hickok that he took his family to Denver during the winter off-season "because the schools [are] better in Denver," adding that he wanted his "kids to get a better education [than] I got." The worker had implied that in the beet-growing areas, farmers and school officials did not care whether Mexican children received an education. Lorena Hickok, Denver, Colorado, to Harry L. Hopkins, Federal Emergency Relief Administrator, Washington, D.C., June 23, 1934, Lorena Hickok Papers, Box 11 (May–August 1934), Franklin D. Roosevelt Presidential Library, Hyde Park, New York, p. 5.

28. Johnson, "Wages, Employment Conditions, and Welfare," p. 328; Lorena Hickok, Denver, Colorado, to Harry L. Hopkins, Federal Emergency Relief Administrator, Washington, D.C., June 23, 1934, Lorena Hickok Papers, Box 11 (May–August 1934), Franklin D. Roosevelt Presidential Library, Hyde Park, New York, pp. 5–6. Hickok was told that heart disease was a common health malady among the children of Mexican beet workers. Ibid.

29. Reisler, *By the Sweat of Their Brow*, p. 89; Mahony, "Some Approaches to the Problems of the Mexican Migratory Beet Laborer in Colorado," pp. 33, 36; Deutsch, *No Separate Refuge*, pp. 133–34, 143, 145; *Violations of Free Speech and Rights of Labor*, p. 219; *Migrant Farm Labor*, p. 6; Schwartz, *Seasonal Farm Labor in the United States*, pp. 132–33; Romero and Margolis, "Tending the Beets," p. 21; Jones, *The Dispossessed*, p. 183.

30. *Violations of Free Speech and Rights of Labor*, p. 453; Deutsch, *No Separate Refuge*, pp. 135–36; Reisler, *By the Sweat of Their Brow*, pp. 84–85; Schwartz, *Seasonal Farm Labor in the United States*, pp. 113–14.

31. Deutsch, *No Separate Refuge*, pp. 129, 133–34, 137–39; Schwartz, *Seasonal Farm Labor in the United States*, p. 115; Romero and Margolis, "Tending the Beets," p. 24.

32. Deutsch, *No Separate Refuge*, pp. 138–39; *Violations of Free Speech and Rights of Labor*, pp. 284–85, 452; *Migrant Farm Labor*, p. 6; Jones, *The Dispossessed*, p. 17; Schwartz, *Seasonal Farm Labor in the United States*, pp. 114–16; Romero and Margolis, "Tending the Beets," p. 24; Lorena Hickok, Denver, Colorado, to Harry L. Hopkins, Federal Emergency Relief Administrator, Washington, D.C., June 17, 1934, Lorena Hickok Papers, Box 11 (May–August 1934), Franklin D. Roosevelt Presidential Library, Hyde Park, New York, p. 3.

33. Schwartz, *Seasonal Farm Labor in the United States*, pp. 9, 53–57; Reisler, *By the Sweat of Their Brow*, pp. 78–79; Webb, *The Migratory-Casual Worker*, pp. 5, 12, 25, 37; *Migrant Farm Labor*, p. 3; Paul S. Taylor and Tom Vasey, *Cali-*

fornia Farm Labor, Social Security Board, Bureau of Research and Statistics, 1937, p. 3; Tomás Almaguer, *Racial Fault Lines: The Historical Origins of White Supremacy in California* (Berkeley: University of California Press, 1994), p. 30; Hahamovitch, *The Fruits of Their Labor,* p. 6; *Migrant Farm Labor,* p. 4.

34. Daniel, *Bitter Harvest,* p. 137; Almaguer, *Racial Fault Lines,* p. 30; Webb, *The Migratory-Casual Worker,* p. 12; Hahamovitch, *The Fruits of Their Labor,* p. 6; *Migrant Farm Labor,* p. 4; Schwartz, *Seasonal Farm Labor in the United States,* pp. 54–57.

35. Weber, *Dark Sweat, White Gold,* p. 32; Corwin and Fogel, "Shadow Labor Force," p. 258; Webb, *The Migratory-Casual Worker,* p. 13; Schwartz, *Seasonal Farm Laborers,* pp. 57–59. One labor department official emphasized that in California, Mexican farm workers had become a "fixed institution." Reisler, *By the Sweat of Their Brow,* p. 78.

36. Reisler, *By the Sweat of Their Brow,* pp. 78–81; Schwartz, *Seasonal Farm Labor in the United States,* pp. 20, 58, 70–71.

37. Reisler, *By the Sweat of Their Brow,* pp. 81–82.

38. *Report of Commission on International and Interracial Factors in the Problems of Mexicans in the United States,* pp. 18–20, 24.

39. Ibid., p. 9; California Mexican Fact-Finding Committee, *Mexicans in California: Report of Governor C. C. Young's Mexican Fact-Finding Committee* (1930; reprint, San Francisco: R. and E. Research Associates, 1970), pp. 175–76; Durón, "Mexican Women and Labor Conflict in Los Angeles," p. 147; Arroyo, "Chicano Participation in Organized Labor," p. 278; David Oberweiser Jr., "The CIO: Vanguard for Civil Rights in Southern California, 1940–46," in *American Labor in the Era of World War II,* ed. Sally M. Miller and Daniel A. Conford (Westport, Conn.: Praeger Publishers, 1995), p. 201; "Subject—Mexicans," January 26, 1934, WPA Writers' Program, Collection 306, Box 58, Special Collections, UCLA, Los Angeles, California. Employment stability among Mexican workers determined their housing, which ranged from a shack in the infamous Hick's Camp in El Monte, located east of Los Angeles, to a four- or five-room bungalow in the city. In the 1930s, 18.6 percent of Mexican families in Los Angeles owned homes, as opposed to 4.8 percent and 8.6 percent for Japanese and Chinese families. Douglas Monroy, "An Essay on Understanding the Work Experience of Mexicans in Southern California, 1900–1939," *Aztlán* 12, no. 1 (Spring 1981), pp. 64–65; Home Missions Council, *A Study of Social and Economic Factors Relating to Spanish-Speaking People in the United States* (n.d., ca. late 1920s), p. 23; U.S. Bureau of the Census, *Fifteenth Census of the United States, 1930: Population, Special Report on Foreign-Born White Families by Country of Birth of Head* (Washington, D.C., 1933), p. 212. As late as 1936, according to an article in the *Labor Herald,* "it was possible for the Los Angeles Chamber of Commerce to advertise in newspapers all over the country that here were conditions dear to every manufacturer's heart . . . a ready supply of labor, that because there were few unions, workers could be made to fight each other for jobs, that wages could be fixed at the lowest possible point, that nearby Mexico was an unfailing source of cheap, submissive labor." Quoted in Arroyo, "Chicano Participation in Organized Labor," p. 278.

40. Durón, "Mexican Women and Labor Conflict in Los Angeles," p. 232; Monroy, "An Essay on Understanding the Work Experience of Mexicans in Southern California," pp. 62–63; State of California, Unemployment Reserves Commission, James L. Mathews, Chairman, *A Study of Seasonal Employment in California* (Sacramento, 1939), pp. 46–53, 67; Schwartz, *Seasonal Farm Labor in the United States*, pp. 29, 34, 38–39, 71; Ruiz, *Cannery Women, Cannery Lives*, pp. 69–70; Sánchez, *Becoming Mexican American*, p. 232; Jones, *The Dispossessed*, p. 176.

41. Monroy, "An Essay on Understanding the Work Experience of Mexicans in Southern California," pp. 63–64; Rose Pesotta, *Bread upon the Waters* (New York: Dodd, Mead & Company, 1945), pp. 19–20; State of California, Unemployment Reserves Commission, *A Study of Seasonal Unemployment in California*, pp. 37, 86; Sánchez, *Becoming Mexican American*, p. 232; California Department of Industrial Relations, Second Biennial Report, 1930–1932 (Sacramento: California State Printing Office, 1932), p. 117; Durón, "Mexican Women and Labor Conflict in Los Angeles," pp. 146–49; Scott Greer, "The Participation of Ethnic Minorities in the Labor Unions of Los Angeles County" (Ph.D. diss., University of California, Los Angeles, 1952), pp. 62–63, 69–70, 73, 89, 104; Schwartz, *Seasonal Farm Laborers*, p. 59.

42. Statement of Ernesto Galarza, Chief of the Division of Labor and Social Information of the Pan American Union, before the Select Committee of the House of Representatives to Investigate the Interstate Migration of Destitute Citizens, Gardner Jackson Papers, Box 1, AAA-1934, Franklin D. Roosevelt Presidential Library, Hyde Park, New York, pp. 1–2; Jones, *The Dispossessed*, pp. 170–71.

43. Robert R. McKay, "The Texas Cotton Acreage Control Law of 1931 and Mexican Repatriation," *West Texas Historical Association Yearbook* 59 (1983), p. 143; Donald Holley, *The Second Great Emancipation: The Mechanical Cotton Picker, Black Migration, and How They Shaped the Modern South* (Fayetteville: University of Arkansas Press, 2000), p. 57.

44. McKay, "The Texas Cotton Acreage Control Law of 1931 and Mexican Repatriation," p. 148; Holley, *The Second Great Emancipation*, p. 58. According to the San Antonio Spanish-language newspaper *La Prensa*, the planned reduction of cotton acreage for 1932 created widespread unemployment among Mexicans in south Texas. McKay, "The Texas Cotton Acreage Control Law of 1931 and Mexican Repatriation," p. 151.

45. Holley, *The Second Great Emancipation*, p. 159; Dionicio Nodín Valdés, *Barrios Norteños: St. Paul and Midwestern Mexican Communities in the Twentieth Century* (Austin: University of Texas Press, 2000), p. 101; Valdés, *Al Norte*, pp. 81–82; Hoffman, *Unwanted Mexican Americans*, p. 33; Jones, *The Dispossessed*, pp. 222–23.

46. Valdés, *Barrios Norteños*, p. 102; Valdés, *Al Norte*, pp. 81–82; Vargas, *Proletarians of the North*, p. 170; Fred R. Johnson, State Relief Administrator, Lansing, Michigan, to Harry L. Hopkins, Federal Emergency Relief Administrator, Washington, D.C., August 10, 1933, Office File 15, Department of Labor, Franklin D. Roosevelt Presidential Library, Hyde Park, New York.

47. Eshref Shevky, "Village Dependence on Migratory Labor in the Upper Rio Grande Valley," July 31, 1937, Case File 196/302, U.S. Mediation and Conciliation Service, RG 280, NA, p. 1; Albert G. Simms, Albuquerque, New Mexico, to

Walter S. Gifford, Director, President's Organization on Unemployment Relief, Washington, D.C., January 4, 1932, State Files, New Mexico, Series 10, Box 1111, PECE/POUR, Hoover Papers, RG 73, Herbert Hoover Presidential Library, West Branch, Iowa; Suzanne Forrest, *The Preservation of the Village: New Mexico's Hispanics and the New Deal* (Albuquerque: University of New Mexico Press, 1989), pp. 79–80, 99; Deutsch, *No Separate Refuge*, p. 164; Lorena Hickok, California, to Harry L. Hopkins, Federal Emergency Relief Administrator, Washington, D.C., June 23, 1934, Lorena Hickok Papers, Box 11 (May–August 1934), Franklin D. Roosevelt Presidential Library, Hyde Park, New York, p. 2.

48. Charles C. Gates, Denver, Colorado, to Walter S. Gifford, Director, President's Organization on Unemployment Relief, Washington, D.C., November 18, 1931, State Files, Colorado, Series 10, Box 1109, PECE/POUR, Hoover Papers, RG 73, Herbert Hoover Presidential Library, West Branch, Iowa; "Families on Relief in Coal Mining Areas," Harry Hopkins Papers, Container 49, Franklin D. Roosevelt Presidential Library, Hyde Park, New York; Forrest, *The Preservation of the Village*, p. 99; Deutsch, *No Separate Refuge*, pp. 163–65, 168.

49. "California," September 11, 1931, State Files, California, Series 10, Box 1109, PECE/POUR, Hoover Papers, RG 73, Herbert Hoover Presidential Library, West Branch, Iowa; George P. Clements, Manager, Agricultural Department, Los Angeles Chamber of Commerce, Los Angeles, California, to Charles P. Visel, Employment Coordinator, City Hall, Los Angeles, California, January 10, 1930, WPA Writers' Program, Collection 306, Box 58, Special Collections, UCLA, Los Angeles, California; George P. Clements, Manager, Agricultural Department, Los Angeles Chamber of Commerce, Los Angeles, California, to Arthur Arnoll, Manager and Secretary, Los Angeles Chamber of Commerce, Los Angeles, California, January 23, 1930, WPA Writers' Program, Collection 306, Box 58, Special Collections, UCLA, Los Angeles, California.

50. Reisler, *By the Sweat of Their Brow*, p. 229; Gilbert G. González, *Labor and Community: Mexican Citrus Worker Villages in a Southern California County, 1900–1950* (Urbana: University of Illinois Press, 1994), pp. 72–74; McWilliams, *Factories in the Field*, p. 285.

51. Atholl McBean, President's Organization on Unemployment Relief, San Francisco, California, to Walter S. Gifford, Director, President's Organization on Unemployment Relief, Washington, D.C., November 18, 1931, State Files, California, Series 10, Box 1109, PECE/POUR, Hoover Papers, RG 73, Herbert Hoover Presidential Library, West Branch, Iowa.

52. Leonardo Macías, Jr. "Mexican Immigration and Repatriation during the Great Depression" (master's thesis, Arizona State University, 1992), p. 80; Reisler, *By the Sweat of Their Brow*, p. 54; Michael Burawoy, "The Functions and Reproduction of Migrant Labor: Comparative Material from Southern Africa and the United States," *American Journal of Sociology* 81, no. 5 (March 1976), pp. 1065–66; Vargas, *Proletarians of the North*, pp. 78–80; *Report of Commission on International and Interracial Factors in the Problems of Mexicans in the United States*, p. 9.

53. Chávez Leyva, "Faithful Hard-Working Mexican Hands," p. 69; Reisler, *By the Sweat of Their Brow*, p. 228; Barrera, *Race and Class in the Southwest*, p.

107; Valdés, *Barrios Norteños*, p. 91; Vargas, *Proletarians of the North*, pp. 169–70; Sánchez, *Becoming Mexican American*, p. 211.

54. Forrest, *The Preservation of the Village*, pp. 81, 99; Deutsch, *No Separate Refuge*, p. 175.

55. Deutsch, *No Separate Refuge*, pp. 175–76. The dependence of Mexican American seasonal workers on public works projects for subsistence in Colorado's Arkansas Valley area, notes historian Sarah Deutsch, led local Anglos to name the projects "Mexican Projects" and to refer derogatorily to the state sales tax that funded the projects as the "Mexican bonus." Ibid., p. 175.

56. Louis Bloch, Secretary and Director of Surveys, State Unemployment Commission, "Tentative Report on the Activities of Certain California Counties and Municipalities in Meeting Their Problems of Emergency Unemployment Relief," November 13, 1931, pp. 2, 7, 10, State Files, California, Series 10, PECE/POUR, Hoover Papers, RG 73, Herbert Hoover Presidential Library, West Branch, Iowa; "Summary, Los Angeles County Welfare Department," Fiscal Year Ending June 30, 1931, State Files, California, Series 10, PECE/POUR, Hoover Papers, RG 73, Herbert Hoover Presidential Library, West Branch, Iowa; Sánchez, *Becoming Mexican American*, pp. 211–12; "Racial Minorities Survey—Mexicans," p. 348, WPA Writers' Program, Collection 306, Box 58, Special Collections, UCLA, Los Angeles, California; Clarence H. Matson, Manager, Department of Foreign Commerce and Shipping, Los Angeles Chamber of Commerce, Los Angeles, California, to Leo S. Fonarow, Victor Clothing Company, Los Angeles, California, May 14, 1931, WPA Writers' Program, Collection 306, Box 58, Special Collections, UCLA, Los Angeles, California.

57. Sánchez, *Becoming Mexican American*, p. 211; Memorandum, "Activities and Plans by Public and Private Agencies to Provide Unemployment Relief," San Francisco, California, September 11, 1931, p. 2, State Files, California, Series 10, PECE/POUR, Hoover Papers, RG 73, Herbert Hoover Presidential Library, West Branch, Iowa; Governor James Rolphe Jr., Governor's Office, Sacramento, California, to D. M. Reynolds, Vice President, Security First National Bank, Los Angeles, California, September 12, 1931, State Files, California, Series 10, PECE/POUR, Hoover Papers, RG 73, Herbert Hoover Presidential Library, West Branch, Iowa; George P. Clements, Manager, Agricultural Department, Los Angeles Chamber of Commerce, Los Angeles, California, to Arthur Arnoll, Manager and Secretary, Los Angeles Chamber of Commerce, Los Angeles, California, February 25, 1931, WPA Writers' Program, Collection 306, Box 58, Special Collections, UCLA, Los Angeles, California.

58. Brian Kelley, *Race, Class, and Power in the Alabama Coalfields, 1908–1921* (Urbana: University of Illinois Press, 2001), pp. 82–83; Barrera, *Race and Class in the Southwest*, pp. 73–74; Reisler, *By the Sweat of Their Brow*, p. 209; Macías, "Mexican Immigration and Repatriation," pp. 22–23; Abraham Hoffman, *Unwanted Mexican Americans in the Great Depression, 1929–1939* (Tucson: University of Arizona Press, 1974), p. 35; Francisco E. Balderrama, *In Defense of La Raza: The Los Angeles Mexican Consulate and the Mexican Community, 1929 to 1936* (Tucson: University of Arizona Press, 1982), p. ix; Valdés, *Barrios Norteños*, p. 32; Vargas, *Proletarians of the North*, p. 190.

59. Marcelo M. Suárez-Orozco, ed., *Crossings: Mexican Immigration in Interdisciplinary Perspectives* (Cambridge, Mass.: David Rockefeller Center for Latin American Studies, Harvard University, 1998), p. 318.

60. Barrera, *Race and Class in the Southwest*, p. 73; Corwin and Fogel, "Shadow Labor Force," p. 261; Sasha Lewis, *Slave Trade Today: American Exploitation of Illegal Aliens* (Boston: Beacon Press, 1979), pp. 136–37. Persons previously deported and apprehended reentering the United States would be charged with a felony punishable by up to a two-year imprisonment. Reisler, *By the Sweat of Their Brow*, pp. 214–15; Hoffman, *Unwanted Mexican Americans in the Great Depression*, p. 33; Macías, "Mexican Immigration and Repatriation," p. 25.

61. Cleofas Calleros, Mexican Border Representative, Bureau of Immigration, National Catholic Welfare Conference, El Paso, Texas, to Bruce M. Mohler, Director, Bureau of Immigration, National Catholic Welfare Conference, Washington, D.C., n.d., Box 29, Accession 933, Cleofas Calleros Collection—Alien Registration, Special Collections, University of Texas at El Paso Library.

62. Emile Pozzo, Member of the Board, Bank of America, Los Angeles, California, to Arthur Arnoll, Manager and Secretary, Los Angeles Chamber of Commerce, Los Angeles, California, May 8, 1931, WPA Writers' Program, Collection 306, Box 58, Special Collections, UCLA, Los Angeles, California; Reisler, *By the Sweat of Their Brow*, p. 231; Macías, "Mexican Immigration and Repatriation," pp. 25–26; Hoffman, *Unwanted Mexican Americans*, p. 39; Francisco E. Balderrama and Raymond Rodríguez, *Decade of Betrayal: Mexican Repatriation in the 1930s* (Albuquerque: University of New Mexico Press, 1995), p. 53; Valdés, *Barrios Norteños*, p. 96; Vargas, *Proletarians of the North*, p. 188; Lewis, *Slave Trade Today*, pp. 95–96.

63. Macías, "Mexican Immigration and Repatriation," p. 26; Hoffman, *Unwanted Mexican Americans*, p. 39; Balderrama and Rodríguez, *Decade of Betrayal*, pp. 58–59.

64. Macías, "Mexican Immigration and Repatriation," pp. 25–26; Hoffman, *Unwanted Mexican Americans*, p. 16. In a telegram to the U.S. Coordinator of Unemployment Relief, Col. Arthur M. Woods, Visel stated his plans: "We note press notices this morning. Four hundred thousand deportable aliens. U.S. estimates 5 percent in this district. We can pick them all up through police and sheriff channels. Local U.S. Department of Immigration personnel not sufficient to handle. You advise please as method of getting rid. We need their jobs for needy citizens." Balderrama and Rodríguez, *Decade of Betrayal*, p. 53.

65. Manuel, "The Mexican Population of Texas," p. 38; Tom Vasey and Josiah C. Folsom, *Survey of Agricultural Labor Conditions in Karnes County, Texas*, U.S. Farm Security Administration, U.S. Department of Agriculture, 1937, pp. 1–2, 5–6, 15; Barrera, *Race and Class in the Southwest*, p. 81. See also Chester P. Mysliwiec, "A History of Karnes County, Texas" (master's thesis, University of Texas, 1952), and Robert H. Thonhoff, "History of Karnes County" (master's thesis, Southwest Texas State College, 1963).

66. R. Reynolds McKay, "The Federal Deportation Campaign in Texas: Mexican Deportations from the Lower Rio Grande Valley during the Great Depression," *Borderlands Journal* 5 (Fall 1981), p. 97; Valdés, *Barrios Norteños*, p. 90; Foley, *The White Scourge*, p. 175; R. Reynolds McKay, "Texas Mexican Repatriation

during the Great Depression" (Ph.D. Diss., University of Oklahoma, 1982), pp. 200–6, 232–44; McKay, "The Texas Cotton Acreage Control Law of 1931 and Mexican Repatriation," p. 143. See also Karl E. Ashburn, "The Texas Cotton Acreage Control Law of 1931–32," *Southwestern Historical Quarterly* 61 (July 1957).

67. Marilyn D. Rhinehart and Thomas H. Kreneck, " 'In the Shadow of Uncertainty': Texas Mexicans and Repatriation in Houston during the Great Depression," *Houston Review* 10 (1988), p. 4; Macías, "Mexican Immigration and Repatriation," pp. 30, 32–34; Jones, *The Dispossessed*, p. 222; Pycior, *LBJ and Mexican Americans*, p. 28. For a study of the repatriation of one Mexican coal-mining community in Texas, see R. Reynolds McKay, "The Impact of the Great Depression on Immigrant Mexican Labor: Repatriation of the Bridgeport, Texas, Coalminers," *Social Science Quarterly* 65 (June 1984), pp. 354, 357, 360, 365.

68. Macías, "Mexican Immigration and Repatriation," pp. 29–32, 34, 50; McKay, "The Federal Deportation Campaign in Texas," pp. 95–97; McKay, "The Texas Cotton Acreage Control Law of 1931 and Mexican Repatriation," pp. 152–53; Deutsch, *No Separate Refuge*, pp. 164–65; Oren Frary, Office of the Town Clerk, Miami, Arizona, to W. Jett Lauck, President's Organization on Unemployment Relief, Washington, D.C., October 23, 1931, Arizona, Box 1100, Series 7, PECE/POUR—Office Files of Fred Croxton-Barrett, PECE/POUR, Hoover Papers, RG 73, Herbert Hoover Presidential Library, West Branch, Iowa; State Chairman, President's Organization on Unemployment Relief, Phoenix, Arizona, to Walter S. Gifford, Director, President's Organization on Unemployment Relief, Washington, D.C., November 16, 1931, State Files, Arizona, Series 10, PECE/POUR, Hoover Papers, RG 73, Herbert Hoover Presidential Library, West Branch, Iowa.

69. Macías, "Mexican Immigration and Repatriation," pp. 35, 56; A. M. Davis, Chairman, Maricopa County, President's Organization on Unemployment Relief, Phoenix, Arizona, to State Chairman, President's Organization on Unemployment Relief, Phoenix, Arizona, November 18, 1931, State Files, Arizona, Series 10, PECE/POUR, Hoover Papers, RG 73, Herbert Hoover Presidential Library, West Branch, Iowa; State Chairman, President's Organization on Unemployment Relief, Phoenix, Arizona, to Walter S. Gifford, Director, President's Organization on Unemployment Relief, Washington, D.C., November 16, 1931, State Files, Arizona, Series 10, PECE/POUR, Hoover Papers, RG 73, Herbert Hoover Presidential Library, West Branch, Iowa.

70. Emile Pozzo, Member of the Board, Bank of America, Los Angeles, California, to Arthur Arnoll, Manager and Secretary, Los Angeles Chamber of Commerce, Los Angeles, California, May 8, 1931, WPA Writers' Program, Collection 306, Box 58, Special Collections, UCLA, Los Angeles, California; Macías, "Mexican Immigration and Repatriation," pp. 26–27, 29; Hoffman, *Unwanted Mexican Americans*, p. 16; Sánchez, *Becoming Mexican American*, pp. 210, 213, 215–16, 221; Valdés, *Barrios Norteños*, p. 90.

71. Macías, "Mexican Immigration and Repatriation," pp. 36–38; Neil Betten and Raymond A. Mohl, "From Discrimination to Repatriation: Mexican Life during the Great Depression," *Pacific Historical Review* 42 (August 1973), pp. 379–80.

72. Valdés, *Barrios Norteños*, pp. 87, 92–93, 95; Vargas, *Proletarians of the North*, p. 186; Lea D. Taylor, President, Chicago Federation of Settlements, Chi-

cago, Illinois, to William N. Doak, Secretary, U.S. Department of Labor, Washington, D.C., January 25, 1932, File 167/255–C/Deportations, RG 174, NA. For examples of how Ford's Mexican autoworkers in Detroit coped with the hardships of the early years of the Depression, see Vargas, *Proletarians of the North*, pp. 190–94.

73. Sánchez, *Becoming Mexican American*, pp. 213, 216, 221; Valdés, *Barrios Norteños*, pp. 90, 95–96, 125–26; Vargas, *Proletarians of the North*, pp. 176–84; Lewis, *Slave Trade Today*, p. 99.

74. Box 5, National Catholic Welfare Conference Case Files, 1904–1958 (hereafter referred to as NCWCCF), Special Collections, University of Texas at El Paso Library.

75. In the mining community near Santa Rita, New Mexico, the parish priest of the Santa Rita Catholic Church reported that over 200 requests for birth certificates were made in 1932. Father Joseph N. O'Toole, Church of Santa Rita, Santa Rita, New Mexico, to Cleofas Calleros, Mexican Border Representative, Bureau of Immigration, National Catholic Welfare Conference, El Paso, Texas, January 14, 1934, Box 3, MS 173, NCWCCF, Special Collections, University of Texas at El Paso Library.

76. Colonel MacCormack, U.S. Commissioner of Immigration and Naturalization, to Cleofas Calleros, Mexican Border Representative, Bureau of Immigration, National Catholic Welfare Conference, El Paso, Texas January 30, 1934, Box 29, Accession 933, Cleofas Calleros Collection—Alien Registration, pp. 1–2, Special Collections, University of Texas at El Paso Library.

77. Thomas Mahony, Knights of Columbus, Colorado State Council, Longmont, Colorado, to Cleofas Calleros, Mexican Border Representative, Bureau of Immigration, National Catholic Welfare Conference, El Paso, Texas, March 1933, Box 3, File G, MS 173, NCWCCF, Special Collections, University of Texas at El Paso Library.

78. Eileen Ward, Executive Secretary, Catholic Social Services, Phoenix, Arizona, to Cleofas Calleros, Mexican Border Representative, Bureau of Immigration, National Catholic Welfare Conference, El Paso, Texas, January 23, 1934, Box 6, File M, MS 173, NCWCCF, Special Collections, University of Texas at El Paso Library.

79. Box 3, File G, MS 173, NCWCCF, Special Collections, University of Texas at El Paso Library.

80. Box 5, File J, MS 173, NCWCCF, Special Collections, University of Texas at El Paso Library; Cleofas Calleros to National Council of Catholic Women, Galveston, Texas, October 21, 1936, Box 28, Accession 933, Cleofas Calleros Collection, pp. 1–2, Special Collections, University of Texas at El Paso Library.

81. Charles W. Sult, State Registrar of Vital Statistics, Arizona State Board of Health, Phoenix, Arizona, to Cleofas Calleros, Mexican Border Representative, Bureau of Immigration, National Catholic Welfare Conference, El Paso, Texas, June 25, 1931, Box 5, MS 173, NCWCCF, Special Collections, University of Texas at El Paso Library. For information on Cleofas Calleros, see Mario T. García, "Mexican Americans and the Politics of Citizenship: The Case of El Paso, 1936," *New Mexico Historical Review* 59, no 2 (1984), pp. 187–204. For the controversy over the classification of El Paso Mexicans in the city birth and death records, see Foley, *The White Scourge*, p. 210.

82. Cleofas Calleros, Mexican Border Representative, Bureau of Immigration, National Catholic Welfare Conference, El Paso, Texas, to Bruce M. Mohler, Director, Bureau of Immigration, National Catholic Welfare Conference, Washington, D.C., December 1, 1930, and December 28, 1933, Box 5, File L, MS 173, NCWCCF, Special Collections, University of Texas at El Paso Library; Cleofas Calleros, Mexican Border Representative, Bureau of Immigration, National Catholic Welfare Conference, El Paso, Texas, to Morris J. Boretz, editor, *El Continental*, El Paso, Texas, January 28, 1931, Box 7, Accession 933, Cleofas Calleros Collection—Alien Registration, Special Collections, University of Texas at El Paso Library; L. H. Manning & Company, El Paso, Texas, to Cleofas Calleros, Mexican Border Representative, Bureau of Immigration, National Catholic Welfare Conference, El Paso, Texas, March 25, 1930, Box 8, Accession 933, Cleofas Calleros Collection—Alien Registration, Special Collections, University of Texas at El Paso Library; A.V. Martínez, General Consul of Mexico, Mexico City, Mexico, to Cleofas Calleros, Mexican Border Representative, Bureau of Immigration, National Catholic Welfare Conference, El Paso, Texas, July 23, 1929, Box 29, Accession 933, Cleofas Calleros Collection—Alien Registration, Special Collections, University of Texas at El Paso Library.

83. Balderrama and Rodríguez, *Decade of Betrayal*, p. 60.

84. The district directors of the U.S. Immigration Bureau were authorized to admit temporary visitors to the United States for one year and, upon application by the alien, to extend the temporary visit to two years. Cleofas Calleros, Mexican Border Representative, Bureau of Immigration, National Catholic Welfare Conference, El Paso, Texas, to Bruce M. Mohler, Director, Bureau of Immigration, National Catholic Welfare Conference, Washington, D.C., January 30, 1934, Box 29, Accession 933, Cleofas Calleros Collection—Alien Registration, pp. 1–2, Special Collections, University of Texas at El Paso Library.

85. Macías, "Mexican Immigration and Repatriation," p. 63; Gutiérrez, *Walls and Mirrors*, p. 72. From 1930 to 1939, Mexicans represented 46.3 percent of all deportations from the United States, though they made up less than 1 percent of the total U.S. population. Balderrama and Rodríguez, *Decade of Betrayal*, p. 53.

86. Macías, "Mexican Immigration and Repatriation," p. 64; Gutiérrez, *Walls and Mirrors*, p. 73; Director, Bureau of Immigration, Washington, D.C., to Miss Alice W. O'Connor, Chairman, Committee on Social Pressures, National Council on Naturalization and Citizenship, Boston, Massachusetts, August 11, 1936, Box 2, Accession 933, Cleofas Calleros Collection, Special Collections, University of Texas at El Paso Library; *Report of Commission on International and Interracial Factors in the Problems of Mexicans in the United States*, p. 19.

CHAPTER TWO
GAINING STRENGTH THROUGH THE UNION:
MEXICAN LABOR UPHEAVALS IN THE ERA OF THE NRA

1. Harvey A. Levenstein, "The AFL and Mexican Immigration in the 1920s: An Experiment in Labor Diplomacy," *Hispanic American Historical Review* 48

(May 1968), pp. 207–19; *Report of Commission on International and Interracial Factors in the Problems of Mexicans in the United States*, p. 31.

2. Gutiérrez, *Walls and Mirrors*, pp. 76–78, 80–81, 85; Joan W. Moore and Alfredo Cuéllar, *Mexican Americans—Ethnic Groups in American Life Series* (Englewood Cliffs, N.J.: Prentice Hall, 1970), p. 143. Wanting credibility, favoring moderation, and being careful not to incite Anglo retaliation, LULAC became a cautious advocate for social and economic improvement. It remained a weak and relatively ineffective organization until after World War II, when, like the NAACP, it adopted a legal approach and began filing suits against discrimination.

3. James R. Barrett, *William Z. Foster and the Tragedy of American Radicalism* (Urbana: University of Illinois Press, 1999), pp. 169–71; Edward P. Johanningsmeier, *Forging American Communism: The Life of William Z. Foster* (Princeton, N.J.: Princeton University Press, 1994), pp. 239, 257, 261.

4. Gigi Peterson, "Grassroots Good Neighbors: Connections between Mexican and U.S. Labor and Civil Rights Activists, 1936–1945" (Ph.D. diss., University of Washington, 1998), pp. 97–98, 109–10; Barry Carr, *Marxism and Communism in Twentieth-Century Mexico* (Lincoln: University of Nebraska Press, 1993), p. 37; Dorothy Healey and Maurice Isserman, *Dorothy Healey Remembers: A Life in the Communist Party* (New York: Oxford University Press, 1990), p. 46.

5. *Daniel, Bitter Harvest*, p. 278; Douglas Monroy, "Anarquismo y Comunismo: Mexican Radicalism and the Communist Party in Los Angeles during the 1930s," *Labor History* 24 (Winter 1983), pp. 52–53; Arroyo, "Chicano Participation in Organized Labor," p. 278; Mario T. García, *Memories of Chicano History: The Life and Narrative of Bert Corona* (Berkeley: University of California Press, 1994), p. 126; Jamieson, *Labor Unionism in American Agriculture*, p. 19.

6. Weber, *Dark Sweat, White Gold*, pp. 82, 105, 113; Hahamovitch, *The Fruits of Their Labor*, p. 139; Nelson-Cisneros, "La clase trabajadora en Tejas," p. 247; Schwartz, *Seasonal Farm Labor in the United States*, p. 154; Jamieson, *Labor Unionism in American Agriculture*, pp. 16–18, 34. In the years 1933 through 1936, farm workers tended to win their strikes because the economic and labor-supply situations favored them slightly. In the country as a whole, farm workers lost three out of ten strikes; in California, one out of six. *Violations of Free Speech and Rights of Labor*, pp. 172, 174–75.

7. Weber, *Dark Sweat, White Gold*, p. 110; Hahamovitch, *The Fruits of Their Labor*, p. 140; Jamieson, *Labor Unionism in American Agriculture*, pp. 41–42. For their part, truck farmers and other smaller growers dreaded unions because they feared bankruptcy. *Violations of Free Speech and Rights of Labor*, pp. 170–71.

8. Weber, *Dark Sweat, White Gold*, pp. 95, 97.

9. Jamieson, *Labor Unionism in American Agriculture*, pp. 271–72; Yolanda Chávez Leyva, "Años de desperación: The Great Depression and the Mexican American Generation in El Paso, Texas, 1929–1935," (master's thesis, University of Texas at El Paso, 1989), pp. 47–49.

10. Chávez Leyva, "Años de desperación," pp. 50–55.

11. Emilio Zamora, *The World of the Mexican Worker in Texas* (College Station: Texas A&M University Press, 1993), pp. 133–39, 159–61, 200–202.

12. Chávez Leyva, "Años de desperación," pp. 56–58.

13. Ibid., pp. 59–61.

14. Ibid., pp. 62–64.

15. Ibid., p. 64.

16. Deutsch, *No Separate Refuge*, p. 157; Harold V. Knight, *Working in Colorado: A Brief History of the Colorado Labor Movement* (Boulder: University of Colorado, Center for Labor Education and Research, 1971), pp. 104–9; John Saké Gambs, *The Decline of the I.W.W.* (New York: Russell & Russell, 1966), pp. 143–53; Jamieson, *Labor Unionism in American Agriculture*, pp. 236–37; Donald J. McClurg, "The Colorado Coal Strike of 1927—Tactical Leadership of the IWW," *Labor History* 4 (Winter 1966), pp. 70–75; Charles J. Bayard, "The 1927–1928 Colorado Coal Strike," *Pacific Historical Review* 32 (August 1963), pp. 237–45; Melvyn Dubofsky, *We Shall Be All: A History of the Industrial Workers of the World* (Chicago: Quadrangle Books, 1969), pp. 475–77; Maier B. Fox, *United We Stand: The United Mine Workers of America, 1890–1990* (Washington, D.C.: International Union, United Mine Workers of America, 1990), p. 292.

17. Deutsch, *No Separate Refuge*, pp. 157–58; Forrest, *The Preservation of the Village*, p. 98.

18. Deutsch, *No Separate Refuge*, pp. 170–71; Knight, *Working in Colorado*, pp. 114–15; Jamieson, *Labor Unionism in American Agriculture*, pp. 237–39. The Beet Workers Association set up locals in North Dakota, Minnesota, and Michigan before collapsing. Valdés, *Al Norte*, p. 39.

19. James F. Wickens, "Depression and the New Deal in Colorado," in John Braeman, Robert H. Bremner, and David Brody, eds., *The New Deal: The States and Local Levels*. Vol. 2 (Columbus: Ohio State University Press, 1975), pp. 272–73; Deutsch, *No Separate Refuge*, pp. 170–71; Forrest, *The Preservation of the Village*, p. 98.

20. Deutsch, *No Separate Refuge*, pp. 154–56, 171–72; Nelson-Cisneros, "UCAPAWA and Chicanos in California," p. 455; Harvey Klehr, *The Heyday of American Communism* (New York: Basic Books, 1984), p. 149; Jamieson, *Labor Unionism in American Agriculture*, pp. 240–41; McClurg, "The Colorado Coal Strike of 1927—Tactical Leadership of the IWW," pp. 79, 91; Bayard, "The 1927–1928 Colorado Coal Strike," p. 240.

21. Deutsch, *No Separate Refuge*, pp. 169, 172–73; Klehr, *The Heyday of American Communism*, p. 149; Forrest, *The Preservation of the Village*, pp. 97–98; Gutiérrez, *Walls and Mirrors*, p. 106; Vargas, *Proletarians of the North*, pp. 194–97; Jamieson, *Labor Unionism in American Agriculture*, pp. 240–41.

22. One Colorado educator had this to say about the knowledge of the state's Mexican Americans, their plight as beet workers, and the contradictions in the American belief in fair play: "Logic suggests the impossibility of indoctrinating them [with the cultural patterns] of the Nordics and still expect[ing] them to perform a type of labor and live under conditions which the Nordic standards taboo. Neither can it be expected that they will willingly relegate themselves to the status of second-class citizens in a country where equal opportunity, regardless of race, is a symbol of opportunity." Jamieson, *Labor Unionism in American Agriculture*, p. 235.

23. Wickens, "Depression and the New Deal in Colorado," pp. 274–75.

24. Ibid., p. 278; Jamieson, *Labor Unionism in American Agriculture*, p. 242. Irate Colorado citizens railed constantly against the "Mexican foreigners" on government work relief, and their anger was conveyed in letters to President Roosevelt: "The Mexican beet worker is on the county and state [relief] as soon as their

work is done. . . . The C.W.A. . . . is going to the Mexican beet worker. . . . I can see no reason for [the] United States supporting foreigners in these hard times as the city of Denver and the state of Colorado are doing." Clarence Dudley, Denver, Colorado, to President Franklin Delano Roosevelt, Washington, D.C., March 16, 1934, File 2037, Transient Labor, 1933–1939, Franklin D. Roosevelt Presidential Library, Hyde Park, New York.

25. Lorena Hickok, Denver, Colorado, to Harry L. Hopkins, Federal Emergency Relief Administrator, Washington, D.C., June 17, 1934, Lorena Hickok Papers, Box 11 (May–August 1934), Franklin D. Roosevelt Presidential Library, Hyde Park, New York, p. 5. Despite the bellicose complaints by Colorado Anglo residents, farmers, and local relief officials, most beet workers preferred to work. At the start of the beet season in one northern Colorado county, the number of families on work relief projects dropped by almost half, from 600 to 350. The families returned to the beet fields after being told by county officials that government work projects were actually relief and that every person who accepted this work when they could get work was keeping others from being helped. The families were unsure whether they were going to be paid, and the fact that only a dozen families had been given grocery orders dramatized the problem of widespread poverty. Wickens, "Depression and the New Deal in Colorado," pp. 285–86.

26. Wickens, "Depression and the New Deal in Colorado," p. 295.

27. Ibid., pp. 285–86; Weber, *Dark Sweat, White Gold*, p. 127; Jamieson, *Labor Unionism in American Agriculture*, pp. 234, 242; Moreno, "Social Equality and Industrialization," p. 72; Ruth Scandrett, Denver, Colorado, to Mrs. Beyer, Agricultural Adjustment Administration, Washington, D.C., October 1, 1934, Gardner Jackson Papers, Box 1, AAA-1934, Franklin D. Roosevelt Presidential Library, Hyde Park, New York, p. 1; Lorena Hickok, California, to Harry L. Hopkins, Federal Emergency Relief Administrator, Washington, D.C., June 23, 1934, Lorena Hickok Papers, Box 11 (May–August 1934), Franklin D. Roosevelt Presidential Library, Hyde Park, New York, p. 7; Jesse Lummis, Denver, Colorado, to Harry L. Hopkins, Federal Emergency Relief Administrator, Washington, D.C., August 9 and 15, 1933, Office File 15, Department of Labor, 1933, Franklin D. Roosevelt Presidential Library, Hyde Park, New York.

28. Jamieson, *Labor Unionism in American Agriculture*, p. 243; Weber, *Dark Sweat, White Gold*, pp. 113, 129; Johnson, "Wages, Employment Conditions, and Welfare," pp. 338–39; Lorena Hickok, Denver, Colorado, to Harry L. Hopkins, Federal Emergency Relief Administrator, Washington, D.C., June 17, 1934, Lorena Hickok Papers, Box 11 (May–August 1934), Franklin D. Roosevelt Presidential Library, Hyde Park, New York, p. 5; Harry L. Hopkins, Federal Emergency Relief Administrator, Washington, D.C., to President Roosevelt, The White House, August 16, 1933, Office File 15, Department of Labor 1933, Franklin D. Roosevelt Presidential Library, Hyde Park, New York. In 1935, the Bureau of Home Economics, U.S. Department of Agriculture, noted that the money needed to buy an adequate diet was $110 per family member per year. Johnson, "Wages, Employment Conditions, and Welfare," p. 339. Writing to President Roosevelt of his decision, Hopkins stated: "It seems to me it is indefensible for relief funds to be used to supplement the wages of workers in the beet fields and I am taking steps to correct this at once." Wickens, "Depression and the New Deal in Colorado," p. 295.

29. Jamieson, *Labor Unionism in American Agriculture*, p. 244; Deutsch, *No Separate Refuge*, p. 173.

30. Elizabeth Faue, "Paths of Unionization: Community, Bureaucracy, and Gender in the Minneapolis Labor Movement of the 1930s," in *Work Engendered: Toward a New History of American Labor*, ed. Ava Baron (Ithaca, N.Y.: Cornell University Press, 1991), p. 319; Chávez Leyva, "Faithful Hard-Working Mexican Hands," pp. 65, 68–70.

31. Captain Carroll M. Counts, District Intelligence Office, El Paso, Texas, to Captain Snow, Department Intelligence Office, Fort Sam Houston, Texas, November 20, 1919, Case File 10634/699–1, Box 3648, RG 165, NA; Chávez Leyva, "Faithful Hard-Working Mexican Hands," pp. 65–68. Support for the NRA among Tejanos in El Paso was already widespread; it was reported that even tortilla street vendors had signed the NRA pledge. Ibid.

32. Chávez Leyva, "Años de desperación, p. 17.

33. Chávez Leyva, "Faithful Hard-Working Mexican Hands," p. 70.

34. Ibid., pp. 71–72.

35. Ibid., pp. 72–73; Chávez Leyva, "Años de desperación," p. 45.

36. "We needed work here, and here were all these people coming from the other side," Porras recalled. "So, I got the smart idea and organized the Domestic Worker's Association—all women, local, from here." Chávez Leyva "Faithful Hard-Working Mexican Hands," pp. 70–71.

37. Nelson-Cisneros, "La clase trabajadora en Tejas," p. 256.

38. Ibid., pp. 256–57.

39. Ibid. Many ex-Finck Cigar workers later worked on a WPA sewing project headed by Mrs. Ernst. Ibid.

40. Melissa Hield, "Union-Minded: Women in the Texas ILGWU, 1933–1950," *Frontiers* 4 (1979), pp. 61–64; Mary Loretta Sullivan and Bertha Blair, *Women in Texas Industries. Hours, Wages, and Working Conditions, and Home Work*. United States Department of Labor, Women's Bureau Bulletin No. 126 (Washington, D.C.: Government Printing Office, 1936), p. 7; Nelson-Cisneros, "La clase trabajadora en Tejas," pp. 254–55; *International Ladies' Garment Workers' Local Union No. 123 et al. v. Dorothy Frocks Co.*, No. 10046, 97 S.W. 2d 379 (Texas App. 1936).

41. Exhibit 10225, "American Federation of Labor, Washington, D.C.," Los Angeles Police Department, Office of Intelligence Bureau, Metropolitan Division, November 4, 1933, Senate Committee on Education and Labor, Violations of Free Speech and Rights of Labor, 76th Cong., *Documents Relating to Intelligence Bureau or Red Squad of Los Angeles Police Department* (Washington, D.C.: Government Printing Office, 1940), p. 23524; *Los Angeles Citizen*, October 6, 1933, p. 6; Durón, "The ILGWU Dressmakers' Strike of 1933," pp. 145, 149; Sánchez, *Becoming Mexican American*, pp. 227–28, 232, 234; John Laslett and Mary Tyler, *The ILGWU in Los Angeles, 1907–1988* (Inglewood, Calif.: Ten Star Press, 1989), pp. 30–31; Faue, "Paths of Unionization," p. 310.

42. Pesotta, *Bread upon the Waters*, pp. 23, 42; Durón, "The ILGWU Dressmakers' Strike of 1933," pp. 149–51; Louis and Richard Perry, *A History of the Los Angeles Labor Movement, 1911–1941* (Berkeley: University of California Press,

1963), p. 243; Sánchez, *Becoming Mexican American*, p. 232; Laslett and Tyler, *The ILGWU in Los Angeles*, pp. 31–32; Faue, "Paths to Unionization," p. 302.

43. Pesotta, *Bread upon the Waters*, pp. 19–20, 22; Durón, "The ILGWU Dressmakers' Strike of 1933," pp. 151–52; Sánchez, *Becoming Mexican American*, p. 227; Laslett and Tyler, *The ILGWU in Los Angeles*, pp. 32–33.

44. Pesotta, *Bread upon the Waters*, pp. 26–29, 31–32; Durón, "The ILGWU Dressmakers' Strike of 1933," pp. 152–53; Sánchez, *Becoming Mexican American*, pp. 232–34; Laslett and Tyler, *The ILGWU in Los Angeles*, pp. 32–33; Douglas Monroy, *Rebirth: Mexican Los Angeles from the Great Migration to the Great Depression* (Berkeley: University of California Press, 1999), pp. 235, 237; Faue, "Paths of Unionization," p. 304; Exhibit 10322, "Assignment Officers Garment Strike Detail: Two Officers," Los Angeles Police Department, Office of Intelligence Bureau, Metropolitan Division, November 9, 1933, *Documents Relating to Intelligence Bureau or Red Squad of Los Angeles Police Department*, p. 23588.

45. Douglas Monroy, "La Costura en Los Angeles, 1933–1939: The ILGWU and the Politics of Domination," in *Mexican Women in the United States*, ed. Magdalena Mora and Adelaida R. Del Castillo (Los Angeles: UCLA Chicano Studies Research Center, 1980), p. 173; Monroy, *Rebirth*, p. 234; Pesotta, *Bread upon the Waters*, p. 31; Durón, "The ILGWU Dressmakers' Strike of 1933," p. 153; Laslett and Tyler, *The ILGWU in Los Angeles*, p. 34.

46. *Los Angeles Times*, October 13, 1933, part 2, p. 2; *La Opinión*, October 20, 1933, p. 6; Pesotta, *Bread upon the Waters*, p. 58; *Los Angeles Citizen*, October 27, 1933, p. 1; Durón, "The ILGWU Dressmakers' Strike of 1933," pp. 154–55; Sánchez, *Becoming Mexican American*, p. 227; Monroy, *Rebirth*, pp. 108, 236; Laslett and Tyler, *The ILGWU in Los Angeles*, pp. 34–35. Pinkerton detectives reported that a Communist Party executive member was present at an underground meeting of all organizers of the NTWIU in downtown Los Angeles. Exhibit 10317, "Memo. Re Strike Plans," Los Angeles Police Department, Office of Intelligence Bureau, Metropolitan Division, October 17, 1933, *Documents Relating to Intelligence Bureau or Red Squad of Los Angeles Police Department*, p. 23583.

47. Monroy, *Rebirth*, p. 236; Monroy, "La Costura en Los Angeles," p. 173; Pesotta, *Bread upon the Waters*, p. 31; Durón, "The ILGWU Dressmakers' Strike of 1933," p. 154; Sánchez, *Becoming Mexican American*, p. 227; Exhibit 10319, "Statement of George Jennings, 450 So. Benton Way, FE 4696 (landlady's phone) taken in office Intelligence Bureau, LAPD, Saturday Oct. 21, 1933, 1:06 P.M.; in connection with transporting a 'load' of non-striking employees from 860 So. L.A. St. to Pico & Main, Friday, Oct. 20–33," Los Angeles Police Department, Office of Intelligence Bureau, Metropolitan Division, October 17, 1933, *Documents Relating to Intelligence Bureau or Red Squad of Los Angeles Police Department*, pp. 23583–85.

48. Durón, "The ILGWU Dressmakers' Strike of 1933," pp. 155–56; Laslett and Tyler, *The ILGWU in Los Angeles*, p. 36; *La Opinión*, October 17, 1933, pp. 1, 6; Pesotta, *Bread upon the Waters*, p. 42; Exhibit 10320, "Memo. Re Picketing Activities 850 So. Broadway & Along Broadway between 8th and 9th this afternoon," Los Angeles Police Department, Office of Intelligence Bureau, Metropolitan Division, October 30, 1933, *Documents Relating to Intelligence*

Bureau or Red Squad of Los Angeles Police Department, p. 23587; Exhibit 10323, "Memo. Request Detail 834 So. Broadway," Los Angeles Police Department, Office of Intelligence Bureau, Metropolitan Division, November 9, 1933, *Documents Relating to Intelligence Bureau or Red Squad or Los Angeles Police Department*, p. 23588.

49. *Los Angeles Times*, October 17, 1933, part 2, p. 1, October 26, 1933, part 2, p. 1, and October 27, 1933, part 2, p. 8; Pesotta, *Bread upon the Waters*, p. 52; Durón, "The ILGWU Dressmakers' Strike of 1933," pp. 156–57; *Unions Mean Higher Wages: The Story of the Lafollette Committee Hearings in Los Angeles*, Los Angeles Industrial Union Council—CIO, February 1940, p. 4; Exhibit 10322, "Assignment Officers Garment Strike Detail: Two Officers," Los Angeles Police Department, Office of Intelligence Bureau, Metropolitan Division, November 9, 1933, *Documents Relating to Intelligence Bureau or Red Squad of Los Angeles Police Department*, p. 23588.

50. Pesotta, *Bread upon the Waters*, p. 54; Monroy, *Rebirth*, p. 238; Monroy, "La Costura en Los Angeles," p. 172; Perry and Perry, *A History of the Los Angeles Labor Movement*, p. 279; Durón, "The ILGWU Dressmakers' Strike of 1933," pp. 157–58; Sánchez, *Becoming Mexican American*, p. 234; Laslett and Tyler, *The ILGWU in Los Angeles*, pp. 35–36.

51. Durón, "The ILGWU Dressmakers' Strike of 1933," p. 158; Sánchez, *Becoming Mexican American*, pp. 234–35; Faue, "Paths of Unionization," pp. 318–19.

52. Communist Party of the United States, *The Way Out: A Program for American Labor* (New York: Workers Library Publishers, 1934), pp. 10–11; Sánchez, *Becoming Mexican American*, p. 240.

53. Exhibit 10295, "RE: Scheduled Upholsterer's Strike," Los Angeles Police Department, Office of Intelligence Bureau, Metropolitan Division, June 6, 1933, *Documents Relating to Intelligence Bureau or Red Squad of Los Angeles Police Department*, p. 23573; Sánchez, *Becoming Mexican American*, pp. 240–41. In the fall of 1933, Locals 241 and 244 of the Amalgamated Meat Cutters and Butchers of America convened a meeting in downtown Los Angeles to hear a speech by an NRA official from Washington, D.C. A third of the packinghouse workers at the meeting were Mexicans employed by Wilson & Company. The NRA representative told the workers what the NRA was going to do for the working classes and explained how it planned to handle the "chiseler" employers. The packinghouse workers voted to strike the next day. They were handed pro-union literature as well as stickers to post on trucks, in meat markets, and in other strategic places. The Cudahy Plant was next targeted for a strike. Exhibits 10334 and 10335, "RE: Packing house Strike," Los Angeles Police Department, Office of Intelligence Bureau, Metropolitan Division, October 26 and 27, 1933, *Documents Relating to Intelligence Bureau or Red Squad of Los Angeles Police Department*, pp. 23592–93.

54. Teresa R. Statler-Keener, "Progressives, Communists and the National Miners Union: Left-Wing Confrontation with the United Mine Workers of America, 1923–1933" (master's thesis, Indiana University of Pennsylvania,

1994), p. 81; Louis Colman, *Night Riders in Gallup* (New York: International Labor Defense, 1935), p. 7; Barrett, *William Z. Foster and the Tragedy of American Radicalism*, p. 174; Johanningsmeier, *Forging American Communism*, pp. 260–61; A. Markoff, "Building the Party in the Mine Strike Area," *Party Organizer* 4, no. 7 (August 1931), p. 8.

55. Lorena Hickok, Denver, Colorado, to Harry L. Hopkins, Federal Emergency Relief Administrator, Washington, D.C., June 17, 1934, Lorena Hickok Papers, Box 11 (May–August 1934), Franklin D. Roosevelt Presidential Library, Hyde Park, New York, p. 4; William Pickens, "The New Deal in New Mexico," in *The New Deal*, vol. 2, *The State and Local Levels*, ed. John Braeman, Robert H. Bremner, and David Brody (Columbus: Ohio State University Press, 1975), pp. 316, 319; Harry R. Rubenstein, "The Great Gallup Coal Strike of 1933," *New Mexico Historical Review* 52 (1977), pp. 174–75; Philip Stevenson, "Deporting Jesús," *Nation* 143 (July 18, 1936), p. 68; Harry R. Rubenstein, "Political Regression in New Mexico: The Destruction of the National Miners' Union in Gallup," in *Labor in New Mexico: Unions, Strikes, and Social History since 1881*, ed. Robert Kern (Albuquerque: University of New Mexico Press, 1983), pp. 92–93, 96; Theodore Draper, "Communists and Miners: 1928–1933," *Dissent* 19 (Spring 1972), p. 375.

56. Robin D. G. Kelley, *Hammer and Hoe: Alabama Communists during the Great Depression* (Chapel Hill: University of North Carolina Press, 1990), pp. 57–58, 64; Daniel Letwin, *The Challenge of Interracial Unionism: Alabama Coal Miners, 1878–1921* (Chapel Hill: University of North Carolina Press, 1998), pp. 42–44; Rubenstein, "Political Regression in New Mexico," p. 96; Rubenstein, "The Great Gallup Coal Strike of 1933," p. 175; Pat Toohey, *N.R.A., Martial Law, "Insurrection"* (New York: Workers Library Publishers, 1934), p. 8; Report of F. S. Hogan, Chairman, Bituminous Coal Labor Board, Division V, January 30–31, 1934, Consolidated Files on Industries Governed by Approved Codes, Code No. 24: Bituminous Coal Folder: Division V, Code Authority, Box 1000, p. 5, RG 9, NA; "Gallup Coal Strike," November, 1933, p. 7, Governor Hockenhull Papers, New Mexico State Records Center and Archives (hereafter referred to as NMSRCA).

57. Anselmo Arellano, "The People's Movement: Las Gorras Blancas," in *The Contested Homeland: A Chicano History of New Mexico*, ed. Erlinda Gonzales-Berry and David Maciel (Albuquerque: University of New Mexico Press, 2000), pp. 64–69; Governor M. C. Mechem, Santa Fe, New Mexico, to George R. Craig, U.S. District Attorney, Albuquerque, New Mexico, April 17, 1922, Mail and Files Division, 16–130–49–205–194–32, RG 60, NA; William E. Forbath, *Law and the Shaping of the American Labor Movement* (Cambridge, Mass.: Harvard University Press, 1991), pp. 95–96; Rubenstein, "Political Regression in New Mexico," p. 96; Toohey, *N.R.A., Martial Law, "Insurrection,"* pp. 9–10; F. O. Matthiessen, "The New Mexican Workers' Case," *New Republic* (May 8, 1933), p. 362; "Gallup Coal Strike," November, 1933, pp. 21, 31–32, Governor Hockenhull Papers, NMSRCA; Henry Rolf Brown, Commanding General, New Mexico National Guard, to Governor M. C. Mechem, April 14, 1922, Governor Mechem Papers, NMSRCA; George R. Craig, United States Attorney for New Mexico, to United States Attorney General, May 8, 1922, File 155–49–220547–1, Mail and

Files Division, Department of Justice, RG 60, NA; Helen Zeese Papanikolas, "Unionism, Communism, and the Great Depression: The Carbon County Coal Strike of 1933," *Utah Historical Quarterly* 41 (1973), p. 277; Barrett, *William Z. Foster and the Tragedy of American Radicalism*, pp. 173, 175.

58. Rubenstein, "Political Regression in New Mexico," p. 93; Toohey, *N.R.A., Martial Law, "Insurrection,"* p. 10; Papanikolas, "Unionism, Communism, and the Great Depression," pp. 256–57; Charles W. Grubbs, "Strike Situation Gallup, New Mexico, Coal Mining Area," p. 1, Governor Hockenhull Papers, NMSRCA; Report of F. S. Hogan, Chairman, Bituminous Coal Labor Board, Division V, January 30–31, 1934, Consolidated Files on Industries Governed by Approved Codes, Code No. 24: Bituminous Coal Folder: Division V, Code Authority, Box 1000, pp. 2–3, RG 9, NA.

59. W. J. Richardson, Secretary, Roswell Central Committee Unemployed Councils, Roswell, New Mexico, to Governor Arthur Seligman, Santa Fe, New Mexico, June 25, 1933, "New Deal," Governor Arthur Seligman Papers, 1933, NMSCRA; Spanish American Club, Clovis, New Mexico, to Governor Arthur Seligman, Santa Fe, New Mexico, June 26, 1933, Governor Arthur Seligman Papers, 1933, "New Deal," NMSRCA.

60. Statler-Keener, "Progressives, Communists and the National Miners Union," pp. 49–52; "The Fundamental Principles of the National Miners' Union," p. 1, Governor Arthur Seligman Papers, 1933, "Gallup Coal Strike— Misc. Newspaper Publicity," NMSRCA; Rubenstein, "Political Regression in New Mexico," p. 93; Toohey, *N.R.A., Martial Law, "Insurrection,"* p. 12; Harry Mavrogenis, "To the People of Gallup," n.d., Governor Hockenhull Papers, NMSRCA; Report of F. S. Hogan, Chairman, Bituminous Coal Labor Board, Division V, January 30–31, 1934, Consolidated Files on Industries Governed by Approved Codes, Code No. 24: Bituminous Coal Folder: Division V, Code Authority, Box 1000, p. 2, RG 9, NA; Kelley, *Hammer and Hoe*, p. 60; Allan Kent Powell, *The Next Time We Strike: Labor in Utah's Coal Fields, 1900–1933* (Logan: Utah State University Press, 1985), pp. 166–94; Melvyn Dubofsky and Warren Van Tine, *John L. Lewis* (Urbana: University of Illinois Press, 1986), p. 123; Papanikolas, "Unionism, Communism, and the Great Depression," p. 264; Barrett, *William Z. Foster and the Tragedy of American Radicalism*, p. 176.

61. Forrest, *The Preservation of the Village*, p. 98; Deutsch, *No Separate Refuge*, p. 173; James B. Swayne, "A Survey of the Economic, Political and Legal Aspects of the Labor Problem in New Mexico" (master's thesis, University of New Mexico, 1935), p. 32; D. H. Dinwoodie, "Deportation: The Immigration Service and the Chicano Labor Movement in the 1930s," *New Mexico Historical Review* 52 (1977), p. 193; Erna Furgusson, *Murder and Mystery in New Mexico* (Albuquerque, N.M.: Merle Armitage Editions, 1948), p. 172; Papanikolas, "Unionism, Communism, and the Great Depression," p. 258; Barrett, *William Z. Foster and the Tragedy of American Radicalism*, p. 175.

62. Jack Stachel, "Our Trade Union Policy," *Communist* 14 (November 1934), pp. 1093–1101; William Z. Foster, "Breakthrough in Industrial Organization," *Political Affairs* 48 (September–October 1969), pp. 67–68; Earl Browder, "Why an Open Letter to Our Party Membership," *Communist* 12 (August 1933), pp. 707–15; Carl I. Meyerhuber Jr., *Less than Forever: The Rise and Decline of Union*

Solidarity in Western Pennsylvania, 1914–1948 (London: Associated University Press, 1987), pp. 99, 106; Rubenstein, "The Great Gallup Coal Strike of 1933," p. 176; Rubenstein, "Political Regression in New Mexico," pp. 94–95; John J. Watt, "Launching the National Miners Union," *Labor Unity* (October 1928), pp. 2–6; Harry Mavrogenis, "To the People of Gallup," n.d., Governor Hockenhull Papers, NMSRCA. On the failed unionizing efforts of the National Miners Union in Carbon County, Utah, see Papanikolas, "Unionism, Communism, and the Great Depression," pp. 260, 265.

63. Report of F. S. Hogan, Chairman, Bituminous Coal Labor Board, Division V, January 30–31, 1934, Consolidated Files on Industries Governed by Approved Codes, Code No. 24: Bituminous Coal Folder: Division V, Code Authority, Box 1000, p. 3, RG 9, NA; Barrett, *William Z. Foster and the Tragedy of American Radicalism*, pp. 174–75; Draper, "Communists and Miners," p. 378.

64. Johanningsmeier, *Forging American Communism*, p. 259; Rubenstein, "The Great Gallup Coal Strike of 1933," p. 176; Rubenstein, "Political Regression in New Mexico," p. 96.

65. Rubenstein, "The Great Gallup Coal Strike of 1933," p. 181; Rubenstein, "Political Regression in New Mexico," pp. 95–96, 99; Statler-Keener, "Progressives, Communists and the National Miners Union," p. 48; Toohey, *N.R.A., Martial Law, "Insurrection,"* p. 14; Kelley, *Hammer and Hoe*, p. 64; Papanikolas, "Unionism, Communism, and the Great Depression," pp. 260, 266, 269–70, 298; Markoff, "Building the Party in the Mine Strike Area," pp. 9, 11.

66. Telegram, John L. Lewis, Washington, D.C., to Governor Arthur Seligman, Santa Fe, New Mexico, August 30, 1933, Governor Arthur Seligman Papers, 1933, "Gallup Coal Strike," NMSRCA; Governor Arthur Seligman, Santa Fe, New Mexico, to John L. Lewis, Washington, D.C., September 1 and 2, 1933, Governor Arthur Seligman Papers, 1933, "Gallup Coal Strike," NMSRCA; Kelley, *Hammer and Hoe*, p. 30; Rubenstein, "Political Regression in New Mexico," p. 99; Toohey, *N.R.A., Martial Law, "Insurrection,"* pp. 15–16; John L. Lewis, United Mine Workers Union, to Governor Hockenhull, August 30, 1933, Governor Hockenhull Papers, NMSRCA; Harry Mavrogenis, "To the People of Gallup," n.d., Governor Hockenhull Papers, NMSRCA; Papanikolas, "Unionism, Communism, and the Great Depression," p. 268; Johanningsmeier, *Forging American Communism*, p. 26.

67. Statler-Keener, "Progressives, Communists and the National Miners Union," pp. 61–62; Toohey, *N.R.A., Martial Law, "Insurrection,"* p. 19; Rubenstein, "The Great Gallup Coal Strike of 1933," p. 178; Matthiessen, "The New Mexican Workers' Case," p. 362; Papanikolas, "Unionism, Communism, and the Great Depression," p. 270; Draper, "Communists and Miners," p. 379; Markoff, "Building the Party in the Mine Strike Area," p. 10.

68. Charles W. Grubbs, Gallup, New Mexico, to L. H. Peebles, U.S. Department of Commerce, Bureau of Foreign and Domestic Commerce, Los Angeles, California, n.d., Governor Arthur Seligman Papers, 1933, "Gallup Coal Strike," NMSRCA; Rubenstein, "Political Regression in New Mexico," p. 97; Rubenstein, "The Great Gallup Coal Strike of 1933," p. 178; Statler-Keener, "Progressives, Communists and the National Miners Union," p. 60; Toohey, *N.R.A., Martial Law, "Insurrection,"* pp. 20–21; "Fundamental and Organization Principles of

the National Miners Union," Governor Hockenhull Papers, NMSRCA; Papanikolas, "Unionism, Communism, and the Great Depression," p. 258; GDB, May 11, 1935, p. 2; Markoff, "Building the Party in the Mine Strike Area," p. 12.

69. Charles W. Grubbs, Gallup, New Mexico, to L. H. Peebles, U.S. Department of Commerce, Bureau of Foreign and Domestic Commerce, Los Angeles, California, n.d., Governor Arthur Seligman Papers, 1933, "Gallup Coal Strike," NMSRCA; Rubenstein, "The Great Gallup Coal Strike of 1933," p. 178; Rubenstein, "Political Regression in New Mexico," p. 97; " 'Proclamation' for Martial Law," Governor Arthur Seligman Papers, NMSRCA.

70. A. Alvarado, Sub-District Executive Board, National Miners Union, Gallup, New Mexico, to Governor Arthur Seligman, Santa Fe, New Mexico, September, 3, 1933, Governor Arthur Seligman Papers, 1933, "Protests against martial law," NMSRCA.

71. Rubenstein, "Political Regression in New Mexico," pp. 99–100; Papanikolas, "Unionism, Communism, and the Great Depression," p. 266; Lt. Colonel Charles G. Sage, 111th Cavalry, District Commander, Gallup, New Mexico, to Governor Arthur Seligman, Santa Fe, New Mexico, September 22, 1933, Governor Arthur Seligman Papers, 1933, "Gallup Coal Strike," NMSRCA. For information on the work of the Communist Party among farmers during the Third Period, see Klehr, *The Heyday of American Communism*, pp. 135–52.

72. Toohey, *N.R.A., Martial Law, "Insurrection,"* pp. 25–26.

73. Kelley, *Hammer and Hoe*, p. 76; *Gallup Independent*, September 2, 1933; Toohey, *N.R.A., Martial Law, "Insurrection,"* p. 30.

74. Toohey, *N.R.A., Martial Law, "Insurrection,"* pp. 30–31; Rubenstein, "The Great Gallup Coal Strike of 1933," pp. 31–33, 182; Rubenstein, "Political Regression in New Mexico," p. 97; "Fundamental and Organization Principles of the National Miners Union," Governor Hockenhull Papers, NMSRCA.

75. Charles W. Grubbs, Gallup, New Mexico, to L. H. Peebles, U.S. Department of Commerce, Bureau of Foreign and Domestic Commerce, Los Angeles, California, n.d., Governor Arthur Seligman Papers, 1933, "Gallup Coal Strike," NMSRCA; Rubenstein, "Political Regression in New Mexico," p. 100; Toohey, *N.R.A., Martial Law, "Insurrection,"* p. 34; Rubenstein, "The Great Gallup Coal Strike of 1933," p. 180.

76. Captain Alfonso B. Martínez, Troop B, 111th Cavalry, Mentmore, New Mexico, to District Commander, Gallup, New Mexico, September 8, 1933, Governor Arthur Seligman Papers, 1933, "Gallup Coal Strike," NMSRCA; Robert F. Roberts, Sub-District Executive Board, National Miners Union, to Governor Arthur Seligman, Santa Fe, New Mexico, September 10, 1933, Governor Arthur Seligman Papers, 1933, "Gallup Coal Strike—Correspondence," NMSRCA; Statler-Keener, "Progressives, Communists and the National Miners Union," p. 64; Papanikolas, "Unionism, Communism, and the Great Depression," p. 261.

77. Lt. Colonel Charles G. Sage, 111th Cavalry, District Commander, Gallup, New Mexico, to Governor Arthur Seligman, Santa Fe, New Mexico, September 22, 1933, Governor Arthur Seligman Papers, 1933, "Gallup Coal Strike," NMSRCA.

78. Horace Moses, GAMERCO, to Governor Arthur Seligman, Santa Fe, New Mexico, September 23, 1933, Governor Arthur Seligman Papers, "Gallup Coal Strike," NMSRCA.

79. Brigadier Osborne C. Wood, Gallup, New Mexico, to Gallup Sub-District Board, National Miners Union, Gallup, New Mexico, September 22, 1933, Governor Arthur Seligman Papers, 1933, "National Guard Actions," NMSRCA; Rubenstein, "Political Regression in New Mexico," p. 100; *Gallup Independent*, September 2, 1933.

80. *Gallup Independent*, September 2, 1933; Papanikolas, "Unionism, Communism, and the Great Depression," p. 283; Toohey, *N.R.A., Martial Law, "Insurrection,"* p. 35; González, *Mexican Consuls and Labor Organizing*, p. 78.

81. *Gallup Independent*, October 12, 1933; Lt. Colonel Charles G. Sage, 111th Cavalry, District Commander, Gallup, New Mexico, to Governor Arthur Seligman, Santa Fe, New Mexico, September 22, 1933, Governor Arthur Seligman Papers, 1933, "Gallup Coal Strike," NMSRCA.

82. Strike Bulletin, Governor Hockenhull Papers, 1933, "Gallup Coal Strike—Misc.," NMSRCA; NMU Strike Bulletin, September 24, 1933, Governor Arthur Seligman Papers, 1933, "Gallup Coal Strike," NMSRCA; *Gallup Independent*, October 12, 1933.

83. *Gallup Independent*, October 12, 1933.

84. Ibid.; Klehr, *The Heyday of American Communism*, pp. 57–58, 65–68; Franklin Folsom, *Impatient Armies of the Poor: The Story of Collective Action of the Unemployed, 1808–1942* (Niwot: University Press of Colorado, 1991), pp. 292–93, 295–97; Mexican Consul General Enrique A. González, El Paso, Texas, to Governor A. W. Hockenhull, Santa Fe, New Mexico, October 16, 1933, Governor Hockenhull Papers, 1933, "Gallup Coal Strike—Misc.," NMSRCA.

85. *Gallup Independent*, October 12, 1933.

86. *Gallup Independent*, October 14, 1933.

87. Ibid.

88. The Santa Fe Railroad, one of the state's largest taxpayers, was interested in the Gallup strike. The Santa Fe Railroad got its coal from Gallup and hauled large coal tonnages from there to other points. *Gallup Independent*, October 14, 1933.

89. Ibid.

90. Ibid.

91. National Miners Union, Gallup, New Mexico, to Governor A. W. Hockenhull, Santa Fe, New Mexico, November 27, 1933, Governor Hockenhull Papers, 1933, "Gallup Coal Strike—Misc.," NMSRCA; Report of F. S. Hogan, Chairman, Bituminous Coal Labor Board, Division V, January 30–31, 1934, Consolidated Files on Industries Governed by Approved Codes, Code No. 24: Bituminous Coal Folder: Division V, Code Authority, Box 1000, p. 1, RG 9, NA; Rubenstein, "Political Regression in New Mexico," p. 100; Furgusson, *Murder and Mystery in New Mexico*, pp. 172–73.

92. Report of F. S. Hogan, Chairman, Bituminous Coal Labor Board, Division V, January 30–31, 1934, Consolidated Files on Industries Governed by Approved Codes, Code No. 24: Bituminous Coal Folder: Division V, Code Authority, Box 1000, pp. 8, 11, RG 9, NA; Rubenstein, "Political Regression in New Mexico,"

pp. 100–1; Swayne, "A Survey of the Economic, Political and Legal Aspects of the Labor Problem in New Mexico," pp. 33–34, 69. New Mexico's CWA jobs program initially employed 8,250, but by March 1934 it employed 11,992 at a cost of $2,356,221. Pickens, "The New Deal in New Mexico," p. 323.

93. Colonel Clyde E. Ely, Raton, New Mexico, to Governor A. W. Hockenhull, Santa Fe, New Mexico, January 18, 1933, Governor Hockenhull Papers, 1933, "Gallup Coal Strike—National Guard," NMSRCA; Statler-Keener, "Progressives, Communists and the National Miners Union," p. 83; Klehr, *The Heyday of American Communism*, pp. 132–33; Rubenstein, "Political Regression in New Mexico," p. 101; Barrett, *William Z. Foster and the Tragedy of American Radicalism*, p. 176; Draper, "Communists and Miners," p. 391.

94. Report of F. S. Hogan, Chairman, Bituminous Coal Labor Board, Division V, January 30–31, 1934, Consolidated Files on Industries Governed by Approved Codes, Code No. 24: Bituminous Coal Folder: Division V, Code Authority, Box 1000, p. 4, RG 9, NA; GDB, May 18, 1935, p. 3.

95. Barrett, *William Z. Foster and the Tragedy of American Radicalism*, p. 176; Wickens, "Depression and the New Deal in Colorado," p. 275; Statler-Keener, "Progressives, Communists and the National Miners Union," pp. 86–87; Bulletin, January 15, 1934, 10110–2668–52, Box 28558, U.S. Department of Justice, RG 60, NA.

96. "Gallup Coal Strike," November, 1933, p. 36, Governor Hockenhull Papers, NMSRCA; Pickens, "The New Deal in New Mexico," p. 323; GDB, May 11, 1935, p. 2.

97. Statler-Keener, "Progressives, Communists and the National Miners Union," p. 89; Draper, "Communists and Miners," p. 391.

98. Statler-Keener, "Progressives, Communists and the National Miners Union," p. 89; Draper, "Communists and Miners," p. 391; Barrett, *William Z. Foster and the Tragedy of American Radicalism*, p. 176; Rubenstein, "The Great Gallup Coal Strike of 1933," p. 188; Report of F. S. Hogan, Chairman, Bituminous Coal Labor Board, Division V, January 30–31, 1934, Consolidated Files on Industries Governed by Approved Codes, Code No. 24: Bituminous Coal Folder: Division V, Code Authority, Box 1000, pp. 4, 18–20, RG 9, NA; Katherine Gay, "Background of the Gallup Strike," *Nation* 140 (November 1933), p. 512; Stevenson, "Deporting Jesús," pp. 68–69; Furgusson, *Murder and Mystery in New Mexico*, pp. 171–73; GDB, May 11, 1935, p. 2.

99. Furgusson, *Murder and Mystery in New Mexico*, pp. 176–78; GDB, May 11, 1935, p. 2.

100. GDB, May 18, 1935, p. 3.

101. GDB, June 29, 1935, p. 2.

102. GDB, May 11, 1935, p. 2.

103. Bulletin of the American Committee for the Protection of the Foreign Born, July 1936, pp. 2, 11, American Committee for the Protection of the Foreign Born, Folder 17, International Labor Defense Collection, 512, Colorado Historical Society, Denver, Colorado; Chairman, State Farmers Conference, Denver Colorado, to Governor Ed G. Johnson, Denver, Colorado, May 13, 1934, Folder 18, Miscellaneous Correspondence and Handbills, RE: Labor and Trade Union

Activities, 1934–1935, International Labor Defense Collection, 512, Colorado Historical Society, Denver, Colorado.

104. GDB, October 12, 1935, p. 1.

105. GDB, June 29, 1935, pp. 3–4.

106. Margarita C. Pedroza to Governor Clyde C. Tingley, July 22, 1936 Governor Tingley Papers, NMSRCA. See also "Petition of Margarita C. Pedroza, C. Ortiz, and C. Espinoza" to Governor Clyde C. Tingley, July 22, 1936, Governor Tingley Papers, NMSRCA.

CHAPTER THREE
"DO YOU SEE THE LIGHT?": MEXICAN AMERICAN
WORKERS AND CIO ORGANIZING

1. J. R. Steelman, Commissioner of Conciliation, San Antonio, Texas, to H. L. Kerwin, Director of Conciliation, U.S. Department of Labor, Washington, D.C., April 20, 1935, File 182/326, RG 280, NA; John H. Yeaman, Laredo Chamber of Commerce, Laredo, Texas, to J. R. Steelman, Commissioner of Conciliation, San Antonio, Texas, April 18, 1935, File 182/327, RG 280, NA; Nelson-Cisneros, "La clase trabajadora en Tejas," p. 252; Ed Idar, "The Labor Movement in Laredo," p. 2, Mexican American Workers, Folder 13, Box 2E309, Labor Movement in Texas Collection, Center for American History, University of Texas, Austin, Texas.

2. Murray Emanuel Polakoff, "The Development of the Texas State CIO Council" (Ph. D. dissertation, Columbia University, 1955), pp. 54–55.

3. Robert M. Utley, *Lone Star Justice: The First Century of the Texas Rangers* (New York: Oxford University Press, 2002), p. 243.

4. Jamieson, *Labor Unionism in American Agriculture*, pp. 273–74; J. R. Steelman, Commissioner of Conciliation, San Antonio, Texas, to H. L. Kerwin, U.S. Department of Labor, Washington, D.C., April 20, 1935, Case File 182/326, RG 280, NA; Romeyn Wormuth, American Consul, Nuevo Laredo, Mexico, to Secretary of State, Washington, D.C., May 4, 1935, 811.5045/179, Box 5112, RG 59, NA; José Jacobs, Laredo, Texas, to Senator La Follette, La Follette Subcommittee of Senate Committee on Education and Labor, Washington, D.C., May 5, 1936, p. 3, Mexican American Workers, Laredo, Texas, Folder 12, Box 2E309, Labor Movement in Texas Collection, Center for American History, University of Texas, Austin, Texas; Nelson-Cisneros, "La clase trabajadora en Tejas," p. 246.

5. Romeyn Wormuth, American Consul, Mexico City, D.F., Mexico, to Secretary of State, Washington, D.C., May 4, 1935, RE: Strike of Mexican Laborers in the Onion District of Texas, Department of State Decimal File 1930–39, 811.5045/179 H-TH, Box 5112, RG 59, NA; Herndon W. Goforth, American Consul, Matamoras, Tamaulipas, Mexico, to Secretary of State, Washington, D.C., May 7, 1935, RE: Strike of Mexican Laborers in the Onion District of Texas—Webb County Section, Department of State Decimal File 1930–39, 811.5045/180 H-DP, Box 5112, RG 59, NA; J. R. Steelman, Commissioner of Conciliation, San Antonio, Texas, to H. L. Kerwin, Director of Conciliation, U.S. Department of Labor, Washington, D.C., April 20, 1935, File 182/326, RG 280, NA.

6. J. R. Steelman, Commissioner of Conciliation, San Antonio, Texas, to H. L. Kerwin, U.S. Department of Labor, Washington, D.C., April 20, 1935, Case File 182/326, RG 280, NA; Romeyn Wormuth, American Consul, Nuevo Laredo, Mexico, to Secretary of State, Washington, D.C., May 4, 1935, 811.5045/179, Box 5112, RG 59, NA; Jamieson, *Labor Unionism in American Agriculture*, pp. 274–75; Nelson-Cisneros, "La clase trabajadora en Tejas," p. 248; Nelson-Cisneros, "UCAPAWA Organizing Activities in Texas," pp. 73–74.

7. Nelson-Cisneros, "La clase trabajadora en Tejas," pp. 151–52; González, *Mexican Consuls and Labor Organizing*, p. 201.

8. Jamieson, *Labor Unionism in American Agriculture*, pp. 154–55; Peterson, "Grassroots," pp. 35, 110–11. On October 13, 1935, Tejanos held a convention organized by the Communist Party (La Covención Constitutivo Pro Derechos Mexicanos de Tejas) and passed a resolution for the secession of south Texas and the border region.

9. Carr, *Marxism and Communism in Twentieth-Century Mexico*, pp. 97–98; Exhibit 10404, August 12, 1936, Los Angeles Police Department, Office of Intelligence Bureau, Metropolitan Division, Senate Committee on Education and Labor, Violations of Free Speech and Rights of Labor. 76th Cong. *Documents Relating to Intelligence Bureau or Red Squad of Los Angeles Police Department*, p. 23637.

10. "Report on the Conference for the Organization of the Agricultural Workers in South Texas," January 23, 1937, pp. 1–5, Mexican American Workers, Folder 13, Box 2E309, Labor Movement in Texas Collection, Center for American History, University of Texas, Austin, Texas; José Jacobs, Laredo, Texas, to Senator La Follette, La Follette Subcommittee of Senate Committee on Education and Labor, Washington, D.C., May 5, 1936, pp. 3–4, Mexican American Workers, Folder 12, Box 2E309, Labor Movement in Texas Collection, Center for American History, University of Texas, Austin, Texas; F. B. Mallon, Lieutenant Colonel, General Staff, Headquarters Eight Crops Area, Fort Sam Houston, Texas, to Assistant Chief of Staff, G-2, War Department, Washington, D.C., March 13, 1936, Military Intelligence Division File 2657–g–657186, RG 165, NA; Jamieson, *Labor Unionism in American Agriculture*, p. 275. The Agricultural Workers Union continued to organize Laredo's Tejano workers. More joined the union every week. Although the AWU grew in membership, it lapsed for lack of leadership. The last full-time organizer had been Clemente N. Idar. Nelson-Cisneros, "La clase trabajadora en Tejas," pp. 252–53.

11. F. B. Mallon, Lieutenant Colonel, General Staff, Headquarters Eight Crops Area, Fort Sam Houston, Texas, to Assistant Chief of Staff, G-2, War Department, Washington, D.C., March 13, 1936, Military Intelligence Division File 2657–g–657186, RG 165, NA.

12. Ibid.

13. "Report on the Conference for the Organization of the Agricultural Workers in South Texas," January 23, 1937, pp. 1–5, Mexican American Workers, Folder 13, Box 2E309, Labor Movement in Texas Collection, Center for American History, University of Texas, Austin, Texas; González, *Mexican Consuls and Labor Organizing*, pp. 46–47; F. B. Mallon, Lieutenant Colonel, General Staff, Headquarters Eight Crops Area, Fort Sam Houston, Texas, to Assistant Chief of Staff, G-2, War Department, Washington, D.C., March 18, 1936, Military Intelligence Division File 2657–g–657186, RG 165, NA.

14. "Report on the Conference for the Organization of the Agricultural Workers in South Texas," January 23, 1937, pp. 1–5, Mexican American Workers, Folder 13, Box 2E309, Labor Movement in Texas Collection, Center for American History, University of Texas, Austin, Texas; Nelson-Cisneros, "La clase trabajadora en Tejas," pp. 248–49; Nelson-Cisneros, "UCAPAWA Organizing Activities in Texas," pp. 73–74; Jamieson, *Labor Unionism in American Agriculture*, pp. 276–77; Peterson "Grassroots," p. 156; Juan Gomez-Quiñones, *Mexican American Labor, 1790–1990* (Albuquerque: University of New Mexico Press, 1994), pp. 147–49.

15. Ed Idar, "The Labor Movement in Laredo," pp. 1–3, Mexican American Workers, Folder 13, Box 2E309, Labor Movement in Texas Collection, Center for American History, University of Texas, Austin, Texas; Jamieson, *Labor Unionism in American Agriculture*, pp. 276–78; Nelson-Cisneros, "La clase trabajadora en Tejas," pp. 249–50; Nelson-Cisneros, "UCAPAWA Organizing Activities in Texas," pp. 73–74; Gomez-Quiñones, *Mexican American Labor*, p. 144.

16. Ed Idar, "The Labor Movement in Laredo," pp. 1–3, Mexican American Workers, Folder 13, Box 2E309, Labor Movement in Texas Collection, Center for American History, University of Texas, Austin, Texas; Jamieson, *Labor Unionism in American Agriculture*, pp. 276–78; Nelson-Cisneros, "La clase trabajadora en Tejas," pp. 249–50; Nelson-Cisneros, "UCAPAWA Organizing Activities in Texas," pp. 73–74; Gomez-Quiñones, *Mexican American Labor*, p. 144; Weber, *Dark Sweat, White Gold*, p. 180.

17. Jamieson, *Labor Unionism in American Agriculture*, p. 278; Polakoff, "The Development of the Texas State CIO Council," p. 109.

18. Sarah Deutsch, "Gender, Labor History, and Chicano/a Ethnic Identity," *Frontiers* 14 (1994), pp. 1–2.

19. Green Peyton, *San Antonio: City in the Sun* (New York: McGraw-Hill, 1946), p. 169; David Lewis Filewood, "Tejano Revolt: The Significance of the 1938 Pecan Shellers Strike" (master's thesis, University of Texas at Arlington, 1994), p. 23; Richard Croxdale, "The 1938 San Antonio Pecan Shellers' Strike," in *Women in the Texas Workforce*, ed. Richard Croxdale and Melissa Hield (Austin: People's History in Texas, 1979), p. 30; George and Latane Lambert Papers, Collection 127, Labor History Archives, University of Texas at Arlington Library, Arlington, Texas, p. 25; Harry Koger Papers, Collection 66, Labor History Archives, University of Texas at Arlington Library, Arlington, Texas, p. 2. Emma Tenayuca used community as a model to recruit workers to the union. Her organizing strategies, which she utilized successfully as an Unemployed Councils relief worker and as secretary of the Workers' Alliance, relied on family and kinship networks at the neighborhood level as channels for organizing.

20. George and Latane Lambert Papers, Collection 127, Labor History Archives, University of Texas at Arlington Library, Arlington, Texas, p. 25.

21. Filewood, "Tejano Revolt," p. 85.

22. Croxdale, "The 1938 San Antonio Pecan Shellers' Strike," p. 27; Roberto Calderón and Emilio Zamora, *Chicana Voices: Intersections of Race, Class, and Gender* (Austin: Center for Mexican American Studies, 1986), pp. 37–38; author interview with Emma Tenayuca, May 3, 1990.

23. Author interview with Emma Tenayuca, May 3, 1990.

24. Calderón and Zamora, *Chicana Voices*, pp. 37–38; author interview with Emma Tenayuca, May 3, 1990.

25. Raúl Ramos, "Así Fue: La Huelga de los Nueceros de San Antonio, Texas, Febrero 1938" (senior thesis, Princeton University, 1989), p. 11; author interview with Emma Tenayuca, May 3, 1990. The classic study of the Gregorio Cortez ballad is Américo Paredes, *'With His Pistol in His Hand': A Border Ballad and Its Hero* (Austin: University of Texas Press, 1958).

26. Author interview with Emma Tenayuca, May 3, 1990; Julia Kirk Black-welder, *Women of the Depression: Caste and Culture in San Antonio, 1929–1939* (College Station: Texas A&M University Press, 1984), p. 147; Peyton, *San Antonio: City in the Sun*, p. 169.

27. Montejano, *Anglos and Mexicans in the Making of Texas*, pp. 164–65, 189–90; Robert J. Thomas, *Citizenship, Gender, and Work: Social Organization of Industrial Agriculture* (Berkeley: University of California Press, 1985), p. 148; Farm Placement Service, *Origins and Problems of Texas Migratory Farm Labor*, Texas State Employment Service, Texas Unemployment Compensation Commission, Austin, Texas, September 1940, pp. 20, 42; Richard A. García, *Rise of the Mexican American Middle Class: San Antonio, 1929–1941* (College Station: Texas A&M University Press, 1991), p. 58.

28. Anthony J. Badger, *The New Deal: The Depression Years, 1933–1940* (New York: Noonday Press, 1989), p. 182; Filewood, "Tejano Revolt," p. 12; Montejano, *Anglos and Mexicans in the Making of Texas*, pp. 218–19; George O. Coalson, *The Development of the Migratory Farm Labor System in Texas, 1900–1954* (San Francisco: R. and E. Research Associates, 1977), p. 58; author interview with Emma Tenayuca, May 4, 1990; Lyndon Gayle Knippa, "San Antonio II: The Early New Deal," in *Texas Cities and the Great Depression*, ed. W. W. Newcomb, Miscellaneous Papers 3 (Austin: Texas Memorial Museum, 1973), p. 80; Ramos, "Así Fue," p. 8.

29. Montejano, *Anglos and Mexicans in the Making of Texas*, p. 265.

30. J. R. Steelman, Commissioner of Conciliation, San Antonio, Texas, to H. L. Kerwin, U.S. Department of Labor, Washington, D.C., April 20, 1935, Case File 182/326, RG 280, NA; Romeyn Wormuth, American Consul, Nuevo Laredo, Mexico, to Secretary of State, Washington, D.C., May 4, 1935, 811.5045/179, Box 5112, RG 59, NA; Sharon Hartman Strom, "Challenging 'Women's Place': Feminism, the Left, and Industrial Unionism in the 1930s," *Feminist Studies* 9 (Summer 1980), pp. 361–62; Sullivan and Blair, *Women in Texas Industries*, pp. 47–48, 57.

31. Filewood, "Tejano Revolt," p. 27. The ex–coal miner Juan Peña helped form a UCAPAWA farm workers' local union in Laredo. D. H. Dinwoodie, "The Rise of the Mine-Mill Union in Southwestern Copper," in *American Labor in the Southwest: The First One Hundred Years*, ed. James C. Foster (Tucson: University of Arizona Press, 1982), p. 48.

32. Blackwelder, *Women of the Depression*, pp. 103–4; Calderón and Zamora, *Chicana Voices*, p. 33; García, *Rise of the Mexican American Middle Class*, p. 60; Chris Strachwitz and James Nicolopulos, comps., *Lydia Mendoza: A Family Autobiography* (Houston: Arte Publico Press, 1993), pp. 68–70; Filewood, "Tejano Revolt," pp. 34–36. Tenayuca claimed that what motivated her to join the

picket line was seeing a photograph of San Antonio Police Chief A. West putting on a new pair of boots and boasting that if the women cigar workers walked out, he would use those boots. Author interview with Emma Tenayuca, May 3, 1990.

33. Nelson-Cisneros, "La clase trabajadora en Tejas," pp. 255–56; *Houston Chronicle*, June 3, 1938.

34. Nelson-Cisneros, "La clase trabajadora en Tejas," pp. 255–56.

35. Taylor told Tenayuca once, "You know, Emma, these Mexicans are never going to amount to anything." Author interview with Emma Tenayuca, May 4, 1990.

36. Ramos, "Así Fue," p. 9; Blackwelder, *Women of the Depression*, pp. 144–45; Filewood, "Tejano Revolt," pp. 41–42; Irene Ledesma, "Texas Newspapers and Chicana Workers' Activism, 1919–1974," *Western Historical Quarterly* 26 (Autumn 1995), p. 318; WPA Central Files, Texas 1935–1936, Box 2618, Folder 641, 199/1189, No. 3168–5A, RG 69, NA. Along with conservative interests in the Lone Star State, San Antonio's political bosses had targeted Congressman Maury Maverick for defeat in the Democratic primary. Judith Kaaz Doyle, "Maury Maverick and Radical Politics in San Antonio, Texas, 1938–1941," *Journal of Southern History* 53 (May 1987), p. 203. Allies in the strikebreaking effort were Father John Lopez of the National Catholic Welfare Conference and Rebecca Taylor of the ILGWU, who remained outspoken in her criticism of Tenayuca. For her part, Taylor drove around with the police pointing out union activists as likely communists. García, *Rise of the Mexican American Middle Class*, p. 63; author interview with Emma Tenayuca, May 4, 1990; Filewood, "Tejano Revolt," pp. 82–83.

37. Peyton, *San Antonio: City in the Sun*, p. 147; Filewood, "Tejano Revolt," pp. 29, 32–33, 37–39; Ramos, "Así Fue," p. 6; Blackwelder, *Women of the Depression*, p. 145; Coalson, *The Development of the Migratory Farm Labor System in Texas*, p. 58; Klehr, *The Heyday of American Communism*, pp. 50–56; author interview with Emma Tenayuca, May 4, 1990. For works on the Unemployed Councils, see Daniel Leab, " 'United We Eat': The Creation and Organization of the Unemployed Councils," *Labor History* 8 (Fall 1967), pp. 300–15, and Roy Rosenzweig, "Organizing the Unemployed: The Early Years of the Great Depression, 1929–33," *Radical America* 10 (July–August 1976), pp. 37–60.

38. *People's Press*, January 23, 1937; author telephone interview with Emma Tenayuca, February 20, 1990; Fraser M. Ottanelli, *The Communist Party of the United States: From the Depression to World War II* (New Brunswick, N.J.: Rutgers University Press, 1991), pp. 35–36. As noted, during the cotton-picking season, relief agencies dropped hundreds of Mexicans from relief rolls or referred them to additional kinds of farm work. At the end of the harvest season, case workers told the Mexicans they were ineligible for WPA relief because they had been employed the previous year. Cut off from relief, these laborers added to the problem of rising unemployment in San Antonio. Emma Tenayuca, Secretary, West Side Unemployed Council, San Antonio, Texas, to Harry L. Hopkins, National Director, Works Progress Administration, Washington, D.C., WPA Central Files, Texas 1935–1936, Box 2615, Folder 641, RG 69, NA.

39. Author interview with Emma Tenayuca, May 4, 1990.

40. Author interview with Emma Tenayuca, May 3, 1990; Folsom, *Impatient Armies of the Poor*, pp. 421–22; "La Pasionaria de Texas," *Time* 31 (February 28, 1938), p. 17; Klehr, *The Heyday of American Communism*, p. 273; Monroy, "Anarquismo y Comunismo," p. 55; Dinwoodie, "Deportation," pp. 193–94; Gilbert Mers, *Working the Waterfront: The Ups and Downs of a Rebel Longshoreman* (Austin: University of Texas Press, 1988), p. 122.

41. Dinwoodie, "Deportation," pp. 193–94.

42. Author interview with Emma Tenayuca, May 3, 1990; *People's Press*, March 6, 1937; Hoffman, *Unwanted Mexican Americans in the Great Depression*, p. 120.

43. Folsom, *Impatient Armies of the Poor*, pp. 422–23; *San Antonio Light*, June 30, 1937; Calderón and Zamora, *Chicana Voices*, p. 33; author interview with Emma Tenayuca, May 4, 1990; Richard H. Pells, *Radical Visions and American Dreams: Culture and Thought in the Depression Years* (New York: Harper Torchbooks, 1973), p. 259.

44. *People's Press*, July 10, 1937; Kelley, *Hammer and Hoe*, pp. 191–92.

45. Polakoff, "The Development of the Texas State CIO Council," pp. 141–45; Don Carleton, *Red Scare! Right-Wing Hysteria, Fifties Fanaticism, and Their Legacy in Texas* (Austin: University of Texas Press, 1985), pp. 27–28; Filewood, "Tejano Revolt," p. 85; Ledesma, "Texas Newspapers and Chicana Workers' Activism," p. 319; author interview with Emma Tenayuca, May 5, 1990; Klehr, *The Heyday of American Communism*, p. 273; Mers, *Working the Waterfront*, pp. 122, 124.

46. Ramos, "Así Fue," p. 26; Filewood, "Tejano Revolt," p. 72; Ledesma, "Texas Newspapers and Chicana Workers' Activism," p. 318; *People's Press*, July 10 and 24, 1937; author interview with Emma Tenayuca, May 5, 1990.

47. Nelson-Cisneros, "La clase trabajadora en Tejas," p. 253; Ramos, "Así Fue," pp. 13–14, 20; Jamieson, *Labor Unionism in American Agriculture*, p. 278; Ledesma, "Texas Newspapers and Chicana Workers' Activism," p. 317; García, *Rise of the Mexican American Middle Class*, pp. 55, 60–62; *Current*, May 22, 1986; Blackwelder, *Women of the Depression*, pp. 141, 148–49; Filewood, "Tejano Revolt," pp. 46–50, 58; Sullivan and Blair, *Women in Texas Industries*, p. 78; Albert Camarillo, *Chicanos in California: A History of Mexican Americans in California* (San Francisco: Boyd & Fisher Publishing Company, 1984), p. 59. Mexicans made up about 52.2 percent of San Antonio's relief rolls; half of these (22.8 percent, or 16,324 individuals) were Mexican nationals, and the remainder (about 29.4 percent, or 21,032) were Mexican Americans. Knippa, "San Antonio II," p. 87.

48. Nelson-Cisneros, "UCAPAWA Organizing Activities in Texas," pp. 77–78; Filewood, "Tejano Revolt," pp. 70, 72–73; Clyde Johnson Papers, *The Green Rising*, Reel 13, Special Collections, UCLA, p. 14; *People's Press*, August 14, 1937.

49. Jamieson, *Labor Unionism in American Agriculture*, p. 280; Blackwelder, *Women of the Depression*, pp. 141, 148–49; *Current*, May 22, 1986; Filewood, "Tejano Revolt," pp. 79–80; George and Latane Lambert Papers, Collection 127, Labor History Archives, University of Texas at Arlington Library, Arlington, Texas, pp. 19, 29; García, *Rise of the Mexican American Middle Class*, p. 62;

Report of District 3, *UCAPAWA Year Book*, 1938, p. 22, Case File 195/114, RG 280, NA.

50. Author interview with Emma Tenayuca, May 3, 1990; Ramos, "Así Fue," p. 26.

51. Nelson-Cisneros, "La clase trabajadora en Tejas," pp. 156–57; Peterson, "Grassroots," pp. 18–19, 110–11.

52. Montejano, *Anglos and Mexicans in the Making of Texas*, p. 244; Filewood, "Tejano Revolt," pp. 86–88; Polakoff, "The Development of the Texas State CIO Council," p. 109. The call for Catholic clergy to join a crusade against international communism was the result of a 1937 Catholic encyclical, "Divini Redemptoris." Gary Gerstle, *Working-Class Americanism: The Politics of Labor in a Textile City, 1914–1960* (New York: Cambridge University Press, 1989), p. 250.

53. Blackwelder, *Women of the Depression*, p. 141; Peyton, *San Antonio: City in the Sun*, p. 170; Filewood, "Tejano Revolt," pp. 85–86; author interview with Emma Tenayuca, May 4, 1990; Gerstle, *Working-Class Americanism*, pp. 250–52; García, *Rise of the Mexican American Middle Class*, pp. 169–73.

54. Ramos, "Así Fue," pp. 57–58.

55. Ibid., pp. 33, 52–53; Filewood, "Tejano Revolt," pp. 76–77, 112–13; Ledesma, "Texas Newspapers and Chicana Workers' Activism," p. 319; Report of District 3, *UCAPAWA Year Book*, 1938, p. 22, Case File 195/114, RG 280, NA; Polakoff, "The Development of the Texas State CIO Council," p. 109.

56. The CTM delegates did get an agreement from Texas organized labor to counter anti-Cárdenas propaganda in the United States. Gigi Peterson, "Compañeros across the Border: The Mexican Labor-Left and Its U.S. Connections, 1936–1940" (unpublished seminar paper, Department of History, University of Washington, Spring 1992), p. 20; WPA Central Files, Texas 1935–1936, Box 2618, Folder 641, 199/1189, No. 3168–5A, RG 69, NA.

57. *Houston Labor Journal*, January 27, 1939, n.p.

58. García, *Rise of the Mexican American Middle Class*, p. 63; Blackwelder, *Women of the Depression*, pp. 141–49; Filewood, "Tejano Revolt," pp. 82–83; Strom, "Challenging 'Women's Place,' " pp. 368–69; Ramos, "Así Fue," p. 25; Faue, "Paths of Unionization," pp. 296–301; Polakoff, "The Development of the Texas State CIO Council," p. 109.

59. Filewood, "Tejano Revolt," p. 106; George and Latane Lambert Papers, Collection 127, Labor History Archives, University of Texas at Arlington Library, Arlington, Texas, pp. 18–19.

60. George and Latane Lambert Papers, Collection 127, Labor History Archives, University of Texas at Arlington Library, Arlington, Texas, pp. 18–19; Ramos, "Así Fue," p. 33; author interview with Emma Tenayuca, May 3, 1990.

61. Harry Koger Papers, Collection 66, Labor History Archives, University of Texas at Arlington Library, Arlington, Texas, p. 6; author interview with Emma Tenayuca, May 3 and 5, 1990; Jamieson, *Labor Unionism in American Agriculture*, p. 280.

62. Ramos, "Así Fue," p. 73; Filewood, "Tejano Revolt," pp. 90–93; Jamieson, *Labor Unionism in American Agriculture*, p. 280; Polakoff, "The Development of the Texas State CIO Council," p. 109. The hot-tempered police chief

overplayed the communist ties to the strike to discredit everyone involved in assisting the pecan shellers, particularly Emma Tenayuca and UCAPAWA president Donald Henderson. Kilday despised Tenayuca, and the Tejana likewise had a low opinion of the racist Irish police chief. Tenayuca believed that as an Irishman and as a Catholic, Kilday in his threatening behavior toward and attacks on Mexicans demanding equality betrayed the cause of ethnic solidarity and what she knew of the centuries-long Irish struggle for liberation. "Kilday was the most stupid man I had ever met. His brother was a priest. All the damning the [Irish] got from the English, you think they'd learn something!" Author interview with Emma Tenayuca, May 4, 1990.

63. Ramos, "Así Fue," pp. 73–74; Blackwelder, *Women of the Depression*, p. 141; Filewood, "Tejano Revolt," pp. 93–96; Ledesma, "Texas Newspapers and Chicana Workers' Activism," p. 318; Harry Koger Papers, Collection 66, Labor History Archives, University of Texas at Arlington Library, Arlington, Texas, p. 2; George and Latane Lambert Papers, Collection 127, Labor History Archives, University of Texas at Arlington Library, Arlington, Texas, pp. 23–24, 28–29; author interview with Emma Tenayuca, May 4, 1990. The city of San Antonio denied that police had used unnecessary force in dispersing crowds or had arrested anyone for peaceful picketing. In fact, presiding Judge S. G. Tayloe wrote his decision before all the evidence had been presented; he had already decided that the police were within their rights to prohibit any picketing during the walkout. *San Antonio Light*, February 24, 1938, p. 7A. See also *Martinez et al. v. Kilday et al.*, No. 10420, 117 S.W. 2d 151 (Texas App. 1938).

64. García, *Rise of the Mexican American Middle Class*, p. 63.

65. Blackwelder, *Women of the Depression*, p. 142; Filewood, "Tejano Revolt," pp. 114–15; Jamieson, *Labor Unionism in American Agriculture*, p. 281.

66. Nelson-Cisneros, "UCAPAWA Organizing Activities in Texas," pp. 77–78; *UCAPAWA News*, July 1939, p. 8; Jamieson, *Labor Unionism in American Agriculture*, p. 281; Selden C. Menefee and Orin C. Cossmore, *The Pecan Shellers of San Antonio*, Federal Works Agency, WPA Division of Research (Washington, D.C.: Government Printing Office, 1940), p. 16; Arthur Shapiro, "The Workers of San Antonio, Texas, 1900–1940" (Ph.D diss., University of Texas at Austin, 1952), pp. 115–16; Ramos, "Así Fue," pp. 85–86; Filewood, "Tejano Revolt," p. 120; Amador G. González to WPA Administration, November 29, 1938, WPA Central Files: State, 1934–1944 Texas 641 N-2 1937–1938, San Antonio, Box 2618, RG 69, NA.

67. Nelson-Cisneros, "UCAPAWA Organizing Activities in Texas," pp. 78–79; *UCAPAWA News*, December 1939, p. 16, September/October 1940, p. 12, October 27, 1941, p. 6, and September 1, 1943, p. 3. The pecan workers finally received a raise in 1943 as a result of the increase in the federal minimum wage to forty cents an hour. Pecan Workers' Local 172 continued in existence at least until 1946.

68. Filewood, "Tejano Revolt," p. 102; *People's Press*, March 19, 1938.

69. For an excellent elaboration on this theme, see Gutiérrez, *Walls and Mirrors*.

70. Monroy, "Anarquismo y Comunismo," p. 52; Forrest, *The Preservation of the Village*, pp. 154–55; Mark Naison, *Communists in Harlem during the Depression* (New York: Grove Press, 1983), pp. 256–57.

71. Carleton, *Red Scare!* p. 29. Tenayuca's appearance on the Communist Party ticket no doubt surprised her longtime friend the liberal Texan Maury Maverick, who had been rebuked by the San Antonio city machine as a servant of the communists and as a racial reformer. Doyle, "Maury Maverick and Radical Politics in San Antonio, Texas," p. 217.

72. Montejano, *Anglos and Mexicans in the Making of Texas*, pp. 117–19; Kelley, *Hammer and Hoe*, p. 13. Fifteen years later, Spanish-speaking party members would struggle against national CPUSA leaders to gain recognition for Mexicans as an oppressed national minority. Healey and Isserman, *Dorothy Healey Remembers*, p. 70; Monroy, "Anarquismo y Comunismo," p. 50.

73. Emma Tenayuca and Homer Brooks, "The Mexican Question in the Southwest," *Communist* 18 (March 1939), pp. 257–68; Monroy, "Anarquismo y Comunismo," pp. 42–44; author interview with Emma Tenayuca, May 3, 1990; Calderón and Zamora, *Chicana Voices*, pp. 34–35; García, *Mexican Americans*, pp. 153–54; Peterson, "Grassroots," pp. 183–84.

74. Peterson, "Grassroots," p. 184.

75. García, *Mexican Americans*, p. 154. The Communist Party had considered Mexicans a national minority as early as 1932. According to an article in the *Western Worker*, "[Mexicans] are a national minority and if we are to win the Mexican worker to our Party, we must orient and develop our tactics to suit this situation." *Western Worker*, July 1, 1932.

76. Naison, *Communists in Harlem during the Depression*, pp. 256–57; Richard B. Henderson, *Maury Maverick: A Political Biography* (Austin: University of Texas Press, 1970), pp. 214–16; Harry Koger Papers, Collection 66, Labor History Archives, University of Texas at Arlington Library, Arlington, Texas, p. 3; George and Latane Lambert Papers, Collection 127, Labor History Archives, University of Texas at Arlington Library, Arlington, Texas, pp. 21–22; Ledesma, "Texas Newspapers and Chicana Workers' Activism," p. 321; author interview with Emma Tenayuca, May 3, 1990.

77. Author interview with Emma Tenayuca, May 3, 1990; Healey and Isserman, *Dorothy Healey Remembers*, pp. 80–82; Ottanelli, *The Communist Party of the United States*, pp. 183–85.

78. Homer Brooks later died of a heart attack in Los Angeles. Author interview with Emma Tenayuca, May 4, 1990.

79. Ottanelli, *The Communist Party of the United States*, pp. 182–83. Emma Tenayuca later learned of the "Great Terror"—Stalin's arrest, torture, and murder of Bolsheviks. This news was extremely upsetting to Emma because most of these Soviet crimes occurred during the years 1937–39, the heyday of her activism. She lamented, "Khrushchev's announcement horrified the world, it horrified me." Author interview with Emma Tenayuca, May 4, 1990.

80. The situation among the pecan shellers was different because UCAPAWA Local 172 effectively used the strike tactic and was politically active. Nelson-Cisneros, "UCAPAWA Organizing Activities in Texas," pp. 81–82; Jamieson, *Labor Unionism in American Agriculture*, p. 221.

81. Nelson-Cisneros, "UCAPAWA and Chicanos in California," p. 456.

82. Ibid., p. 458; Deutsch, *No Separate Refuge*, p. 171.

83. Isaac Durán, President, Agricultural Workers Union, Scottsbluff, Nebraska, to President Franklin Delano Roosevelt, Washington, D.C., July 21, 1937, Office File 241, Sugar, July–August 1937, Franklin D. Roosevelt Presidential Library, Hyde Park, New York.

84. *Violations of Free Speech and Rights of Labor*, pp. 175, 447–48; "Time Factors in Sugar Beet Union Labor Situation in Rocky Mountain States," U.S. Mediation and Conciliation Service, U.S. Department of Labor, Washington, D.C., Case File 196/139, RG 280, NA.

85. *Violations of Free Speech and Rights of Labor*, pp. 442, 444–45; Committee of the Spanish Defense Council, Denver, Colorado, to Labor Secretary Francis Perkins, Washington, D.C., October 19, 1940, Case File 196/3399, RG 280, NA.

86. Weber, *Dark Sweat, White Gold*, p. 189; Valdés, *Barrios Norteños*, pp. 113–14; Louise Año Nuevo Kerr, "Chicanas in the Great Depression," in *Between Borders: Essays on Mexicana/Chicana History*, ed. Adelaida R. Del Castillo (Encino, Calif.: Floricanto Press, 1990), pp. 262–65.

87. Jamieson, *Labor Unionism in American Agriculture*, p. 140; Stanley White, U.S. Mediation and Conciliation Service, U.S. Department of Labor, Washington, D.C., to John R. Steelman, Director, U.S. Mediation and Conciliation Service, U.S. Department of Labor, Washington, D.C., October 26, 1938, pp. 1, 8, Case File 195/123, RG 280, NA.

88. Jamieson, *Labor Unionism in American Agriculture*, pp. 124–26; Nelson-Cisneros, "UCAPAWA and Chicanos in California," p. 457; Exhibit 10254, "MEMORANDUM: Re Truck and Agricultural Workers Union," March 28, 1936, Los Angeles Police Department, Office of Intelligence Bureau, Metropolitan Division, Senate Committee on Education and Labor, Violations of Free Speech and Rights of Labor. 76th Cong., *Documents Relating to Intelligence Bureau or Red Squad of Los Angeles Police Department*, p. 23545.

89. Monroy, "Work Experience of Mexicans in Southern California," p. 61; Faith N. Williams and Alice C. Hanson, *Money Disbursements of Wage Earners and Clerical Workers in Five Cities in the Pacific Region, 1934–1936: Mexican Families in Los Angeles*, U.S. Department of Labor, Bureau of Labor Statistics Bulletins, no. 639, part 2 (Washington, D.C.: Government Printing Office, 1939), pp. 87–88, 100. Another factor lessening the annual migration was that a local labor supply in the San Joaquin Valley had been created by the development of small farm worker communities on the outskirts of the Valley's towns and villages.

90. Weber, *Dark Sweat, White Gold*, p. 190; Nelson-Cisneros, "UCAPAWA and Chicanos in California," p. 466.

91. Weber, *Dark Sweat, White Gold*, p. 149; Daniel, *Bitter Harvest*, pp. 272–73; Stanley White, U.S. Mediation and Conciliation Service, U.S. Department of Labor, Washington, D.C., to John R. Steelman, Director, U.S. Mediation and Conciliation Service, U.S. Department of Labor, Washington, D.C., October 26, 1938, p. 2, Case File 195/123, RG 280, NA.

92. Ruiz, *Cannery Women, Cannery Lives*, p. 73.

93. Ibid., pp. 74–76; Sánchez, *Becoming Mexican American*, pp. 242–44; Nelson-Cisneros, "UCAPAWA and Chicanos in California," pp. 463–64.

94. Ruiz, *Cannery Women, Cannery Lives*, p. 76; Sánchez, *Becoming Mexican American*, pp. 243–44; Nelson-Cisneros, "UCAPAWA and Chicanos in California," pp. 463–64. The Teamsters would later use brutal violence against César Chávez's farm workers' union in the 1970s as the two groups competed for contracts and members in the California farmland area. Steven Brill, *The Teamsters* (New York: Pocket Books, 1978), pp. 402–5.

95. Sánchez, *Becoming Mexican American*, pp. 243–44; Nelson-Cisneros, "UCAPAWA and Chicanos in California," pp. 463–64; Ruiz, *Cannery Women, Cannery Lives*, pp. 76–77.

96. Ruiz, *Cannery Women, Cannery Lives*, pp. 79–81.

97. Ibid., pp. 77–79; Sánchez, *Becoming Mexican American*, pp. 243–44; Nelson-Cisneros, "UCAPAWA and Chicanos in California," pp. 463–64; Exhibit 10432, "Re: Labor Trouble at Cal. Walnut Growers Asso. 1745 and 2180 E. 7th St." October 9, 1935, Los Angeles Police Department, Office of Intelligence Bureau, Metropolitan Division, Senate Committee on Education and Labor, Violations of Free Speech and Rights of Labor. 76th Cong., *Documents Relating to Intelligence Bureau or Red Squad of Los Angeles Police Department*, p. 23550. As UCAPAWA's chief organizer in Los Angeles, Moreno encouraged Cal San employees to combat the discriminatory hiring practices of the Shapiro brothers. Pressure from Local 75 in early 1942 forced the Shapiros to hire blacks. Ruiz, *Cannery Women, Cannery Lives*, pp. 77–79.

98. Ruiz, *Cannery Women, Cannery Lives*, pp. 81–82; Nelson-Cisneros, "UCAPAWA and Chicanos in California," p. 465. Workers at Cal San gained wage increases and improved working conditions, as well as a badly needed company nursery for its female cannery and food processing workers. Worker solidarity remained strong. In 1943, UCAPAWA organizers Dixie Tiller, Luisa Moreno, and Pat Verble founded the Citrus Workers Organizing Committee (CWOC) and spearheaded successful organizing campaigns by workers at onion dehydration plants and packing sheds in Southern California and in the San Joaquin Valley. By early 1945, UCAPAWA had won thirty-one NLRB representation elections. Ruiz, *Cannery Women, Cannery Lives*, p. 79.

99. "Report to the Second International Conference of UCAPAWA—Donald Henderson, General President," Case File 195/114, RG 280, NA; Ruiz, *Cannery Women, Cannery Lives*, pp. 81–82; Nelson-Cisneros, "UCAPAWA and Chicanos in California," p. 465.

100. Ruiz, *Cannery Women, Cannery Lives*, p. 83. In 1938, Eduardo Quevedo Sr. ran unsuccessfully for city council. Sánchez, *Becoming Mexican American*, p. 250.

101. U.S. Works Progress Administration, California, *Los Angeles County Vegetable Growers Survey* (Washington, D.C.: U.S. Works Progress Administration, 1935), p. 29.

102. Exhibit 10367, "Memorandum for Chief Davis," September 30, 1937, Los Angeles Police Department, Office of Intelligence Bureau, Metropolitan Division, Senate Committee on Education and Labor, Violations of Free Speech and Rights of Labor. 76th Cong., *Documents Relating to Intelligence Bureau or Red Squad of Los Angeles Police Department*, pp. 23613–14.

103. García, *Memories of Chicano History*, pp. 89, 92–93; Ann Fagan Ginger and David Christiano, eds., *The Cold War against Labor*, vol. 1 (Berkeley, Calif.: Meiklejohn Civil Liberties Institute, 1987), pp. 434–35; Harvey A. Young, Alhambra, California, to The White House, Washington, D.C., April 7, 1935, Criminal Division, U.S. Department of Justice, RG 60, NA.

104. Thomas Göbel, "Becoming American: Ethnic Workers and the Rise of the CIO," *Labor History* 29, no. 2 (Spring 1988), pp. 195–96.

105. Neuvo-Kerr, "Chicanas in the Great Depression," pp. 263–65; Vargas, *Proletarians of the North*, p. 207; Rick Halpern, *Down on the Killing Floor: Black and White Workers in Chicago's Packinghouses, 1904–1954* (Urbana: University of Illinois Press, 1997), pp. 139, 186.

CHAPTER FOUR
ADVOCATES OF RACIAL DEMOCRACY: MEXICAN AMERICAN WORKERS FIGHT
FOR LABOR AND CIVIL RIGHTS IN THE EARLY WORLD WAR II YEARS

1. Daniel, *Chicano Workers and the Politics of Fairness*, p. 140; Zieger, *The CIO, 1935–1955*, pp. 154, 158.

2. Zieger, *The CIO, 1935–1955*, pp. 112, 153, 160; Kryder, *Divided Arsenal*, pp. 126–28; Lichtenstein, *Labor's War at Home*, p. 48; Denning, *The Cultural Front*, pp. 7–9; Roderick N. Ryon, "An Ambiguous Legacy: Baltimore Blacks and the CIO, 1936–1941," *Journal of Negro History* 65, no. 1 (Winter 1980), p. 22.

3. Vernon H. Jensen, *Collective Bargaining in the Nonferrous Metals Industry* (Berkeley: Institute of Industrial Relations, University of California, 1955), p. 11; D. H. Dinwoodie, "The Rise of the Mine-Mill Union in Southwestern Copper," in *American Labor in the Southwest: The First One Hundred Years*, ed. James C. Foster (Tucson: University of Arizona Press, 1982), pp. 47–48.

4. Jensen, *Collective Bargaining in the Nonferrous Metals Industry*, p. 8; Dinwoodie, "The Rise of the Mine-Mill Union in Southwestern Copper," pp. 46–47, 49.

5. Arroyo, "Chicano Participation in Organized Labor," pp. 278–79, 290; David Oberweiser, Jr., "The CIO: Vanguard for Civil Rights in Southern California, 1940–46," in Sally M. Miller and Daniel A. Conford, eds., *American Labor in the Era of World War II* (Westport, Conn.: Praeger Publishers, 1995), pp. 200–213; Denning, *The Cultural Front*, p. 14.

6. Kryder, *Divided Arsenal*, p. 104; Richard W. Steele, " 'No Racials': Discrimination against Ethnics in American Defense Industry, 1940–42," *Labor History* 32, no. 1 (Winter 1991), p. 80; Arroyo, "Chicano Participation in Organized Labor," pp. 291–92; Oberweiser, "The CIO: A Vanguard for Civil Rights in Southern California, 1940–46," pp. 203–4.

7. Vernon H. Jensen, *Nonferrous Metals Industry Unionism, 1932–1954: A Story of Leadership Controversy* (Ithaca, N.Y.: Cornell University Press, 1954), pp. 12–13; Jensen, *Collective Bargaining in the Nonferrous Metals Industry*, pp. 17–19; Dinwoodie, "The Rise of the Mine-Mill Union in Southwestern Copper," p. 48; Michael E. Sherman, Commissioner of Conciliation, Santa Fe, New Mex-

ico, to Hugh L. Kerwin, Director of Conciliation, U.S. Department of Labor, Washington, D.C., March 26, 1936, pp. 1–3, File 182/1800, RG 280, NA.

8. Ryon, "An Ambiguous Legacy," p. 21; Dinwoodie, "The Rise of the Mine-Mill Union in Southwestern Copper," p. 47; Richard Melzer, *Madrid Revisited: Life and Labor in a New Mexican Mining Camp in the Years of the Great Depression* (Sante Fe, N.M.: Lightening Tree Press, 1986), pp. 24, 33–35.

9. Dinwoodie, "The Rise of the Mine-Mill Union in Southwestern Copper," pp. 50–51; Jensen, *Nonferrous Metals Industry Unionism*, p. 48.

10. Captain Carroll M. Counts, District Intelligence Officer, to Captain Snow, Department Intelligence Officer, District Intelligence Office, Fort Sam Houston, Texas, November 20, 1919, Case File 10634/699–1, Box 3648, RG 165, NA; Dinwoodie, "The Rise of the Mine-Mill Union in Southwestern Copper," p. 48; García, *Mexican Americans*, p. 176; Peterson, "Grassroots," pp. 157–58.

11. García, *Mexican Americans*, pp. 178–79; Ryon, "An Ambiguous Legacy," p. 23; Frank Arnold, "Humberto Silex: CIO Organizer from Nicaragua," *Southwest Economy and Society* 4 (1978), p. 5; oral interview with Humberto Silex by Oscar J. Martínez and Art Sadin, April 28, 1978, Institute of Oral History, University of El Paso, El Paso, Texas, p. 16; City of El Paso, to President Franklin D. Roosevelt, Washington, D.C., February 6, 1936, WPA Central Files, State 1935–1944, Box 2614, Folder 641, El Paso, Texas, RG 69, NA; "Facts relative to the Deportation Proceedings Brought against Humberto Silex," Box 133, Folder 41, p. 1, Los Angeles CIO Council Files (Philip "Slim" Connelly Files), Urban Archives Center, California State University, Northridge, California.

12. García, *Mexican Americans*, pp. 179–80; Ryon, "An Ambiguous Legacy," p. 23; "Facts Relative to the Deportation Proceedings Brought against Humberto Silex," Box 133, Folder 41, p. 2, Los Angeles CIO Council Files (Philip "Slim" Connelly Files), Urban Archives Center, California State University, Northridge, California.

13. García, *Mexican Americans*, p. 180; Dinwoodie, "The Rise of the Mine-Mill Union in Southwestern Copper," pp. 48–49; Peterson, "Grassroots," p. 158; Arnold, "Humberto Silex," pp. 6–7; oral interview with Humberto Silex by Oscar J. Martínez and Art Sadin, April 28, 1978, Institute of Oral History, University of El Paso, El Paso, Texas, pp. 3–4.

14. Dinwoodie, "The Rise of the Mine-Mill Union in Southwestern Copper," p. 51; García, *Mexican Americans*, pp. 181–82.

15. García, *Mexican Americans*, p. 182; Jensen, *Nonferrous Metals Industry Unionism*, pp. 21–22; Peterson, "Grassroots," pp. 58–60; Arnold, "Humberto Silex," p. 7; Oral interview with Humberto Silex by Oscar J. Martínez and Art Sadin, April 28, 1978, Institute of Oral History, University of El Paso, El Paso, Texas, p. 4.

16. García, *Mexican Americans*, pp. 182–83; Peterson, "Grassroots," p. 159; Arnold, "Humberto Silex," pp. 6–7; "Facts relative to the Deportation Proceedings Brought against Humberto Silex," Box 133, Folder 41, p. 2, Los Angeles CIO Council Files (Philip "Slim" Connelly Files), Urban Archives Center, California State University, Northridge, California; oral interview with Humberto Silex by Oscar J. Martínez and Art Sadin, April 28, 1978, Institute of Oral History, University of El Paso, El Paso, Texas, p. 26.

17. García, *Mexican Americans*, pp. 183–84.

18. Ibid., p. 184.

19. Ibid., pp. 184–85.

20. Ibid., pp. 185–86.

21. Ibid., p. 186; Zieger, *The CIO, 1935–1955*, pp. 155–56; Kryder, *Divided Arsenal*, p. 127; Dinwoodie, "The Rise of the Mine-Mill Union in Southwestern Copper," p. 53; Arnold, "Humberto Silex," p. 8; Jensen, *Collective Bargaining in the Nonferrous Metals Industry*, p. 27; Jensen, *Nonferrous Metals Industrial Unionism*, p. 89. At the CIO's November 1942 convention, CIO president Philip Murray named a Mine-Mill official to the union's new Committee to Abolish Racial Discrimination. According to Mine-Mill president Reid Robinson, "nothing could be more dangerous to our trade-union movement . . . than a breakdown of the no-strike policy, despite the problems confronted by workers." Zieger, *The CIO, 1935–1955*, pp. 152, 156.

22. García, *Mexican Americans*, pp. 187–88; Ryon, "An Ambiguous Legacy," p. 25; Arnold, "Humberto Silex," p. 8; "Facts relative to the Deportation Proceedings Brought against Humberto Silex," Box 133, Folder 41, p. 1, Los Angeles CIO Council Files (Philip "Slim" Connelly Files), Urban Archives Center, California State University, Northridge, California.

23. García, *Mexican Americans*, p. 189. In October 1943, Local 501 received a favorable decision from the War Labor Board granting a wage increase of eleven and a half cents an hour retroactive to October 1942. Each worker received back pay of almost $200. As an expression of their loyalty to the war effort, union members purchased several hundred dollars' worth of war bonds with some of their wage increase and voted unanimously to donate one day's pay to the community war chest. Ibid.

24. Ibid., pp. 189–90.

25. Dinwoodie, "The Rise of the Mine-Mill Union in Southwestern Copper," p. 52.

26. García, *Mexican Americans*, pp. 188–89; Arnold, "Humberto Silex," p. 9; Peterson, "Grassroots," p. 160.

27. Steele, "No Racials," pp. 70–75; Zieger, *The CIO, 1935–1955*, p. 179.

28. Zieger, *The CIO, 1935–1955*, pp. 128, 155–57.

29. Denning, *The Cultural Front*, pp. 16–17; Oberweiser, "The CIO: A Vanguard for Civil Rights in Southern California, 1940–46," pp. 201–2; García, *Memories of Chicano History*, pp. 105–7.

30. Arroyo, "Chicano Participation in Organized Labor," pp. 290–91; Oberweiser, "The CIO: A Vanguard for Civil Rights in Southern California, 1940–46," pp. 201–2.

31. Arroyo, "Chicano Participation in Organized Labor," p. 291; Oberweiser, "The CIO: A Vanguard for Civil Rights in Southern California, 1940–46," pp. 201–3.

32. Oberweiser, "The CIO: A Vanguard for Civil Rights in Southern California, 1940–46," pp. 202–3; E. Frederick Anderson, *The Development of Leadership and Organization Building in the Black Community of Los Angeles from 1900 through World War II* (Saratoga, Calif.: Century Twenty-One Publishing, 1980), p. 85. The ILWU also helped defend Festus Coleman, an African American

falsely charged with rape in San Francisco. Corona took the Coleman case to the Los Angeles CIO Industrial Union Council, which set up the Coleman Defense Committee. Coleman was sentenced to death. A valid confession, incriminating a policeman, proved Coleman innocent, and he was released after serving over four years in prison. Oberweiser, "The CIO: A Vanguard for Civil Rights in Southern California, 1940–46," p. 203.

33. Zieger, *The CIO, 1935–1955*, p. 154; Martin Bauml Duberman, *Paul Robeson* (New York: Alfred A. Knopf, 1988), pp. 247, 249; García, *Memories of Chicano History*, pp. 108–9, 113–14, 124–25; Oberweiser, "The CIO: A Vanguard for Civil Rights in Southern California, 1940–46," p. 201; Peterson, "Grassroots," pp. 184–85; García, *Mexican Americans*, pp. 146–47; Gutiérrez, *Walls and Mirrors*, pp. 110–11; Camarillo, *Chicanos in California*, pp. 58–60; Monroy, *Rebirth*, p. 258; Program of the Congress of Spanish-Speaking Peoples, Gardner Jackson Papers, Box 16, Franklin D. Roosevelt Presidential Library, Hyde Park, New York, pp. 1–2.

34. García, *Mexican Americans*, pp. 146–47; García, *Memories of Chicano History*, p. 109; Sánchez, *Becoming Mexican American*, pp. 244–45; Gutiérrez, *Walls and Mirrors*, pp. 110–11; Camarillo, *Chicanos in California*, pp. 58–60; Monroy, *Rebirth*, p. 258; Program of the Congress of Spanish-Speaking Peoples, Gardner Jackson Papers, Box 16, Franklin D. Roosevelt Presidential Library, Hyde Park, New York, pp. 1–2; Peterson, "Grassroots," pp. 184–85; Lichtenstein, *Labor's War at Home*, p. 27.

35. Lichstenstein, *Labor's War at Home*, p. 30; García, *Mexican Americans*, p. 148; García, *Memories of Chicano History*, p. 109; Sánchez, *Becoming Mexican American*, p. 244; Polakoff, "The Development of the Texas State CIO Council," p. 386.

36. García, *Mexican Americans*, pp. 148–49; García, *Memories of Chicano History*, pp. 109–10; Sánchez, *Becoming Mexican American*, p. 245; Louise Moreno, Los Angeles, California, to Gardner Jackson, AAA, Washington, D.C., March 13 and 23, 1939, Gardner Jackson Papers, Box 16, Franklin D. Roosevelt Presidential Library, Hyde Park, New York; Louise Moreno, Albuquerque, New Mexico, to Gardner Jackson, AAA, Washington, D.C., February 28, 1939, Gardner Jackson Papers, Box 16, Franklin D. Roosevelt Presidential Library, Hyde Park, New York, pp. 1–2.

37. García, *Mexican Americans*, pp. 147–48; Sánchez, *Becoming Mexican American*, p. 245; Louise Moreno, Los Angeles, California, to Gardner Jackson, AAA, Washington, D.C., March 13 and 23, 1939, Gardner Jackson Papers, Box 16, Franklin D. Roosevelt Presidential Library, Hyde Park, New York; Louise Moreno, Albuquerque, New Mexico, to Gardner Jackson, AAA, Washington, D.C., February 28, 1939, Gardner Jackson Papers, Box 16, Franklin D. Roosevelt Presidential Library, Hyde Park, New York, pp. 1–2.

38. García, *Memories of Chicano History*, p. 94; Denning, *The Cultural Front*, p. 12.

39. García, *Memories of Chicano History*, pp. 96, 126–28; *Jose Angel Ocon, Appellant, v. Herman R. Landon, District Director, Immigration and Naturalization Service, Respondent*, 218 F. 2d 320 (U.S. App. 1954).

40. García, *Memories of Chicano History*, p. 127; García, *Mexican Americans*, pp. 149–50; Monroy, *Rebirth*, p. 258; Sánchez, *Becoming Mexican American*, pp. 245–46; Peterson, "Grassroots," p. 185; Josephine Fierro de Bright, Los Angeles, California, to Gardner Jackson, AAA, Washington, D.C., April 10, 1939, Gardner Jackson Papers, Box 16, Franklin D. Roosevelt Presidential Library, Hyde Park, New York.

41. Zieger, *The CIO, 1935–1955*, pp. 85–88.

42. Sánchez, *Becoming Mexican American*, pp. 247–48; García, *Memories of Chicano History*, pp. 111–12; Peterson, "Grassroots," p. 185.

43. Zieger, *The CIO, 1935–1955*, pp. 39–40; Ottanelli, *The Communist Party of the United States*, pp. 119–20; Sánchez, *Becoming Mexican American*, p. 247; Kevin Leonard, "Years of Hope, Days of Fear: The Impact of World War II on Race Relations in Los Angeles" (Ph. D. dissertation, University of California, Davis, 1992), p. 38; Polakoff, "The Development of the Texas State CIO Council," pp. 38, 44–45; Josephine Fierro de Bright, Los Angeles, California, to Gardner Jackson, AAA, Washington, D.C., April 10, 1939, Gardner Jackson Papers, Box 16, Franklin D. Roosevelt Presidential Library, Hyde Park, New York, p. 3; Louise Moreno, Los Angeles, California, to Gardner Jackson, AAA, Washington, D.C., March 13, 1939, Gardner Jackson Papers, Box 16, Franklin D. Roosevelt Presidential Library, Hyde Park, New York.

44. Peterson, "Grassroots," p. 185; Gardner Jackson, AAA, Washington, D.C., to Louise Moreno, Albuquerque, New Mexico, February 21, 1939, Gardner Jackson Papers, Box 16, Franklin D. Roosevelt Presidential Library, Hyde Park, New York; Gardner Jackson, AAA, Washington, D.C., to Dr. A. L. Campa, Acting Executive, Congress of Mexican and Spanish American Peoples, Albuquerque, New Mexico, February 21, 1939, Gardner Jackson Papers, Box 16, Franklin D. Roosevelt Presidential Library, Hyde Park, New York, pp. 1–2.

45. García, *Mexican Americans*, p. 149; Gutiérrez, *Walls and Mirrors*, p. 111; Peterson, "Grassroots," p. 185; Ruiz, *Cannery Women, Cannery Lives*, p. 55; García, *Memories of Chicano History*, p. 94; Lary May, *Recasting Culture: Culture and Politics in the Age of the Cold War* (Chicago: University of Chicago Press, 1989), pp. 133–36; Denning, *The Cultural Front*, p. 89.

46. García, *Memories of Chicano History*, pp. 110–14; García, *Mexican Americans*, p. 151; Selden C. Menefee, *Assignment: USA* (New York: Reynal & Hitchcock, Inc., 1943), p. 186.

47. Edward L. Barrett Jr., *The Tenney Committee: Legislative Investigation of Subversive Activities in California* (Ithaca, N.Y.: Cornell University Press, 1951), pp. 2, 7–9.

48. Sánchez, *Becoming Mexican American*, pp. 245–46; Gutiérrez, *Walls and Mirrors*, pp. 111–13; Camarillo, *Chicanos in California*, p. 63; Leonard, "Years of Hope, Days of Fear," pp. 48–49.

49. Peterson, "Grassroots," pp. 188–89; Leonard, "Years of Hope, Days of Fear," pp. 48–49. The Peoples' Congress's contact with the Mexican Left was monitored by the U.S. government. One federal government examiner in 1942 noted a packet of publications sent from the Universidad Obrera in Mexico City, Mexico, to Fierro, and U.S. censors extracted one pamphlet titled "Como Actuan los Nazis en México" ("How the Nazis Operate in Mexico"). Peterson, "Grassroots," p. 189.

50. Lichtenstein, *Labor's War at Home*, p. 27; Duberman, *Paul Robeson*, p. 252; García, *Mexican Americans*, p. 151; García, *Memories of Chicano History*, pp. 111, 115–16; Sánchez, *Becoming Mexican American*, p. 248.

51. President's Official File, "Union Nacional Sinarquista," July 1943, U.S. Department of Justice, 10B, Box 23, Franklin D. Roosevelt Presidential Library, Hyde Park, New York, pp. 8, 10, 21; Allan Chase, *Falange: The Axis Secret Army in the Americas* (New York: G. P. Putnam's Sons, 1943), p. 167.

52. President's Official File, "Union Nacional Sinarquista," July 1943, U.S. Department of Justice, 10B, Box 23, Franklin D. Roosevelt Presidential Library, Hyde Park, New York, pp. 15–20. With regard to their activities, the Sinarquista officials in the U.S. stated that they would "instill in their members respect for law and order . . . and constantly recommend and prescribe the most honest way of living and the loyal obedience and support of the authorities and laws of the United States." Ibid., p. 16.

53. Ibid., p. 30; Chase, *Falange*, pp. 169–70, 174; Division of Inter-American Activities, Coordinator of Inter-American Affairs, "Confidential Report of the Conference on the Spanish-Speaking Minority Program in the Southwest," held in Washington, D.C., July 12–14, 1943, 4245G, Box 4, FEPC, Franklin D. Roosevelt Presidential Library, Hyde Park, New York, pp. 3, 8.

54. Menefee, *Assignment: USA*, p. 187; President's Official File, "Union Nacional Sinarquista," July 1943, U.S. Department of Justice, 10B, Box 23, Franklin D. Roosevelt Presidential Library, Hyde Park, New York, pp. 32–33.

55. Division of Inter-American Activities, Coordinator of Inter-American Affairs, "Confidential Report of the Conference on the Spanish-Speaking Minority Program in the Southwest," held in Washington, D.C., July 12–14, 1943, 4245G, Box 4, FEPC, Franklin D. Roosevelt Presidential Library, Hyde Park, New York, pp. 3, 8; President's Official File, "Union Nacional Sinarquista," July 1943, United States Department of Justice, 10B, Box 23, Franklin D. Roosevelt Presidential Library, Hyde Park, New York, pp. 33–35.

56. President's Official File, "Union Nacional Sinarquista," July 1943, United States Department of Justice, 10B, Box 23, Franklin D. Roosevelt Presidential Library, Hyde Park, New York, pp. 36–37.

57. Ibid., pp. 36–37.

58. The Justice Department found no evidence in support of these allegations by the Communist Party regarding profascist activity in Texas. Ibid., pp. 38–39.

59. Ibid., pp. 33–35; Division of Inter-American Activities, Coordinator of Inter-American Affairs, "Confidential Report of the Conference on the Spanish-Speaking Minority Program in the Southwest," held in Washington, D.C., July 12–14, 1943, 4245G, Box 4, FEPC, Franklin D. Roosevelt Presidential Library, Hyde Park, New York, p. 8.

60. Denning, *The Cultural Front*, p. 18; Kelley, *Hammer and Hoe*, p. 23; Peterson, "Grassroots," pp. 226, 232. Carey McWilliams led the SLDC. With widespread community support, McWilliams in October 1944 would ask the district court of appeals to review the case and reverse the conviction of all the defendants "for lack of evidence." Arroyo, "Chicano Participation in Organized Labor," p. 293.

61. Peterson, "Grassroots," pp. 195–97.

62. Oberweiser, "The CIO: A Vanguard for Civil Rights in Southern California, 1940–46," p. 205. These activists from various backgrounds included Mexican American attorney Manuel Ruiz Jr., a lifelong Republican. Ibid., p. 202.

63. Arroyo, "Chicano Participation in Organized Labor," pp. 293–94; R. H. Turner and S. J. Surace, "Zoot-Suiters and Mexicans: Symbols in Crowd Behavior," *American Journal of Sociology* 62 (July 1962), p. 20.

64. Arroyo, "Chicano Participation in Organized Labor," p. 294; Oberweiser, "The CIO: A Vanguard for Civil Rights in Southern California, 1940–46," p. 206; Ginger and Christiano, eds., *The Cold War against Labor*, vol. 1, pp. 434–35.

65. Denning, *The Cultural Front*, p. 403; Zieger, *The CIO, 1935–1955*, p. 253; President's Official File, "Union Nacional Sinarquista," July 1943, U.S. Department of Justice, 10B, Box 23, Franklin D. Roosevelt Presidential Library, Hyde Park, New York, pp. 32–33, 40–41.

66. California Senate, *Report, Joint Fact-Finding Committee on Un-American Activities in California* (Sacramento, 1943), p. 207.

67. Interestingly, an editorial in the *Los Angeles Times* on December 26, 1942, stated, "These Sinarchists . . . in Mexico oppose the Communists and communism and hence would naturally be considered by Pinkos as Fascists, for to a Communist every non-Communist is a Fascist." President's Official File, "Union Nacional Sinarquista," July 1943, U.S. Department of Justice, 10B, Box 23, Franklin D. Roosevelt Presidential Library, Hyde Park, New York, pp. 41–42. During the Los Angeles grand jury hearings on the Sleepy Lagoon murders, Oscar Fuss would testify that "a subversive group known as the Sinarquistas . . . exploit all the legitimate grievances of the Mexican people for their particular purposes. . . . The cause[s] for unrest among Hispanic youth are not found in the unions but in the slums of Jim-town and Happy Valley where Latinos receive less relief than other Americans on the theory that Mexican Americans are accustomed to a lower standard of living." Oberweiser, "The CIO: A Vanguard for Civil Rights in Southern California, 1940–46," p. 205.

68. Peterson, "Grassroots," pp. 210–12.

69. Ibid., p. 211.

70. Ibid., pp. 96, 191; Chase, *Falange*, pp. 162, 174–75.

71. Kenneth O'Reilly, "The Roosevelt Administration and Black America: Federal Surveillance Policy and Civil Rights during the World War II Years," *Phylon* 48, no. 1 (1987), p. 20; J. Edgar Hoover Report to the FBI, 1942, Division of Inter-American Activities, Coordinator of Inter-American Affairs, "Confidential Report of the Conference on the Spanish-Speaking Minority Program in the Southwest," held in Washington, D.C., July 12–14, 1943, 4245G, Box 4, FEPC, Franklin D. Roosevelt Presidential Library, Hyde Park, New York, pp. 23–25.

72. J. Edgar Hoover Report to the FBI, 1942, Division of Inter-American Activities, Coordinator of Inter-American Affairs, "Confidential Report of the Conference on the Spanish-Speaking Minority Program in the Southwest," held in Washington, D.C., July 12–14, 1943, 4245G, Box 4, FEPC, Franklin D. Roosevelt Presidential Library, Hyde Park, New York, pp. 21–28, 30. Since August 30, 1942, Sinarquista members in the United States had contributed less than $5,000 to the headquarters in Mexico City. The U.S. Justice Department determined that La Union Nacional Sinarquista was not a threat to America's internal security. Ibid., p. 26.

73. Oberweiser, "The CIO: A Vanguard for Civil Rights in Southern California, 1940–46," p. 205; Peterson, "Grassroots," pp. 96, 191; Chase, *Falange*, p. 163; García, *Memories of Chicano History*, p. 116; Gutiérrez, *Walls and Mirrors*, p. 114; Camarillo, *Chicanos in California*, p. 64.

74. Oberweiser, "The CIO: A Vanguard for Civil Rights in Southern California, 1940–46," pp. 206–7.

75. Arroyo, "Chicano Participation in Organized Labor," p. 292; Ryon, "Ambiguous Legacy," pp. 22–23; Anderson, *The Development of Leadership and Organization Building in the Black Community of Los Angeles*, pp. 88–93. In addition, the ADC and UAW Local 887, with support from the black community, won reinstatement of a black worker at North American Aircraft with full seniority and back pay. The black worker had been fired for talking to a white woman worker. Oberweiser, "The CIO: A Vanguard for Civil Rights in Southern California, 1940–46," p. 204.

76. Kryder, *Divided Arsenal*, p. 47; Lichtenstein, *Labor's War at Home*, p. 45; Arroyo, "Chicano Participation in Organized Labor," pp. 292–93; Oberweiser, "The CIO: A Vanguard for Civil Rights in Southern California, 1940–46," pp. 204–5; Anderson, *The Development of Leadership and Organization Building in the Black Community of Los Angeles*, pp. 92–93. In August, ADC secretary Cayton recommended changing this committee's name to the Minorities Committee (MC) to better reflect its activities. Arroyo, "Chicano Participation in Organized Labor," p. 292.

77. Anderson, *The Development of Leadership and Organization Building in the Black Community of Los Angeles*, pp. 94–95.

78. "News Survey of the Month," *Inter-American* 2, no. 8 (August 1943), p. 6.

79. O' Reilly, "The Roosevelt Administration and Black America," pp. 19–20.

80. Oberweiser, "The CIO: A Vanguard for Civil Rights in Southern California, 1940–46," p. 205. The *Labor Herald* noted, "The twin circumstance of greater concentration on the Negro problem and the strongly anti-union influence of the fascist Sinarquist movement . . . dangerously strong in the Mexican community resulted in the greater success of the CIO in the Black community." Ibid.

81. Ryon, "An Ambiguous Legacy," p. 30.

CHAPTER FIVE
THE LIE OF "AMERICA'S GREATEST GENERATION": MEXICAN AMERICANS FIGHT AGAINST PREJUDICE, INTOLERANCE, AND HATRED DURING WORLD WAR II

1. Gerald Nash, "Spanish-Speaking Americans in Wartime," in *American West Transformed* (Bloomington: Indiana University Press, 1985), p. 107; "On the Home Front," *Inter-American* 3, no. 4 (April 1944), p. 40; "Fair Employment Practices Act Hearings," in *Are We Good Neighbors?* comp. Alonso S. Perales (1948; reprint, New York: Arno Press, 1974), p. 93; W. Rex Crawford, "The Latin American in the United States," *Annals of the American Academy of Political and Social Science* 223 (September 1942), pp. 123, 127; Carey McWilliams, "The Forgotten Mexican," *Common Ground* 3 (Spring 1943), p. 65; Richard Polenberg, *War and Society: The United States, 1941–1945* (New York: J. B. Lippon-

cott Company, 1972), p. 129; Harvard Sitkoff, "Racial Militancy and Interracial Violence in the Second World War," *Journal of American History* 58, no. 3 (December 1971), p. 665; Jones, *The Dispossessed*, p. 178; Robin Fitzgerald Scott, "Wartime Labor Problems and Mexican-Americans in the War," in *The Mexican Americans: An Awakening Minority*, ed. Manuel P. Servín, 2nd ed. (Beverly Hills, Calif.: Glencoe Press, 1974), pp. 134, 136; Eileen Boris, " 'You Wouldn't Want One of 'Em Dancing with Your Wife': Racialized Bodies on the Job in World War II," *American Quarterly* 50, no. 1 (1998), pp. 79–80.

2. Polenberg, *War and Society*, pp. 99–100, 113; Kryder, *Divided Arsenal*, pp. 208, 216, 256–57; Zieger, *The CIO, 1935–1955*, p. 149; Valdés, *Barrios Norteños*, p. 134; Sitkoff, "Racial Militancy and Interracial Violence in the Second World War," p. 670; James N. Gregory, *American Exodus: The Dust Bowl Migration and Okie Culture in California* (New York: Oxford University Press, 1989), pp. 168–69; Honey, *Southern Labor and Black Civil Rights*, p. 202; "Committee of 100," *No Larger Ambition: The Story of the "Committee of 100"* (New York: "Committee of 100," 1946), pp. 1–2.

3. Division of Inter-American Activities, Coordinator of Inter-American Affairs, "Confidential Report of the Conference on the Spanish-Speaking Minority Program in the Southwest," held in Washington, D.C., July 12–14, 1943, 4245G, Box 4, FEPC, Franklin D. Roosevelt Presidential Library, Hyde Park, New York, p. 32.

4. The CIO, the AFL, the War Manpower Commission, the Coordinator of Inter-American Affairs, the Office of War Information, the Labor Department, the Farm Security Administration, the Fair Employment Practices Committee, the Federal Council of Churches, the U.S. Army, the Board of Economic Warfare, and the Confederación Regional Obrera Mexicana, as well as various Mexican American social organizations, all voiced concern. "Memorandum on a Proposal to Coordinate Activities and Programs Relating to Spanish-Speaking Minorities in the United States," November 20, 1942, Box 47, Gardner Jackson Papers, Franklin D. Roosevelt Presidential Library, Hyde Park, New York, pp. 1–2; Jonathan Daniels, Administrative Assistant to the President, Washington, D.C., to Nelson A. Rockefeller, Coordinator of Inter-American Affairs, Washington, D.C., July 29, 1943, 4245G, Box 6, FEPC, Franklin D. Roosevelt Presidential Library, Hyde Park, New York; Nelson A. Rockefeller, Coordinator of Inter-American Affairs, Washington, D.C., to Jonathan Daniels, Administrative Assistant to the President, Washington, D.C., August 3, 1943, 4245G, Box 6, FEPC, Franklin D. Roosevelt Presidential Library, Hyde Park, New York.

5. Lloyd H. Fisher, *The Problem of Violence: Observations on Race Conflict in Los Angeles* (New York: American Council on Race Relations, 1945), p. 19.

6. Merl E. Reed, "The FEPC and the Federal Agencies in the South," *Journal of Negro History* 65, no. 1 (Winter 1980), p. 54.

7. McWilliams, "The Forgotten Mexican," p. 69; Malcolm Ross, *All Manner of Men* (New York: Greenwood Press, 1948), p. 269; Honey, *Southern Black Labor and Civil Rights*, pp. 187, 194; "Fair Employment Practices Act Hearings," p. 95; "Statement of Dr. Carlos E. Castañeda, Regional Director, Fair Employment Practice Committee, Region 10, San Antonio, Texas," in *Are We Good Neighbors?* comp. Alonso S. Perales (1948; reprint, New York: Arno Press, 1974),

p. 102; Herschal T. Manuel, "Comments on the Education of Children of Spanish-Speaking Ancestry in Texas," in Coordinator of Inter-American Affairs, Committee Reports of the Conference on Educational Problems in the Southwest—With Special Reference to the Educational Problems in Spanish-Speaking Communities, held at Santa Fe, New Mexico, August 19–24, 1943, p. 1; Division of Inter-American Activities, Coordinator of Inter-American Affairs, "Confidential Report of the Conference on the Spanish-Speaking Minority Program in the Southwest," held in Washington, D.C., July 12–14, 1943, 4245G, Box 4, FEPC, Franklin D. Roosevelt Presidential Library, Hyde Park, New York, p. 17; Crawford, "The Latin American in the United States," p. 125; "A Proposal Concerning the Spanish Speaking People in the United States," Submitted by the Institute of Ethnic Affairs, Washington, D.C., n.d., p. 20, Box 16, R.E. Smith, Office of Civil Defense, George I Sánchez Papers, NLBLAC, University of Texas, Austin (hereafter referred to as "A Proposal Concerning the Spanish Speaking People in the United States").

8. Kryder, *Divided Arsenal*, p. 215; Honey, *Southern Black Labor and Civil Rights*, p. 192; *Farm Labor Program in Texas, 1943–1947* (College Station: Texas A&M College Extension Service, 1947), Dan Kilgore Collection, Special Collections and Archives, Texas A&M University, Corpus Christi, Texas, p. 3 (hereafter referred to as *Farm Labor Program in Texas*).

9. David M. Kennedy, *Freedom from Fear: The American People in Depression and War, 1929–1945* (New York: Oxford University Press, 1999), pp. 633–34; Paul T. Murray, "Blacks and the Draft: A History of Institutional Racism," *Journal of Black Studies* 2, no. 1 (September 1971), p. 61; Pycior, *LBJ and Mexican Americans*, p. 53. On August 21, 1942, the Zapata County Selective Service Board, made up of three Anglo ranchers and a businessman, intentionally classified Tejano County Judge Manuel B. Bravo class III-A as a way to remove him from office. J. Gilberto Quezada, *Border Boss: Manuel B. Bravo and Zapata County* (College Station: Texas A&M Press, 1999), p. 80.

10. "No Mexicans Allowed," *Inter-American* 2, no. 9 (September 1943), p. 8; Otey M. Scruggs, "Texas and the Bracero Program, 1942–1947," *Pacific Historical Review*, 32, no. 3 (August 1963), p. 254; *Farm Labor Program in Texas*, pp. 4, 8; Pauline R. Kibbe, *Latin Americans in Texas* (Albuquerque: University of New Mexico Press, 1946), pp. 171–73; Kryder, *Divided Arsenal*, pp. 209–10; Jones, *The Dispossessed*, pp. 175, 177; Kennedy, *Freedom from Fear*, p. 777.

11. Kryder, *Divided Arsenal*, pp. 210, 216; *Farm Labor Program in Texas*, pp. 5, 8–9; Kibbe, *Latin Americans in Texas*, pp. 173–74, 182–84; Leocadio Durán, Rosenberg, Texas, to Governor Coke Stevenson, Austin, Texas, October 16, 1943, Box 67, American Civil Liberties Union, George I. Sánchez Papers, Nettie Lee Benson Latin American Collection (hereafter referred to as NLBLAC), University of Texas, Austin.

12. Scruggs, "Texas and the Bracero Program, 1942–1947," p. 255; Pycior, *LBJ and Mexican Americans*, p. 53; Murray, "Blacks and the Draft," p. 66; Division of Inter-American Activities, Coordinator of Inter-American Affairs, "Confidential Report of the Conference on the Spanish-Speaking Minority Program in the Southwest," held in Washington, D.C., July 12–14, 1943, 4245G, Box 4, FEPC, Franklin D. Roosevelt Presidential Library, Hyde Park, New York, pp. 14–16; George I. Sánchez, University of Texas, Austin, to Elmore R. Torn, Regional Mobilization

Officer, Eighth Civil Defense Region, Office of Civil Defense, Dallas, Texas, January 1, 1942, Box 16, Elmore R. Torn, Office of Civil Defense, George I. Sánchez Papers, NLBLAC, University of Texas, Austin. A similar pattern of discriminatory practices by local draft boards prevailed against Mexican Americans in the Midwest. Valdés, *Barrios Norteños*, p. 131.

13. Pecos County Water Improvement District No. 1 to the Public, July 7, 1943, County 4245G, Box 4, FEPC, Franklin D. Roosevelt Presidential Library, Hyde Park, New York, pp. 1–2; Luis L. Ruplán, Consul of Mexico, Mexico City, Mexico, to Dr. George I. Sánchez, University of Texas, Austin, Texas, April 23, 1943, 4245G, Box 3, FEPC, Franklin D. Roosevelt Presidential Library, Hyde Park, New York, p. 10; M. R. González, Fort Stockton, Texas, to M. C. González, Executive Secretary, LULAC, San Antonio, Texas, October 15, 1943, Box 67, American Civil Liberties Union, George I. Sánchez Papers, NLBLAC, University of Texas, Austin; "A Proposal Concerning the Spanish Speaking People in the United States," p. 25.

14. Pecos County Water Improvement District No. 1 to the Public, July 7, 1943, County 4245G, Box 4, FEPC, Franklin D. Roosevelt Presidential Library, Hyde Park, New York, pp. 1–2; Luis L. Ruplán, Consul of Mexico, Mexico City, Mexico, to Dr. George I. Sánchez, University of Texas, Austin, Texas, April 23, 1943, 4245G, Box 3, FEPC, Franklin D. Roosevelt Presidential Library, Hyde Park, New York, pp. 11–12, 14; M. C. González, Executive Secretary, LULAC, San Antonio, Texas, to George I. Sánchez, University of Texas, Austin, April 8, 1943, Box 68, Legal Cases (Texas Civil Rights Fund), George I. Sánchez Papers, NLBLAC, University of Texas, Austin; George I. Sánchez, University of Texas, Austin, to Mr. Ross, USO, Del Rio, Texas, May 31, 1943, Box 68, Legal Cases, Re: Discrimination in Employment, George I. Sánchez Papers, NLBLAC, University of Texas, Austin; Sitkoff, "Racial Militancy and Interracial Violence in the Second World War," p. 670; Kryder, *Divided Arsenal*, p. 141; Scott, "Wartime Labor Problems and Mexican-Americans in the War," p. 137.

15. Kennedy, *Freedom from Fear*, p. 770; Ernest G. Trimble to Lawrence W. Cramer, n.d., 4245G, Box 3, FEPC, Franklin D. Roosevelt Presidential Library, Hyde Park, New York, pp. 1–5; Jones, *The Dispossessed*, p. 177; Polakoff, "The Development of the Texas State CIO Council," pp. 161, 386–87; Zamora, "The Failed Promise of Wartime Opportunity for Mexicans in the Texas Oil Industry," p. 337.

16. Texas State Employment Service, 1940; Selden C. Menefee, *Mexican Migratory Workers of South Texas: Crystal City, 1938* (Washington, D.C.: Government Printing Office, 1943), p. 53; Montejano, *Anglos and Mexicans in the Making of Texas*, p. 219; Valdés, *Barrios Norteños*, pp. 129–31; Kryder, *Divided Arsenal*, pp. 107, 217; Valdés, *Al Norte*, p. 91; Vargas, *Proletarians of the North*, p. 208; Polakoff, "The Development of the Texas State CIO Council," pp. 386–87.

17. Valdés, *Barrios Norteños*, pp. 136–37, 140–42, 149; Kryder, *Divided Arsenal*, pp. 102–3.

18. Richard A. Santillán, "Rosita the Riveter: Midwest Mexican American Women during World War II," *Perspectives in Mexican American Studies* 2 (1989), p. 115. Along with other Mexican American women, these midwestern

Spanish-speaking women war workers also aided the war effort by organizing war bond drives, working with the local Red Cross, collecting scrap metal, and forming social clubs modeled after the USO. Ibid.

19. Ibid., p. 116; Jacqueline Jones, *Labor of Love, Labor of Sorrow: Black Women, Work and the Family, from Slavery to the Present* (New York: Vintage Books, 1986), p. 238.

20. Zieger, *The CIO, 1935–1955*, p. 149; Lichtenstein, *Labor's War at Home*, p. 74; Ruiz, *Cannery Women, Cannery Lives*, pp. 81–82; Polakoff, "The Development of the Texas State CIO Council," p. 115.

21. "Fair Employment Practices Act Hearings," p. 95; Deutsch, *No Separate Refuge*, p. 205; McWilliams, "The Forgotten Mexican," pp. 71–73, 75; "Spanish-Americans in the Southwest and the War Effort," Special Services Division, Bureau of Intelligence, Office of War Information, 4245G, Box 7, FEPC, Franklin D. Roosevelt Presidential Library, Hyde Park, New York, p. 7; R. A. Gerken, Archbishop of Santa Fe, Santa Fe, New Mexico, to Senator Dennis Chávez, Washington, D.C., March 13, 1942, Franklin D. Roosevelt Presidential Library, Hyde Park, New York, p. 1; Senator Dennis Chávez, Washington, D.C., to R. A. Gerken, Archbishop of Santa Fe, Santa Fe, New Mexico, March 17, 1942, Franklin D. Roosevelt Presidential Library, Hyde Park, New York, p. 2.

22. Raúl Morín, *Among the Valiant: Mexican Americans in World War II and Korea* (Los Angeles: Borden Publishing Company, 1963), p. 23; "Spanish-Americans in the Southwest and the War Effort," Special Services Division, Bureau of Intelligence, Office of War Information, 4245G, Box 7, FEPC, Franklin D. Roosevelt Presidential Library, Hyde Park, New York, p. 9; Senator Dennis Chávez, Washington, D.C., to R. A. Gerken, Archbishop of Santa Fe, Santa Fe, New Mexico, March 17, 1942, Franklin D. Roosevelt Presidential Library, Hyde Park, New York, p. 1; Barron B. Beshoar, "Report from the Mountain States," *Common Ground* 4 (Spring 1944), p. 25. A large number of Mexican Americans from New Mexico volunteered for service in the armed forces to help their besieged National Guard comrades in the Philippines. Charles P. Loomis, "Wartime Migration from the Rural Spanish Speaking Villages of New Mexico," *Rural Sociology* 7 (December 1942), p. 390 n. 10; McWilliams, "The Forgotten Mexican," p. 78.

23. Loomis, "Wartime Migration from New Mexico," pp. 386–87; "Spanish-Americans in the Southwest and the War Effort," Special Services Division, Bureau of Intelligence, Office of War Information, 4245G, Box 7, FEPC, Franklin D. Roosevelt Presidential Library, Hyde Park, New York, p. 6.

24. Loomis, "Wartime Migration from New Mexico," pp. 388–90.

25. Pycior, *LBJ and Mexican Americans*, p. 29; Henry A. Gonzáles, "Vocational Trade and Industrial Education in New Mexico," in Coordinator of Inter-American Affairs, Committee Reports of the Conference on Educational Problems in the Southwest—With Special Reference to the Educational Problems in Spanish-Speaking Communities, held in Santa Fe, New Mexico, August 19–24, 1943, 4512, Coordinator of Inter-American Affairs, Franklin D. Roosevelt Presidential Library, Hyde Park, New York, pp. 11–13; George I. Sánchez, University of Texas, Austin, to Elmer R. Torn, Regional Mobilization Officer, Eighth Civil Defense Region, Office of Civil Defense, Dallas, Texas, February 2, 1942, and March 31,

1943, Box 16, Elmore R. Torn, Office on Civil Defense, George I. Sánchez Papers, NLBLAC, University of Texas, Austin.

26. Kryder, *Divided Arsenal*, p. 105; Nina Otero Warren, "Adult Education Activities of Works Progress Administration," in Office of the Coordinator of Inter-American Affairs, "Conference on the Problems of Education Among Spanish-Speaking Populations of Our Southwest," held in Santa Fe, New Mexico, August 19–24, 1943, 4512, Coordinator of Inter-American Affairs, Franklin D. Roosevelt Presidential Library, Hyde Park, New York, pp. 16–17; Max Salazar, "Development of Opportunities for Spanish American Youth through NYA," in Office of the Coordinator of Inter-American Affairs, "Conference on the Problems of Education among Spanish Speaking Populations of Our Southwest," held in Santa Fe, New Mexico, August 19–24, 1943, 4512, Coordinator of Inter-American Affairs, Franklin D. Roosevelt Presidential Library, Hyde Park, New York, pp. 18–19.

27. Nina Otero Warren, "Adult Education Activities of Works Progress Administration," in Office of the Coordinator of Inter-American Affairs, "Conference on the Problems of Education among Spanish-Speaking Populations of Our Southwest," held in Santa Fe, New Mexico, August 19–24, 1943, 4512, Coordinator of Inter-American Affairs, Franklin D. Roosevelt Presidential Library, Hyde Park, New York, pp. 16–17; Quincy Guy Burris, "Institute of the Air," in Office of the Coordinator of Inter-American Affairs, "Conference on the Problems of Education among Spanish-Speaking Populations of Our Southwest," held in Santa Fe, New Mexico, August 19–24, 1943, 4512, Coordinator of Inter-American Affairs, Franklin D. Roosevelt Presidential Library, Hyde Park, New York, pp. 6–7; J. T. Reid, "Taos County Project," in Office of the Coordinator of Inter-American Affairs, "Conference on the Problems of Education among Spanish-Speaking Populations of Our Southwest," held in Santa Fe, New Mexico, August 19–24, 1943, 4512, Coordinator of Inter-American Affairs, Franklin D. Roosevelt Presidential Library, Hyde Park, New York, pp. 10–11, 24; George I. Sánchez, University of Texas, Austin, to Elmer R. Torn, Regional Mobilization Officer, Eighth Civil Defense Region, Office of Civil Defense, Dallas, Texas, February 2, 1942, and May 5, 1943, Box 16, Elmore R. Torn, Office of Civil Defense, George I. Sánchez Papers, NLBLAC, University of Texas, Austin.

28. Wilhelmina Hill, "Education of Spanish-Speaking Americans in Colorado and Wyoming," in Office of the Coordinator of Inter-American Affairs, "Conference on the Problems of Education among Spanish-Speaking Populations of Our Southwest," held in Santa Fe, New Mexico, August 19–24, 1943, 4512, Coordinator of Inter-American Affairs, Franklin D. Roosevelt Presidential Library, Hyde Park, New York, p. 2.

29. Ibid., pp. 2–5, 7–9; Beshoar, "Report from the Mountain States," p. 24.

30. Nash, "Spanish-Speaking Americans in Wartime," p. 109; Beshoar, "Report from the Mountain States," p. 25; "A Proposal Concerning the Spanish Speaking People in the United States," pp. 21, 25.

31. Beshoar, "Report from the Mountain States," pp. 25–27.

32. Ibid, p. 27; Polenberg, *War and Society*, p. 119; John Morton Blum, *V Was for Victory* (New York: Harcourt Brace Jovanovich, 1976), p. 212; Nelson A. Rockefeller, Coordinator of Inter-American Affairs, Washington, D.C., to M. H. McIntyre, Secretary to the President, The White House, November 25, 1943,

4512, Coordinator of Inter-American Affairs, July–December 1943, Franklin D. Roosevelt Presidential Library, Hyde Park, New York; Tom C. Clark, Assistant Attorney General, U.S. Department of Justice, Washington, D.C., to Thomas J. Morrissey, U.S. Attorney, Denver, Colorado, November 12, 1943, 4512, Coordinator of Inter-American Affairs, July–December 1943, Franklin D. Roosevelt Presidential Library, Hyde Park, New York, p. 1.

33. Nelson A. Rockefeller, Coordinator of Inter-American Affairs, Washington, D.C., to M. H. McIntyre, Secretary to the President, The White House, November 25, 1943, 4512, Coordinator of Inter-American Affairs, July–December 1943, Franklin D. Roosevelt Presidential Library, Hyde Park, New York; Nash, "Spanish-Speaking Americans in Wartime," p. 110; Polenberg, *War and Society*, p. 115; Blum, *V Was for Victory*, p. 213; Daniel, *Chicano Workers and the Politics of Fairness*, pp. 107–9; Alexa B. Henderson, "FEPC and the Southern Railway Case: An Investigation into the Discriminatory Practices of Railroads during World War II," *Journal of Negro History* 61, no. 2 (April 1976), p. 182; Christine Marín, "La Asociacion Hispano-Americana de Madres y Esposas: Tucson's Mexican American Women in World War II," in *Renato Rosaldo Lecture Series*, vol. 1 (1983–84), ed. Ignacio M. García, et al. (Tucson: University of Arizona, 1985), pp. 7, 11; "Fair Employment Practices Act Hearings," p. 95; "Statement of Dr. Carlos E. Castañeda," p. 99; J. Edgar Hoover, Director, Federal Bureau of Investigation (hereafter referred to as FBI), Washington, D.C., to Jonathan Daniels, Administrative Assistant to the President, Washington, D.C., March 29, 1944, 4245G, Box 6, FEPC, Franklin D. Roosevelt Presidential Library, Hyde Park, New York, pp. 1–2; Affidavit of Jesús Contreras, October 30, 1941, Box 68, Legal Cases, Re: Discrimination in Employment, George I. Sánchez Papers, NLBLAC, University of Texas, Austin.

34. Daniel, *Chicano Workers and the Politics of Fairness*, pp. 69–70; Ross, *All Manner of Men*, p. 265; J. Edgar Hoover, Director, FBI, Washington, D.C., to Jonathan Daniels, Administrative Assistant to the President, Washington, D.C., March 29, 1944, 4245G, Box 6, FEPC, Franklin D. Roosevelt Presidential Library, Hyde Park, New York, pp. 2–6.

35. Daniel, *Chicano Workers and the Politics of Fairness*, pp. 63, 68, 96, 164; Jonathan D. Rosenbaum, *Copper Crucible: How the Arizona Miners' Strike of 1983 Recast Labor-Management Relations in America* (New York: ILR Press, 1988), p. 31; J. Edgar Hoover, Director, FBI, Washington, D.C., to Jonathan Daniels, Administrative Assistant to the President, Washington, D.C., March 29, 1944, 4245G, Box 6, FEPC, Franklin D. Roosevelt Presidential Library, Hyde Park, New York, pp. 6–8, 10.

36. E. G. Trimble, Field Investigator, Fair Employment Practices Commission, to Lawrence W. Cramer, Executive Secretary, Committee on Fair Employment Practice, n.d., 4245G, Box 3, FEPC, Franklin D. Roosevelt Presidential Library, Hyde Park, New York, pp. 3–4; Zieger, *The CIO, 1935–1955*, p. 171.

37. Daniel, *Chicano Workers and the Politics of Fairness*, p. 61. The Miami Copper Company and the Inspiration Copper Company held labor board elections because they did not have contracts with unions. E. G. Trimble, Field Investigator, Fair Employment Practices Commission, to Lawrence W. Cramer, Executive Secretary, Committee on Fair Employment Practices, n.d., 4245G, Box 3, FEPC,

Franklin D. Roosevelt Presidential Library, Hyde Park, New York, p. 4; "Statement of Dr. Carlos E. Castañeda," p. 99.

38. Daniel, *Chicano Workers and the Politics of Fairness*, p. 63; "Fair Employment Practices Act Hearings," p. 93; "Statement of Dr. Carlos E. Castañeda," p. 99; Mark F. Ethridge, Chairman, Committee on Fair Employment Practices, Social Security Building, Washington, D.C., to President Franklin D. Roosevelt, The White House, December 12, 1941, 4245G, Box 3, FEPC, Franklin D. Roosevelt Presidential Library, Hyde Park, New York. On January 23, 1942, President Roosevelt authorized the FEPC to investigate in a more restrictive manner those cases in which noncitizens alleged that they had been discriminated against because of their national origin. See President Franklin D. Roosevelt, The White House, to Mark F. Ethridge, Chairman, Committee on Fair Employment Practices, Social Security Building, Washington, D.C., January 3, 1942, 4245G, Box 3, FEPC, Franklin D. Roosevelt Presidential Library, Hyde Park, New York. The FEPC field representatives received numerous reports of discrimination from Spanish-speaking miners employed by the Phelps Dodge Corporation at mines and smelters around Douglas, Bisbee, and Clifton, Arizona, and at El Paso; the Miami Copper Company in Miami, Arizona; the Inspiration Consolidated Copper Company (owned by Anaconda, the nation's second-largest copper producer); the International Smelter & Refining Company in Inspiration, Arizona; the Nevada Consolidated Copper Company (owned by the Kennecott Company, the biggest American copper producer); mines in Ray, Arizona, and Hurley, New Mexico; the United States Potash Company in Carlsbad, New Mexico; and the McKee Construction Company of El Paso. E. G. Trimble, Field Investigator, Fair Employment Practices Commission, to Lawrence W. Cramer, Executive Secretary, Committee on Fair Employment Practices, n.d., 4245G, Box 3, FEPC, Franklin D. Roosevelt Presidential Library, Hyde Park, New York, p. 2.

39. E. G. Trimble, Field Investigator, Fair Employment Practices Commission, to Lawrence W. Cramer, Executive Secretary, Committee on Fair Employment Practices, n.d., 4245G, Box 3, FEPC, Franklin D. Roosevelt Presidential Library, Hyde Park, New York, p. 3; Affidavit of Alberto Salazar, Ajo, Arizona, May 12, 1942, 4245G, Box 3, FEPC, Franklin D. Roosevelt Presidential Library, Hyde Park, New York; Daniel, *Chicano Workers and the Politics of Fairness*, pp. 72, 132–33.

40. Daniel, *Chicano Workers and the Politics of Fairness*, p. 130; E. G. Trimble, Field Investigator, Fair Employment Practices Commission, to Lawrence W. Cramer, Executive Secretary, Committee on Fair Employment Practices, n.d., 4245G, Box 3, FEPC, Franklin D. Roosevelt Presidential Library, Hyde Park, New York, pp. 4–5.

41. E. G. Trimble, Field Investigator, Fair Employment Practices Commission, to Lawrence W. Cramer, Executive Secretary, Committee on Fair Employment Practices, n.d., 4245G, Box 3, FEPC, Franklin D. Roosevelt Presidential Library, Hyde Park, New York, p. 5.

42. Nash, "Spanish-Speaking Americans in Wartime," pp. 107–8; "Fair Employment Practices Act Hearings," p. 94; Division of Inter-American Activities, Coordinator of Inter-American Affairs, "Confidential Report of the Conference on the Spanish-Speaking Minority Program in the Southwest," held in Washing-

ton, D.C., July 12–14, 1943, 4245G, Box 4, FEPC, Franklin D. Roosevelt Presidential Library, Hyde Park, New York, p. 12.

43. Division of Inter-American Activities, Coordinator of Inter-American Affairs, "Confidential Report of the Conference on the Spanish-Speaking Minority Program in the Southwest," held in Washington, D.C., July 12–14, 1943, 4245G, Box 4, FEPC, Franklin D. Roosevelt Presidential Library, Hyde Park, New York, pp. 10–12; "On the Home Front," p. 40; Marco Almazán, "The Mexicans Keep 'Em Rolling," *Inter-American* 4, no. 10 (October 1945), p. 36; González, *Labor and Community*, p. 56; Leonard, "Years of Hope, Days of Fear," p. 74; Zieger, *The CIO, 1935–1955*, p. 149; Kryder, *Divided Arsenal*, pp. 103, 106, 109; Los Angeles Urban League, *This Is the Problem: Report of the Los Angeles Urban League for the Year 1944–45* (Los Angeles: Los Angeles Urban League, 1945), p. 2.

44. Memorandum from Lewis W. Jones and Clarence Glick to Alan Cranston, June 16, 1943, 4245G, Box 7, FEPC, Franklin D. Roosevelt Presidential Library, Hyde Park, New York, pp. 1–3; Nash, "Spanish-Speaking Americans in Wartime," pp. 108–9; Leonard, "Years of Hope, Days of Fear," pp. 21, 25, 74–75. Approximately 64,262 Mexicans lived in the Los Angeles metropolitan district, and 36,840 Mexicans lived in the city of Los Angeles. Division of Inter-American Activities, Coordinator of Inter-American Affairs, "Confidential Report of the Conference on the Spanish-Speaking Minority Program in the Southwest," held in Washington, D.C., July 12–14, 1943, 4245G, Box 4, FEPC, Franklin D. Roosevelt Presidential Library, Hyde Park, New York, p. 12.

45. Zieger, *The CIO, 1935–1955*, p. 158; Oberweiser, "The CIO: A Vanguard for Civil Rights in Southern California, 1940–46," p. 207; Anderson, *The Development of Leadership and Organization Building in the Black Community of Los Angeles*, p. 97.

46. Folsom, *Impatient Armies of the Poor*, pp. 266–71; Oberweiser, "The CIO: Vanguard for Civil Rights in Southern California, 1940–46," p. 207; Arroyo, "Chicano Participation in Organized Labor," p. 294; "A Proposal Concerning the Spanish Speaking People in the United States," p. 18.

47. Leonard, "Years of Hope, Days of Fear," pp. 47, 179, 120, 301; Oberweiser, "The CIO: A Vanguard for Civil Rights in Southern California 1940–46," pp. 208–9; Division of Inter-American Activities, Coordinator of Inter-American Affairs, "Confidential Report of the Conference on the Spanish-Speaking Minority Program in the Southwest," held in Washington, D.C., July 12–14, 1943, 4245G, Box 4, FEPC, Franklin D. Roosevelt Presidential Library, Hyde Park, New York, p. 12.

48. "Across the Tracks," *Time*, September 6, 1943, p. 25; Oberweiser, "The CIO: A Vanguard for Civil Rights in Southern California, 1940–46," pp. 208–9.

49. Fisher, "The Problem of Violence," p. 13.

50. McWilliams, "The Forgotten Mexican," p. 70.

51. Kryder, *Divided Arsenal*, p. 229; Polenberg, *War and Society*, pp. 129–130; Blum, *V Was for Victory*, p. 205; Sitkoff, "Racial Militancy and Interracial Violence in the Second World War," p. 671; "News Survey of the Month," *Inter-American* 2, no. 8 (August 1943), pp. 5–6; Vicki L. Ruiz, *From Out of the Shadows: Mexican Women in Twentieth-Century America* (New York: Oxford University Press, 1998), p. 84; "Mexican Youth Gangs," FBI Survey of Racial Conditions

in the United States, Section 2—Pacific Coast Section, September 24, 1943, President's Official File, 10B, Box 12, Franklin D. Roosevelt Presidential Library, Hyde Park, New York, p. 382.

52. Blum, *V Was for Victory*, pp. 205–6; "News Survey of the Month," p. 5; Ruiz, *From Out of the Shadows*, p. 83; "Mexican Youth Gangs," FBI Survey of Racial Conditions in the United States, Section 2—Pacific Coast Section, September 24, 1943, President's Official File, 10B, Box 12, Franklin D. Roosevelt Presidential Library, Hyde Park, New York, pp. 382–87; Leonard, "Years of Hope, Days of Fear," pp. 135–36. Some of the committee members belonged to the Citizens' Committee for the Defense of Mexican American Youth. Leonard, "Years of Hope, Days of Fear," p. 161.

53. Blum, *V Was for Victory*, p. 206; Oberweiser, "The CIO: A Vanguard for Civil Rights in California, 1940–46," pp. 208–9; Fisher, "The Problem of Violence," p. 14.

54. Division of Inter-American Activities, Coordinator of Inter-American Affairs, "Confidential Report of the Conference on the Spanish-Speaking Minority Program in the Southwest," held in Washington, D.C., July 12–14, 1943, 4245G, Box 4, FEPC, Franklin D. Roosevelt Presidential Library, Hyde Park, New York, pp. 34–37; "Mexican Youth Gangs," FBI Survey of Racial Conditions in the United States, Section 2—Pacific Coast Section, September 24, 1943, President's Official File, 10B, Box 12, Franklin D. Roosevelt Presidential Library, Hyde Park, New York, pp. 380–81.

55. "Mexican Youth Gangs," FBI Survey of Racial Conditions in the United States, Section 2—Pacific Coast Section, September 24, 1943, President's Official File, 10B, Box 12, Franklin D. Roosevelt Presidential Library, Hyde Park, New York, pp. 383–84; Report of the American Consul General on the Tour of Los Angeles, California, by Mexican Consul Gerald A. Mokma, August 3, 1943, 4245G, Box 7, FEPC, Franklin D. Roosevelt Presidential Library, Hyde Park, New York, pp. 1–2; Murray, "Blacks and the Draft," p. 63; Camarillo, *Chicanos in California*, p. 72. About 48 percent of those in the army's 12-week special training were of Mexican ancestry. Scott, "Wartime Labor Problems and Mexican-Americans in the War," pp. 138–40. Over 80 percent of the aliens who registered with the Selective Service in Arizona, New Mexico, and Texas were Mexican. Hugh Carter and Bernice Doster, "Social Characteristics of Aliens from the Southwest Registered for Selective Service during World War II," *Immigration and Naturalization Service Monthly Review* 8 (1951), p. 90.

56. Kryder, *Divided Arsenal*, p. 103; Ruiz, *Cannery Women, Cannery Lives*, p. 120; Leonard, "Years of Hope, Days of Fear," pp. 75–76; Daniel, *Chicano Workers and the Politics of Fairness*, pp. 11–12; Polenberg, *War and Society*, p. 116; Steele, "No Racials," p. 80; "Employment Discrimination Report," December 1940, Community Relations Committee, Jewish Federation Council, Box 19, Folder 9 (hereafter referred to as CRC Collection), Special Collections, Urban Archives Center, California State University, Northridge, California; Camarillo, *Chicanos in California*, p. 72; Nash, "Spanish-Speaking Americans in Wartime," p. 109.

57. Steele, "No Racials," p. 80; Kryder, *Divided Arsenal*, pp. 104, 108, 111; "Statement of Dr. Carlos E. Castañeda," pp. 99–100; Council of Civic Unity, 1941, 1943, Box 12, Folder 7, CRC Collection, Special Collections, Urban Archives Cen-

ter, California State University, Northridge, California, pp. 4–5; Division of Inter-American Activities, Coordinator of Inter-American Affairs, "Confidential Report of the Conference on the Spanish-Speaking Minority Program in the Southwest," held in Washington, D.C., July 12–14, 1943, 4245G, Box 4, FEPC, Franklin D. Roosevelt Presidential Library, Hyde Park, New York, pp. 10–12; Marie M. Hughes, "Statement of Southern California's Educational and Community Projects Related to the Latin Americans," in Office of the Coordinator of Inter-American Affairs, "Conference on the Problems of Education among Spanish-Speaking Populations of Our Southwest," held in Santa Fe, New Mexico, August 19–24, 1943, 4512, Coordinator of Inter-American Affairs, Franklin D. Roosevelt Presidential Library, Hyde Park, New York, p. 5; Mark F. Ethridge, Chairman, Office of Production Management, Washington, D.C., to President Roosevelt, The White House, October 27, 1941, 4245G, Box 3, FEPC, Franklin D. Roosevelt Presidential Library, Hyde Park, New York, p. 1.

58. Peterson, "Grassroots," p. 235; Arroyo, "Chicano Participation in Organized Labor," pp. 295–96; Ginger and Christiano, *The Cold War against Labor*, vol. 1, p. 435.

59. Kryder, *Divided Arsenal*, pp. 108–9; Oberweiser, "The CIO: A Vanguard for Civil Rights in Southern California 1940–46," p. 209; Leonard, "Years of Hope, Days of Fear," pp. 111, 135; Ruiz, *From Out of the Shadows*, p. 82; "No Mexicans Allowed," p. 8. Arthur E. Wood, Local Manager, USES, WMC, to Clarence Johnson, Field Representative, Negro Manpower Service, WMC, February 3, 1943, WMC (Johnson Files), 1941–1946, Box 2, Folder 2, Bratt Collection, Southern California Library for Social Studies and Research, Los Angeles, California. West Coast war industries tempted between 400 and 500 Mexican contract laborers to abandon the agricultural fields. The Farm Security Administration quickly notified the U.S. Bureau of Immigration, whose agents found these deserters and gave them the option of fulfilling their contracts or returning to Mexico. Carey McWilliams, "They Saved the Crops," *Inter-American* 2, no. 8 (August 1943), pp. 12–13.

60. "Minutes of the Eighth Monthly Committee Meeting, October 9, 1944," Los Angeles Committee for Interracial Progress, Box 19, Folder 9, CRC Collection, Special Collections, Urban Archives Center, California State University, Northridge, California, pp. 2–4; W. N. Cunningham, Chief of Placement, USES, WMC, to Arthur E. Wood, Chief of Operations, USES, WMC, March 10, 1945, Discrimination Cases, 1944–1946, Box 1, Folder 11, Bratt Collection, Southern California Library for Social Studies and Research, Los Angeles, California, p. 3.

61. Leonard, "Years of Hope, Days of Fear," pp. 110–11; Honey, *Southern Black Labor and Civil Rights*, pp. 287–88.

62. Sitkoff, "Racial Militancy and Interracial Violence in the Second World War," pp. 678–79; Peter J. Kellogg, "Civil Rights Consciousness in the 1940s," *Historian* 42 (November 1979), p. 27.

63. "Memorandum of Conference," November 1, 1943, Inter-Racial Relations, September–November 1943, Box 111, Folder 17, CRC Collection, Special Collections, Urban Archives Center, California State University, Northridge, California, p. 1; Fisher, "The Problem of Violence," p. 16.

64. Scott, "Wartime Labor Problems and Mexican-Americans in the War," pp. 136–37; "Discrimination against Spanish-Speaking Citizens Must Cease," December 14, 1944, Local 665, Los Angeles Police Employees' Union, Inter-Racial Relations, September–December 1944, Box 111, Folder 12, CRC Collection, Special Collections, Urban Archives Center, California State University, Northridge, California, p. 1.

65. Division of Inter-American Activities, Coordinator of Inter-American Affairs, "Confidential Report of the Conference on the Spanish-Speaking Minority Program in the Southwest," held in Washington, D.C., July 12–14, 1943, 4245G, Box 4, FEPC, Franklin D. Roosevelt Presidential Library, Hyde Park, New York, pp. 5–6.

66. Peterson, "Grassroots," pp. 193, 213–14.

67. Ibid., pp. 214–15.

68. Leonard, "Years of Hope, Days of Fear," pp. 136–37.

69. Ruiz, *Cannery Women, Cannery Lives*, pp. 55–56.

70. Hahamovitch, *The Fruits of Their Labor*, pp. 163–65.

71. Pycior, *LBJ and Mexican Americans*, p. 25; U.S. Congressman Richard M. Kleberg, Washington, D.C., to President Roosevelt, The White House, June 10, 1941, President's Office File 258, Franklin D. Roosevelt Presidential Library, Hyde Park, New York, pp. 1–2; McWilliams, "They Saved the Crops," p. 14.

72. Paul H. Appleby, Undersecretary, U.S. Department of Agriculture, Washington, D.C., to Brigadier General Edwin M. Watson, Secretary to the President, The White House, June 28, 1941, President's Office File 258, Franklin D. Roosevelt Presidential Library, Hyde Park, New York, p. 1.

73. Ibid., pp. 2–3; President Franklin Delano Roosevelt, The White House, to Congressman Richard M. Kleberg, Washington, D.C., July 1, 1941, Franklin D. Roosevelt Presidential Library, Hyde Park, New York, pp. 1–2; Ernesto Galarza, *Merchants of Labor: The Bracero Story* (Santa Barbara, Calif.: McNally & Loftin, 1964), p. 41.

74. Paul H. Appleby, Undersecretary, U.S. Department of Agriculture, Washington, D.C., to Brigadier General Edwin M. Watson, Secretary to the President, The White House, June 28, 1941, President's Office File 258, Franklin D. Roosevelt Presidential Library, Hyde Park, New York, p. 4; President Franklin Delano Roosevelt, The White House, to Congressman Richard M. Kleberg, Washington, D.C., July 1, 1941, Franklin D. Roosevelt Presidential Library, Hyde Park, New York, pp. 2–3.

75. Hahamovitch, *The Fruits of Their Labor*, pp. 168–69; M. H. McIntire, Secretary to the President, The White House, to R. A. Grant, Southeastern Montana Counties Association, May 4, 1942, President's Office File 241, Sugar 1942, Franklin D. Roosevelt Presidential Library, Hyde Park, New York; Fred Cummings, Fort Collins, Colorado, to M. H. McIntire, Secretary to the President, The White House, June 24, 1942, President's Office File 241, Sugar 1942, Franklin D. Roosevelt Presidential Library, Hyde Park, New York.

76. "Memorandum on Manpower Mobilization Involving Mexican Workers," November 25, 1942, Box 47, Gardner Jackson Papers, Franklin D. Roosevelt Presidential Library, Hyde Park, New York, p. 1.

77. Leonard, "Years of Hope, Days of Fear," p. 73; Laurence I. Hewes Jr., Regional Director, Farm Security Administration, U.S. Department of Agriculture, to C. B. Baldwin, Administrator, Farm Security Administration, U.S. Department of Agriculture, Washington, D.C., n.d., Box 47, Gardner Jackson Papers, Franklin D. Roosevelt Presidential Library, Hyde Park, New York, p. 1; " 'Braceros' to the United States," *Tiempo*, October 2, 1942, p. 23; Almazán, "The Mexicans Keep 'Em Rolling," p. 23.

78. Laurence I. Hewes Jr., Regional Director, Farm Security Administration, U.S. Department of Agriculture, to C. B. Baldwin, Administrator, Farm Security Administration, U.S. Department of Agriculture, Washington, D.C., n.d., Box 47, Gardner Jackson Papers, Franklin D. Roosevelt Presidential Library, Hyde Park, New York, p. 2.

79. Gardner Jackson, "Memorandum on Arizona Long Staple Cotton Situation," President's Office File 258, Cotton 1942–1945, Franklin D. Roosevelt Presidential Library, Hyde Park, New York p. 2; "Sinarquistas Plan Subversive Campaign," *Mexican Labor News* 8 (December 15, 1942), Box 47, Gardner Jackson Papers, Franklin D. Roosevelt Presidential Library, Hyde Park, New York, pp. 1–2; Galarza, *Merchants of Labor*, p. 52.

80. Ruiz, *Cannery Women, Cannery Lives*, p. 56; McWilliams, "They Saved the Crops," p. 12.

81. Theodore A. Chacón, Wilmar, California, to George I. Sánchez, University of Texas, Austin, July 12, 1941, Box 68, Legal Cases, Re: Discrimination in Employment, George I. Sánchez Papers, NLBLAC, University of Texas, Austin.

82. Sitkoff, "Racial Militancy and Interracial Violence in the Second World War," pp. 670–71, 675–76; Richard M. Dalfiume, "The 'Forgotten Years' of the Negro Revolution," *Journal of American History* 55, no. 1 (June 1968), pp. 103, 105.

83. Menefee, *Assignment: USA*, p. 168.

84. The Rosenwald Foundation offered its support in establishing an Office of Race Relations. "Office of Race Relations," S. K. Padover, Assistant to the Secretary, U.S. Department of the Interior, Washington, D.C., June 29, 1943, Fair Employment Practices Committee, Box 6, Franklin D. Roosevelt Presidential Library, Hyde Park, New York, pp. 1–2.

85. Ibid., pp. 3–4; James B. Cobb, President, National Alliance of Postal Employees, Washington, D.C., June 20, 1943, 4245G, FEPC, Box 6, Franklin D. Roosevelt Presidential Library, Hyde Park, New York, pp. 1–4.

86. Polenberg, *War and Society*, p. 117; Sitkoff, "Racial Militancy and Interracial Violence in the Second World War," p. 677; "Office of Race Relations," S. K. Padover, Assistant to the Secretary, U.S. Department of the Interior, Washington, D.C., June 29, 1943, FEPC, Box 6, Franklin D. Roosevelt Presidential Library, Hyde Park, New York, pp. 2–3; Jonathan Daniels, Administrative Assistant to the President, Washington, D.C., to Monsignor Francis Haas, Committee on Fair Employment Practices, Washington, D.C., July 28, 1943, FEPC, Box 4, Franklin D. Roosevelt Presidential Library, Hyde Park, New York; "Office of Race Relations," S. K. Padover, Assistant to the Secretary, U.S. Department of the Interior, Washington, D.C., June 30, 1943, FEPC, Box 6, Franklin D. Roosevelt Presidential Library, Hyde Park, New York, pp. 1–2.

87. "Work Stoppages," Fair Employment Practices Committee, 4245G, FEPC, Box 8, Franklin D. Roosevelt Presidential Library, Hyde Park, New York, pp. 1–4; M. C. González, San Antonio, Texas, to Ben F. Foster, U.S. District Attorney, San Antonio, Texas, June 30, 1943, Box 67, American Civil Liberties Union, George I. Sánchez Papers, NLBLAC, University of Texas, Austin; George I. Sánchez to Elmore R. Torn, Regional Mobilization Officer, Eighth Civil Defense Region, Office of Civil Defense, Dallas, Texas, June 3, 1943, Box 16, R. E. Smith, Office of Civil Defense, George I. Sánchez Papers, NLBLAC, University of Texas, Austin. In a letter to professor Sánchez, attorney M. C. González expressed his hesitation, as a longtime LULAC member, to connect himself with the ACLU, an organization "which in this part of the state is considered radical." González cautioned Sánchez, "We must not be stampeded into anything like this . . . because such a step might brand us as pursuing [the] ideals [of an] organization [that] is known to be affiliated with the CIO and radical groups." M. C. González, San Antonio, Texas, to George I. Sánchez, University of Texas, Austin, December 30, 1942, Box 67, American Civil Liberties Union, George I. Sánchez Papers, NLBLAC, University of Texas, Austin.

88. George Weaver, Congress of Industrial Organizations, Washington, D.C., to Jonathan Daniels, Office of the President, The White House, July 8, 1943, 4245G, Box 8, FEPC, Franklin D. Roosevelt Presidential Library, Hyde Park, New York; Juan Gómez-Quiñones, *Roots of Chicano Politics, 1600–1940* (Albuquerque: University of New Mexico Press, 1990), p. 397; Nash, "Spanish-Speaking Americans in Wartime," p. 121; McWilliams, "The Forgotten Mexican," p. 78; Arroyo, "Chicano Participation in Organized Labor," p. 296; Oberweiser, "The CIO: A Vanguard for Civil Rights in Southern California, 1940–46," p. 210.

89. Kryder, *Divided Arsenal*, p. 100; Sitkoff, "Racial Militancy and Interracial Violence in the Second World War," p. 672; Zieger, *The CIO, 1935–1955*, pp. 152, 154–55; Boris, "You Wouldn't Want One of 'Em Dancing with Your Wife," p. 83; "Work Stoppages," Fair Employment Practices Committee, 4245G, FEPC, Box 8, Franklin D. Roosevelt Presidential Library, Hyde Park, New York, pp. 1–4.

90. Oberweiser, "The CIO: A Vanguard for Civil Rights in Southern California, 1940–46," p. 211.

91. Ibid., p. 210; Zieger, *The CIO, 1935–1955*, pp. 180–81.

92. Zieger, *The CIO, 1935–1955*, pp. 179, 181–83, 186; Arroyo, "Chicano Participation in Organized Labor," p. 296; "Discrimination against Spanish-Speaking Citizens Must Cease," December 14, 1944, Local 665, Los Angeles Police Employees' Union, Inter-Racial Relations, September–December 1944, Box 111, Folder 12, CRC Collection, Special Collections, Urban Archives Center, California State University, Northridge, California, p. 1.

93. Zieger, *The CIO, 1935–1955*, pp. 181, 186; Arroyo, "Chicano Participation in Organized Labor," pp. 296–97. "Bulldog" Hawkins, in 1934 the first black elected to the California Assembly, had worked in the San Pedro shipyards during the war and was legislative director of the California CIO. Oberweiser, "The CIO: A Vanguard for Civil Rights in Southern California, 1940–46," pp. 210–11.

94. Nash, "Spanish-Speaking Americans in Wartime," pp. 123–24; Victor Borella, Director, Department of Information Services, Coordinator of Inter-American Affairs, Washington, D.C., to Jonathan Daniels, Administrative Assistant to the President, Washington, D.C., August 15, 1943, 4245G, Box 6, FEPC, Franklin D. Roosevelt Presidential Library, Hyde Park, New York, pp. 1–2; Division of Inter-American Activities, Coordinator of Inter-American Affairs, "Confidential Report of the Conference on the Spanish-Speaking Minority Program in the Southwest," held in Washington, D.C., July 12–14, 1943, 4245G, Box 4, FEPC, Franklin D. Roosevelt Presidential Library, Hyde Park, New York, p. 2.

95. Nelson A. Rockefeller, Coordinator of Inter-American Affairs, Washington, D.C., to President Franklin Delano Roosevelt, The White House, August 16, 1943, 4512, Coordinator of Inter-American Affairs, July–December 1943, Franklin D. Roosevelt Presidential Library, Hyde Park, New York; Division of Inter-American Activities, Coordinator of Inter-American Affairs, "Confidential Report of the Conference on the Spanish-Speaking Minority Program in the Southwest," held in Washington, D.C., July 12–14, 1943, 4245G, Box 4, FEPC, Franklin D. Roosevelt Presidential Library, Hyde Park, New York, pp. 20–21; Wilhelmina Hill, "Education of Spanish-Speaking Americans in Colorado and Wyoming," in Office of the Coordinator of Inter-American Affairs, "Conference on the Problems of Education among Spanish-Speaking Populations of Our Southwest," held in Santa Fe, New Mexico, August 19–24, 1943, 4512, Coordinator of Inter-American Affairs, Franklin D. Roosevelt Presidential Library, Hyde Park, New York, p. 2.

96. Division of Inter-American Activities, Coordinator of Inter-American Affairs, "Confidential Report of the Conference on the Spanish-Speaking Minority Program in the Southwest," held in Washington, D.C., July 12–14, 1943, 4245G, Box 4, FEPC, Franklin D. Roosevelt Presidential Library, Hyde Park, New York, pp. 30–31.

97. Boris, "You Wouldn't Want One of 'Em Dancing With Your Wife," p. 99.

98. Scott, "Wartime Labor Problems and Mexican-Americans in the War," pp. 134, 137; "A Proposal Concerning the Spanish Speaking People in the United States," p. 17; Memorandum from J. Watt Page, Brigadier General, U.S. Army, State Director of Selective Service, Austin, Texas, to all Local Draft Boards, Designation of "Mexicans" on S.S. Forms, Box 16, R. E. Smith, Office of Civilian Defense, George I. Sánchez Papers, NLBLAC, University of Texas, Austin; George I. Sánchez to R. E. Smith, Houston, Texas, May 14, 1943, Box 16, R. E. Smith, Office of Civil Defense, George I. Sánchez Papers, NLBLAC, University of Texas, Austin. Selective Service boards were instructed not to use the term "Mexican" on an inductee's papers unless the individual was a citizen of Mexico. George I. Sánchez, University of Texas, Austin, to R. D. Thorp, Chief of Police, Austin, Texas, February 23, 1942, Box 68, Legal Cases, Re: Discrimination in Employment, George I. Sánchez Papers, NLBLAC, University of Texas, Austin; "A Proposal Concerning the Spanish Speaking People in the United States," p. 29.

99. Scott, "Wartime Labor Problems and Mexican-Americans in the War," p. 136.

CHAPTER SIX
LABOR RIGHTS ARE CIVIL RIGHTS: THE EMERGENCE OF THE MEXICAN AMERICAN
CIVIL RIGHTS STRUGGLE

1. Santillán, "Rosita the Riveter," p. 148.
2. Ibid.; Scott, "Wartime Labor Problems and Mexican-Americans in the War," p. 141.
3. Morín, *Among the Valiant*, p. 87.
4. Zaragosa Vargas, "In the Years of Darkness and Torment: The Early Mexican American Struggle for Civil Rights, 1945–1963," *New Mexico Historical Review* 76, no. 4 (October 2001), pp. 385–86; Philip S. Foner, *Organized Labor and the Black Worker, 1619–1981* (New York: International Publishers, 1981), pp. 270, 272–73. From 1940 to 1950, the rural population of Texas declined by 12 percent. Polakoff, "The Development of the Texas State CIO Council," p. 348.
5. Vargas, "In the Years of Darkness and Torment," p. 394.
6. Santillán, "Rosita the Riveter," p. 147; Daniel Horowitz, *Betty Friedan and the Making of the Feminine Mystique: The American Left, the Cold War, and Modern Feminism* (Amherst: University of Massachusetts Press, 1998), p. 125.
7. Martha Biondi, *To Stand and Fight: The Struggle for Civil Rights in Postwar New York City* (Cambridge, Mass.: Harvard University Press, 2003), pp. 1–4; Robert J. Norrell, "Caste in Steel: Jim Crow Careers in Birmingham, Alabama," *Journal of American History* 73, no. 3 (December 1986), pp. 685, 692; Ruth Needleman, *Black Freedom Fighters in Steel: The Struggle for Democratic Unionism* (Ithaca, N.Y.: Cornell University Press, 2003), p. 142.
8. Ginger and Christiano, *The Cold War against Labor*, vol. 1, p. 435.
9. García, *Mexican Americans*, pp. 190–93; "Facts relative to the Deportation Proceedings Brought against Humberto Silex," Box 133, Folder 41, pp. 1–3, Los Angeles CIO Council Files (Philip "Slim" Connelly Files), Urban Archives Center, California State University, Northridge, California.
10. "Facts relative to the Deportation Proceedings Brought against Humberto Silex," Box 133, Folder 41, pp. 1, 5, Los Angeles CIO Council Files (Philip "Slim" Connelly Files), Urban Archives Center, California State University, Northridge, California.
11. García, *Mexican Americans*, pp. 192, 198; "Facts relative to the Deportation Proceedings Brought against Humberto Silex," Box 133, Folder 41, pp. 3–4, Los Angeles CIO Council Files (Philip "Slim" Connelly Files), Urban Archives Center, California State University, Northridge, California.
12. Arnold, "Humberto Silex," pp. 11–13.
13. Ibid. One cowed Mexican CIO member actually refused to run for union office out of fear that he would be singled out for deportation and that his application for U.S. citizenship would be denied. "Facts relative to the Deportation Proceedings Brought against Humberto Silex," Box 133, Folder 41, pp. 4–5, Los Angeles CIO Council Files (Philip "Slim" Connelly Files), Urban Archives Center, California State University, Northridge, California.
14. "Facts relative to the Deportation Proceedings Brought against Humberto Silex," Box 133, Folder 41, p. 5, Los Angeles CIO Council Files (Philip "Slim" Connelly Files), Urban Archives Center, California State University, Northridge,

California; Natalie Gross, Chairman, Silex Defense Committee, to Philip Connelly, CIO Council, Los Angeles, California, August 12, 1946, 2A34, Los Angeles CIO Council Files (Philip "Slim" Connelly Files), Urban Archives Center, California State University, Northridge, California; García, *Mexican Americans*, pp. 186–89.

15. Santillán, "Rosita the Riveter," p. 148; Foner, *Organized Labor and the Black Worker, 1619–1981*, p. 291; Jones, *Labor of Love, Labor of Sorrow*, p. 256; Elaine Tyler May, *Homeward Bound: American Families in the Cold War Era* (New York: Basic Books, 1988), pp. 76, 89; Art Pries, *Labor's Giant Step: Twenty Years of the CIO* (New York: Pioneer Publishers, 1964), p. 350; Kate Ecklund, "Latina Packinghouse Workers: The Story of These Immigrant Women Workers Is a Neglected Chapter in St. Paul History," *Union Advocate* 101, no. 6 (August 4, 1997), pp. 5–6.

16. Bernard Valdéz, Taos Latin American Service Club, Taos, New Mexico, to Gilberto Valadéz, Mexican American Movement, Placentia, California, April 29, 1946, Mexican American Movement (MAM) Collection, Box 1, Urban Archives Center, California State University, Northridge, California.

17. R. L. Chambers, "The New Mexico Pattern," *Common Ground* 9, no. 4 (Summer 1949), p. 21.

18. *Hollywood Citizen News*, October 7, 1946; *Los Angeles Times*, October 8, 1946; *Daily People's World*, October 17, 1946; *Los Angeles Examiner*, October 30, 1946. FEPC California Initiative, Box 108, Folder 20, Los Angeles CIO Council Files (Philip "Slim" Connelly Files), Urban Archives Center, California State University, Northridge, California.

19. Ben S. Berry, Executive Committee of the Council for Civic Unity of Los Angeles, to Governor Earl Warren, State Capitol, Sacramento, California, December 19, 1946, Box 120, Folder 5, Community Relations Committee Collection, Jewish Federation Council, Part II, Urban Archives Center, California State University, Northridge, California, pp. 1–2. This civil rights body pointed out that if racial minority groups realized that no aid against intolerance would come from the recognized political parties, they would look to un-American influences ready to take advantage of their feelings of injustice to foster hatred and dissension that could be used to undermine the country. Ibid.

20. Carlos E. Castañeda, University of Texas, Austin, to George I. Sánchez, University of Texas, Austin, December 5, 1946, Box 16, George I. Sánchez Papers, NLBLAC, University of Texas, Austin; Polakoff, "The Development of the Texas State CIO Council," p. 394; Ricardo Romo, "George I. Sánchez and the Civil Rights Movement: 1940–1960," *La Raza Law Journal* 1, no. 3 (Fall 1986), pp. 351–53; Juan Gómez-Quiñones, *Chicano Politics: Reality and Promise, 1940–1990* (Albuquerque: University of New Mexico Press, 1990), p. 37.

21. "The Story of the Killing of Herman Burns," p. 1, Los Angeles CIO Council Files (Philip "Slim" Connelly Files), Urban Archives Center, California State University, Northridge, California. Julius Burns was beaten unconscious and collapsed over his dead brother's body. Ibid.

22. Ibid., p. 2; Camarillo, *Chicanos in California*, p. 78; Mobilization for Democracy Reports, February 1945 to November 1946, Box 124, Folder A2, Los Angeles CIO Council Files (Philip "Slim" Connelly Files), Urban Archives Center, California State University, Northridge, California. The Los Angeles Police De-

partment investigated itself on all charges of police brutality, in accordance with the policy of Mayor Fletcher Bowron's Police Commission.

23. Mobilization for Democracy Reports, February 1945 to November 1946, Box 124, Folder A2, Los Angeles CIO Council Files (Philip "Slim" Connelly Files), Urban Archives Center, California State University, Northridge, California.

24. For example, the mother of an eight-year-old boy reported that he came home with a questionnaire that had been passed out in class by his teacher. Some of the questions included: Do you or do you not care to have a Negro as your teacher? Do you or do you not believe that Negroes and Mexicans start race riots? Do you or do you not believe that the Jewish religion should continue? Meanwhile, We the Mothers Mobilize for America, Inc., was formed. This racist, right-wing organization's purpose was to defend the constitutional rights of besieged whites and true Americanism by opposing the black and Mexican American civil rights organizations, particularly alleged communist organizations that pleaded "their alien cause as an American Ideal." Partial Questionnaire in the Beverly Hills Elementary School District, January 15, 1945, Discrimination Cases, 1944–1946, Box 1, Folder 11, War Manpower Commission (Bratt Files), 1934–1948, Southern California Library for Social Studies and Research, Los Angeles, California; Adelle Cox's "We, the Mothers Mobilize for America, Inc.," January–July, 1946 (Labor), Box 113, Folder 22, Community Relations Committee Collection, Jewish Federation Council, Part II, Urban Archives Center, California State University, Northridge, California.

25. Becky M. Nicolaides, *My Blue Heaven: Life and Politics in the Working-Class Suburbs of Los Angeles, 1920–1965* (Chicago: University of Chicago Press, 2002), pp. 210–11.

26. Ibid., p. 192.

27. "Special Circular—The California Council for Civic Unity," August 1946 (Council for Civic Unity, 1945, 1946), Box 120, Folder 5, Community Relations Committee Collection, Jewish Federation Council, Part II, Urban Archives Center, California State University, Northridge, California, p. 1; Mobilization for Democracy Reports, February 1945 to November 1946, Los Angeles CIO Council Files (Philip "Slim" Connelly Files), Urban Archives Center, California State University, Northridge, California; LA-CIO Council Committees, Minorities/FEPC correspondence, Reports, 1945, 1946, 2a-9, Los Angeles CIO Council Files (Philip "Slim" Connelly Files), Urban Archives Center, California State University, Northridge, California. For example, J. R. Chávez represented Local 9 of the Industrial Union of Marine and Shipbuilders of America, Frank Romero and Isador Armenta spoke on behalf of ILWU Local 26, Frank Lopez served as secretary of the "Anti-Discrimination in Unions" panel, and Armenta chaired the "Community-wide Activities" panel. The conference panels addressed many issues pertinent to the city's racial minorities: police violence; housing for veterans, mobilizing the public against restrictive covenants, and the implementation of a long-range housing program to ensure low-cost housing for racial minorities; the increase in discrimination by employers against blacks and Mexican Americans; the persistent failure of the U.S. Employment Services agency to serve all minority job applicants; the reluctance of CIO unions to eliminate racial discrimination; the need for nondiscrimination clauses in union contracts and for the

adherence of employers and union members to these clauses; the forging of a campaign to collect signatures in order to place on the November ballot a measure to provide for a state FEPC; and the importance of concrete union educational programs to ensure the success of a fair employment practices bill. Proceedings of Anti-Discrimination Conference, held at CIO Building, March 10, 1946, p. 1, 2A1B, Los Angeles CIO Council Files (Philip "Slim" Connelly Files), Urban Archives Center, California State University, Northridge, California.

28. Ibid., pp. 5–6. The Rose Hill shooting case was brought up as a recent example of police brutality. After a white citizen shot a Mexican, this individual stated that the investigating police officer egged him on, advising that in the future he should do a better job by killing his Mexican victim. Ibid., p. 10.

29. Ibid., p. 6.

30. Ibid., pp. 2, 4, 6, 10. As a member of the CIO's Joint Anti-Fascist Refugee Committee, Armando Davila, business agent of UFWA Local 576, brought up the fate of antifascist refugees in North Africa and the deportation to Spain of Spanish refugee children currently residing in Mexico. Correspondence of Joint Anti-Fascist Refugee Committee, January 1943–September 1945, 2A-9, 2A-30, Los Angeles CIO Council Files (Philip "Slim" Connelly Files), Urban Archives Center, California State University, Northridge, California.

31. Bruce Nelson, *Divided We Stand: American Workers and the Struggle for Black Equality* (Princeton, N.J.: Princeton University Press, 2000), pp. 218–19; Institute of Ethnic Affairs, "A Proposal Concerning the Spanish Speaking People in the United States," Washington, D.C., n.d., p. 18, Box 1, Mexican American Movement (MAM) Collection, Urban Archives Center, California State University, Northridge, California; Valdés, *Barrios Norteños*, p. 150.

32. Ross, *All Manner of Men*, p. 270; Blum, *V Was for Victory*, p. 198. The GI Bill of Rights provision of free education was made doubly difficult for blacks, Mexican Americans, and Jewish Americans by the quotas and barriers colleges placed on these minority veterans. Minority veterans also encountered housing discrimination in college and university towns. For example, Tejano World War II veterans enrolled at the University of Texas at Austin were turned away from rooming houses because Anglo landlords refused to rent to Mexicans. Ross, *All Manner of Men*, p. 270.

33. Karen Tucker Anderson, "Last Hired, First Hired: Black Women Workers during World War II," *Journal of American History*, 69, no. 1 (June 1982), p. 95; Santillán, "Rosita the Riveter," p. 147.

34. "Rough Analysis of Placements of Non-Whites in Los Angeles," Discrimination Cases, 1944–1946, Box 1, Folder 11, War Manpower Commission (Bratt Files), 1943–1948, Southern California Library for Social Studies and Research, Los Angeles, California.

35. Ibid.

36. Ibid.; FEPC (Fair Employment Practices Committee) and Miscellaneous Minority, 1942–1946, Box 1, Folder 18, p. 1, War Manpower Commission (Bratt Files), 1943–1948, Southern California Library for Social Studies and Research, Los Angeles, California; Foner, *Organized Labor and the Black Worker, 1619–1981*, p. 269.

37. FEPC (Fair Employment Practices Committee) and Miscellaneous Minority, 1942–1946, Box 1, Folder 18, pp. 2–3, War Manpower Commission (Bratt Files), 1943–1948, Southern California Library for Social Studies and Research, Los Angeles, California; Zamora, "The Failed Promise of Wartime Opportunity for Mexicans in the Texas Oil Industry," p. 325.

38. Joel Seidman, *American Labor from Defense to Reconversion* (Chicago: University of Chicago Press, 1953), pp. 250–51.

39. Norrell, "Caste in Steel," pp. 675, 677, 683, 694; Needleman, *Black Freedom Fighters in Steel*, pp. 52–53, 103; Nelson, *Divided We Stand*, pp. 206, 211, 240; Vargas, "In the Years of Darkness and Torment," p. 396.

40. Vargas, "In the Years of Darkness and Torment," p. 396.

41. Nelson, *Divided We Stand*, pp. 219, 288; Vargas, "In the Years of Darkness and Torment," p. 396; Honey, *Southern Labor and Black Civil Rights*, p. 216; Polakoff, "The Development of the Texas State CIO Council," p. x.

42. The following one-minute radio announcement ran daily from October 22 through November 4, 1946, and was a paid political announcement contracted for by the Committee to Vote "No" on Proposition 11: "Don't be misled! VOTE NO ON PROPOSITION 11. This act would be unfair to the worker, to the union, to the employer. It would foster discrimination, intolerance, hatred. . . . It says you must work with anyone that the Commission directs, regardless of his color, race, creed or nationality. People can be jailed without a trial by jury for disobeying the mandate of a political commission. VOTE NO ON PROPOSITION 11. Committee to Vote No on Proposition #11." Joseph Roos, Los Angeles, California, to Eugene Block, San Francisco, California, October 18, 1946, pp. 1–2, FEPC California Initiative, Box 108, Folder 20, Los Angeles CIO Council Files (Philip "Slim" Connelly Files), Urban Archives Center, California State University, Northridge, California.

43. Pries, *Labor's Giant Step*, p. 333.

44. Ibid., pp. 335, 337, 358, 377.

45. David Caute, *The Great Fear: The Anti-Communist Purge under Truman and Eisenhower* (New York: Simon and Schuster, 1979), pp. 215, 229; Foner, *Organized Labor and the Black Worker, 1619–1981*, p. 277; Polakoff, "The Development of the Texas State CIO Council," pp. 392–93.

46. Ann Fagan Ginger and David Christiano, *The Cold War against Labor*, vol. 2 (Berkeley, Calif.: Meiklejohn Civil Liberties Institute, 1987), p. 594; Ginger and Christiano, *The Cold War against Labor*, vol. 1, p. 434. Armando Davila was finally deported in the early 1950s. Ginger and Christiano, *The Cold War against Labor*, vol. 1, p. 436.

47. Vargas, "In the Years of Darkness and Torment," p. 392.

48. Ginger and Christiano, *The Cold War against Labor*, vol. 1, pp. 433–34.

49. Ibid.; Division of Inter-American Activities, Coordinator of Inter-American Affairs, "Confidential Report of the Conference on the Spanish-Speaking Minority Program in the Southwest," held in Washington, D.C., July 12–14, 1943, 4245G, Box 4, FEPC, Franklin D. Roosevelt Presidential Library, Hyde Park, New York, pp. 12–14; Zieger, *The CIO, 1935–1955*, p. 183.

50. Polakoff, "The Development of the Texas State CIO Council," pp. 382 n. 67, 390–92, n. 96 and n. 97.

51. Pycior, *LBJ and Mexican Americans*, pp. 61–62, 64–66.

52. Vargas, "In the Years of Darkness and Torment," p. 397.

53. Ibid.

54. Ibid., p. 399; Ginger and Christiano, *The Cold War against Labor*. vol. 1, p. 435.

55. Foner, *Organized Labor and the Black Worker, 1619–1981*, p. 311. In Denver, as part of "Bill of Rights Week" in late December 1950, during the busy Christmas shopping season, fifteen black, Mexican American, and white members of the Civil Rights Congress dressed as minutemen and, with fife and drum and carrying American flags, paraded through that city's downtown streets with banners that read, "Repeal the McCarran Act." Vargas, "In the Years of Darkness and Torment," p. 400.

56. Vargas, "In the Years of Darkness and Torment," pp. 400–1.

57. Ibid., pp. 388–90; George I. Sánchez and Lyle Saunders, "Wetbacks," a Preliminary Report to the Advisory Committee, Study of Spanish-Speaking People, University of Texas, Austin, 1949, pp. 24, 26; "Illegal Alien Labor," in *Readings on La Raza, the Twentieth Century*, ed. Matt S. Meier and Feliciano Rivera (New York: Hill and Wang, 1974), p. 189; Américo Paredes, "Texas' Third Man: The Texas Mexican," *Race* 4, no. 1 (1963), pp. 55–56; Pauline R. Kibbe, "The Economic Plight of Mexicans," in *Ethnic Relations in the United States*, ed. Edward C. McDonagh and Eugene S. Richards (New York: Appleton-Century Crofts, 1953), pp. 190–91; Montejano, *Anglos and Mexicans in the Making of Texas*, p. 273.

58. Sánchez and Saunders, "Wetbacks," p. 34; Polakoff, "The Development of the Texas State CIO Council," p. 389.

59. Vargas, "In the Years of Darkness and Torment," pp. 389–90.

60. Sánchez and Saunders, "Wetbacks," p. 34. These two labor bodies would also tackle the issue of growing economic discrimination against Tejanos; they agreed to cooperate in alleviating existing wage differentials between Anglo and Tejano workers along the Texas-Mexico border as a way to raise the living standards of Tejanos. Polakoff, "The Development of the Texas State CIO Council," p. 389.

61. Bernard Valdéz, Taos Latin American Service Club, Taos, New Mexico, to Gilberto Valadéz, Mexican American Movement, Placentia, California, April 29, 1946, Mexican American Movement (MAM) Collection, Box 1, Urban Archives Center, California State University, Northridge, California.

62. Polakoff, "The Development of the Texas State CIO Council," pp. 389–90.

63. Foner, *Organized Labor and the Black Worker, 1619–1981*, pp. 287–88.

CONCLUSION

1. Leo Grebler, Joan W. Moore, and Ralph C. Guzmán, *The Mexican-American People: The Nation's Second Largest Minority* (New York: Free Press, 1970), pp. 36, 51, 85–86. The movement of workers from Mexico across the border included immigrants seeking permanent residence, legally admitted temporary laborers, commuters, and undocumented workers. Ibid., p. 37.

2. Ibid., p. 85. The largest number of repatriates, about 132,000, came from Texas; the second-largest number was expelled from California; and the Indiana-Illinois area ranked third in the number of repatriations.

3. Ibid., p. 91.

4. As in the case of blacks, the internationalist beliefs of these erstwhile Mexican American fighters for social justice foreshadowed the outlook of 1960s Chicano radical activists, who supported wars of national liberation throughout the Third World. Biondi, *To Stand and Fight*, pp. 274–75.

5. Norrell, "Caste in Steel," pp. 685, 692; Needleman, *Black Freedom Fighters in Steel*, p. 142.

6. Norrell, "Caste in Steel, " pp. 670, 679, 691; Needleman, *Black Freedom Fighters in Steel*, pp. 52–53, 103.

7. Norrell, "Caste in Steel," pp. 675, 677, 683, 694; Needleman, *Black Freedom Fighters in Steel*, pp. 52–53, 103; Nicolaides, *My Blue Heaven*, pp. 253, 286.

8. Law enforcement officers gained immunity from prosecution because they often charged their victims with a crime, usually resisting arrest or assaulting a police officer. It was not unusual for Mexican Americans to be shot during arrests.

9. Sánchez and Saunders, "Wetbacks," p. 192. That the grim and desperate situation of segregated housing was an inescapable fact of life in Los Angeles was revealed in 1958, when 80 percent of this city's racial minority groups surveyed stated that they "would move out of their present neighborhoods if they could." Nicolaides, *My Blue Heaven*, p. 192.

10. Grebler, Moore, and Guzmán, *The Mexican-American People*, p. 267. As late as 1955, some Los Angeles County real estate boards expelled members for selling to Mexican Americans. Through the practice of redlining, banks kept maps of the racial composition of communities, drawing black or mixed areas in red as bad investments. For example, in Los Angeles, red ratings or downgrades were given to the Mexican communities of East Los Angeles, Highland Park, Chavez Ravine, Elysian Park, "Dogtown" (near downtown), and the San Gabriel area. Nicolaides, *My Blue Heaven*, p. 193.

11. Grebler, Moore, and Guzmán, *The Mexican-American People*, pp. 155, 160; Charles E. Silberman, *Crisis in Black and White* (New York: Vintage Books, 1964), p. 198.

12. Sánchez and Saunders, "Wetbacks," pp. 28, 38. For example, in 1957 Congress enacted Public Law 78 because of the manpower shortages brought on by the Korean conflict. Grebler, Moore, and Guzmán, *The Mexican-American People*, p. 67.

13. Grebler, Moore, and Guzmán, *The Mexican-American People*, pp. 41, 54, 73–74.

14. Ibid., p. 67. Cities along the border and in the interior of the Southwest were losing the fight to Americanize Mexican American youth because a constant influx of Mexican children who spoke no English poured into the schools. Sánchez and Saunders, "Wetbacks," pp. 29–30.

15. Grebler, Moore, and Guzmán, *The Mexican-American People*, p. 55.

16. One overriding issue of concern was overcoming widespread voter fraud in south Texas, where Tejanos cast their vote at the orders of Anglo border bosses.

Robert A. Caro, *The Years of Lyndon Johnson: Master of the Senate* (New York: Alfred A. Knopf, 2002), p. 745.

17. Grebler, Moore, and Guzmán, *The Mexican-American People*, pp. 7–9.

18. Ibid., p. 7.

19. Ibid., pp. 4, 592. Indeed, one of the emerging figures of the civil rights movement would be César Chávez, whose farm worker union movement would lead the call for economic and social justice for the Mexican American population.

20. Silberman, *Crisis in Black and White*, pp. 139–40.

Index

POLITICS AND SOCIETY IN TWENTIETH-CENTURY AMERICA

Civil Defense Begins at Home: Militarization Meets Everyday Life in the Fifties
BY LAURA MCENANEY

Cold War Civil Rights: Race and the Image of American Democracy
BY MARY L. DUDZIAK

Divided We Stand: American Workers and the Struggle for Black Equality
BY BRUCE NELSON

Poverty Knowledge: Social Science, Social Policy, and the Poor in Twentieth-Century U.S. History
BY ALICE O'CONNOR

Suburban Warriors: The Origins of the New American Right
BY LISA MCGIRR

The Politics of Whiteness: Race, Workers, and Culture in the Modern South
BY MICHELLE BRATTAIN

State of the Union: A Century of American Labor
BY NELSON LICHTENSTEIN

Changing the World: American Progressives in War and Revolution
BY ALAN DAWLEY

Dead on Arrival: The Politics of Healthcare in Twentieth-Century America
BY COLIN GORDON

For All These Rights: Business, Labor, and the Shaping of America's Public-Private Welfare State
BY JENNIFER KLEIN

The Radical Middle Class: Populist Democracy and the Question of Capitalism in Progressive Era Portland, Oregon
BY ROBERT D. JOHNSTON

American Babylon: Race and the Struggle for Postwar Oakland
BY ROBERT O. SELF

The Other Women's Movement: Workplace Justice and Social Rights in Modern America
BY DOROTHY SUE COBBLE

Impossible Subjects: Illegal Aliens and the Making of Modern America
BY MAY M. NGAI

More Equal Than Others: America from Nixon to the New Century
BY GODFREY HODGSON

Cities of Knowledge: Cold War Science and the Search for the Next Silicon Valley
BY MARGARET PUGH O'MARA

Labor Rights Are Civil Rights: Mexican American Workers in Twentieth-Century America
BY ZARAGOSA VARGAS